Britain's Railways

Rail Atlas
1890

Tony Dewick

Ian Allan

PUBLISHING

INTRODUCTION

This atlas takes as its starting point the classic *Pre-Grouping Atlas and Gazetteer* and, for Ireland, the Channel Islands and the Isle of Man, my own *Complete Atlas of Railway Station Names* (both published by Ian Allan). It sets out to show the railways of the British Isles on 1 January 1890 and includes all stations open to passengers, together with many goods stations, viaducts, tunnels and other railway locations, with the lines distinguished by their owning company. The fact that a line was owned by a particular company is not, of course, an indication that it operated its own trains, and information is given in the Index to Companies on those which were worked by other railway companies. It was, however, beyond the scope of this work to indicate the many lines, particularly of the major companies, over which other railways enjoyed running powers.

Although most of the main components of the railway network of these islands were already in place by 1890, this work identifies some major gaps, often quite surprising to a railway enthusiast familiar with the network at its greatest extent. The relatively late construction of the Great Central's London extension, or the West Highland line of the North British, is quite well known. Perhaps more unexpected, except to the railway historian, is the absence of the London & South Western's independent route from Lydford (then spelt Lidford) into Plymouth and its lines into Cornwall; of the Great Western's route between Birmingham and Cheltenham; and the GW's line to Fishguard and the associated lines across the Irish Sea from the port of Rosslare. The remoter parts of western Ireland had yet to gain extensive networks, both of narrow and Irish standard gauge. The railway map of certain areas, such as the Black Country and the Liverpool and Manchester corridor, had already almost reached its full extent, whereas that of others, like the Nottinghamshire/Derbyshire coalfield and the Glasgow suburbs, were still at an embryonic stage. In the last two cases, this was all to change by the end of the century, through the penetration of the former by the Manchester, Sheffield and Lincolnshire (to be renamed the Great Central in 1897) and, in the latter,

the extensions of the Caledonian north of the Clyde. To the modern railway enthusiast the railway map looks quite odd without the direct GW line from London to High Wycombe and the Aynho cut-off, the Midland's Hope Valley line, the Highland's direct route to Inverness over Slochd Summit, and the Forth Bridge and its associated lines running deep into Fife. London's first tube line, the world's first underground electric railway, the City & South London, was to open at the end of the year. Its success resulted in the 'Tube Mania' of the following year.

The following lines which missed inclusion in this atlas were opened during the course of 1890 (in some cases passenger services may have been introduced later than the opening date for goods):

Dalmeny to Inverkeithing
  (including the Forth Bridge) (NB): 4 March
Chester (Northgate) to Connah's Quay (MS&L):
  31 March
Connah's Quay to Buckley Junction (WM&CQ):
  31 March
Market Weighton to Driffield (NE): 18 April
Bridge of Earn to Mawcarse (NB): 4 May
Kidlington to Blenheim & Woodstock (GW):
  19 May
Cowdenbeath Jc. to Kelty (NB): 2 June
Inverkeithing to Burntisland (NB): 2 June
Dalmeny to Corstorphine (NB): 2 June
Dalmeny to Winchburgh Jc. (NB): 2 June
Lidford to Devonport (PD&SWJn): 2 June
Ripley to Heanor (Mid.): 2 June
Kilwinning to Irvine (Cal.): 2 June
Cymmer to Treherbert (R&SB): 2 July
Brookwood to Bisley Camp (L&SW): 14 July
Bridgwater to Edington Road (L&SW): 21 July
Netherthorpe to Pleasley (throughout) (Mid.):
  1 September
Holmfield to Halifax St. Paul's (throughout) (HHL):
  5 September
Attymon Junction to Loughrea (MGW): 1 December
King William Street to Stockwell (C&SL):
  18 December

First published 2005

ISBN 0 7110 3031 6

© Ian Allan Publishing Ltd 2005

Published by Ian Allan Publishing

an imprint of Ian Allan Publishing Ltd, Hersham, Surrey KT12 4RG.

Printed by Ian Allan Printing Ltd, Hersham, Surrey KT12 4RG.

Code: 0506/B2

Harrow to Stanmore (L&NW): 18 December
Ballinascarthy to Timoleague (T&CL): 20 December
Lucan, Leixlip & Celbridge Steam Tramway
Fairbourne Miniature Railway

A table listing all passenger stations opened, closed or
re-named during the course of 1890, is to be found on
pages 72 and 73 (I am greatly indebted to *The
Directory of Railway Stations* by R. V. J. Butt for
much of this information and, indeed, this invaluable
book has been a constant source of reference in
preparing this work.)

In 1890 railways were the principal means of
longer distance communication for both goods and
passengers. An interesting indication of the
importance of railways at that time can be gained from
Baedeker's guide to Great Britain of that year. Its
itineraries are predominantly railway based and, for
the railway enthusiast, provide fascinating
descriptions of the lines taken. It also contains
interesting information about the length and cost of
journeys at the time. London to Brighton (Victoria
and London Bridge portions combining at East
Croydon) took between 1¼ and 3 hours (fares 10s
(£0.50), 6s 6d (£0.32½) or 4s 2½d (£0.21)); Paddington
to Bristol, 2½ to 4¾ hours, fares 20s 10d (£1.04), 15s
7d (£0.78), 9s 10½d (£0.49); Bristol to Derby, 3¼ to 4¾
hours, fares 18s (£0.90), 10s 4d (£0.52) (the Midland
had already abolished second class); London to
Berwick-on-Tweed, 7 to 9 hours, 47s (£2.35), 37s 8d
(£1.88), 28s 2½d (£1.41). Anglo-Scottish schedules
had only recently been improved following the Race
to the North of 1888. Fares look cheap but would in
fact have been very expensive to the average working
man on a few shillings a week. Journeys were long,
dirty and probably quite uncomfortable: coaches were
wooden bodied, often rigid four or six wheelers, with
no refreshment facilities or toilets (20 minute stops for
these needs being made by long distance trains at
stations such as Preston), and the first corridor trains
were not introduced until 1892. Apart from on a
couple of very minor electrically operated tramways,
all trains were hauled by steam locomotives. The GW
was still using Gooch broad gauge 4-2-2s (until the
final demise of the 7ft 0¼in gauge in 1892) and Dean
157-166 class 2-2-2s on the narrow gauge; the LSWR
had recently introduced the Drummond 'T9' class
4-4-0; the GNR had its famous Stirling Singles; the
LNWR Webb's 2-4-0 'Precedents'; the Midland
Johnson's handsome 4-2-2 express engines (which
they were still building); the Metropolitan's original
4-4-0Ts, used by both the Metropolitan and the
Metropolitan District Railways, were the standard
motive power on London's, still exclusively steam
powered underground. On the operational safety front,
a recent development had been the Regulation of
Railways Act of 1889, which finally enforced the
interlocking of points and signals and the block
system, and automatic continuous brakes for
passenger trains.

In terms of number of passenger stations (those
which were joint or were owned by companies that did
not work their own trains are not included) the largest
railway companies in 1890 were: L&NW (593
stations), GW (584), NE (531), Midland (443),
NB (354), GE (334), Caledonian (258), L&SW (255),
L&Y (246) and GN (213). In terms of mileage,
however, the GW was the largest, followed by the
L&NW, Midland, NE, GE, GN, L&SW and L&Y.
Total railway mileage in Great Britain was 20,073.
The GE, however, carried by far the greatest number
of passengers, reflecting the importance of its London
suburban services, with the L&NW some way behind
in second place.

It is also interesting to consider the wider social,
political and economic climate in which the railways
of 1890 operated. Britain and all of Ireland were one
nation, of course, the United Kingdom of Great
Britain and Ireland, under the imperial rule of Queen
Victoria, who had been on the throne since 1837 and
was to reign for another 11 years. The British Empire
encompassed Canada, India and Australia, and the
Scramble for Africa was underway. The Conservative
Lord Salisbury was Prime Minister. Europe was
enjoying a period of relative peace, the last major
European war having been the Franco-Prussian War of
1870-71. Britain was a major manufacturing country
and a large producer of coal and steel; in the industrial
areas of Britain the railway network had evolved to
serve these industries, and carrying passengers was
often secondary. For long distance travel the railway's
only real competitor was river and coastal shipping
and the remaining canals. Road transport was still
predominantly horse-powered and slow and in urban
areas the railways were yet to face competition from
electric tramways, although many horse or steam-
operated urban tramways existed by this time.

Although this picture of railway supremacy and
expansion appears rosy, this atlas shows the already
wasteful duplication of lines and stations which was
very shortly to burden the railways with mounting
losses. In 1890 there were at least 400 cities, towns
and villages served by two or more railway companies
with separate, often unconnected, passenger stations.
Many of these places, such as Gretna, Aylsham and
Cleator Moor, were quite small places. And yet this
duplication of lines was to continue to increase into
the early years of the twentieth century. It is perhaps
no coincidence that the majority of lines built after
1890, even in growing urban areas (apart from
London), were also those first to close, many to
passengers within 20-30 years of opening. In so many
cases it is in fact the original lines of the early to mid
nineteenth century which have survived. This atlas,
therefore, provides a fascinating snapshot of the
railway system of the British Isles, before the final
major burst of railway construction around the end of
the century and the slow contraction thereafter until
the relative stability and even moderate growth of the
past 30 years.

BIBLIOGRAPHY

General

Author	Title	Publisher	Date
Hyde, Ralph	The A to Z of Victorian London (reprint of Bacon's contemporary atlas)	Harry Margary	1987
	6 inch County Maps of England and Wales	Ordnance Survey	1850s-1900s
	1 inch maps of Scotland	Ordnance Survey	1850s-1900s
	1 inch maps of Ireland	Ordnance Survey	1850s-1900s
	The Harmsworth Encyclopaedia (8 vols)	Amalgamated & Thomas Nelson	c1905
	The Village London Atlas 1822-1903	Alderman	1986
	Baedeker's Great Britain 1890 (reprint)	Old House Books	2004

Railways

Author	Title	Publisher	Date
Anderson, VR & Fox, GK	An Historical Survey of the Chester & Holyhead Railway	OPC	1984
Awdry, Christopher	Encyclopaedia of British Railway Companies	Guild Publishing	1990
Barrie, DS	The Barry Railway	Oakwood	1962
Barrie, DSM	South Wales (Regional History of Railways Vol 12)	David & Charles	1980
Baughan, Peter E	North and Mid Wales (Regional History of Railways Vol 11)	David & Charles	1982
Blackburn, A & Mackett, J	The Freshwater, Yarmouth & Newport Railway	Branch Line Handbooks	1966
Bonsor, NRP	The Jersey Railway	Oakwood	1962
Bonsor, NRP	The Jersey Eastern Railway	Oakwood	1965
Bonsor, NRP	The Guernsey Railway	Oakwood	1967
Bridges, Alan	Industrial Locomotives of Scotland	Industrial Railway Society	1976
Briwnant-Jones, Gwyn	Railway through Talerddig	Gomer	1990
Butt, RVJ	The Directory of Railway Stations	Patrick Stephens	1995
Carter, Ernest	An Historical Geography of the Railways of the British Isles	Cassell	1959
Christiansen, Rex	Thames & Severn (Regional History of Railways Vol 13)	David & Charles	1981
Christiansen, Rex	The West Midlands (Regional History of Railways Vol 7)	David St John Thomas	1991
Clinker, CR	Register of Closed Passenger Stations & Goods Depots - England, Scotland & Wales 1830-1977	Avon Anglia	1977
Connor, JE & Halford, BL	Forgotten Stations of Greater London	Town & Country	1972
Cook, RA & Hoole, K	North Eastern Railway Historical Maps	Railway & Canal Historical Society	1975
Course, Edwin	The Railways of Southern England :The Main Lines	BT Batsford	1973
Course, Edwin	The Railways of Southern England: Secondary & Branch Lines	BT Batsford	1974
Cozens, Lewis	The Corris Railway	Private	1949
Croughton, G, Kidner, RW, Young, A	Private and Untimetabled Railway Stations	Oakwood	1982
Crowther, GL	National Atlas showing Canals, Navigable Rivers, Mineral Tramroads, Railways and Street Tramways (8 vols)	Preston	1980s
Davison, MF	Blyth & Tyne (Part 2)	John Sinclair	1990
Devereux, Charles	Railways of Sevenoaks	Oakwood	1977
Dewick, Tony	Complete Atlas of Railway Station Names	Ian Allan	2002
Goode, CT	The Great Northern & Great Eastern Joint Railway	Private	1989
Gordon, DI	The Eastern Counties (Regional History of Railways Vol 5)	David & Charles	1990
Greville, MD & Spence, Jeoffry	Closed Passenger Lines of Great Britain 1827-1947	Railway & Canal Historical Society	1974
Hajducki, S Maxwell	Railway Atlas of Ireland	David & Charles	1974
Hateley, Roger	Industrial Locomotives of South Western England	Industrial Railway Society	1977
Holt, Geoffrey O	The North West (Regional History of Railways Vol 10)	David & Charles	1978
Hoole, K	The North East (Regional History of Railways Vol 4)	David & Charles	1978
Jackson, Alan A	Volk's Railway Brighton 1883-1964	Light Railway Transport League	1964
Jackson, Alan A	London's Termini	David & Charles	1969
Jenkins, SC & Quayle, HI	The Oxford, Worcester & Wolverhampton Railway	Oakwood	1977
Johnson, Stephen	Johnson's Atlas & Gazetteer of the Railways of Ireland	Midland	1997
Joy, David	The Lake Counties (Regional History of Railways Vol 14)	David & Charles	1983
Joy, David	South & West Yorkshire (Regional History of Railways Vol 8)	David & Charles	1984
Kidner, RW	The Narrow Gauge Railways of Wales (9th ed)	Oakwood	1970
Kingdom, Anthony R	The Plymouth & Turnchapel Railway	ARK	1996
Leleux, Robin	The East Midlands (Regional History of Railways Vol 9)	David & Charles	1984
Lister, MD	The Railways of Port Sunlight & Bromborough Port	Oakwood	1980
Marshall, Peter F	The Railways of Dundee	Oakwood	1996
Mellentin, Julian	Kendal & Windermere Railway	Dalesman	c1980
Mitchell, Vic & Smith, Keith	Woking to Southampton	Middleton	1988
Mitchell, Vic & Smith, Keith	Dover to Ramsgate	Middleton	1990
Mitchell, Vic & Smith, Keith	Charing Cross to Dartford	Middleton	1990
Mulligan, Fergus	One Hundred & Fifty Years of Irish Railways	Appletree	1990
Nock, OS	The Railway Enthusiast's Encyclopedia	Arrow	1970
Norris, John	The Stratford & Moreton Tramway	Railway & Canal Historical Society	1987
O'Cuimin, Padraig	The Baronial Lines of the MGWR	Transport Research Associates	1972
Patterson, EM	The Belfast & County Down Railway	Oakwood	1958
Patterson, EM	The Great Northern Railway of Ireland	Oakwood	1962
Peacock, Thomas B	Railways to Tintern and Coleford	LPC	1952

Price, MRC	The Llanelly & Mynydd Mawr Railway	Oakwood	1992
Rolt, LTC	Railway Adventure	David & Charles	1961
Rowledge, JWP	Ireland (Regional History of Railways Vol 16)	Atlantic Transport	1995
Swindale, Dennis L	Branch Line to Southminster	Halstead Press	1981
Thomas, David St John	West Country Railway History (Regional History of Railways Vol.1)	David & Charles	1973
Thomas, John	Scotland The Lowlands & the Borders (Regional History of Railways Vol 6)	David & Charles	1971
Thomas, John & Turnock, David	North of Scotland (Regional History of Railways Vol 15)	David & Charles	1989
Vaughan, John	The Newquay Branch	OPC	1991
Vincent, Mike	Reflections on the Portishead Branch	OPC	1983
Whetmath, CFD	The Bodmin & Wadebridge Railway	Branch Line Handbooks	1967
White, HP	Southern England (Regional History of Railways Vol 2)	David & Charles	1982
White, HP	Greater London (Regional History of Railways Vol 3)	David & Charles	1987
Whitehead, RA & Simpson, FD	The Colne Valley & Halstead Railway	Oakwood	1988
Wright, Neil R	The Railways of Boston	Richard Kay	1971
Wrottesley, AJ	The Midland & Great Northern Joint Railway	David & Charles	1970
Wrottesley, John	Great Northern Railway Vol.2	Batsford	1979
	A History of the Middleton Railway Leeds	MRPS/MRT	1973
	Airey's Railway Map of Cumberland and Westmorland		1870
	Airey's Railway Map of Gloucestershire & Oxfordshire		1893
	Airey's Railway Map of Lancashire		1888
	Airey's Railway Map of Lancashire & District		1881
	Airey's Railway Map of London & Its Suburbs		1886
	Airey's Railway Map of London & Its Suburbs		1894
	Airey's Railway Map of Scotland		1891
	Airey's Railway Map of South Wales		1889
	Airey's Railway Map of the Derbyshire & Nottinghamshire District		1884
	Airey's Railway Map of the Durham & Northumberland District		1894
	Airey's Railway Map of the East of England		1886-93
	Airey's Railway Map of Yorkshire & District		1892
	Bradshaw Britain & Ireland		1890
	British Railway Maps of Yesteryear	Ian Allan	1991
	British Railways Pre-Grouping Atlas and Gazetteer	Ian Allan	1972
	Handbook of Stations	Henry Oliver	1895
	Railway Diagrams of London & Its Suburbs	Railway Clearing House	1888
	Railway Junction Diagrams	Railway Clearing House	1888
	Railway Junction Diagrams	Railway Clearing House	1895
	Railway Timetables in the National Archives Collection (various)		1889-1891
	The Railway Clearing House Handbook of Railway Stations 1904	David & Charles (reprint)	1970

INDEX OF RAILWAY COMPANIES

GY&C	Glasgow, Yoker & Clydebank
H&CJt	Hammersmith & City Joint (GW and MET., worked by MET.)
H&OJt	Halifax & Ovenden Joint (GN and L&Y)
H&WN	Hunstanton & West Norfolk (worked by GE)
Halesowen	Halesowen (worked by GW and MID.)
Hall's Tm.	Hall's Tramroad (worked by GW)
Harborne	Harborne (worked by L&NW)
Hayling	Hayling (worked by LB&SC)
HB&WRJn	Hull, Barnsley & West Riding Junction Railway & Dock
H'castle	Horncastle (worked by GN)
Helston	Helston (worked by GW)
HHL	Halifax High Level & North & South Junction (worked by GN and L&Y)
HR	Highland
IoM	Isle of Man
IoW	Isle of Wight
IoWC	Isle of Wight Central
IV	Ilen Valley (worked by CB&SC)
JE	Jersey Eastern
Jersey	Jersey
K&B	Kilsyth & Bonnybridge (worked by CAL. and NB)
K&E	Kington & Eardisley (worked by GW)
K&N	Kanturk & Newmarket (worked by GS&W)
K&T	Kilmarnock & Troon (worked by G&SW)
Killin	Killin (worked by CAL.)
KJn	Kilkenny Junction (worked by W&L)
KLDock	King's Lynn Dock Co. (worked by GE)
KT&H	Kettering, Thrapstone & Huntingdon (worked by MID.)
L&A	Lanarkshire & Ayrshire (worked by CAL.)
L&B	Listowel & Ballybunion
L&C	Liskeard & Caradon
L&D	Limavady & Dungiven (worked by B&NC)
L&E	Limerick & Ennis (worked by W&L)
L&EC	Louth & East Coast (worked by GN)
L&F	Limerick & Foynes (worked by W&L)
L&G	London & Greenwich (worked by SE)
L&IDocks	London & India Docks Joint Committee
L&K	Limerick & Kerry (worked by W&L)
L&L	Liskeard & Looe (worked by L&C)
L&LS	Londonderry & Lough Swilly
L&MM	Llanelly & Mynydd Mawr
L&NW	London & North Western
L&SW	London & South Western
L&Y	Lancashire & Yorkshire
LB&SC	London, Brighton & South Coast
LC&D	London, Chatham & Dover
L'derry	Londonderry
Lee Moor	Lee Moor Tramway
Letterkenny	Letterkenny (worked by L&LS)
Ll&C	Llangollen & Corwen (worked by GW)
LL&CST	Lucan, Leixlip & Celbridge Steam Tramway (worked by D&LST)
Lm&K	Leominster & Kington (worked by GW)
London Necropolis Co.	London Necropolis Company
Longdendale	Longdendale (Manchester Corporation)
LP&HC	Londonderry Port & Harbour Commissioners
LS&PJc	Liverpool, Southport & Preston Junction (worked by WLancs)
LT&S	London, Tilbury & Southend
Ludlow & Clee Hill	Ludlow & Clee Hill (worked by GW and L&NW)
LUJt	Lancashire Union Joint (L&NW and L&Y)
Lydd	Lydd
M&C	Maryport & Carlisle
M&D	Merrybent & Darlington
M&DJn.	Mold & Denbigh Junction (worked by L&NW)
M&E	Mellis & Eye (worked by GE)
M&M	Manchester & Milford
M&SWJn.	Midland & South Western Junction
Marl.	Marlborough (worked by GW)
Marland Lt.	Marland Light
Mawddwy	Mawddwy
MD&HB	Mersey Docks & Harbour Board
MER.	Mersey
MET.	Metropolitan
MET.-DIS.	Metropolitan District
MGW	Midland Great Western
MH&P	Muswell Hill & Palace (worked by GN)
MID.	Midland
Middleton	Middleton
Mid-Wales	Mid-Wales (worked by CAM.)
Milford	Milford (worked by GW)
Millwall Ex.	Millwall Extension (worked by GE and dock companies)
Minehead	Minehead (worked by GW)
MJt	Methley Joint (GN, L&Y and NE)
MK(B-StMC)	Mid-Kent (Bromley to St. Mary Cray) (worked by LC&D)
MN	Manx Northern
MS&L	Manchester, Sheffield & Lincolnshire
MSJ&A	Manchester South Junction & Altrincham (MS&L and L&NW, worked by MS&L)
MW&SJc	Much Wenlock & Severn Junction (worked by GW)
N&B	Neath & Brecon (worked by MID.)
N&BJn.	Northampton & Banbury Junction
N&GR&C	Nottingham & Grantham Railway & Canal (worked by GN)
N&MD	Nantwich & Market Drayton (worked by GW)
N&RJt.	Nantybwch & Rhymney Joint (L&NW and Rhym.)
N&SWJn	North & South Western Junction (L&NW, MID. and NL)
NB	North British
NE	North Eastern
Newent	Newent (worked by GW)
Newport	Newport (worked by NB)
NL	North London
Nott. Sub.	Nottingham Suburban (worked by GN)
NP&F	North Pembrokeshire & Fishguard
NS	North Staffordshire
NWNG	North Wales Narrow Gauge
O&AT	Oxford & Aylesbury Tramroad
O&IJt	Otley & Ilkley Joint (MID. and NE)
OA&G	Oldham, Ashton-under-Lyne & Guide Bridge Junction (L&NW and MS&L)
Oldbury	Oldbury (worked by GW)
Oy.	Oystermouth
P&D	Plymouth & Dartmoor
P&T	Pembroke & Tenby (worked by GW)
P&WJt	Portpatrick & Wigtownshire Joint (CAL., G&SW, MID. and L&NW)
Padarn	Padarn
PC&BT	Portmadoc, Croesor & Beddgelert Tram
PC&N	Pontypridd, Caerphilly & Newport (worked by A(N&SW)D&R)
PD&SWJn	Plymouth, Devonport & South Western Junction (worked by L&SW)
Penrhyn	Penrhyn
Pensnett	Pensnett
Pentewan	Pentewan
Princetown	Princetown (worked by GW)
PS&NW	Potteries, Shrewsbury & North Wales
PsT	Portstewart Tramway
Q&MJt.	Quaker's Yard & Merthyr Joint (GW and Rhym.)
R&E	Ravenglass & Eskdale
R&H	Royston & Hitchin (worked by GN)
R&KF	Rowrah & Kelton Fell (Mineral)
R&M	Ross & Monmouth (worked by GW)
R&NJn	Rathkeale & Newcastle Junction (worked by W&L)
R&SB	Rhondda & Swansea Bay
Ramsey	Ramsey (worked by GN)

Redruth & C'water	Redruth & Chasewater	Van	Van
Rhym.	Rhymney	VE	Volks Electric
RPT	Ryde Pier & Tramway	VoL	Vale of Llangollen (worked by GW)
S&A	Strathendrick & Aberfoyle (worked by NB)	W&B	Wivenhoe & Brightlingsea (worked by GE)
S&D Jt.	Somerset & Dorset Joint (L&SW and MID.)	W&C	Whitland & Cardigan (worked by GW)
S&E	Stamford & Essendine (worked by GN)	W&CI	Waterford & Central Ireland (worked by W&L)
S&F	Spilsby & Firsby (worked by GN)	W&F	Wainfleet & Firsby (worked by GN)
S&HJt	Shrewsbury & Hereford Joint (GW and L&NW)	W&L	Waterford & Limerick
S&KJt	Swinton & Knottingley Joint (MID. and NE)	W&PJt.	Weymouth & Portland Joint (GW/L&SW,
S&MJt	Sheffield & Midland Joint (MID. and MS&L)		worked by L&SW)
S&SLt	Schull & Skibbereen Light	W&R	Weatherhill & Rookhope (worked by Weardale
S&W	Sutton & Willoughby (worked by GN)		Iron Company)
S&WJt	Severn & Wye & Severn Bridge Joint (GW and	W&RT	Warrenpoint & Rostrevor Tramway
	MID.)	W&S	Watton & Swaffham (worked by GE)
S&WnJt	Shrewsbury & Wellington Joint (GW and	W&SJc	Wellington & Severn Junction (worked by GW)
	L&NW)	W&T	Waterford & Tramore
S&WpJt	Shrewsbury & Welshpool Joint (GW and	W&W	Waterford & Wexford (worked by DW&W)
	L&NW)	Wantage	Wantage Tramway
S(I)	Southern (of Ireland) (worked by W&L)	WC	Waterloo Colliery
Saundersfoot	Saundersfoot Railway & Harbour	WC&EJt	Whitehaven, Cleator & Egremont Joint (FUR.
Sc&Wby	Scarborough & Whitby (worked by NE)		and L&NW)
Scole Tramway	Scole Tramway	WClare	West Clare
SE	South Eastern	WD	West Donegal
SH&D	Seacombe, Hoylake & Deeside	WD&L	Waterford, Dungarvan & Lismore
Sidmouth	Sidmouth (worked by L&SW)	Wenlock	Wenlock (worked by GW)
SJ	Solway Junction (worked by CAL.)	West Somerset	West Somerset (worked by GW)
SL&NC	Sligo, Leitrim & Northern Counties	West Somerset Mineral	West Somerset Mineral
Snailbeach Dist.	Snailbeach District	Whit.	Whittingham
Southwold	Southwold	Whiteinch	Whiteinch (worked by NB)
SSM&WC	South Shields, Marsden & Whitburn Colliery	Wirral	Wirral
Stocksbridge	Stocksbridge	Witney	Witney (worked by GW)
SWMin.	South Wales Mineral	WJn	Wigan Junction (worked by MS&L)
T&CL	Timoleague & Courtmacsherry Light	WLancs	West Lancashire
T&F	Tralee & Fenit (worked by W&L)	WLEJt	West London Extension Joint (L&NW, GW,
T&HJc	Tottenham & Hampstead Junction (worked by		LB&SC and L&SW)
	GE and MID.)	WLJt	West London Joint (GW and L&NW)
T&ND	Tiverton & North Devon (worked by GW)	WM&CQ	Wrexham, Mold & Connah's Quay
T&W	Thetford & Watton (worked by GE)	WR&GJt	West Riding & Grimsby Joint (GN and MS&L)
Talyllyn	Talyllyn	WSS&D	Wolverton, Stony Stratford & District Light
TBJt.	Taff Bargoed Joint (GW and Rhym.)	Wye Valley	Wye Valley (worked by GW)
TV	Taff Vale		

Note on the maps

As mentioned in the introduction, the maps in this work have been based on those in the classic *Pre-Grouping Atlas of Great Britain* (itself derived from Airey's contemporary maps of the 19th and early 20th century). Lines of different companies are shown in different colours or styles (eg, broken lines) to distinguish them one from another, maintaining consistency with the *Pre-Grouping Atlas* wherever possible. There is no other significance in the colour or style of line used for a particular company and the same colours and styles are used for a number of different railways (e.g., blue for the Cheshire Lines Committee and the Great Eastern) where no confusion is likely. Company abbreviations are given against the lines at frequent intervals and a key to these is provided in the Index to Railway Companies, which also gives information on those which did not operate their own trains but were operated by larger concerns, many which were to eventually absorb them completely.

All passenger stations are shown, using a coloured dot with the name in capitals. Other railway locations, such as major goods stations, collieries, works, summits and junctions, are indicated by a thin black line with the name in title case, although this atlas does not attempt to show them all. Names have been indicated by a number and a footnote elsewhere on the page, where space has been tight. All named railway locations on the maps are listed in the index, similarly using capitals for passenger stations, with company name and map reference (and footnote number where applicable). Some geographical features such as lakes and mountains are named on the maps but these are not included in the index. Counties have been shown on the maps with names and boundaries as they were in 1890.

Cartography by Maidenhead Cartographics, Berks.

DIAGRAM OF MAPS

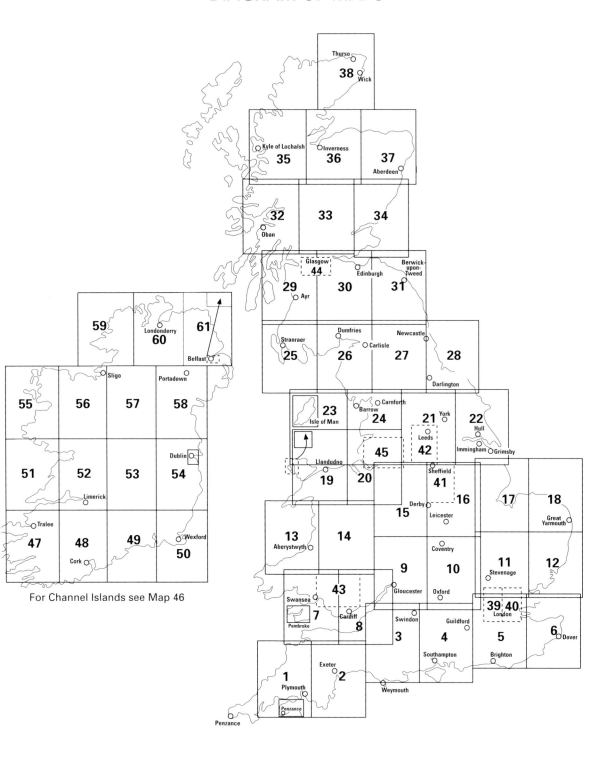

For Channel Islands see Map 46

1 2 Seven 3 4 5

A

B

C

D

E

F

G

Inset (Plymouth):

KEYHAM ADMIRALTY PLATFORM (military)
P&D
Marland Light Railway
Peter's Marland
PLYMOUTH NORTH RD. (Joint)
Devonport Jc.
Laira Jc.
MUTLEY
West Jc.
North Rd. Jc.
Friary Jc.
DEVONPORT
Cornwall Jc.
Friary (Goods)
L. & S.W. Goods
North Quay
Sutton Harbour
Stonehouse Pool
MILLBAY
PLYMOUTH DOCKS (boat trains)
Cattewater Harbour

D D E

HOLSWORTHY
DUNSLAND CROSS
HALWILL JUNC.
ASHBURY
ASHWATER
TOWER HILL
LIFTON
LAUNCESTON
CORYTON
LIDFORD
MARYTAVY
TAVISTOCK
HORRABRIDGE

C O R N W A L L

Wenford Bridge
L & SW (Bodmin & Wadebridge Rly.)
WADEBRIDGE
Grogley Jc.
Ruthern Bridge
BODMIN
Boscarne Jc.
G.W.
BODMIN ROAD
Brownqueen Tun.
DOUBLEBOIS
Cheesewring Quarry
RILLATON BRIDGE (unadvertised)
Minions
TOKENBURY CORNER (unadvertised)
SOUTH CARADON (Private)
Kit Hill
East Cornwall Mineral Rly.
RAILWAY TERRACE (unadvertised)
ST. CLEER (unadvertised)
Calstock Quay
MOORSWATER
LISKEARD
COOMBE
MENHENIOT
ST GERMANS
SALTASH
Royal Albert Bridge
NORTH ROAD
DEVONPORT
MILLBAY
PLYMOUTH
CAUSELAND
SANDPLACE
LOOE
L. & L.R.
P&D

Harbour
NEWQUAY
St. Dennis Jc.
VICTORIA for ROCHE
Tolcarn Jc.
ST. COLUMB RD.
Carbis
BUGLE
BRIDGES
LOSTWITHIEL
Melangoose Mill
Drinnick Mill
Treverrin Tun.
Cornwall Minerals Railway
Treamble
East Wheal Rose
ST. BLAZEY
PAR
BURNGULLOW
ST. AUSTELL
FOWEY
GRAMPOUND ROAD
ST AUSTELL (unadvertised)
Pentewan Railway
PENTEWAN (unadvertised)

Polperro Tun.
G.W.
TICKET PLATFORM
Buckshead Tun.
CHACEWATER
TRURO
Newham (Goods)
SCORRIER GATE
Penwithers Jc.
Point Quay
PERRANWELL
Redruth & Chasewater Rly.
PENRYN
FALMOUTH

Inset (West Cornwall):

E F

ST. IVES
CARBIS BAY
LELANT
HAYLE
ST. ERTH
MARAZION ROAD
PENZANCE
Wharves
CAMBORNE
GWINEAR ROAD
G.W.
Roskear
Crofty
Redruth Jc.
REDRUTH
Portreath (Goods)
CHACEWATER
SCORRIER GATE
CARN BREA
Tresavean
PRAZE
Helston Railway
NANCEGOLLAN
HELSTON

L & S.W.

EGGESFORD

V   O   N   S   H   I   R   E

LAPFORD

MORCHARD ROAD
COPPLESTONE

T. & N.D.
BolhamJc.
BURLESCOMBE
TIVERTON
CULMSTOCK
HEMYOCK
TIVERTON JUNC.
UFFCULME
CADELEIGH & BICKLEIGH
CULLOMPTON
UP EXE & SILVERTON
THORVERTON
SILVERTON
HELE & BRADNINCH
Honiton Summit
Honiton Tun.
JOINT CHARD TOWN

SAMPFORD COURTENAY
L & S.W.
NORTH TAWTON
BOW (DEVON)
YEOFORD JUNC.
Coleford Jc.
CREDITON
BRAMPFORD SPEKE
SIDMOUTH JUNC.
HONITON
AXMINSTER

OKEHAMPTON
ST. CYRES
STOKE CANON
WHIMPLE
SEATON JUNC.
COLYTON TOWN

Meldon Jc.
Summit
Cowley Bridge Jc.
ST. DAVIDS
ST. THOMAS
EXETER
Exmouth Jc.
QUEEN STREET
City Basin
PINHOE
BROAD CLYST
OTTERY ST MARY
TIPTON ST JOHN'S
Sidmouth Rly.
COLYFORD
SEATON & BEER

Yes Tor
BRIDESTOWE

MORETONHAMPSTEAD
Teign House
EXMINSTER
TOPSHAM
Harbour
WOODBURY ROAD
LYMPSTONE
SIDMOUTH

ASHTON
G.W.
LUSTLEIGH
TRUSHAM
STARCROSS
EXMOUTH
BOVEY
CHUDLEIGH
DAWLISH
HEATHFIELD
TEIGNGRACE
TEIGNMOUTH

PRINCETOWN
Princetown Rly.
DOUSLAND
YELVERTON
ASHBURTON
NEWTON ABBOT
Aller Jc.
KINGSKERSWELL
B.T. & S.D. Rly.
Summit
Dainton Tun.
TORRE
TORQUAY

BICKLEIGH
Lee Moor
Lee Moor Tramway
CORNWOOD
BUCKFASTLEIGH
STAVERTON (DEVON)
Ashburton Jc.
Marley Tun.
BRENT
Quay
PAIGNTON
MARSH MILLS
PLYMPTON
Tavistock Jc.
Hemerdon Bank
IVYBRIDGE
Wrangaton Summit
KINGSBRIDGE ROAD
Rattery Bank
TOTNES
BRIXHAM
CHURSTON
KINGSWEAR

1   2   3   Nine   4   5

PORTISHEAD
Pier
AVONMOUTH
SHIREHAMPTON
SEA MILLS
FILTON
FISH PONDS
Westerleigh Jc.
G.W.
Portbury
PILL
CLIFTON DOWN
BRISTOL
STAPLEHILL
MANGOTSFIELD
WARMLEY
MID.
CHIPPENHAM
Calne Rly.
W I L T S
CLIFTON BR.
TEMPLE MEADS
St. Annes Wood Tun.
Brislington Tun.
BITTON
BLACK DOG SIDING (Private)
CLEVEDON
FLAX BOURTON
SEE INSET
BRISLINGTON
KEYNSHAM
KELSTON for SALTFORD
BOX
Box Tun.
CORSHAM
Thingley Jc.
CALNE
NAILSEA
SALTFORD
Middle Hill Tun.
YATTON
G.W.
PENSFORD
WESTON
Twerton Tun.
TWERTON
Mid.
G.W.
BATHAMPTON
MELKSHAM
CONGRESBURY
PUXTON
Worle Jc.
WORLE
Frys Bottom Col.
Devonshire Tun.
Combe Down Tun.
BATH
HOLT JUNC.
SEEND
DEVIZES
WOODBOROUGH
WESTON - SUPER - MARE
SANDFORD & BANWELL
CLUTTON
Greyfield Col.
CAMERTON
MIDFORD
LIMPLEY STOKE
BRADFORD
Uphill Jc.
BLEADON & UPHILL
WINSCOMBE
HALLATROW
FRESHFORD
Bradford Jc.
TROWBRIDGE
AXBRIDGE
CHEDDAR
WELTON
S. & D.
RADSTOCK
WELLOW
BRENT KNOLL
DRAYCOTT
MIDSOMER NORTON
G.W.
MELLS
WESTBURY
BURNHAM
Level Crossing
HIGHBRIDGE
LODGE HILL
Chilcompton Tun.
CHILCOMPTON
BASON BRIDGE
WOOKEY
BINEGAR
Vobster
G.W.
EDINGTON ROAD
Masbury Summit
MASBURY
FROME
WARMINSTER
DUNBALL
SHAPWICK
WELLS (G.W.)
WELLS PRIORY RD (S. & D.)
Winsor Hill Tun.
CRANMORE
WANSTROW
HEYTESBURY
Docks
BRIDGWATER
POLSHAM
(G.W.)
CHARLTON RD.
(S. & D.)
SHEPTON MALLET
WEST PENNARD
PYLLE
WITHAM
CODFORD
ASHCOTT
GLASTONBURY & STREET
EVERCREECH NEW
WYLYE
S O M E R S E T
EVERCREECH JUNC.
S. & D. J.
BRUTON
WISHFORD
COLE
CASTLE CARY
(L. & S.W. & MID.)
DINTON
WILTON
G.W.
ATHELNEY
G.W.
WINCANTON
TISBURY
L. & S.W.
L. & S.W.
DURSTON
SPARKFORD
GILLINGHAM
SEMLEY
LANGPORT
MARSTON
Goods S. & D.
Buckhorn Weston Tun.
MARTOCK
TEMPLECOMBE
HATCH
G.W.
MONTACUTE
PEN MILL
Summit
LOWER PLT. (S. & D)
MILBORNE PORT
HENSTRIDGE
ILMINSTER
YEOVIL
TOWN Joint
Clifton Mayb'nk Jc.
SHERBORNE
STALBRIDGE
L. & S.W.
STURMINSTER NEWTON
DAGGENS ROAD
YEOVIL JUNC.
Clifton Maybank (Goods)
S. & D. Jt.
SUTTON BINGHAM
L. & S.W.
SHILLINGSTONE
VERWOOD
JOINT
CHARD
CREWKERNE
YETMINSTER
(L. & S.W. & MID.)
TOWN
Hewish Summit
BLANDFORD
WEST MOORS
CHARD JUNC.
EVERSHOT
Summit
D O R S E T S H I R E
SPETISBURY
BAILEY GATE
WIMBORNE
Bridport Rly.
TOLLER
MAIDEN NEWTON
Corfe Mullen Jc.
POWERSTOCK
GRIMSTONE & FRAMPTON
BROADSTONE JUNC.
BRIDPORT
EAST STREET
HAMWORTHY JUNC.
POOLE
EAST
WEST BAY
DORCHESTER (G.W.)
Goods (L. & S.W.)
L. & S.W.
HAMWORTHY
PARKSTONE
BOURNE-MOUTH
Dorchester Jc.
(L. & S.W.)
MORETON
WAREHAM
Arne
PORTESHAM
Abbotsbury Rly.
Bincombe Summit
WOOL
L. & S.W.
Worgret Junc.
Goathorn Pier
ABBOTSBURY
BROADWAY
Bincombe Tuns.
Furzebrook Tmy.
Goathorn Rly.
UPWEY JUNC.
West Creech
Norden
CORFE CASTLE
Portland Jc.
TOWN QUAY
WEYMOUTH
SWANAGE
RODWELL
W. & P. Jt.
(L. & S. W. & G.W. Jt.)
PORTLAND

Inset (Bristol)
Sneyd Park Jc.
CLIFTON DOWN
B. P. & P.
ASHLEY HILL
MONTPELIER
Ashley Hill Jc.
STAPLETON RD.
CLIFTON
BRISTOL
ST. PHILIP'S
Kingswood Jc.
CLIFTON BRIDGE
Wapping Wharf
Gds.
Lower Yard Goods
Lawrence Hill Jc.
LAWRENCE HILL
TEMPLE MEADS
Joint
Dr. Days Bridge Jc.
Pylle Hill (Gds)
Feeder Br. Jc.
BEDMINSTER
Bedminster Jc.

Eight

Two

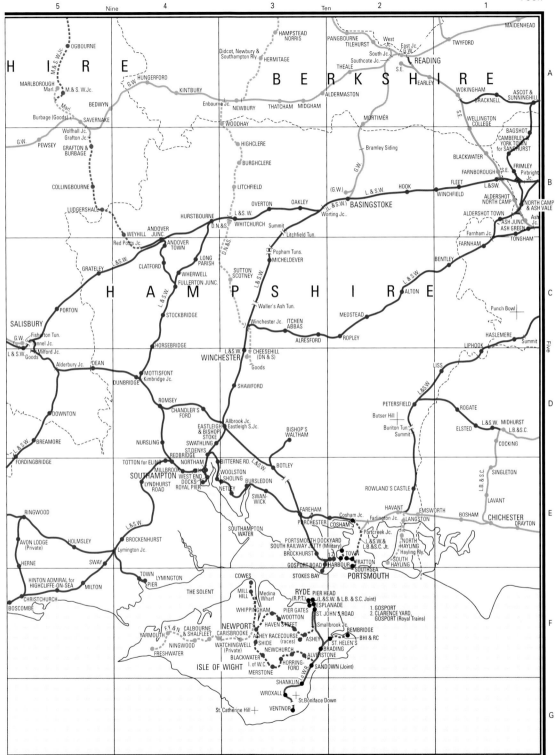

5   Nine   4   3   Ten   2   1

H I R E

OGBOURNE

MARLBOROUGH
Marl. M & S. W Jc.

BEDWYN

Burbage (Goods)
SAVERNAKE

G.W. PEWSEY
Wolfhall Jc.
Grafton Jc.
GRAFTON & BURBAGE

COLLINGBOURNE

LUDGERSHALL

WEYHILL

GRATELEY

SALISBURY
G.W. Fisherton Tun.
Tunnel Jc.
L & S.W. Milford Jc.
Goods

Alderbury Jc.
DEAN

PORTON

ANDOVER JUNC
ANDOVER TOWN

Red Potts Jc.

CLATFORD
LONG PARISH

WHERWELL
FULLERTON JUNC.

STOCKBRIDGE

HORSEBRIDGE

DUNBRIDGE
Kimbridge Jc.
MOTTISFONT

ROMSEY

CHANDLER'S FORD

NURSLING

HUNGERFORD

KINTBURY

Enbourne Jc.
NEWBURY   THATCHAM   MIDGHAM

WOODHAY

HIGHCLERE

BURGHCLERE

LITCHFIELD

OVERTON   OAKLEY

HURSTBOURNE
WHITCHURCH   Summit
L & S.W.
D.N.&.S.

SUTTON SCOTNEY

Popham Tuns.
MICHELDEVER

Waller's Ash Tun.

Winchester Jc.
ITCHEN ABBAS

CHEESEHILL
(DN & S)
WINCHESTER
Goods

SHAWFORD

BISHOP'S WALTHAM

B E R K S H I R E

HAMPSTEAD NORRIS

Didcot, Newbury &
Southampton Rly
HERMITAGE

PANGBOURNE
TILEHURST   West Jc.   East Jc.
G.W.
Southcote Jc.   READING
Theale   S.E.

ALDERMASTON

MORTIMER

Bramley Siding

(G.W.)   L & S.W.   HOOK
(L & S.W.)   BASINGSTOKE
Worting Jc.
Litchfield Tun.

MEDSTEAD

ALRESFORD   ROPLEY

MAIDENHEAD

TWYFORD

EARLEY

WOKINGHAM   ASCOT & SUNNINGHILL
BRACKNELL
S.E.
WELLINGTON COLLEGE
BAGSHOT
CAMBERLEY & YORK TOWN
for SANDHURST

BLACKWATER
S.E.
FARNBOROUGH   FRIMLEY
Pirbright Jc.
FLEET   L & S.W.
WINCHFIELD   ALDERSHOT NORTH CAMP
NORTH CAMP & ASH VALE
ALDERSHOT TOWN   Ash
ASH JUNC.   Jc.
ASH GREEN

Farnham Jc.

FARNHAM   TONGHAM

BENTLEY

ALTON

Punch Bowl

HASLEMERE

LIPHOOK   Summit
Five
LISS

H A M P S H I R E

L & S.W.

L & S.W.

L & S.W.

PETERSFIELD

ROGATE

Butser Hill   L&S.W.   MIDHURST
ELSTED   L.B.&S.C.
Buriton Tun.
Summit   COCKING

L.B. & S.C.
SINGLETON

LAVANT

CHICHESTER
DRAYTON

DOWNTON

BREAMORE

FORDINGBRIDGE
L & S.W.

EASTLEIGH & BISHOPSTOKE
Allbrook Jc.
Eastleigh S.Jc.
SWATHLING
ST.DENYS
REDBRIDGE
TOTTON for ELING
NORTHAM   BITTERNE RD.   BOTLEY
MILLBROOK   L.&S.W.
SOUTHAMPTON   WOOLSTON
WEST END   SHOLING
DOCKS   BURSLEDON
LYNDHURST   ROYAL PIER   NETLEY
ROAD   SWAN-WICK

ROWLAND'S CASTLE

HAVANT   EMSWORTH
BOSHAM

RINGWOOD

AVON LODGE
(Private)

HOLMSLEY

HERNE   SWAY

HINTON ADMIRAL for
HIGHCLIFFE-ON-SEA

CHRISTCHURCH
BOSCOMBE

BROCKENHURST

Lymington Jc.
L & S.W.

TOWN
LYMINGTON
PIER
MILTON

FAREHAM

PORTCHESTER

SOUTHAMPTON
WATER

THE SOLENT

COWES

MILL
HILL

WHIPPINGHAM

Medina
Wharf
PIER GATES
WOOTTON

NEWPORT
CARISBROOKE
YARMOUTH   CALBOURNE
& SHALFLEET
NINGWOOD   WATCHINGWELL
(Private)
FRESHWATER   BLACKWATER
I. of W.C.
MERSTONE

ISLE OF WIGHT

St. Catherine Hill

HAVEN STREET

ASHEY RACECOURSE
(races)   SHIDE
NEWCHURCH
HORRINGFORD
C.&N.
SANDOWN (Joint)

WROXALL
St.Boniface Down

VENTNOR

COSHAM   Cosham Jc.
Farlington Jc.
Portcreek Jc.
LANGSTON
PORTSMOUTH DOCKYARD
SOUTH RAILWAY JETTY (Military)   L.&S.W.&
L.B.&S.C. Jt.
BROCKHURST   TOWN
GOSPORT ROAD   HARBOUR   FRATTON
Stokes Bay   SOUTHSEA
PORTSMOUTH

NORTH
HAYLING
Hayling Rly
SOUTH
HAYLING

RYDE
(R.P.T.)   PIER HEAD
(L.&S.W. & L.B. & S.C. Joint)
ESPLANADE
ST. JOHN'S ROAD
Smallbrook   BEMBRIDGE
ASHEY   BHI & RC
ST. HELEN'S
BRADING
ALVERSTONE
I.W.N.R.
SHANKLIN

1. GOSPORT
2. CLARENCE YARD,
   GOSPORT (Royal Trains)

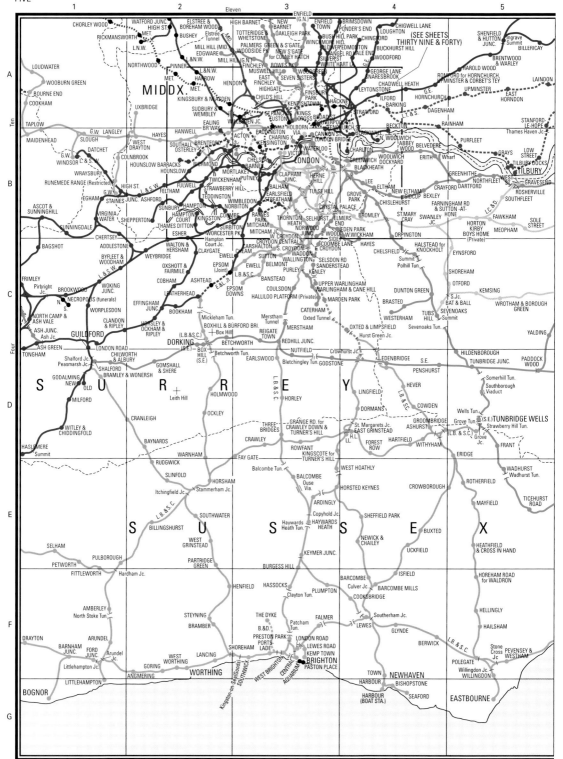

5   4   3   Twelve   2   1

WOODHAM FERRIS
BATTLESBRIDGE
FAMBRIDGE
ALTHORNE
BURNHAM-ON-CROUCH
WICKFORD JUNC.
G.E.
HOCKLEY
RAYLEIGH
ROCHFORD
L.T. & S.
PITSEA
BENFLEET   LEIGH
PRITTLEWELL
(G.E.)
L.T. & S.
(L.T. & S.)
Canvey Island
SHOEBURYNESS
SOUTHEND-ON-SEA

THAMES HAVEN
(Workmen)

A

CLIFFE
Hoo Jc.
HIGHAM   SHARNAL STR.
Higham Tun.
Strood Tun.
ROCHESTER & STROOD
STROOD
Rochester Br. Jc.
CUXTON
Fort Pitt Tun.
Dockyard
NEW BROMPTON (GILLINGHAM)
Gillingham Tun.
Chatham Tun.
CHATHAM
RAINHAM
NEWINGTON
King's Ferry Bri.
Middle Jc.
West Jc.   SITTINGBOURNE
East Jc.
TEYNHAM
Quay
FAVERSHAM
Faversham Jc.
Graveney (Goods)
Tyler Hill Tun.
S.E.

PORT VICTORIA
SHEERNESS DOCKYARD
SHEERNESS-ON-SEA
QUEENBOROUGH PIER
QUEENBOROUGH
Isle of Sheppey

WHITSTABLE (S.E.)
WHITSTABLE-ON-SEA
HERNE BAY & HAMPTON-ON-SEA
STURRY for HERNE BAY
GROVE FERRY
L.C. & D.
BIRCHINGTON-ON-SEA
ST. LAWRENCE (PEGWELL BAY)
Minster East Jc.
Minster West Jc.
MINSTER JUNC.
MARGATE & CLIFTONVILLE
WESTGATE-ON-SEA
(S.E.)   MARGATE
EAST
BROADSTAIRS
RAMSGATE (S.E.)
RAMSGATE & ST. LAWRENCE-ON-SEA

B

SNODLAND
AYLESFORD
MALLING   Preston Hall Tuns.
(L.C.&D.)   BEARSTED
BARMING
BARRACKS
TOVIL   (S.E.)   HOLLINGBOURNE
EAST FARLEIGH
WATERINGBURY
MAIDSTONE
HARRIETSHAM
LENHAM
L.C. & D.
CHARING

CANTERBURY
SOUTH CANTERBURY
L.C. & D.
SELLING
Selling Tun.
CHILHAM
CHARTHAM
BRIDGE
BISHOPSBOURNE
BEKESBOURNE
ADISHAM
SANDWICH
DEAL
WALMER
S.E./L.C.&D. Joint

K   E   N   T

C

MARDEN   STAPLEHURST
HEADCORN
S.E.
PLUCKLEY
L.C. & D.
ASHFORD   S.E.

HOTHFIELD
WYE
SMEETH
Sandling Tun.
SANDLING JUNC.
WESTENHANGER
HAM STREET

ELHAM
LYMINGE
Saltwood Tun.
RADNOR PARK
Martello Tun.
Abbotscliff Tun.
Shakespeare Tun.
SHORNCLIFFE CAMP
HYTHE
SANDGATE
TOWN & HARBOUR
Archcliffe Jc.
TOWN
FOLKESTONE
HARB.
Foord Via.
SHEPHERDS WELL
Lydden Tun.
KEARSNEY
Deal Jc.
Buckland Jc.
Charlton Tun.
PRIORY
DOVER
ADMIRALTY PIER
MARTIN MILL
Guston Tun.
Priory Tun.
Harb. Tun.

D

ETCHINGHAM
ROBERTSBRIDGE
Mountfield Tun.
BATTLE
Bopeep Tunnel
Ore Tun.
WEST ST. LEONARDS
Bopeep Jc.
ORE
Mount Pleasant Tun.
BEXHILL
WEST MARINA
WARRIOR SQUARE
ST. LEONARDS
HASTINGS (Joint)
Hastings Tun.

APPLEDORE
BROOKLAND
Lydd Rly.
NEW ROMNEY & LITTLESTONE-ON-SEA
LYDD
RYE
Harbour
WINCHELSEA
DUNGENESS

E

F

G

1 2 Thirteen 3 4 Fourteen 5

Gehirrach

Taf Vale Jc. — Cardigan Jc. WHITLAND — ST CLEARS
P&T — SARNAU — CARMARTHEN JUNCTION — DRYSLLWYN
DERWYDD ROAD — LLANDEBIE — PENWYLLT
SEE SHEET NO.

Cwmmawr — Cross Hands — GARNANT — BRYNAMMAN — ABERCRAVE
Mynydd-y-Garreg — Pontyberem — Mountain Branch — GLANAMMAN — YNISCEDWYN — COLBREN JUNC
FERRYSIDE — Tumble — TIRYDAIL — AMMANFORD — GWYS — ONLLWYN
BP & GV — Cwm Blawd — PANTYFFYNNON — SEVEN SISTERS
KIDWELLY — Pont Yates — Gurnos (Gds) — GLYN NEATH
G.V. — Cynheidre — YSTALYFERA — CRYNANT — G.W.
Horeb — Ynisygeinon Jc. — MID
Quay — Trimsaran (Goods) — PONTARDULAIS (Joint) — PONTARDAWE — RESOLVEN
Tycoch Jc. — L & M.M. — GLAM.
G.V. — Pwll Col. Felin Foel — LLAN-GENNECH — CWM CLYDACH — CILFREW PLAT
PEMBREY & BURRY PORT — Victoria Rd (Gds) Dafen — GLAIS — ABERDYLAIS — SWM
Burry Port (Gds) — LLANELLY — BYNEA — DYNEVOR — TREHERBERT
Docks — L & N.W. — GORSEINON — MORRISTON — NEATH — ABER-GWYNFI
Dock Goods — PENCLAWDD — PLAS MARL — NEATH ABBEY — CWM-AVON — CYMMER — NANTYMOEL
LLANMORLAIS — (L & N.W.) — LANDORE — BRITON FERRY — TYWITH — Pwllcarne Col.
GOWERTON — Summit — UP. BANK — MAESTEG — PONTY-RHYLL — TYNEWYDD OGMORE VALE
DUNVANT — COCKETT — HIGH ST. — ABERAVON
KILLAY — RUTLAND ST. — SWAN-SEA BAY — PORT TALBOT — TROEDYRHIEW GARTH — LLANGONOYD — LLANGEINOR
MUMBLES ROAD — Oystermouth Rly. — BLACKMILL
MUMBLES — KENFIG HILL — TONDU — Bryncethin Jc.
PYLE — G.W. — BRIDGEND
PORTHCAWL

HAVERFORDWEST — NARBERTH
G.W. — TEMPLETON
JOHNSTON — Milford Rly. — KILGETTY & BEGELLY — Bonville's Court Col.
MILFORD — SAUNDERSFOOT — Pier
NEW MILFORD — Saundersfoot Rly.
PEMBROKE DOCK — PEMBROKE — TENBY
P. & T. — PENALLY
LAMPHEY — MANORBIER

BRISTOL

ILFRACOMBE
Summit — MORTHOE
L. & S.W.
BRAUNTON
WRAFTON — TOWN — BARNSTAPLE
FREMING-TON — JUNC. — SWIMBRIDGE — FILLEIGH
INSTOW — Devon & Somerset Rly. — BISHOP'S NYMPTON & MOLLAND — DULVERTON
BIDEFORD — CHAPELTON — SOUTH MOLTON — EAST ANSTEY
UMBERLEIGH — Morebath Jc.
BAMPTON
TORRINGTON — PORTSMOUTH ARMS — SOUTH MOLTON ROAD — T. & N.D.
DEVONSHIRE — L & S.W. — Bolham Jc.
Marland Light Rly. — EGGESFORD — TIVERTON
Peter's Marland

One Two

Inset

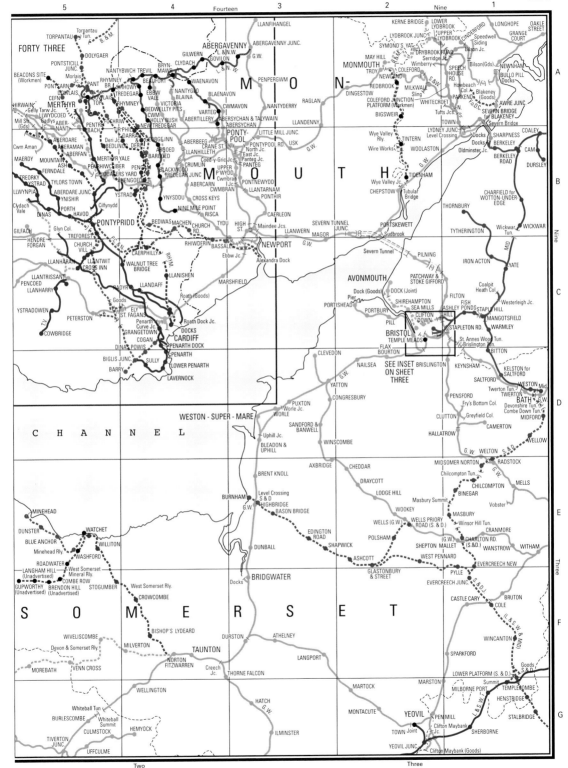

1   2   3   Fifteen   4   5

A

B

Fourteen

C

D

E

Eight

F

G

Three   Four

WORCESTER

WAR

HEREFORD

GLOUCESTER

WILTSHIRE

MONMOUTH

ONIBURY
BROMFIELD
Titterstone Clee
Ludlow & Clee Hill Rly.
Middleton
Bitterley
LUDLOW
Clee Hill
TENBURY
WOOFFERTON
EASTON COURT
G.W.
NEWNHAM BRIDGE
BERRINGTON & EYE
L & K.
S & H, G.W. & L.N.W.
LEOMINSTER
STEENS BRIDGE
FORD BRIDGE
Dinmore Tun.
DINMORE
MORETON-ON-LUGG
CREDENHILL
Barton Jc.
Shelwick Jc.
WITHINGTON
Moorfields
BARRS COURT
BARTON
Barrs Ct Jc.
HEREFORD
Rotherwas Jc.
Red Hill Jc.
L & N.W.
HOLME LACY
TRAM INN
FAWLEY
ROSS
R & M
KERNE BRIDGE
LOWER LYDBROOK
UPPER LYDBROOK
LYDBROOK JUNC.
SYMOND'S YAT
MAY HILL
Serridge Jc.
DRYBROOK ROAD
TROY
MONMOUTH
NEWLAND
Wimberry
COLEFORD
Whimsey Jc.
MILKWALL
Bilson Jc.
SPEECH HOUSE RD.
CINDERFORD
Speedwell Siding
Bilson (Gds)
NEWNHAM
BULLO PILL Docks
REDBROOK
DINGESTOW
Sling
COLEFORD JUNCTION
PLATFORM (Workmen)
PARKEND
Howbeach Col.
Blakeney (Goods)
AWRE JUNC.
WHITECROFT
Tufts Jcs.
S. for BLAKENEY
BIGSWEIR
HARESFIELD
TOWN
LYDNEY JUNC.
Severn Bridge
Docks
Standish Jc.
1 RYEFORD
2 DUDBRIDGE
STONEHOUSE (MID.)
(G.W.)
(G.W.)
FROCESTER
Viaduct
STROUD
COALEY
TINTERN
Wire Works
Level Crossing
WOOLASTON
Oldminster Jc.
SHARPNESS
BERKELEY
Docks
CAM
WOODCHESTER
G.W. CIRENCESTER
E. Glos.Rly.
TIDENHAM
BERKELEY ROAD
DURSLEY
NAILSWORTH
BRIMSCOMBE near CHALFORD
Sapperton Tun. Summit
Tetbury Rd (Gds)
M & S. W.Jc.
FAIRFORD
LECHLADE
Tubular Bridge
CHEPSTOW
Wye Valley Junc.
CHARFIELD for WOTTON-UNDER-EDGE
THORNBURY
CULKERTON
KEMBLE
CERNEY & ASHTON KEYNES
SEVERN TUNNEL JUNC.
Sudbrook
TYTHERINGTON
WICKWAR
Wickwar Tun.
TETBURY
MINETY
M & S. W.Jc.
CRICKLADE
HANNINGTON
HIGHWORTH
Severn Tunnel
PILNING
IRON ACTON
YATE
MALMESBURY
PURTON
STANTON
STRATTON
SHRIVENHAM
AVONMOUTH
AVONMOUTH DOCK Joint
Dock
PATCHWAY
Coalpit Heath Col.
Westerleigh Jc.
SOMERFORD
WOOTTON BASSETT
WORKS (Workmen)
Highworth Jc.
(GW)
Rushey Platt Jc.
SWINDON TOWN
RUSHEY PLATT
Pier
PORTISHEAD
PORTBURY PILL
SHIREHAMPTON
SEA MILLS
See Sheet No 3
FILTON
ASHLEY HILL
FISH PONDS
STAPLE HILL
MANGOTSFIELD
Westerleigh Jc.
DAUNTSEY
CHISELDON

HIGHLEY
STOURBRIDGE TOWN
STOURBRIDGE JUNC.
LYE
HUNNINGTON
HALESOWEN
HARBORNE
SELLY OAK
SOMERSET RD
KINGS HEATH
MOSELEY (Mid)
HAMPTON (Mid)
ARLEY
HAGLEY
Halesowen Rly
BOURNVILLE & STIRCHLEY ST
NORTHFIELD
LIFFORD
HAMPTON-IN-ARDEN (L. & N.W.)
OLTON
BERKSWELL
BEWDLEY
CHURCHILL & BLAKEDOWN
KIDDERMINSTER
RUBERY
Halesowen Jc.
KING'S NORTON
SOLIHULL
CLEOBURY MORTIMER
WYRE FOREST
STOURPORT
HARTLEBURY
Lickey Incline Summit
BLACKWELL
BARNT GREEN
ALVECHURCH
KNOWLE
KINGSWOOD
NEEN SOLLERS
G.W.
Lickey Incline
BROMSGROVE
REDDITCH
HATTON
CLAVERDON
Stoke Works Jc.
STOKE WORKS Goods
STUDLEY & ASTWOOD BANK
COUGHTON
BEARLEY
GREAT ALNE
WILMCOTE
WAR
STRATFORD-ON-AVON
DROITWICH
MID.
Droitwich Road (Goods)
Dunhampstead (Goods)
ALCESTER
WIXFORD
BROOM JUNC.
BROMYARD
KNIGHTWICK
LEIGH COURT
HENWICK
FERNHILL HEATH
FOREGATE ST.
Rainbow Hill Jc.
Tunnel Jc.
WORCESTER
SHRUB HILL
G.W. & MID Joint
Spetchley (Goods)
SALFORD PRIORS
E.R.& Su A Jc. BINTON
BIDFORD
Canal Dock
Goods
MILCOTE
SUCKLEY
Bransford Road Jc.
BRANSFORD RD.
Wharf
NORTON JUNC.
Abbotswood Jc.
STOULTON
PERSHORE
HARVINGTON
LONG MARSTON
Newbold Wharf
MALVERN LINK
GREAT MALVERN
WADBOROUGH
FLADBURY
EVESHAM
MID.
LITTLETON & BADSEY
HONEY-BOURNE
SHIPSTON-ON-STOUR
COLWALL
Malvern Jc.
MALVERN WELLS MID.
G.W.
DEFFORD
BENGEWORTH
G.W.
Campden Tun.
LONGDON ROAD for ILMINGTON
STOKE EDITH
ASHPERTON
ECKINGTON
HINTON
CAMPDEN
BLOCKLEY
UPTON-ON-SEVERN
ASHTON-UNDER-HILL
LEDBURY
R. & L.
RIPPLE
BREDON
BECKFORD
MORETON-IN-MARSH
Summit
G.W.
DYMOCK
TEWKESBURY
Level Crossing
ASHCHURCH
Newent Railway
NEWENT
CLEEVE
ADLESTROP
STOW-ON-THE-WOLD
MITCHELDEAN ROAD
BARBER'S BRIDGE
CHELTENHAM HIGH STREET
G.W.
NOTGROVE & WESTFIELD
CHIPPING NORTON JUNC.
LONGHOPE
OAKLE STREET
MID.
Lansdowne Jc.
CHELTENHAM
LECKHAMPTON
ANDOVERSFORD
BOURTON-ON-THE-WATER
GRANGE COURT
CHURCHDOWN
Over Jc.
MID. & G.W. Jt
Banbury & Cheltenham Direct Rly
Docks
G.W.
CHARLTON KINGS
GLOUCESTER
Tuffley Jc.
BULLO PILL Docks

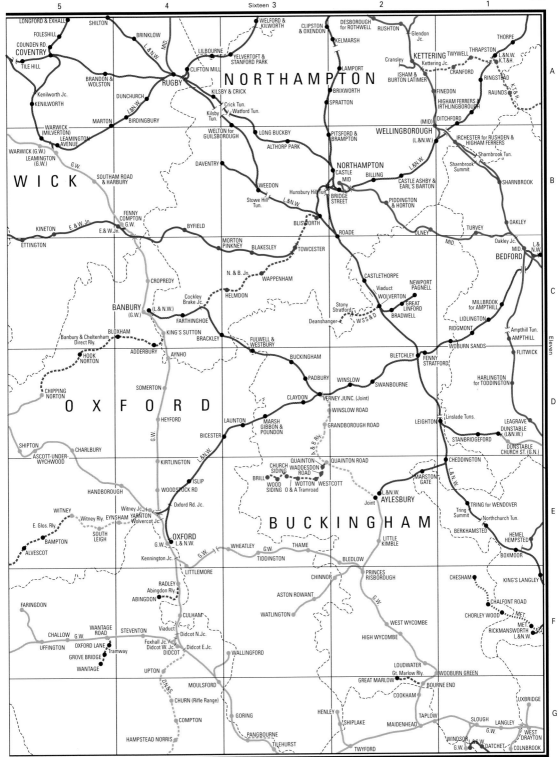

LONGFORD & EXHALL
FOLESHILL
COUNDEN RD.
COVENTRY
TILE HILL
Kenilworth Jc.
KENILWORTH
WARWICK (MILVERTON)
LEAMINGTON AVENUE
WARWICK (G.W.)
LEAMINGTON (G.W.)

WICK

KINETON
ETTINGTON

SHILTON
BRINKLOW
BRANDON & WOLSTON
DUNCHURCH
MARTON
BIRDINGBURY

SOUTHAM ROAD & HARBURY

E. & W. Jn.
E.& W.Jn.

FENNY COMPTON G.W.
CROPREDY

BANBURY (G.W.)

BLOXHAM
Banbury & Cheltenham Direct Rly.
HOOK NORTON

CHIPPING NORTON

OXFORD

L&N.W.
MID.
LILBOURNE
CLIFTON MILL
RUGBY
KILSBY & CRICK
Crick Tun.
Watford Tun.
Kilsby Tun.

L.&N.W.
WELTON for GUILSBOROUGH
DAVENTRY

WEEDON
BYFIELD

MORTON PINKNEY
BLAKESLEY

N. & B. Jn.
WAPPENHAM
HELMDON
Cockley Brake Jc.
FARTHINGHOE
KING'S SUTTON (L & N.W.)
ADDERBURY
AYNHO

SOMERTON

HEYFORD

CHARLBURY
ASCOTT-UNDER-WYCHWOOD

WELFORD & KILWORTH
YELVERTOFT & STANFORD PARK

NORTHAMPTON

LONG BUCKBY
ALTHORP PARK

WELDON & KILWORTH
CLIPSTON & OXENDON
KELMARSH
LAMPORT
PITSFORD & BRAMPTON
SPRATTON

NORTHAMPTON
CASTLE MID.
BILLING
BRIDGE STREET
Hunsbury Hill Tun.
Stowe Hill Tun.
L.&N.W.

BLISWORTH
ROADE
OLNEY

TOWCESTER
CASTLETHORPE
Viaduct
WOLVERTON

Stony Stratford
Deanshanger
WSS&D

FULWELL & WESTBURY

BUCKINGHAM
PADBURY
WINSLOW
SWANBOURNE

CLAYDON
VERNEY JUNC. (Joint)
WINSLOW ROAD
GRANDBOROUGH ROAD

DESBOROUGH for ROTHWELL
RUSHTON
Glendon Jc.
KETTERING Jc.
Cransley
ISHAM & BURTON LATIMER
BRIXWORTH

THORPE
TWYWELL
THRAPSTON
L.&N.W. K.T.&H.
CRANFORD
RINGSTEAD
RAUNDS

KETTERING
Kettering Jc.

FINEDON
HIGHAM FERRERS IRTHLINGBOROUGH
DITCHFORD (MID.)

WELLINGBOROUGH (L.&N.W.)

IRCHESTER for RUSHDEN & HIGHAM FERRERS
Sharnbrook Tun.
Sharnbrook Summit
SHARNBROOK

CASTLE ASHBY & EARL'S BARTON
PIDDINGTON & HORTON

TURVEY
OAKLEY
Oakley Jc.
MID.

BEDFORD
L.& N.W.

MILLBROOK for AMPTHILL
LIDLINGTON
RIDGMONT
Ampthill Tun.
AMPTHILL
FLITWICK

NEWPORT PAGNELL
GREAT LINFORD
BRADWELL

WOBURN SANDS
BLETCHLEY
FENNY STRATFORD

HARLINGTON for TODDINGTON

LEIGHTON
Linslade Tuns.
STANBRIDGEFORD

LEAGRAVE
DUNSTABLE (L.&N.W.)
DUNSTABLE CHURCH ST. (G.N.)

LAUNTON
MARSH GIBBON & POUNDON
BICESTER

KIRTLINGTON
WOODSTOCK RD
ISLIP

A. & B. Rly.

QUAINTON WADDESDON ROAD
BRILL
CHURCH SIDING
WOOD SIDING
WOTTON WESTCOTT
O & A Tramroad

QUAINTON ROAD
CHEDDINGTON
MARSTON GATE
L.&N.W.

AYLESBURY
Joint
TRING for WENDOVER
Tring Summit
Northchurch Tun.

BERKHAMSTED

HEMEL HEMPSTED
BOXMOOR

G.W.

SHIPTON

WITNEY
E. Glos. Rly.
BAMPTON
ALVESCOT

Witney Jc.
Witney Rly. EYNSHAM
YARNTON
Wolvercot Jc.
Oxford Rd. Jc.
OXFORD
G.W. L & N.W.
Kennington Jc.

HANDBOROUGH

SOUTH LEIGH

FARINGDON

CHALLOW G.W.
UFFINGTON
OXFORD LANE
GROVE BRIDGE
WANTAGE

WANTAGE ROAD
STEVENTON
Tramway

RADLEY
Abingdon Rly.
ABINGDON
LITTLEMORE
CULHAM
Viaduct
Didcot N.Jc.
Foxhall Jc.
Didcot W.Jc.
DIDCOT
Didcot E.Jc.
UPTON

DN.&S.
CHURN (Rifle Range)
COMPTON
HAMPSTEAD NORRIS
MOULSFORD

WHEATLEY G.W.
TIDDINGTON

LITTLE KIMBLE

THAME
CHINNOR
ASTON ROWANT
WATLINGTON

BLEDLOW
PRINCES RISBOROUGH

WEST WYCOMBE
HIGH WYCOMBE

G.W.

WALLINGFORD
GORING
PANGBOURNE
TILEHURST

BUCKINGHAM

LOUDWATER
Gt. Marlow Rly.
GREAT MARLOW
BOURNE END
COOKHAM

HENLEY
SHIPLAKE
MAIDENHEAD
TAPLOW
TWYFORD

CHESHAM
CHALFONT ROAD
CHORLEY WOOD
MET.
MET.
RICKMANSWORTH
L.&N.W.

KING'S LANGLEY

WOOBURN GREEN

SLOUGH
LANGLEY
G.W.
WINDSOR G.W. L.&N.W. DATCHET

UXBRIDGE
WEST DRAYTON
COLNBROOK

Eleven

1   2   3   Seventeen   4   5

A

B

C

Ten

D

E

F

G

KINGS CLIFFE
WANSFORD ROAD
CASTOR
New England Sidings
L & N.W. & G.E. G.N.
PETERBOROUGH
DENVER
RYSTON D.& S.F.
ABBEY for WEST DEREHAM
NASSINGTON
WANSFORD
Yarwell Jc.
OVERTON
G.E. G.E.
WHITTLESEA
Fletton (Goods)
Grassmoor Jc.
Whitemoor(Goods)
West Jc.
North Jc.
MARCH
South Jc.
HILGAY FEN
STOKE FERRY
ELTON
Longville Jc.
Yaxley (Goods)
STONEA
MANEA
WIMBLINGTON
LITTLEPORT
BRANDON
OUNDLE
Ramsey Rly
HOLME
ST MARY'S
G.N.
CHATTERIS
BLACK BANK
CHITTISHAM
BURNT FEN
LAKENHEATH
BARNWELL
RAMSEY
HIGH ST. (GE)
WARBOYS
SOMERSHAM
ELY
Dock Jc.
Sutton Branch Jc.
THORPE
THRAPSTON
L.N.W. K.T.&H.
HUNTINGDON
ABBOTTS RIPTON
G.N. & G.E. Jt.
E.& St.I
SUTTON
WILBURTON
STRETHAM
SOHAM
ISLEHAM
MILDENHALL
RAUNDS
KIMBOLTON
Long Stow Siding (Goods)
K.T.&H.
GRAFHAM
HUNTINGDON
G.N. Joint. Mid.
GODMANCHESTER
ST.IVES
Needingworth Jc.
HADDENHAM
EARITH BRIDGE
BLUNTISHAM
FORDHAM
E.& N.
BUCKDEN
OFFORD & BUCKDEN
SWAVESEY
LONG STANTON
BURWELL
Snailwell Jc.
Warren Hill Jc.
Chippenham Jc.
KENNET
HIGHAM
SAXHAM & RISBY
SHARNBROOK
ST. NEOTS
OAKINGTON
WATERBEACH
SWAFFHAM PRIOR
NEWMARKET
WARREN HILL
NEWMARKET WARREN HILL (races)
CAMBRIDGE
HISTON
QUY
BOTTISHAM
OAKLEY
TEMPSFORD
Barnwell Junc.
FULBOURNE
SIX MILE BOTTOM
DULLINGHAM
MID
CAMBRIDGE
BLUNHAM
GAMLINGAY
L & N.W.
OLD NORTH ROAD
LORDS BRIDGE
Shepreth Branch Jc.
BEDFORD
L & NW Level Crossing
G.N.
SANDY
POTTON
SHELFORD
HARSTON
FOXTON
SHEPRETH
PAMPISFORD
LINTON
BARTLOW
HAVERHILL
CAVENDISH
CLARE
STOKE
Oakley Jc.
MID.
CARDINGTON
BIGGLESWADE
WHITTLESFORD
MELDRETH & MELBOURN
C.V.&H.
STURMER
SOUTHILL
ROYSTON
GREAT CHESTERFORD
BIRDBROOK
YELDHAM
MILLBROOK for AMPTHILL
BEDFORD
Ampthill Tun.
AMPTHILL
SHEFFORD
ARLESEY & SHEFFORD RD.
ASHWELL
R.& H.
SAFFRON WALDEN
C.V.& H.
SIBLE & CASTLE HEDINGHAM
FLITWICK
HENLOW
THREE COUNTIES
BALDOCK
AUDLEY END
NEWPORT
HALSTEAD
HARLINGTON for TODDINGTON
LEAGRAVE
MID.Goods
HITCHIN
BUNTINGFORD
WEST MILL
ELSENHAM Summit
DUNSTABLE (L & NW)
DUNSTABLE CHURCH ST.
LUTON Mid.
G.N.
STEVENAGE
BRAUGHING
STANDON
STANSTEAD
EASTON LODGE (private)
DUNMOW
FELSTEAD
BRAINTREE Goods
RAYNE
BISHOP'S STORTFORD
TAKELEY
G.E.
BULFORD
WHITE NOTLEY
NEW MILL END
CHILTERN GREEN
KNEBWORTH
HERTFORD
HADHAM
SAWBRIDGEWORTH
HARPENDEN
Harpenden Jc.
WHEAT-HAMPSTEAD
AYOT
Welwyn N.Tun.
Welwyn S.Tun.
WELWYN
Welwyn Viaduct
COWBRIDGE (G.N.)
WIDFORD
MARDOCK
HARLOW
HATFIELD PEVEREL
REDBOURN
WARE
ST. MARGARETS
BURNT MILL
HERTFORD
HERTINGFORDBURY
COLE GREEN
RYE HOUSE
ROYDON
HEMEL HEMPSTED
ST.ALBANS
L & N.W.
LONDON RD. (G.N.)
HATFIELD
SMALLFORD
Broxbourne Jc.
BROXBOURNE & HODDESDON
CHELMSFORD
BOXMOOR
KING'S LANGLEY
PARK STREET
POTTERS BAR
NORTH WEALD
BLAKE HALL
ONGAR
BRICKET WOOD
RADLETT
Potters Bar Tun.
Hadley N.Tun.
CHESHUNT
EPPING
THEYDON BOIS
INGATESTONE
WOODHAM FERRIS
Watford Tun.
JUNC.
HIGH ST.
WATFORD
ELSTREE & BOREHAM WOOD
Elstree Tun.
HADLEY WOOD
Hadley S. Tun.
G.N.
NEW BARNET
OAKLEIGH PARK
ENFIELD TOWN
WALTHAM CROSS
ENFIELD LOCK
BRIMSDOWN
CHIGWELL LANE
LOUGHTON
SHENFIELD & HUTTON JUNC.
Ingrave Summit
BATTLESBRIDGE
CHORLEY WOOD
RICKMANSWORTH
MET.
L & N.W.
BUSHEY
TOTTERIDGE & WHETSTONE
WINCHMORE HILL
BUSH HILL PARK
LOWER EDMONTON
PONDER'S END
CHINGFORD
BUCKHURST HILL
BILLERICAY

HUNTINGDON

CAMBRIDGE

BEDFORD

HERTFORD

ESSEX

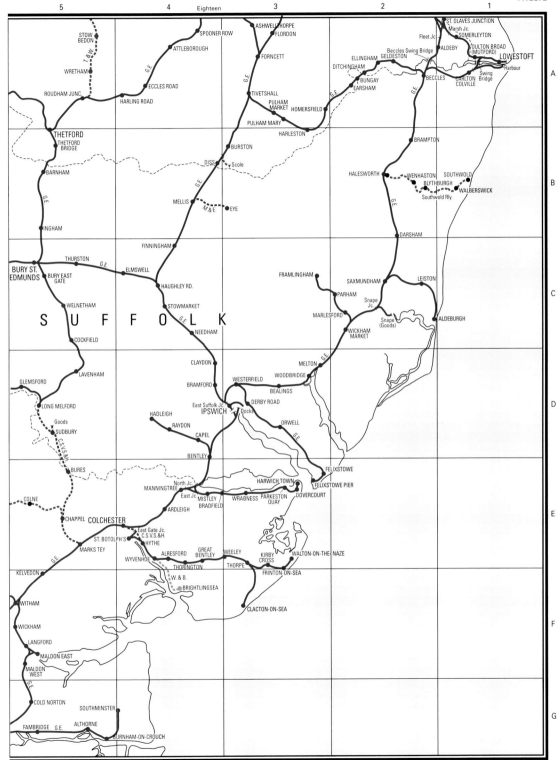

STOW BEDON
SPOONER ROW
ASHWELL THORPE
FLORDON
ST. OLAVES JUNCTION
Marsh Jc.
SOMERLEYTON
OULTON BROAD
(MUTFORD)
LOWESTOFT

ATTLEBOROUGH
FORNCETT
Fleet Jc.
ALDEBY

WRETHAM
T. & W.
ELLINGHAM
Beccles Swing Bridge
GELDESTON
Harbour

DITCHINGHAM
Swing Bridge
CARLTON COLVILLE

ROUDHAM JUNC.
ECCLES ROAD
G.E.
TIVETSHALL
BUNGAY
EARSHAM
BECCLES

HARLING ROAD
PULHAM MARKET
HOMERSFIELD
G.E.

PULHAM MARY

THETFORD
THETFORD BRIDGE
BURSTON
HARLESTON
BRAMPTON

DISS
Scole
G.E.

BARNHAM
HALESWORTH
WENHASTON
SOUTHWOLD
BLYTHBURGH
WALBERSWICK

MELLIS
EYE
M & E.
Southwold Rly.

INGHAM
G.E.
DARSHAM

FINNINGHAM
THURSTON
G.E.
FRAMLINGHAM
SAXMUNDHAM
LEISTON

BURY ST. EDMUNDS
BURY EAST GATE
ELMSWELL
PARHAM
Snape Jc.

HAUGHLEY RD.
MARLESFORD
Snape (Goods)
ALDEBURGH

WELNETHAM
STOWMARKET
WICKHAM MARKET

S U F F O L K
G.E.
NEEDHAM

COCKFIELD

CLAYDON
MELTON

LAVENHAM
BRAMFORD
WESTERFIELD
WOODBRIDGE

GLEMSFORD
BEALINGS

LONG MELFORD
DERBY ROAD

Goods
East Suffolk Jc.
SUDBURY
HADLEIGH
RAYDON
IPSWICH
Docks
ORWELL

C.S.V.S.&H.
CAPEL
G.E.

BURES
BENTLEY
FELIXSTOWE

COLNE
North Jc.
HARWICH TOWN
FELIXSTOWE PIER

MANNINGTREE
WRABNESS
PARKESTON QUAY
DOVERCOURT

East Jc.
MISTLEY
BRADFIELD

CHAPPEL
COLCHESTER
ARDLEIGH

East Gate Jc.
C.S.V.S.&H.
ST. BOTOLPH'S
HYTHE

MARKS TEY
ALRESFORD
GREAT BENTLEY
WEELEY
KIRBY CROSS
WALTON-ON-THE-NAZE

G.E.
WYVENHOE
THORINGTON
THORPE
FRINTON-ON-SEA

KELVEDON
W. & B.
BRIGHTLINGSEA

WITHAM
CLACTON-ON-SEA

WICKHAM

LANGFORD

MALDON EAST
MALDON WEST
G.E.

COLD NORTON
SOUTHMINSTER

FAMBRIDGE
G.E.
ALTHORNE
BURNHAM-ON-CROUCH

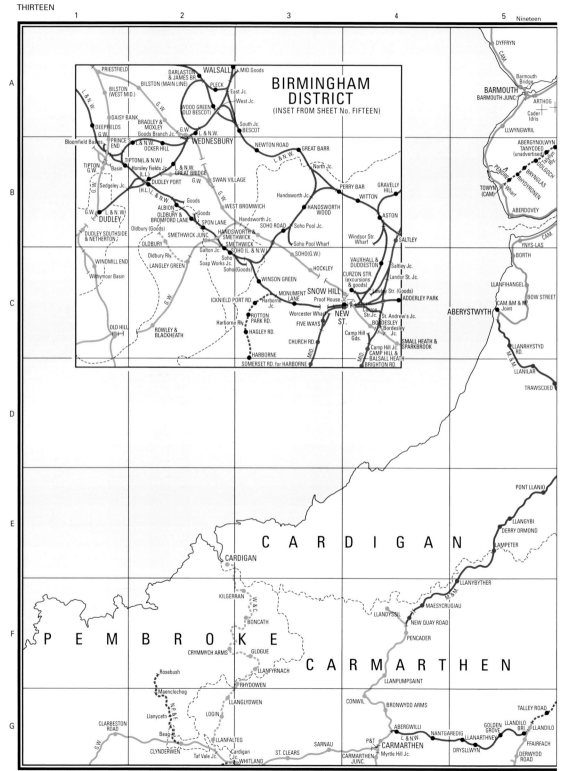

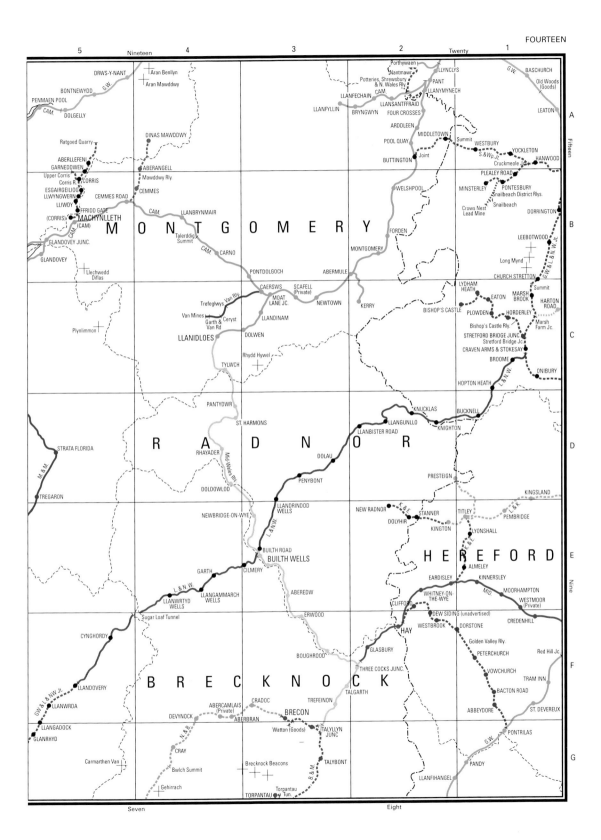

DRWS-Y-NANT
Aran Benllyn
Aran Mawddwy
BONTNEWYDD
G.W.
PENMAEN POOL
CAM.
DOLGELLY

Porthywaen
Nantmawr
Potteries, Shrewsbury & N. Wales Rly.
Old Woods (Goods)
G.W.
BASCHURCH
LLYNCLYS
PANT
LLANYMYNECH
CAM.
LEATON
LLANFECHAIN
LLANSANTFFRAID
BRYNGWYN
FOUR CROSSES
LLANFYLLIN

DINAS MAWDDWY
ARDDLEEN
MIDDLETOWN
Summit
WESTBURY
S.&Wp.Jt.
YOCKLETON
HANWOOD
Cruckmeole Jct.
POOL QUAY
BUTTINGTON
Joint
Ratgoed Quarry
ABERLLEFENI
GARNEDDWEN
ABERANGELL
Upper Corris
Corris R. CORRIS
Mawddwy Rly.
WELSHPOOL
PLEALEY ROAD
PONTESBURY
Snailbeach District Rlys.
ESGAIRGEILIOG
LLWYNGWERN
CEMMES
MINSTERLEY
Snailbeach
LLIWDY
CEMMES ROAD
Crows Nest
Lead Mine
DORRINGTON
FFRIDD GATE
(CORRIS)
MACHYNLLETH
(CAM.)
CAM.
LLANBRYNMAIR
FORDEN
LEEBOTWOOD
GLANDOVEY JUNC.
GW.& L&N.W.
Talerddig
Summit
Long Mynd
GLANDOVEY
CAM.
CARNO
MONTGOMERY
CHURCH STRETTON
Llechwedd
Diflas
PONTDOLGOCH
ABERMULE
Summit
CAERSWS
SCAFELL
(Private)
LYDHAM
HEATH
MARSH
BROOK
HARTON
ROAD
Plynlimmon
Trefeglwys Van Rly.
MOAT
LANE JC.
NEWTOWN
KERRY
EATON
BISHOP'S CASTLE
PLOWDEN
HORDERLEY
Van Mines
Garth & Ceryst
Van Rd
LLANDINAM
Bishop's Castle Rly.
Marsh
Farm Jc.
LLANIDLOES
DOLWEN
STRETFORD BRIDGE JUNC.
Stretford Bridge Jct.
CRAVEN ARMS & STOKESAY
Rhydd Hywel
TYLWCH
BROOME
L&N.W.
ONIBURY

PANTYDWR
HOPTON HEATH
ST. HARMONS
KNUCKLAS
BUCKNELL
STRATA FLORIDA
RHAYADER
Mid-Wales Rly.
LLANGUNLLO
KNIGHTON
M.&M.
R A D N O R
LLANBISTER ROAD
DOLAU
TREGARON
DOLDOWLOD
PENYBONT
PRESTEIGN
KINGSLAND
NEWBRIDGE-ON-WYE
LLANDRINDOD
WELLS
NEW RADNOR
K.&E.
STANNER
TITLEY
L.&K.
PEMBRIDGE
DOLYHIR
KINGTON
LYONSHALL
L&N.W.
BUILTH ROAD
BUILTH WELLS
H E R E F O R D
GARTH
CILMERY
ALMELEY
K.&E.
LLANWRTYD
WELLS
LLANGAMMARCH
WELLS
ABEREDW
EARDISLEY
KINNERSLEY
MOORHAMPTON
WESTMOOR
(Private)
L.&N.W.
WHITNEY-ON-THE-WYE
CLIFFORD
ERWOOD
Sugar Loaf Tunnel
MID.
DEW SIDING (unadvertised)
CREDENHILL
CYNGHORDY
HAY
WESTBROOK
DORSTONE
Golden Valley Rly.
BOUGHROOD
GLASBURY
PETERCHURCH
Red Hill Jc.
LLANDOVERY
THREE COCKS JUNC.
VOWCHURCH
TRAM INN
GW.& L.NW.Jt.
LLANWRDA
B R E C K N O C K
TALGARTH
BACTON ROAD
CRADOC
TREFEINON
ABBEYDORE
ST. DEVEREUX
LLANGADOCK
ABERCAMLAIS
(Private)
BRECON
DEVYNOCK
ABERBRAN
N.&B.
Watton (Goods)
TALYLLYN
JUNC.
G.W.
PONTRILAS
GLANRHYD
CRAY
Carmarthen Van
TALYBONT
PANDY
Brecknock Beacons
Bwlch Summit
B.&M.
Gehirrach
Torpantau
Tun.
LLANFIHANGEL
TORPANTAU

M O N T G O M E R Y

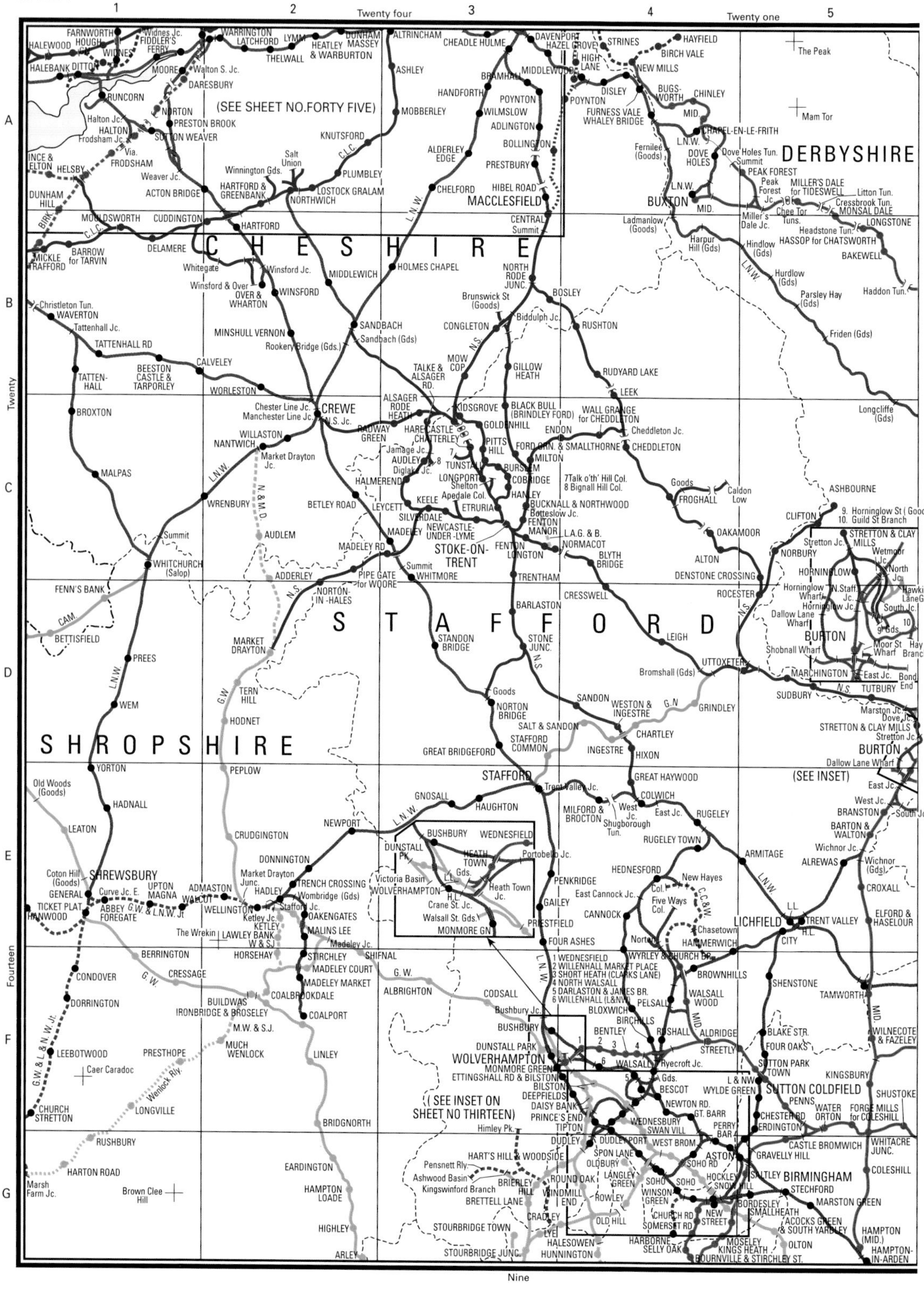

1
2
Twenty four
3
4
Twenty one
5
A
B
C
D
E
F
G
Twenty
Fourteen
Nine
CHESHIRE
DERBYSHIRE
STAFFORD
SHROPSHIRE
(SEE SHEET NO.FORTY FIVE)
FARNWORTH
Widnes Jc.
HALEWOOD
HOUGH
FIDDLER'S FERRY
WIDNES
HALEBANK
DITTON
MOORE
Walton S. Jc.
DARESBURY
RUNCORN
NORTON
PRESTON BROOK
Halton Jc.
HALTON
Frodsham Jc.
SUTTON WEAVER
Via.
INCE & ELTON
HELSBY
FRODSHAM
Weaver Jc.
DUNHAM HILL
ACTON BRIDGE
BIRK.
MOULDSWORTH
CUDDINGTON
C.L.C.
MICKLE TRAFFORD
BARROW for TARVIN
DELAMERE
WARRINGTON
LATCHFORD
LYMM
THELWALL
HEATLEY & WARBURTON
DUNHAM MASSEY
ALTRINCHAM
ASHLEY
MOBBERLEY
KNUTSFORD
Salt Union
Winnington Gds.
PLUMBLEY
HARTFORD & GREENBANK
LOSTOCK GRALAM
NORTHWICH
HARTFORD
Whitegate
Winsford Jc.
Winsford & Over
OVER & WHARTON
WINSFORD
MIDDLEWICH
HOLMES CHAPEL
CHEADLE HULME
DAVENPORT
HAZEL GROVE
STRINES
HAYFIELD
BIRCH VALE
HIGH LANE
NEW MILLS
MIDDLEWOOD
BRAMHALL
HANDFORTH
POYNTON
WILMSLOW
ADLINGTON
ALDERLEY EDGE
BOLLINGTON
PRESTBURY
CHELFORD
HIBEL ROAD
MACCLESFIELD
CENTRAL
Summit
L.N.W.
DISLEY
POYNTON
FURNESS VALE
WHALEY BRIDGE
BUGS-WORTH
CHINLEY
MID.
CHAPEL-EN-LE-FRITH
L.N.W.
Fernilee (Goods)
DOVE HOLES
Dove Holes Tun.
Summit
PEAK FOREST
BUXTON
MID.
Peak Forest Jc.
MILLER'S DALE for TIDESWELL
Litton Tun.
Cressbrook Tun.
MONSAL DALE
Chee Tor Tuns.
Miller's Dale Jc.
Headstone Tun.
LONGSTONE
HASSOP for CHATSWORTH
BAKEWELL
Ladmanlow (Goods)
Harpur Hill (Gds)
Hindlow (Gds)
Hurdlow (Gds)
Parsley Hay (Gds)
Haddon Tun.
Friden (Gds)
The Peak
Mam Tor
Longcliffe (Gds)
NORTH RODE JUNC.
BOSLEY
Brunswick St (Goods)
Biddulph Jc.
CONGLETON
RUSHTON
N.S.
MOW COP
GILLOW HEATH
RUDYARD LAKE
LEEK
Christleton Tun.
WAVERTON
Tattenhall Jc.
TATTENHALL RD
TATTEN-HALL
BEESTON CASTLE & TARPORLEY
CALVELEY
WORLESTON
MINSHULL VERNON
SANDBACH
Sandbach (Gds)
Rookery Bridge (Gds.)
TALKE & ALSAGER RD.
ALSAGER RODE HEATH
BROXTON
Chester Line Jc.
Manchester Line Jc.
CREWE
N.S. Jc.
RADWAY GREEN
HARECASTLE
KIDSGROVE
BLACK BULL (BRINDLEY FORD)
WALL GRANGE for CHEDDLETON
GOLDENHILL
ENDON
Cheddleton Jc.
CHEDDLETON
WILLASTON
NANTWICH
Market Drayton Jc.
CHATTERLEY
Jamage Jc.
AUDLEY
Diglake Jc.
PITTS HILL
FORD GRN. & SMALLTHORNE
MILTON
TUNSTALL
BURSLEM
LONGPORT
Shelton
COBRIDGE
7Talk o'th' Hill Col.
8 Bignall Hill Col.
Apedale Col.
HANLEY
MALPAS
L.N.W.
N.& M.D.
HALMEREND
WRENBURY
BETLEY ROAD
LEYCETT
KEELE
ETRURIA
BUCKNALL & NORTHWOOD
Botteslow Jc.
Goods
FROGHALL
Caldon Low
ASHBOURNE
SILVERDALE
NEWCASTLE-UNDER-LYME
FENTON MANOR
L.A.G. & B.
NORMACOT
OAKAMOOR
CLIFTON
9. Horninglow St (Goods)
10. Guild St Branch
Summit
AUDLEM
MADELEY
STOKE-ON-TRENT
FENTON
LONGTON
BLYTH BRIDGE
ALTON
STRETTON & CLAY MILLS
Stretton Jc.
NORBURY
Wetmoor Jc.
North Jc.
HORNINGLOW
Hawkins Lane Gds.
WHITCHURCH (Salop)
MADELEY RD
PIPE GATE for WOORE
Summit
WHITMORE
TRENTHAM
DENSTONE CROSSING
ROCESTER
Horninglow Wharf
N.Staff. Jc.
Horninglow St. Jc.
South Jc.
FENN'S BANK
ADDERLEY
NORTON-IN-HALES
N.S.
BARLASTON
CRESSWELL
Dallow Lane Wharf
Gds
BURTON
Moor St Wharf
Hay Branch
CAM.
BETTISFIELD
MARKET DRAYTON
STANDON BRIDGE
STONE JUNC.
LEIGH
Shobnall Wharf
MARCHINGTON
East Jc.
Bond End
TUTBURY
PREES
UTTOXETER
Bromshall (Gds)
SUDBURY
L.N.W.
G.W.
TERN HILL
Goods
SANDON
WESTON & INGESTRE
G.N.
GRINDLEY
Marston Jc.
Dove Jc.
WEM
NORTON BRIDGE
HODNET
SALT & SANDON
CHARTLEY
STRETTON & CLAY MILLS
Stretton Jc.
GREAT BRIDGEFORD
STAFFORD COMMON
INGESTRE
HIXON
BURTON
Dallow Lane Wharf
(SEE INSET)
YORTON
PEPLOW
STAFFORD
GREAT HAYWOOD
East Jc.
Old Woods (Goods)
Trent Valley Jc.
COLWICH
West Jc.
GNOSALL
HAUGHTON
MILFORD & BROCTON
Shugborough Tun.
East Jc.
RUGELEY
BRANSTON
South Jc.
HADNALL
BARTON & WALTON
LEATON
NEWPORT
BUSHBURY
WEDNESFIELD
RUGELEY TOWN
Wichnor Jc.
CRUDGINGTON
DUNSTALL PK.
Portobello Jc.
ARMITAGE
ALREWAS
Wichnor (Gds)
DONNINGTON
HEATH TOWN
Coton Hill (Goods)
SHREWSBURY
GENERAL
Market Drayton Junc.
Victoria Basin
Gds.
PENKRIDGE
HEDNESFORD
New Hayes
TICKET PLAT
HANWOOD
Curve Jc. E.
ABBEY FOREGATE
UPTON MAGNA
ADMASTON
WALCOT
HADLEY
TRENCH CROSSING
WOLVERHAMPTON
Heath Town Jc.
East Cannock Jc.
Col.
Five Ways Col.
C.C.& W.
CROXALL
G.W. & L.N.W. Jt
WELLINGTON
Stafford Jc.
Wombridge (Gds)
Crane St. Jc.
GAILEY
CANNOCK
LICHFIELD
TRENT VALLEY
ELFORD & HASELOUR
The Wrekin
Ketley Jc.
KETLEY
LAWLEY BANK
W & S J
OAKENGATES
MALINS LEE
Walsall St. Gds.
MONMORE GN
PRIESTFIELD
Chasetown
Norton
HAMMERWICH
CITY
FOUR ASHES
L.L.
H.L.
BERRINGTON
HORSEHAY
Madeley Jc.
STIRCHLEY
SHIFNAL
1 WEDNESFIELD
2 WILLENHALL MARKET PLACE
3 SHORT HEATH (CLARKS LANE)
4 NORTH WALSALL
5 DARLASTON & JAMES BR.
6 WILLENHALL (L&NW)
WYRLEY & CHURCH BR.
BROWNHILLS
SHENSTONE
CONDOVER
CRESSAGE
MADELEY COURT
MADELEY MARKET
G. W.
ALBRIGHTON
WALSALL WOOD
TAMWORTH
DORRINGTON
BUILDWAS
IRONBRIDGE & BROSELEY
COALBROOKDALE
COALPORT
CODSALL
Bushbury Jc.
BLOXWICH
PELSALL
MID.
G.W. & L & N.W. Jt.
M.W. & S.J.
BUSHBURY
BIRCHILLS
RUSHALL
ALDRIDGE
BLAKE STR.
WILNECOTE & FAZELEY
LEEBOTWOOD
PRESTHOPE
MUCH WENLOCK
LINLEY
DUNSTALL PARK
BENTLEY
FOUR OAKS
Caer Caradoc
Wenlock Rly.
WOLVERHAMPTON
MONMORE GREEN
ETTINGSHALL RD & BILSTON
WALSALL
Ryecroft Jc.
STREETLY
SUTTON PARK
TOWN
KINGSBURY
BILSTON
L & NW
WYLDE GREEN
SUTTON COLDFIELD
SHUSTOKE
CHURCH STRETTON
LONGVILLE
(SEE INSET ON SHEET NO THIRTEEN)
DEEPFIELDS
DAISY BANK
OLDBURY
BESCOT
Gds.
NEWTON RD.
GT. BARR
PENNS
WATER ORTON
FORGE MILLS for COLESHILL
BRIDGNORTH
PRINCE'S END
WEDNESBURY
TIPTON
SWAN VILL
CHESTER RD
ERDINGTON
PERRY BAR
RUSHBURY
Himley Pk.
DUDLEY
DUDLEY PORT
WEST BROM
CASTLE BROMWICH
WHITACRE JUNC.
HART'S HILL & WOODSIDE
SPON LANE
ASTON
GRAVELLY HILL
SOHO RD
EARDINGTON
Pensnett Rly.
HARTON ROAD
Ashwood Basin
ROUND OAK
LANGLEY GREEN
SOHO
HOCKLEY
SALTLEY
BIRMINGHAM
COLESHILL
Marsh Farm Jc.
Brown Clee Hill
HAMPTON LOADE
Kingswinford Branch
BRIERLEY HILL
WINDMILL END
ROWLEY
WINSON GREEN
SNOW HILL
STECHFORD
BRETTELL LANE
CHURCH RD
NEW STREET
MARSTON GREEN
BORDESLEY
SMALLHEATH
ACOCKS GREEN & SOUTH YARDLEY
HIGHLEY
STOURBRIDGE TOWN
CRADLEY
OLD HILL
SOMERSET RD
LYE
HALESOWEN
HARBORNE
MOSELEY
KINGS HEATH
OLTON
HAMPTON (MID.)
ARLEY
STOURBRIDGE JUNC.
HUNNINGTON
SELLY OAK
BOURNVILLE & STIRCHLEY ST.
HAMPTON-IN-ARDEN

SHEFFIELD VICTORIA
MIDLAND
DARNALL
TREETON
WOODHOUSE
WOODHOUSE MILL
BEAUCHIEF
HEELEY
MILL HOUSES
BEIGHTON
KILLAMARSH
KIVETON PARK
DORE & TOTLEY
Bradway Tun.
DRONFIELD
ECKINGTON & RENISHAW
SHIREOAKS
WORKSOP
CHECKER HOUSE
RANSKILL
SUTTON
GAINSBOROUGH
M.S. & L.
South Jc.
North Jc.
G.N. & G.E. Joint
Pye Wipe Jc.
W. Holmes
Durham Ox Jc.
Boultham Jc.
G.N.
MID.
Sincil Jc.
Level Crossing
UNSTON
Broomhouse Tun.
WHITTINGTON
STAVELEY
NETHERTHORPE
CLOWN
WHITWELL
M.S. & L.
Whiskerhill Jc.
RETFORD
Clarborough Jc.
Clarborough Tun.
South Jc.
Level Crossing
STURTON
LEVERTON
COTTAM
TORKSEY
STOW PARK
M.S. & L.E.
Sykes Jc.
SAXILBY
Pye Wipe Jc.
LINCOLN
REEPHAM
LANGWORTH for WRAGBY
SHEEPBRIDGE
ELMTON & CRESWELL
Askham Tun.
WASHINGBOROUGH
CHESTERFIELD
Brampton (Goods)
LANGWITH
TUXFORD
Bracebridge (Gds)
Greetwell Jcs.
BRANSTON & HEIGHINGTON
Sincil Jc.
ROWSLEY
DARLEY
CLAY CROSS
Goods
STRETTON
PLEASLEY
Glapwell Col.
MANSFIELD WOODHOUSE
HYKEHAM
THORPE
SWINDERBY
CROW PARK
POTTER HANWORTH
NOCTON & DUNSTON
MATLOCK BRIDGE
High Tor Tuns
MATLOCK BATH
Willersley Tun.
CROMFORD
Lea Wood Tun.
DOE HILL
TIBSHELF
WESTHOUSES
MANSFIELD
BLIDWORTH
FARNSFIELD
CARLTON-ON-TRENT
COLLINGHAM
WADDINGTON
HARMSTON
BLANKNEY & METHERINGHAM
NAVENBY
Steeplehouse Gds.
High Peak Jc.
WIRKSWORTH
WHATSTANDWELL BRIDGE
AMBERGATE
South Jc.
WINGFIELD
Alfreton Tun.
Wingfield Tun.
BUTTERLEY
PINXTON
SUTTON-IN-ASHFIELD
KIRKBY
(SEE SHEET NO. FORTY ONE)
KIRKLINGTON & EDINGLEY
SOUTHWELL
Level Crossing
NEWARK
G.N.
LEADENHAM
CAYTHORPE
ANCASTER
SLEAFORD
RAUCEBY
IDRIDGEHAY
SHOTTLE
HAZELWOOD
DUFFIELD
BELPER
DENBY
KILBURN
Milford Tun.
COXBENCH
RIPLEY
CODNOR PK
CODNOR PARK NEWSTEAD
EASTWOOD
WATNALL
BESTWOOD COL
BULWELL FOREST
LINBY
HUCKNALL
BULWELL
FISKERTON
ROLLESTON JUNC.
BLEASBY
THURGARTON
COTHAM
CLAYPOLE
HOUGHAM
HONINGTON
BARKSTONE
LITTLE EATON
Little Eaton Jc.
WEST HALLAM
SHIPLEY GATE
ILKESTON
ILKESTON JUNC.
KIMBERLEY
AWSWORTH
BASFORD
Bobbers Mill
SHERWOOD
ST. ANN'S WELL
DAYBROOK
LOWDHAM
BURTON JOYCE
N. & G.R. & C.
Saxondale Jc.
ELTON & ORSTON W.Jc.
E.Jc.
BOTTESFORD
Belvoir Jc.
N.Jc.
Peascliffe Tun.
GRANTHAM
Barr Road Jc.
MICKLEOVER
(FRIARGATE)
DERBY (MID)
BREADSALL
NOTTINGHAM ROAD
Derby N.Jc.
Spondon Jc.
STAPLEFORD & SANDIACRE
RADFORD
LENTON
STANTON GATE
BEESTON
TROWELL
BINGHAM
BINGHAM ROAD
ASLOCKTON
S. Jc.
SEDGEBROOK
Canal Yard
Barr Road Jc.
PEAR TREE & NORMANTON
London Road Jc.
SPONDON
BORROWASH
LONG EATON
ATTENBOROUGH
NOTTINGHAM
EDWALTON
Rectory Jc.
NETHERFLD
RADCLIFFE-ON-TRENT
BARNSTON
REDMILE
Woolsthorpe
GREAT PONTON
ETWALL
EGGINTON JUNC.
East Jc.
West Jc.
Stenson Jc.
Willington Jc.
WILLINGTON for REPTON
CHELLASTON
DRAYCOTT
SAWLEY
SAWLEY JUNC.
Sheet Stores
Long Eaton Jc.
N. Erewash Jc.
TRENT
Trent Jc.
WESTON ON TRENT
PLUMTREE & KEYWORTH
Stanton Tun.
WIDMERPOOL
G.N. & L.N.W.
HARBY & STATHERN
Eastwell
LONG CLAWSON & HOSE
Staveley & Oakes Co's Siding
WALTHAM-ON-THE-WOLD (restricted)
Stoke Tun.
Stoke Summit
CORBY
MELBOURNE
CASTLE DONINGTON
KEGWORTH
HATHERN
UPPER BROUGHTON
OLD DALBY
Grimston Tun.
SCALFORD
Wycombe Jc.
Ticknall
Bretby
SWADLINCOTE
GRESLEY
WOODVILLE
WORTHINGTON
Coleorton Col.
SHEPSHED
DERBY RD
LOUGHBOROUGH
MID.
BARROW-ON-SOAR
BROOKSBY
FRISBY
ASFORDBY (late KIRBY)
Asfordby Tun.
Melton Jc.
GRIMSTON
Holwell (Goods)
Saxelby Tun.
SAXELBY JOINT
SAXBY
MELTON MOWBRAY
WHISSENDINE late WYMONDHAM
LITTLE BYTHAM
MOIRA
Cloud Hill
Coleorton Tramway
WHITWICK
COALVILLE EAST
OVERSEAL & MOIRA
SWANNINGTON
COALVILLE
SILEBY
REARSBY
GREAT DALBY
ASHWELL
ESSENDINE
RUTLAND
OAKHAM
RYHALL & BELMISTHORPE
Netherseal Col.
DONISTHORPE
MEASHAM
HEATHER
SNARESTONE
A. & N. Joint
HUGGLESCOTE
BARDON HILL
BAGWORTH
Syston N.Jc.
Syston E. Jc.
SYSTON
Syston S. Jc.
JOHN O'GAUNT
N.
STAMFORD
S. & E.
MID.
KETTON
POLESWORTH
MARKET BOSWORTH
SHACKERSTONE
SHENTON
ATHERSTONE
STOKE GOLDING
Birch Coppice Col.
Baddesley Col.
Stockingford Col.
Ansley Hall Col.
STOCKINGFORD
Stockingford Tun.
Griff Col.
NUNEATON
CHILVERS COTON
GLENFIELD
Glenfield Tun.
RATBY
DESFORD
KIRBY MUXLOE
Knighton Tun.
Knighton S.Jc.
Knighton N.Jc.
LEICESTER
BELGRAVE RD.
WEST BRI
WELFORD RD.
CAMPBELL ST.
HUMBERSTONE RD
HUMBERSTONE
THURNBY & SCRAPTOFT
INGERSBY
G.N.
Marefield Jcs.
W.
LOSEBY
TILTON
EAST NORTON
Manton Tun.
MANTON for UPPINGHAM
Wing Tun.
Glaston Tun.
LUFFENHAM
UFFORD BRIDGE SIDING
HINCKLEY
L.N.W.
BLABY
NARBOROUGH
HIGHAM-ON-THE-HILL
CROFT
ELMESTHORPE
WIGSTON N.Jc.
WIGSTON GLEN PARVA
Wigston Central Jc.
Wigston S.Jc.
WIGSTON SOUTH
COUNTESTHORPE
GLEN
KIBWORTH
HALLATON
Hallaton Jc.
MEDBOURNE
Seaton Tun.
SEATON & UPPINGHAM
WAKERLEY & BARROWDEN
KING'S CLIFFE
Welland Viaduct
HARRINGWORTH
NASSINGTON
Weddington Jc.
S. Leicester Jc.
BROUGHTON ASTLEY
LANGTON
Kibworth Summit
Welham Jc.
ASHLEY & WESTON
Drayton Jc.
GRETTON
ROCKINGHAM
ARLEY & FILLONGLEY
BEDWORTH
BULKINGTON
ULLESTHORPE for LUTTERWORTH
THEDDINGWORTH
LUBENHAM
L.N.W.
MARKET HARBOROUGH
Desborough Summit
Corby Tun.
WELDON & CORBY
Summit
OUNDLE
HAWKESBURY LANE
SHILTON
WELFORD & KILWORTH
CLIPSTON & OXENDON
DESBOROUGH for ROTHWELL
GEDDINGTON
BARNWELL
LONGFORD & EXHALL
FOLESHILL
BRINKLOW
RUSHTON
Glendon Jc.
NORTHAMPTON
LEICESTER

N O T T - I N G - H A M
L I N C O L N
L E I C E S T E R
R U T L A N D

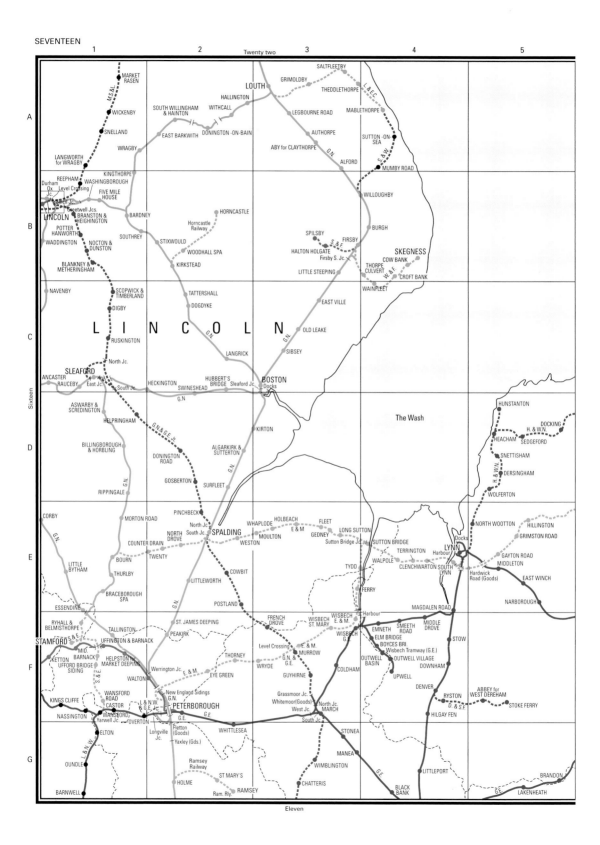

1   2   3   4   5

MARKET RASEN

WICKENBY

M.S.&L.

LOUTH

SALTFLEETBY

GRIMOLDBY

THEDDLETHORPE

L & E.C.

HALLINGTON

WITHCALL

SOUTH WILLINGHAM & HAINTON

SNELLAND

EAST BARKWITH

DONINGTON -ON-BAIN

LEGBOURNE ROAD

MABLETHORPE

WRAGBY

AUTHORPE

ABY for CLAYTHORPE

SUTTON -ON- SEA

LANGWORTH for WRAGBY

G.N.

ALFORD

S. & W.

MUMBY ROAD

KINGTHORPE

REEPHAM

WASHINGBOROUGH

Durham Ox Jc.

Level Crossing

FIVE MILE HOUSE

WILLOUGHBY

Sincil Jc.

Greetwell Jcs.

LINCOLN

BARDNEY

BRANSTON & HEIGHINGTON

HORNCASTLE

Horncastle Railway

BURGH

POTTER HANWORTH

SOUTHREY

SPILSBY

FIRSBY

SKEGNESS

WADDINGTON

STIXWOULD

HALTON HOLGATE

S. & F.

COW BANK

NOCTON & DUNSTON

WOODHALL SPA

Firsby S. Jc.

BLANKNEY & METHERINGHAM

KIRKSTEAD

LITTLE STEEPING

THORPE CULVERT

W. & F.

CROFT BANK

WAINFLEET

NAVENBY

SCOPWICK & TIMBERLAND

TATTERSHALL

DOGDYKE

EAST VILLE

DIGBY

L I N C O L N

RUSKINGTON

G.N.

OLD LEAKE

G.N.

SLEAFORD

North Jc.

LANGRICK

SIBSEY

ANCASTER

RAUCEBY

East Jc.

South Jc.

HECKINGTON

SWINESHEAD

HUBBERT'S BRIDGE

Sleaford Jc.

BOSTON

Docks

ASWARBY & SCREDINGTON

G.N

The Wash

HUNSTANTON

HELPRINGHAM

G.N & G.E Jt.

KIRTON

DOCKING

H. & W.N.

BILLINGBOROUGH & HORBLING

DONINGTON ROAD

ALGARKIRK & SUTTERTON

HEACHAM

SEDGEFORD

GOSBERTON

SURFLEET

G.N

SNETTISHAM

RIPPINGALE

G.N

DERSINGHAM

H. & W.N

CORBY

MORTON ROAD

PINCHBECK

HOLBEACH

FLEET

NORTH WOOTTON

HILLINGTON

WOLFERTON

G.N

COUNTER DRAIN

NORTH DROVE

South Jc.

North Jc.

SPALDING

WHAPLODE

E & M

MOULTON

GEDNEY

LONG SUTTON

SUTTON BRIDGE

GRIMSTON ROAD

LITTLE BYTHAM

BOURN

TWENTY

WESTON

Sutton Bridge Jc.

TERRINGTON

LYNN

Docks

GAYTON ROAD

MIDDLETON

THURLBY

COWBIT

WALPOLE

Harbour

SOUTH LYNN

CLENCHWARTON

EAST WINCH

BRACEBOROUGH SPA

LITTLEWORTH

TYDD

Hardwick Road (Goods)

NARBOROUGH

ESSENDINE

POSTLAND

G.N

FERRY

MAGDALEN ROAD

RYHALL & BELMISTHORPE

ST. JAMES DEEPING

FRENCH DROVE

WISBECH E. & M.

WISBECH ST. MARY

Harbour

TALLINGTON

PEAKIRK

WISBECH

EMNETH

SMEETH ROAD

MIDDLE DROVE

STOW

STAMFORD

S & E

UFFINGTON & BARNACK

Level Crossing

E. & M.

MURROW

G.N. & G.E.

ELM BRIDGE

BOYCES BRI.

KETTON

MID. BARNACK

HELPSTON for MARKET DEEPINGS

Werrington Jc.

E. & M.

WRYDE

Wisbech Tramway (G.E.)

OUTWELL BASIN

OUTWELL VILLAGE

UFFORD BRIDGE SIDING

S & E

EYE GREEN

GUYHIRNE

COLDHAM

UPWELL

DOWNHAM

WALTON

DENVER

ABBEY for WEST DEREHAM

WANSFORD ROAD

New England Sidings G.N.

Grassmoor Jc.

Whitemoor(Goods)

West Jc.

North Jc.

MARCH

RYSTON

D. & S.F.

STOKE FERRY

KINGS CLIFFE

CASTOR

L & N.W.

G.E.J.

PETERBOROUGH

G.E.

South Jc.

HILGAY FEN

NASSINGTON

WANSFORD

Yarwell Jc.

OVERTON

Fletton (Goods)

G.E.

WHITTLESEA

STONEA

ELTON

Longville Jc.

Yaxley (Gds.)

MANEA

G.E

L & N.W.

Ramsey Railway

ST MARY'S

WIMBLINGTON

LITTLEPORT

BRANDON

OUNDLE

HOLME

Ram. Rly.

RAMSEY

CHATTERIS

BLACK BANK

G.E.

LAKENHEATH

BARNWELL

A

B

C

D

E

F

G

Sixteen

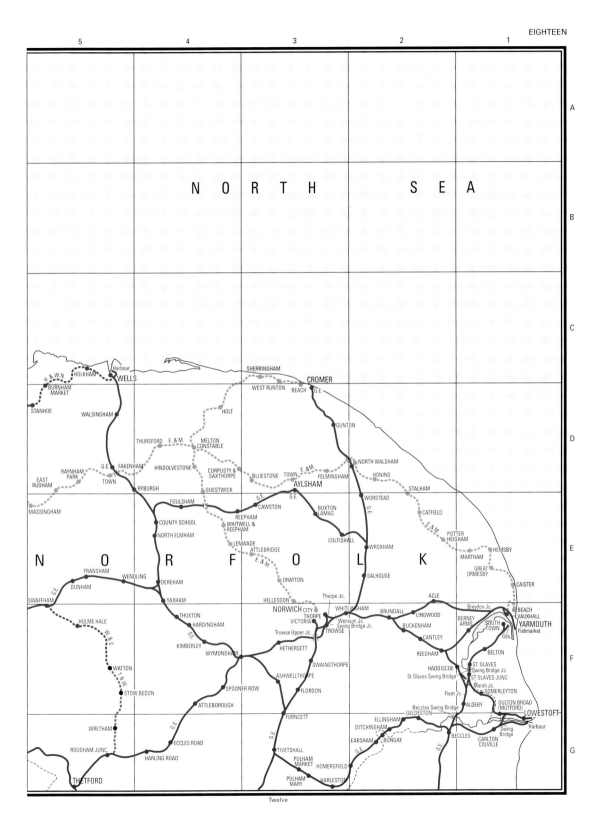

1 2 3 Twenty three 4 5

A
B
C
D
E
F
G

Inset

ADMIRALTY PIER
HOLYHEAD
ANGLESEY
VALLEY
Holyhead Island
L & N W

SEE INSET

AMLWCH
RHOSGOCH
LLANERCHYMEDD
A N G L E S E Y
LLANGWYLLOG
LLANGEFNI
TY CROES
HOLLAND ARMS
BODORGAN
Bodorgan Tuns.
L & N W
GAERWEN
Britannia Tubular Bridge
MENAI BR.
TREBORTH
Dock
PORT DINORWIC
GRIFFITHS CROSSING
PONT RUG
PONTRHYTHALLT
CARNARVON
CWM-Y-GLO
Padarn Rly.
Dinorwic Quarries
TRYFAN JUNC.
WAENFAWR
LLANBERIS
Glyder
BETTWS GARMON
RHOSTRYFAN
SNOWDON RANGER
North Wales N.G.R.
Snowdon
RHYD-DDU

LLANFAIR
Belmont Tun.
Bangor Tun.
BANGOR
PORT PENRHYN (Workmen)
Llandegai Tun.
ABER
FELIN-HEN
Penrhyn Rly.
BETHESDA
PENRHYN QUARRIES (Workmen)

LLANDUDNO
DEGANWY
Tubular Bridge
LLANDUDNO JC.
CONWAY
Penmaenbach Tun.
PENMAENMAWR
LLANFAIRFECHAN
MOCHDRE & PABO
GLAN CONWAY
OLD COLWYN
COLWYN BAY
LLYSFAEN
Penmaenrhos Tun.
LLANDULAS
ABERGELE & PENSARN
RHUDDLAN
ST. ASAPH
TREFNANT
DENBIGH
LLANRHAIADR
RHEWL
RUTHIN
EYARTH

Foryd Pier
Foryd Jc.
FORYD
RHYL
Dyserth
Meliden (Goods)
PRESTATYN
Cwm Branch
L. & M. & D. Jc.
BODFARI
L & N W

TAL-Y-CAFN & EGLWYSBACH
DOLGARROG
LLANRWST & TREFRIW
G & N W
BETTWS-Y-COED
PONT-Y-PANT
ROMAN BRIDGE
DOLWYDDELEN

D E N B I G H
NANTCLWYD
DERWEN

C A R N A R V O N
DINAS JUNC.
LLANWNDA
BRYNGWYN
GROESLON
NANTLLE
PENYGROES
PANT GLAS
Cwm Trwgl
BRYNKIR
YNYS
LLANGYBI
CHWILOG
AFON WEN
ABERERCH
CRICCIETH
PWLLHELI

BLAENAU FESTINIOG
New Rhosydd Quarry
Dinas
L & N.W.
DUFFWS
PC&BT
TAN-Y-GRISIAU
FEST.
B. & F.
MANOD
TAN-Y-BWLCH
DDUALLT
FESTINIOG
Festiniog Rly.
PENRHYN
MAENTWROG RD.
Tremadoc
MINFFORDD
PORTMADOC
Wern (Goods)
Wharf
PORTMADOC HARBOUR
PENRHYNDEUDRAETH
TALSARNAU
TRAWSFYNYDD
HARLECH
LLANBEDR & PENSARN
DYFFRYN
Gorseddau Junc. & Portmadoc Rly.

Festiniog Tun.

M E R I O N E T H S H I R E
CAM
B. & F.
ARENIG
FRONGOCH
Llanderfel Tun.
BALA
Bala Lake
BALA JUNC.
LLANDERFEL
LLANDRILLO
C & B.
CYNWYD
CORWEN
Ll. & C.
GWYDDELWERN

GW
LLANUWCHLLYN
Rhobell Fawr
DRWS-Y-NANT
Aran Benllyn
Aran Mawddwy
BONTNEWYDD
FLAG STA. (private)

A B
1 2
ANGLESEY
Moel Siabod

5 4 3 Twenty four 2 1

Twenty one

Docks
Penwortham Jc. PRESTON JUNC. HOGHTON MILL HILL PORTSMOUTH STANSFIELD HALL
ANSDELL LYTHAM HOWICK BAMBER BRI. CORNHOLME
PLEASINGTON LOWER DARWEN Jc. BAXENDEN Summit Kitson Wood Jc. TODMORDEN
HOWICK LONGTON FARINGTON FENISCOWLES CHERRY TREE Hoddlesden Jc. RAWTEN STALL WATERFOOT for NEWCHURCH BACUP WALSDEN
HESKETH BANK HOOLE MIDGE HALL LEYLAND WITHNELL Hollins (Gds) Hoddlesden (Gds) CLOUGH FOLD FACIT
BANKS HUNDRED END West Lancs. Rly Tarleton Euxton Jc. LOSTOCK HALL BRINSCALL L.U. Jc. DARWEN Grane Rd BRITANNIA
CROSSENS West Lancs Rly L. & Y. Euxton Jc. L. & Y. SPRING VALE HELMSHORE EWOOD BRI. & EDENFIELD SHAW FORTH

SOUTHPORT HESKETH PARK Roe Lane Jc. CHURCHTOWN CROSTON HEAPEY Sough Tun. STUBBINS WHITWORTH BRADLEY
BIRKDALE PALACE MEOLS COP BLOWICK ENTWISTLE HOLCOMBE BROOK SUMMERSEAT WARDLEWORTH BROADLEY
BIRKDALE KEW GDNS. NEW LANE RUFFORD CHORLEY L.U. Jt. TURTON SHAWCLOUGH SMITHY BR
AINSDALE BESCAR LANE COPPULL King William (Gds) GREEN MOUNT TOTTINGTON ROCHDALE MILNROW
WOODVILLE HIRDLEY HILL WHITE BEAR ADLINGTON BROMLEY CROSS BLACK LANE MILTON
FRESHFIELD BURSCOUGH BRI. HOSCAR MOSS STANDISH RED ROCK Astley Bri. (Gds) THE OAKS BOLTON ST HEYWOOD CASTLETON
BARTON & HALSALL LS. & PJ. PARBOLD Standish Jc. BLACKROD HORWICK WOOLFOLD KNOWSLEY STR. BROADFIELD
FORMBY HALSALL APPLEY BRI. BOAR'S HEAD LOSTOCK JUNC. BOLTON L & Y BRADLEY FOLD RADCLIFFE MIDDLETON
ALTCAR RIFLE STA. Hillhouse Jc. SKELMERSDALE GATHURST WIGAN HILTON HOUSE L.N.W. PRESTWICH MIDDLETON JC. WERNETH OLDHAM
HIGHTOWN BURSCOUGH JUNC. TOWN GREEN & AUGHTON Wheley Jc. PLODDER LANE CLIFTON HEATON PK. MOSTON
HALL ROAD ALTCAR & HILLHOUSE Bushey Lane Jc. PEMBERTON HINDLEY FARNWORTH CRUMPSALL DEAN LANE
BLUNDELLSANDS & CROSBY LYDIATE RAINFORD JUNC. BRYNN ATHERTON WALKDEN NEWTON HEATH LONGSIGHT
WATERLOO MAGHULL SEFTON Randle Jc. GARSWOOD TYLDESLEY SWINTON JC. MILES PLATTING VICTORIA LORD RD
SEAFORTH KIRKBY RAINFORD VILLAGE ROOKERY BAMFURLON LEIGH BARTON MOSS PATRICROFT EXCHANGE ARDWICK
AINTREE CRANK MOSS BANK GLAZEBURY ASTLEY SALFORD CENT. ASHBURY
NEW BRIGHTON FAZAKERLEY CARR HILL NEWTON-LE-WILLOWS Golborne MANCHESTER
WALLASEY PRESTON RD ST. HELENS THATTO HEATH LOWTON KENYON JUNC. FLIXTON URMSTON CHORLTON BELLE VUE
SEACOMBE EXCHANGE WATTON-ON-THE-HILL PRESCOT LEA GRN COLLINS GREEN EARLESTOWN JUNC. ASTLEY SALE LEVENSHULME
BIDSTON LIVERPOOL LIME ST. RAINHILL ST. HELEN'S JC. East IRLAM GLAZE BROOK BROOKLANDS DIDSBURY HEATON-MERSEY
MORETON CEN. ROBY HUYTON QUARRY Winwick Jc. PADGATE TIMPERLEY STOCKPORT
MEOLS WOODSIDE ST. MICHAELS HUYTON CLOCK FACE C.L.C. WARRINGTON BROADHEATH NORTHENDEN DAVENPORT
HOYLAKE TOWN CHILDWALL FARNWORTH SANKEY FIDDLERS FERRY ARPLEY HEATLEY DUNHAM MASSEY ALTRINCHAM CHEADLE HULME HAZEL GROVE
WEST KIRBY BIRKENHEAD ROCK FERRY MOSSLEY HILL GATEACRE HOUGH GREEN Widnes Jc. H.L. LATCHFORD LYMM ASHLEY BRAMHALL
BEBINGTON GARSTON ALLERTON WIDNES FIDDLERS FERRY THELWALL HANDFORTH POYNTON (L.N.W.)
SPITAL CRESSINGTON DOCK HUNT'S CROSS DITTON Jc. Walton S. Jc. MOBBERLEY WILMSLOW
THURSTASTON CHURCH RD SPEKE HALEBANK MOORE DARESBURY (SEE SHEET NO. FORTY FIVE) ADLINGTON
BROMBOROUGH GARSTON RUNCORN NORTON KNUTSFORD BOLLINGTON
HESWALL Halton Jc. PRESTON BROOK PRESTBURY
MOSTYN Frodsham Jc. SUTTON WEAVER ALDERLEY EDGE MACCLESFIELD
PARKGATE HOOTON LITTLE SUTTON HALTON WEAVER Jc. PLUMBLEY HIBEL ROAD
HOLYWELL NESTON INCE & ELTON FRODSHAM Weaver Jc. HARTFORD & GREENBANK LOSTOCK GRALAM CHELFORD CENTRAL
BAGILLT HADLOW RD. FRODSHAM ACTON BRIDGE NORTHWICH Summit
FLINT FLINT LEDSHAM ELLESMERE PORT HELSBY Manley (Gds.) HARTFORD NORTH RODE JUNC.
CAERWYS CAPENHURST DUNHAM HILL MOULDS WORTH HANDFORTH
M & D Jn. NANNERCH DELAMERE CHESHIRE Brunswick St. (Goods) BOSLEY
RHYDYMWYN QUAY Buckley Rly. MOLLINGTON Barrow for TARVIN Whitegate Winsford Jc. MIDDLEWICH HOLMES CHAPEL CONGLETON Biddulph Jc.
CONNAH'S QUEENSFERRY CHESTER MICKLE TRAFFORD Winsford & Over OVER & WHARTON WINSFORD GILLOW HEATH
BUCKLEY SANDYCROFT NORTH-GATE (ticket platform) SANDBACH Sandbach (Gds) MOW COP BLACK BULL (BRINDLEY FORD)
MOLD BROUGHTON HALL (Joint) Christleton Tun. MINSHULL VERNON Rookery Bridge (Gds.) CONGLETON
LLONG HOPE EXCHANGE Mold Jc. WAVERTON Tattenhall Jc. CALVELEY TALKE & ALSAGER RD. ALSAGER ROAD N.S.S. KIDSGROVE GOLDENHILL
PADESWOOD & BUCKLEY HOPE Balderton (Goods) TATTENHALL RD BEESTON CASTLE & TARPORLEY WORLESTON CREWE RADWAY GREEN HARE CASTLE CHATTERLEY PITTS HILL FORD GRN & SMALLTHORNE
Coed Talon PENYFFORDD Pulford (Goods) Chester Line Jc. Jamage Jc. AUDLEY TUNSTALL
RUTHIN CAERGWRLE ROSSETT TATTEN-HALL Manchester Line Jc. N.S.S. 1 Talk o'th' Hill Col. Diglake Jc. BURSLEM MILTON
EYARTH BRIDGE END BROXTON WILLASTON 2 Bignall Hill Col. HALMEREND LONGPORT COBRIDGE HANLEY
BRYMBO CEFN-Y-BEDD NANTWICH Market Drayton Jc. BETLEY ROAD BUCKNALL & NORTHWOOD ETRURIA
W.M & C.Q. Ffrwd GRESFORD MALPAS WRENBURY LEYCETT KEELE L.A.G. & B.
Coed Poeth (Goods) GWERSYLLT & WHEATSHEAF SILVERDALE Apedale Col. FENTON MANOR
Minera Moss (Gds.) PLAS POWER MOSS & PENTRE G.W. MADELEY NEWCASTLE UNDER LYME STOKE ON TRENT FENTON
EXCH. WREXHAM CENT Rhos WHITCHURCH (SALOP) MADELEY RD PIPE GATE for WOORE LONGTON NORMACOT
CARROG L.N.W. (Pontcysyllte Tramway) Ponkey Col. RUABON Summit AUDLEM ADDERLEY NORTON-IN-HALES Summit WHITMORE TRENTHAM
GLYNDYFRDWY BERWYN ACREFAIR TREVOR CEFN Dee Viaduct WHITCHURCH BARLASTON
LLANGOLLEN V.o.L. Pontfadog PART OF FLINT MARKET DRAYTON STANDON BRIDGE STONE JUNC.
Glyn Valley Tramway CHIRK Chirk Viaduct FENN'S BANK TERN HILL
Glynceiriog Dolywern FRANKTON WELSHAMPTON BETTISFIELD Goods NORTON BRIDGE
PREESGWEENE GOBOWEN ELLESMERE PREES GREAT BRIDGEFORD STAFFORD COMMON
Gobowen Jc. Summit WEM HODNET PEPLOW STAFFORD
Porthywaen WHITTINGTON (G.W.) SHROPSHIRE GNOSALL
Nantmawr OSWESTRY (G.W.) REDNAL YORTON Trent Valley Jc.
Potteries, Shrewsbury & N. Wales Rly Summit BASCHURCH Old Woods (Goods) HAUGHTON
PANT LLYNCLYS LLANYMYNECH HADNALL
LLANSANTFFRAID CAM.
LLANFECHAIN

FLINT

1   Twenty seven   2   3   4   Twenty eight   5

A

ASKRIGG   REDMIRE   WENSLEY   SPENNI-THORNE   FINGHALL LANE   AINDERBY   LOW   NORTHALLERTON   EARSWICK   KIRBY MOORSIDE

AYSGARTH   LEYBURN   JERVAULX   CRAKEHALL   SCRUTON   LEEMING LANE   OTTERINGTON   Bootham Jc.   Poppleton Jc.   NAWTON   HELMSLEY

N.E.   CONSTABLE BURTON   BEDALE   THIRSK   Town (Goods)   Severus Jc.   Goods   North Jc.   Burton Lane Jc.   YORK   NUNNINGTON

ASHTON   Oldham Road CHARLESTOWN   Oldham Road (Goods)   STALYBRIDGE   MASHAM   SINDERBY   Holgate Bridge Jc.   HOLGATE   Foss Islands (Goods)   GILLING   HOVINGHAM

DROYLSDEN   PARK PARADE   Joint   TANFIELD   TOPCLIFFE   EXCURSION PLATFORM   Chaloners Whin Jc.   COXWOLD

Crownthorn Jc.   O.A.&G.B.   DUKINFIELD   Audenshaw Jc. W.   GUIDE BRIDGE   MELMERBY   BALDERSBY   SESSAY   AMPLEFORTH

ELSLACK   THORNTON   AUDENSHAW   Ashton Moss Jc.   Goods   HOOLEY HILL   RIPON   PILMOOR   HUSHTHWAITE GATE   SLINGSBY

BARNOLDSWICK   MID.   Barnoldswick Rly.   EARBY   Denton Jc.   BRAFFERTON   RASKELF   ALNE   FLAXTON

B

FOULRIDGE   COLNE   BOROUGHBRIDGE   WORMALD GREEN   COPGROVE   TOLLERTON   STRENSALL

L.&Y. Jt.   NELSON   PATELEY BRIDGE   RIPLEY VALLEY   NIDD BRIDGE   HAXBY

Y   O   R   K   S

LEEDS   (Goods)   CENTRAL   WELLINGTON   DACRE   BIRSTWITH   KNARESBOROUGH   GOLDSBOROUGH   SHIPTON   WARTHILL   HOLTBY

ARMLEY   Wellington St   Geldard Jc.   NEW   Three Signal Bri. Jc.   HAMPSTHWAITE   Bilton Road Jc.   Dragon Jc.   ALLERTON   HAMMERTON   WILSTROP SIDING   EARSWICK

Wortley Jc.   HOLBECK   H.L.   Canal Jct.   DARLEY   STARBECK   CATTAL   YORK   Bootham Jc.

ARMLEY & WORTLEY   Leeds Jc.   Hunslet Lane (Goods)   HARROGATE   Goods   HESSAY   MARSTON   Burton Lane Jc.

Wortley W. Jc.   Copley Hill   Engine Shed Jc.   Poppleton Jc.   Severus Jc.   Foss Islands

C

BELL BUSK   GARGRAVE   Farnley Siding   Wortley S. Jc.   WORTLEY & FARNLEY   Crimple Jc.   Crimple Tun.   Poppleton Jc.   Holgate Bridge Jc.   HOLGATE EXCURSION PLATFORM (excursions)

Skipton N. Jc.   EMBSAY   BOLTON ABBEY   Pannal Jc.   PANNAL   SPOFFORTH   Chaloners Whin Jc.

ELSLACK   THORNTON   SKIPTON   ADDINGHAM   WETHERBY   Swing Bridge   NABURN

EARBY   MID.   CONONLEY   STEETON & SILSDEN   ILKLEY   BEN RHYDDING   MID. &N.E. (OTLEY & ILKLEY Jt.)   WEETON   COLLINGHAM BRIDGE   THORP ARCH (BOSTON SPA)   COPMANTHORPE

KILDWICK & CROSSHILLS   O. & I.   BURLEY   Milner Wood Jc.   NEWTON KYME

Worth Valley Bch Jc.   KEIGHLEY   OTLEY   GUISELEY   POOL   ARTHINGTON   BARDSEY   TADCASTER   BOLTON PERCY   ESCRICK

MUMPS   Goods   INGROW   DAMEMS   MENSTON   ESHOLT   Bramhope Tun.   Summit   THORNER & SCARCROFT   STUTTON   ULLESKELF   RICCALL   DUFFIELD GATE   BUBWITH

OLDHAM   CENTRAL   OAKWORTH   GLODWICK RD.   HAWORTH   (GN)   BINGLEY   BAILDON   Bingley Tun.   APPERLEY   CALVERLEY   HORSFORTH   SEE SHEET NO. FORTY TWO   CLIFF COMMON

CLEGG ST.   WERNETH   L.&N.W. Goods   OXENHOPE   DENHOLME   CULLINGWORTH   WILSDEN   FRIZING-HALL   IDLE   INEWLAY   Summit   Cross Gates Jc.   N.E.   CHURCH FENTON   E. Jc.   SELBY   Barlby Jc.   MENTHORPE GATE

D

M.S.&L. Goods   SHIPLEY   ECCLESHILL   BRAMLEY   KIRKSTALL   HEADINGLEY   MARSH LANE   ABERFORD   GARFORTH   SHERBURN   HEMINGBROUGH

SALTAIRE   MANNINGHAM   ARMLEY   WORTLEY   CROSS GATES   MICKLEFIELD   SOUTH MILFORD   WRESSLE

THORNTON   BRADFORD   PUDSEY(L)   LEEDS   HUNSLET   MILFORD JUNC.   GASCOIGNE WOOD JUNC.   Thorp Gates (Gds)

QUEENSBURY   CLAYTON   GT. HORTON   DUDLEY HILL   BIRKENSHAW   BEESTON   CHURWELL   WOODLESFORD   MONK FRYSTON   KIPPAX   LEDSTONE   BURTON SALMON

HOLMFIELD   LOW MOOR   Wyke Tun.   METHLEY

E

STANSFIELD HALL   Hall Royd Jc.   Millwood Tun.   Weasel Hall Tun.   HEBDEN BRI.   MYTHOLMROYD   OVENDEN   WYKE   Wyke Jc.   BIRSTAL   Morley Tun.   TINGLEY   ALTOFTS   CASTLEFORD   FERRYBRIDGE (S.&K.)   TEMPLE HURST   DRAX   BARMBY

EASTWOOD   Horsfall Tun.   Castle Hill Tun.   SOWERBY BRI.   LUDDENDEN FOOT   HALIFAX   CLIFFE   BAILIF BRI.   CLECKHEATON   BATLEY   LOFTHOUSE   NORMANTON   PONTEFRACT   TANSHELF   KNOTTINGLEY L.&Y.& G.N.   WHITLEY BRIDGE   Hensall Jc.   CARLTON

TODMORDEN   WALSDEN   Winterbutlee Tun.   Bank House Tun.   Milner Royd Jc.   COPLEY   GREETLAND   CLIFTON RD.   BRIGHOUSE   DEWSBURY   FLUSH-DYKE   WAKEFIELD   FEATHERSTONE   PONTEFRACT   Balne Moor (Gds)   HENSALL   Gowdall Jc.   SNAITH   RAWCLIFFE

Summit Tun.   RIPPONDEN   WEST VALE   ELLAND   Bradley Wood Jc.   MIRFIELD   OSSETT   SHARLSTON   HECK   BALNE

LITTLEBOROUGH   RISHWORTH   STAINLAND   DEIGHTON   KIRKHEATON   HORBURY   HORBURY JUNC.   SANDAL   CROFTON   ACKWORTH   WOMERSLEY   THORNE (N.E.) (M.S.& L.)

SMITHY BRIDGE   Springwood Jc.   LONGWOOD   HUDDERSFIELD   CRIGGLESTONE   HARE PARK   KIRK SMEATON   NORTON   MOSS

WARDLEWORTH   Rochdale E. Jc.   MILNROW   GOLCAR   L.&N.W.   LOCKWOOD   BERRY BROW   FENAY BRI.   NOSTELL   RYHILL   UPTON   ASKERN

ROCHDALE   ROYTON   NEW HEY   SHAW   SLAITHWAITE   NETHERTON   Robin Hood Tun.   KIRKBURTON   HAIGH   HEMSWORTH   SOUTH ELMSALL   Askern Jc.   Joan Croft Jc.   THORNE (M.S.& L.)

F

ROYTON JUNC.   GLODWICK RD.   Standedge Tun.   MARSDEN   HEALEY HOUSE   BROCKHOLES   CLAYTON WEST   DARTON   STAINCROSS   MOORTHORPE   Shaftholme Jc.   Applehurst   STAINFORTH & HATFIELD

WERNETH   Diggle Jc.   DIGGLE   SADDLEWORTH   STOCKSMOOR   SKELMANTHORPE   STAINCROSS   MONK BRETTON   CUDWORTH   HAMPOLE   CARCROFT & ADWICK-LE-STREET   BRAMWITH   BARNBY DUN

OLDHAM   LEES   GROTTON   UPPER MILL   GREENFIELD   MELTHAM   SHEPLEY   Thurstonland Tun.   DENBY DALE   Cumberworth Tun.   BARNSLEY   FRICKLEY   DARFIELD   ARKSEY   DONCASTER   Balby Jc.

PARK-MOSSLEY   FRIEZLAND   Royal George Tun.   HOLMFIRTH   1. WOODHEAD DAM (workmen)   2. HOLLINS (workmen)   SUMMER LANE   DODWORTH   SILKSTONE   WOMBWELL   BOLTON-ON-DEARNE   Dearne Jc.

BRIT.   O.A.& G.   MICKLEHURST   Scout Tunnel   3. TINTWISTLE (workmen)   4. NEWTON for HYDE   HAZLEHEAD BRIDGE   Wellhouse Tun.   PENISTONE   Barnsley Jc.   WATH   Wath Rd. Jc.   MEXBOROUGH   Warmsworth

DROYLSDEN   ASHTON   STALEY & MILLBROOK   5. GODLEY JUNC.   DUNFORD BRIDGE   Woodhead Tun.   BIRDWELL   SWINTON   KILNHURST   CONISBOROUGH   FINNINGLEY   GN.&G.E.Jt.

G

STOCKPORT   DAVENPORT   STALYBRIDGE   GUIDE BRIDGE   Longdendale Rly.   Dinting Via.   WOODHEAD   Thurgoland Tun.   WORTLEY   WEST WOOD   WATH   SWINTON   KILNHURST   ROSSINGTON   GN.

Denton   HYDE JUNC.   HADFIELD   DINTING   CROWDEN   ARKSEY   DEEPCAR   CHAPELTOWN   PARK GATE   ALDWARKE   BAWTRY

REDDISH   DENTON   HYDE   Apethorne Jc.   GLOSSOP   MOTTRAM & BROADBOTTOM   Mottram Via.   North Jc.   Cherry Tree Lane (Goods) (MID)   DONCASTER   South Jc.   Marsh Gate (Gds)   Balby Jc.   ECCLESFIELD   OUGHTY BRIDGE   HOLMES   ROTHERHAM   SCROOBY

BREDBURY   ROMILEY   ROSE HILL   WOODLEY   STRINES   S. & M. Jt.   Black Carr Jc.   Hexthorpe Jc.   WADSLEY BRIDGE   NEEPSEND   TINSLEY   RANSKILL

MARPLE   HIGH LANE   HAYFIELD   BIRCH VALE   NEW MILLS   Warmsworth (Gds)   BRIGHTSIDE   Tunnel Jc.   SHEFFIELD   VICTORIA   MID.   ATTERCLIFFE   DARNALL   TREETON   WOODHOUSE MILL   Goods   WOODHOUSE

SEE SHEET NO. FORTY FIVE   Fifteen   Sixteen

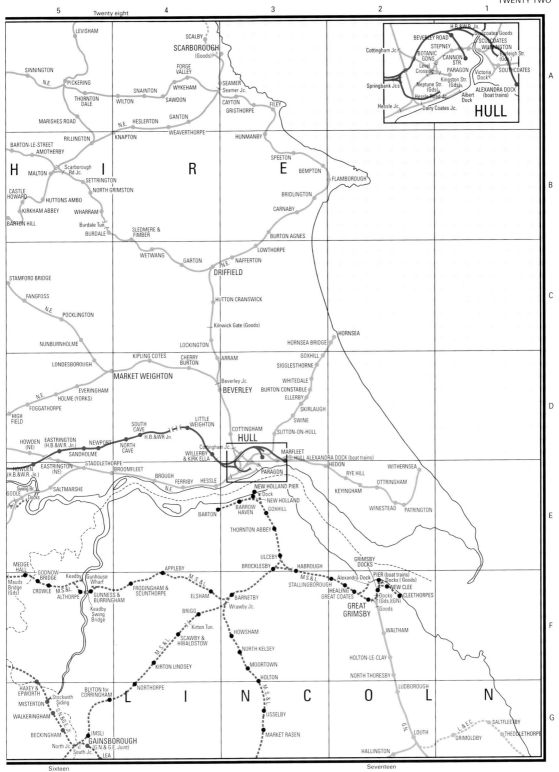
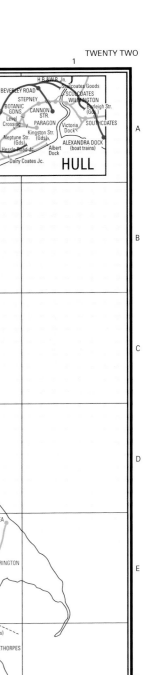

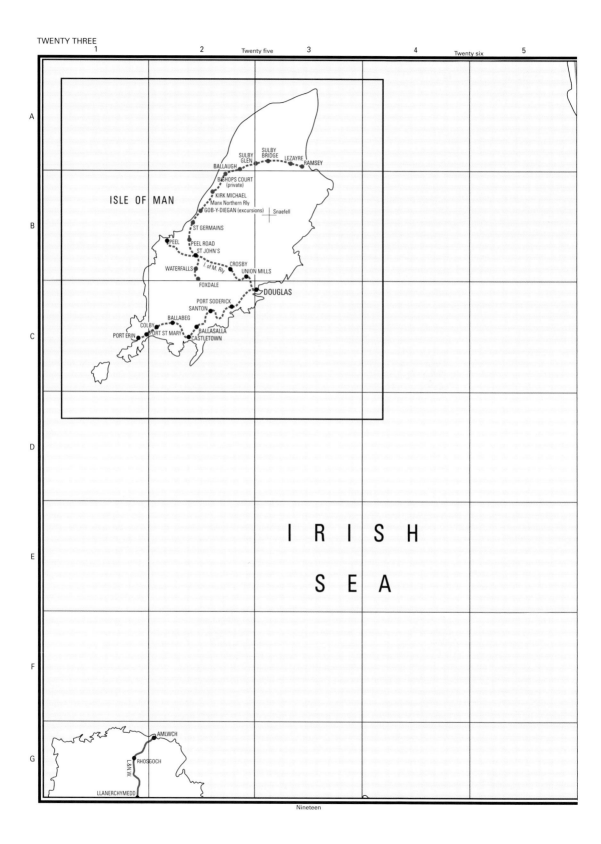

ISLE OF MAN

SULBY
GLEN
SULBY
BRIDGE
LEZAYRE
BALLAUGH
RAMSEY
BISHOPS COURT
(private)
KIRK MICHAEL
Manx Northern Rly
GOB-Y-DIEGAN (excursions)
Snaefell
ST GERMAINS
PEEL
PEEL ROAD
ST JOHN'S
CROSBY
WATERFALLS
I. of M. Rly
UNION MILLS
FOXDALE
DOUGLAS
PORT SODERICK
SANTON
BALLABEG
COLBY
BALLASALLA
PORT ERIN
PORT ST MARY
CASTLETOWN

IRISH
SEA

AMLWCH
L.&N.W.
RHOSGOCH
LLANERCHYMEDD

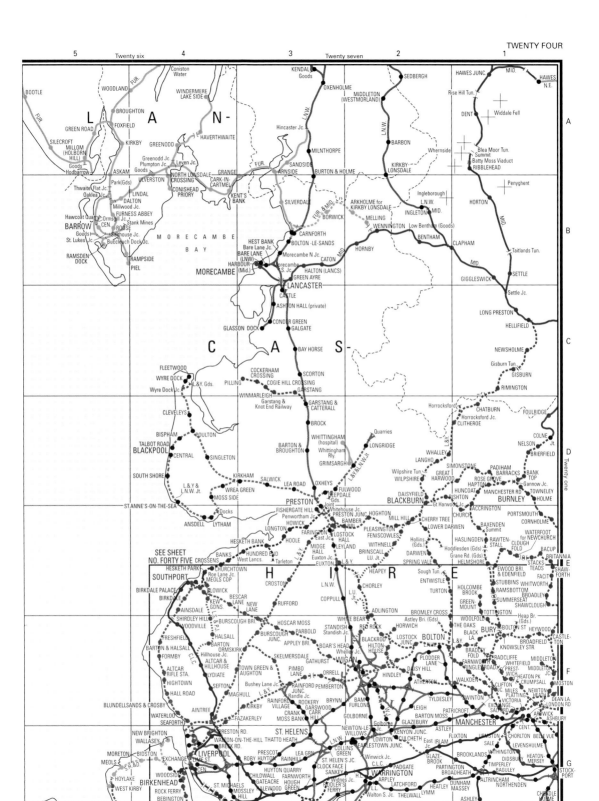

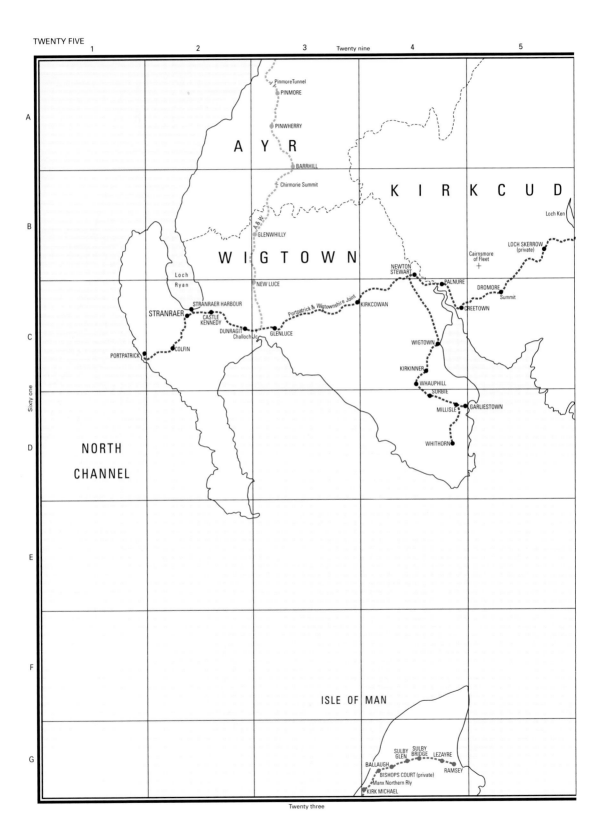

A

PinmoreTunnel
PINMORE

PINWHERRY

A Y R

BARRHILL

Chirmorie Summit

K I R K C U D

Loch Ken

B

A.&.W.

GLENWHILLY

LOCH SKERROW
(private)

W I G T O W N

Loch
Ryan

NEW LUCE

NEWTON
STEWART

Cairnsmore
of Fleet

PALNURE

DROMORE
Summit

Portpatrick & Wigtownshire Joint

KIRKCOWAN

CREETOWN

STRANRAER HARBOUR

STRANRAER

CASTLE
KENNEDY

DUNRAGIT
Challoch Jc.

GLENLUCE

WIGTOWN

C

PORTPATRICK

COLFIN

KIRKINNER

Sixty one

WHAUPHILL
SORBIE

MILLISLE

GARLIESTOWN

WHITHORN

D

NORTH

CHANNEL

E

F

ISLE OF MAN

G

SULBY   SULBY
GLEN   BRIDGE   LEZAYRE

BALLAUGH

RAMSEY

BISHOPS COURT (private)

Manx Northern Rly

KIRK MICHAEL

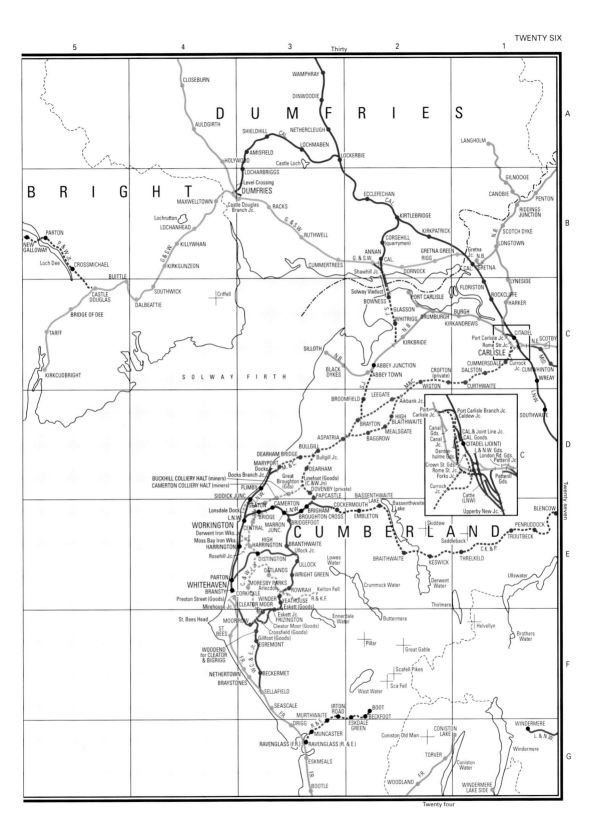

1   Thirty one   2   3   4   5

RICCARTON SAUGHTREE DEADWATER
STEELE ROAD KIELDER
PLASHETTS
N.B.
NEWCASTLETON
N.B. FALSTONE THORNEYBURN
TARSET BELLINGHAM
KERSHOPE FOOT REEDSMOUTH

FONTBURN EWESLEY
LONG WITTON
WOODBURN
SCOT'S GAP
MIDDLETON
KNOWE'S GATE ANGERTON
MELDON
NETHERTON

WIDDRINGTON
LONGHIRST ASHINGTON
NORTH SEATON
MORPETH HEPSCOTT
N.E.
CHOPPINGTON BEDLINGTON BEBSIDE

A

N O R T H U M B E R L A N D

WARK
N.B.
BARRASFORD

PLESSEY
CRAMLINGTON

B

CHOLLERTON
CHOLLERFORD
FOURSTONES
WALL
GILSLAND BARDON HAYDON N.E. Border Counties Jc.
GREENHEAD MILL BRIDGE HEXHAM
HALTWHISTLE
Haltwhistle Tunnel

ANNITSFORD
KILLINGWORTH
FOREST HALL
LEMINGTON GOSFORTH BENTON
NEWBURN
HEDDON-ON-THE-WALL W. JESMOND
NORTH WYLAM JESMOND
West Wylam Jc. SCOTSWOOD CENTRAL
RYTON N.E.
INSET ON
PAGE 28

LOW ROW ELRINGTON
BRAMPTON JUNC. NAWORTH LANGLEY
BRAMPTON FEATHERSTONE STAWARD
TOWN HOW MILL COANWOOD
Brampton Rly. LAMBLEY
HEADS NOOK CATTON ROAD
WETHERAL
COTEHILL SLAGGYFORD

CORBRIDGE Corbridge Tun. MICKLEY PRUDHOE
RIDING MILL STOCKSFIELD

BLAYDON
SWALWELL
BENSHAM
LOW FELL
NEWCASTLE

ROWLANDS GILL LAMESLEY
LINTZ GREEN BIRTLEY
EBCHESTER Tanfield Moor Col.
SHOTLEY BRIDGE Medomsley Col. CHESTER-LE-STREET
CONSETT & BLACKHILL W. Stanley (Gds.)
ROWLEY KNITSLEY PLAWSWORTH

C

ARMATHWAITE
Armathwaite Tun. ALSTON
Baron Wood Tuns.
LAZONBY
LAZONBY Lazonby Tun.
CALTHWAITE MID.
LITTLE SALKELD
PLUMPTON
LANGWATHBY

BOLT'S DOWN WASKERLEY PARK LANCHESTER WITTON
(Workmen) (Workmen) GILBERT DURHAM
Grove Rake Weatherill & BURN HILL ALDIN GRANGE for BEARPARK
Lead Mine Rookhope Rly. JUNC. Relly
Rookhope Parkhead Burnhill Jc. WATERHOUSES USHAW Mill
Stanhope (Goods) Stanley Col. MOOR Jc.
Ironworks BRANDON
Heights Quarry STANHOPE TOW LAW (Wooley Col.)
FROSTERLEY BRANCEPETH
WOLSINGHAM N.E. CROXDALE
Bishopley HARPERLEY CROOK WILLINGTON
BEECHBURN HUNWICK SPENNYMOOR
BYERS GREEN

D

D U R H A M

PENRITH Waste Bank Tun.
Red Hills Culgaith Tun. NEW BIGGIN
Jc. Eamont Bri. Jc. CULGAITH
Eden Valley Jc. CLIFTON TEMPLE
CLIBURN SOWERBY
CLIFTON & KIRKBY THORE
LOWTHER LONG MARTON
(N.E.)
(MID.) APPLEBY
ORMSIDE N.E. WARCOP

MIDDLETON
MICKLETON
ROMALDKIRK
BARNARD BROOMIELAW
COTHERSTONE CASTLE (private) WINSTON
LARTINGTON Tees N.E. GAINFORD Forcett Jc.
Valley PIERCEBRIDGE
Jc.

WITTON-LE-WEAR
WEAR VALLEY JUNC.
BISHOP AUCKLAND ETHERLEY
EVENWOOD COUNDON
Haggerleases WEST SHILDON
COCKFIELD AUCKLAND Simpasture
Jc.
HEIGHINGTON

Merrybent
Jc.

E

W E S T M O R L A N D

SHAP
L.N.W.
Shap Summit
CROSBY GARRETT
SMARDALE
GAISGILL KIRKBY STEPHEN KIRKBY STEPHEN
(MID.) (N.E.)
RAVENSTONEDALE Birkett Tun.
TEBAY
Wild Boar Fell

Helm Tun.
MUSGRAVE Stainmore
Summit
BARRAS BOWES N.E.
Belah Viaduct

High Seat

Forcett Rly.
Forcett Depot
M. & D.
Barton (Goods)
Quarries

MOULTON
SCORTON
RICHMOND CATTERICK
BRIDGE

F

STAVELEY
BURNESIDE LOW GILL
GRAYRIGG
Gds. OXENHOLME
KENDAL SEDBERGH
MIDDLETON
(WESTMORLAND)

Langdale Fell
Aisgill Summit
Bow Fell Shotlock Hill Tun.
Moorcock Tun.
Mossdale Head Tun.
MID.
HAWES JUNC. HAWES N.E.
Rise Hill Tun. ASKRIGG

Great Shunner Fell

Y O R K

REDMIRE
AYSGARTH WENSLEY

LEYBURN
SPENNITHORNE
CONSTABLE BURTON
FINGHALL LANE
JERVAULX
CRAKEHALL
BEDALE

G

Twenty six

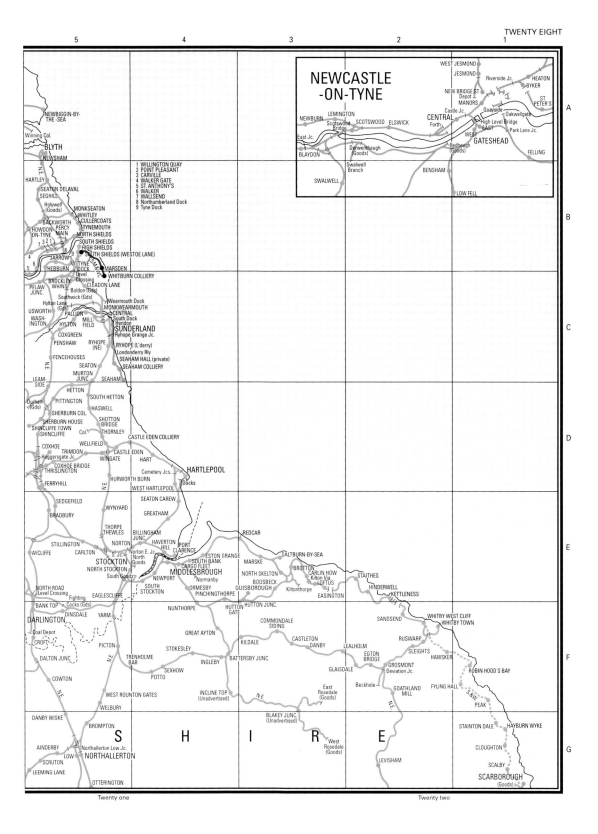

1   Thirty two   3   Thirty three   5
2   4

A

Loch Fyne

Loch Long

Ben Lomond

ABERFOYLE   Lake of Menteith   DOUNE

Loch Goil   GARTMORE   LADYLANDS SIDING   KIPPEN
Loch Lomond   PORT OF MENTEITH   GARGUNNOCK

DUM-   BUCHLYVIE
BARTON

S   T   I   R   L

Gare Loch   DRYMEN   GARTNESS   BALFRON
KILLEARN NEW
CALDARVAN   KILLEARN OLD

Blane Valley Rly.   KILSYTH NEW
BALLOCH PIER   BALLOCH   Campsie Fells   KILSYTH (N.B.)
HELENSBURGH   CRAIGENDORAN   STRATHBLANE   LENNOXTOWN   GAVELL

B   ALEXANDRIA   JAMESTOWN   BLANEFIELD   CAMPSIE GLEN   MILTON
Dalmonach   GARTCOSH
GOUROCK   CARDROSS   RENTON   MILNGAVIE   BALMORE   TORRANCE   KIRKINTILLOCH
GREENOCK PRINCES PIER   DALREOCH   DUMBARTON   Waterside Jc.
FORT MATILDA   GREENOCK CATHCART   BOWLING   KILPATRICK   BEARSDEN   BARDOWIE   SUMMERSTON   LENZIE   Campsie   Bridgend
RAVENSCRAIG   GREENOCK CST   CARTSDYKE   DALMUIR   Milngavie Jc.   MARYHILL   Bch. Jc.   Jc.
LYNEDOCH ST.   PORT GLASGOW   KILBOWIE   CLYDEBANK   STEPS RD   BISHOPBRIGGS
INVERKIP   BOGSTON   LANGBANK   XOKER
UPPER   Upper Port   BISHOPTON   HOUSTON   YOKER   BUCHANAN ST
GREENOCK   Glasgow (Goods)   KILBOWIE   RENFREW   QUEEN ST   BLAIRHILL
WEMYSS BAY   KILMALCOLM   HOUSTON (CROSSLEE)   GOVAN   GLASGOW   CENTRAL   ST.ENOCH   SHETTLESTON
Blackstone Jc.   Linwood   IBROX   CROOKSTON   PAISLEY   PARTICK   MT.VERNON
BRIDGE OF WEIR   ELDERSLIE   POTTERHILL   CROSSMYLOOF   CAMBUSLANG   BROOMHOUSE

C   JOHNSTONE NORTH   JOHN-   NITSHILL   GIFFNOCK   CARMYLE
FIRTH OF   STONE   BARRHEAD   THORNLIEBANK   CATHCART   BLANTYRE
CLYDE   MILLIKEN   CLARKSTON   HIGH BLANTYRE   BOTH-
Hill of Stake   PARK   HOWWOOD   BUSBY   WELL
BUTE   LARGS   LOCHWINNOCH   NEILSTON   THORNTON HALL
CALDWELL   SEE SHEET NO.   EAST   MEIKLE
HAIRMYRES   KILBRIDE   EARNOCK
FORTY FOUR
FAIRLIE PIER   KILBIRNIE   BEITH G. & S.W.
FAIRLIE   GLENGARNOCK (L&A)   BEITH (Joint)   LUGTON   GLASSFORD
GLENGARNOCK & KILBIRNIE   BARRMILL   DUNLOP   STRATHAVEN
Swinlees Branch   GIFFEN
DALRY   AUCHENMADE

D   WEST KILBRIDE   Dalry Jc.   DUNLOP   L   A
Lissens (Gds)   STEWARTON
SALTCOATS   MONTGREENAN   G.B. & K.Jt.
(L&A)   KILWINNING
ARDROSSAN   Dubbs   CUNNINGHAMBEAD
G.&S.W.   Jc.   Doura Main Col.   CROSSHOUSE   Gds   KILMARNOCK
PIER   BOGSIDE Perceton   KILMAURS
SOUTH BEACH   Ardeer   (races)   Branch   Mayfield Branch   NEWMILNS
SALTCOATS (G.&S.W.)   IRVINE   SPRINGSIDE   HURLFORD
STEVENSTON   Harbour   DREGHORN   St Marnocks   GALSTON
ARRAN   GAILES   DRY. GATEHEAD   BRIDGE

E   Harbour   BARASSIE
TROON   MAUCHLINE for   MUIRKIRK
MONKTON   CATRINE
PRESTWICK   ANNBANK   TARBOLTON   LUGAR   CRONBERRY
Falkland Jc.   AUCHINCRUIVE   COMMONDYKE
NEWTON-ON-AYR   Logan Jc.   OLD CUMNOCK
New Harbour   Blackhouse Jc.   TRABBOCH   AUCHINLECK   CUMNOCK
Goods   Hawkhill Jc.   SKARES   DUMFRIES
Old Harbour   AYR   OCHILTREE   HOUSE
DRONGAN   Belston Jc.   NEW CUMNOCK

F   A   Y   R   S   H   I   R   E
DALRYMPLE   Dalrymple Jc.   RANKINSTON
HOLLYBUSH
CASSILLIS   WATERSIDE   Blackcraig
PATNA
MAYBOLE
DALMELLINGTON

G   KILKERRAN   Loch
DAILLY   Doon
KILLOCHAN
GIRVAN   OLD   NEW
Tunnel

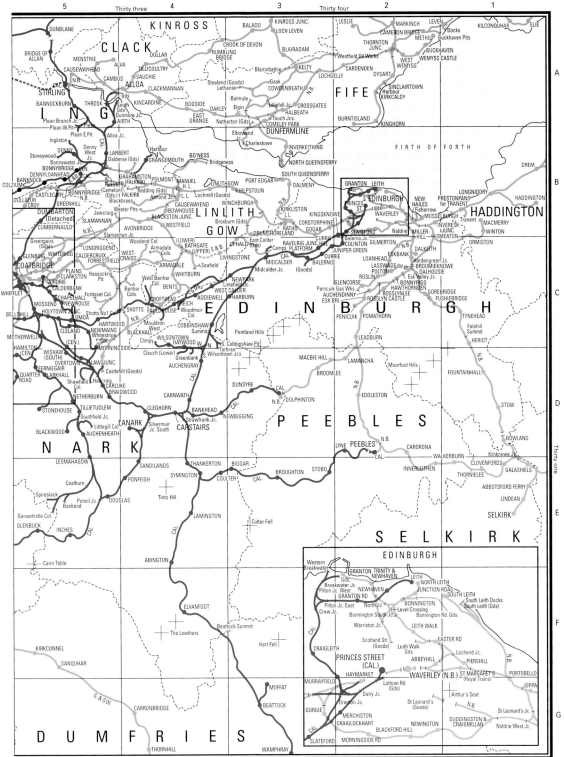

1 2 3 4 5

A

NORTH

SEA

Bass Rock

NORTH BERWICK
DIRLETON
EAST FORTUNE
EAST LINTON
DUNBAR

B

N.B.

INNERWICK
COCKBURNSPATH
St Abb's Head

HADDINGTON

Penmanshiel
Summit Tun.
GRANT'S HOUSE
N.B. RESTON
BURNMOUTH
AYTON
CHIRNSIDE

C

EDROM
DUNS N.B.
BERWICK
Royal Border Bridge
TWEEDMOUTH
SCREMERSTON

BERWICK

MARCHMONT
VELVET HALL
N.E.
NORHAM
WIND MILL HILL
Holy Island

GORDON N.B. GREENLAW
TWIZELL
BEAL

D

EARLSTON
CARHAM
COLDSTREAM
SMEAFIELD
SPROUSTON
SUNILAWS
N.E.
Sprouston Jc.
BELFORD
MELROSE
Ravenswood Jc.
ST BOSWELLS
N.B. KELSO
MINDRUM
Eildon Hills
Kelso Jc.
ROXBURGH
KIRKNEWTON
AKELD
LUCKER

E

RUTHERFORD
MAXTON
KIRKBANK
WOOLER
NEWHAM CHATHILL
N.E.
FALLODON (private)
BELSES
NISBET
ILDERTON
CHRISTON BANK
N.B.
JEDFOOT BRIDGE
JEDBURGH
WOOPERTON
HASSENDEAN
LITTLE MILL

ROXBURGH

HEDGELEY
LONGHOUGHTON
GLANTON
ALNWICK
HAWICK

F

WHITTINGHAM
BILTON
STOBS
EDLINGHAM
WARKWORTH
SHANKEND
AMBLE
N.E.
ROTHBURY
ACKLINGTON BROOMHILL
Whitrope Tun.
N.B.
Summit
BRINKBURN
Amble Branch Jc.
SAUGHTREE Peel Fell
CHEVINGTON

G

RICCARTON
DEADWATER
N.B. STEELE RD. KIELDER
NORTHUMBERLAND
FONTBURN
EWESLEY
WIDDRINGTON

Thirty

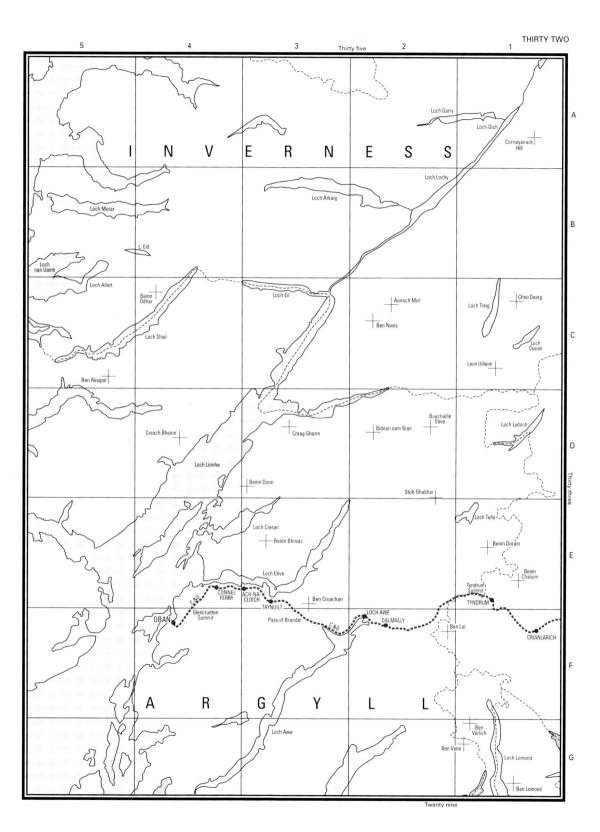

THIRTY TWO

5   4   3   Thirty five   2   1

A

B

C

Thirty three

D

E

F

G

Twenty nine

I N V E R N E S S

Loch Garry
Loch Oich
Corrieyairack Hill
Loch Lochy
Loch Arkaig
Loch Morar
L. Eilt
Loch nan Uamh
Loch Ailort
Beinn Odhar
Loch Eil
Aonach Mor
Loch Treig
Chno Dearg
Ben Nevis
Loch Ossian
Loch Shiel
Leim Uilleim
Ben Resipol
Creach Bheinn
Creag Ghorm
Bidean nam Bian
Buachaille Etive
Loch Lydoch
Loch Linnhe
Beinn Donn
Stob Ghabhar
Loch Tulla
Loch Creran
Beinn Breac
Beinn Dorain
Loch Etive
Beinn Chaluim
Tyndrum Summit
CONNEL FERRY
ACH-NA-CLOICH
Ben Cruachan
TYNDRUM
OBAN
Glencruitten Summit
TAYNUILT
Pass of Brander
LOCH AWE
DALMALLY
Ben Lui
CRIANLARICH
A R G Y L L
Loch Awe
Ben Vorlich
Ben Vane
Loch Lomond
Ben Lomond

H.R.

Carn Mairg   KINGUSSIE

NEWTONMORE

Cairn Gorm

A

I N V E R N E S S   **A B E**

DALWHINNIE

Carn na Caim

B

Loch Ericht

Drumochter Summit
DALNASPIDAL

Loch Garry

H.R.

STRUAN   BLAIR ATHOLE   KILLIECRANKIE   Ben Vrackie

Killiecrankie Tun.

Pass of Killiecrankie

C

PITLOCHRY

GRANDTULLY

H.R.

BALLINLUIG

P E R   **T H**

GUAY

ABERFELDY

DALGUISE

BLAIRGOWRIE

ROSEMOUNT

Inver Tun.

DUNKELD

D

Ben Lawers   Loch Tay

Kingswood Tun.   Summit   MURTHLY   WOODSIDE

LOCH TAY
(KILLIN PIER)

Ballathie
(Goods)   CARGILL

KILLIN

STANLEY

Killin Rly.

CAL

STRATHORD

E

KILLIN JUNC

Ben Chonzie

LUNCARTY

LUIB

GLENOGLEHEAD

TIBBERMUIR
CROSSING

RUTHVEN ROAD CROSSING

Glenoglehead Summit

ALMONDBANK

METHVEN

Almond Valley Jc
NORTH (ticket platform)

METHVEN JUNC. (exchange)

PERTH

Loch Earn

MADDERTY   BALGOWAN

GENERAL
N.B.Goods
PRINCES STR.

LOCHEARNHEAD

CRIEFF

ABERCAIRNY

SOUTH (ticket platform)
Harbour   KINFAUNS

GLENCARSE

KINGSHOUSE   Ben Vorlich

HIGHLANDMAN

INNERPEFFRAY

FORGANDENNY

Hilton Jc.

STRATHYRE

MUTHILL

FORTEVIOT

Moncrieff
Tun.

BRIDGE OF
EARN

F

Benvane

Loch Lubnaig

DUNNING

ABERNETHY

Uamh Bheag

CAL

Loch Katrine

TULLIBARDINE

C.&O.

Pass of Leny

AUCHTERARDER

CURLING POND HALT
(curling events)   BLACKFORD

CRIEFF JUNC.

GATESIDE

Lake of Menteith

Ben Ledi

CALLANDER

Summit

MAWCARSE

Loch Achray

GREENLOANING

MILNATHORT

Loch Vennachar

KINBUCK

KINROSS JUNC.
BALADO

CAL

ABERFOYLE

S.&A.

DOUNE

DUNBLANE

CROOK OF
DEVON

LOCH
LEVEN

Loch
Leven

N.B.

G

GARTMORE

BRIDGE OF ALLAN   MENSTRIE   ALVA   TILLICOULTRY

RUMBLING BRIDGE
DOLLAR

K I N R O S S

BLAIRADAM

Thirty two

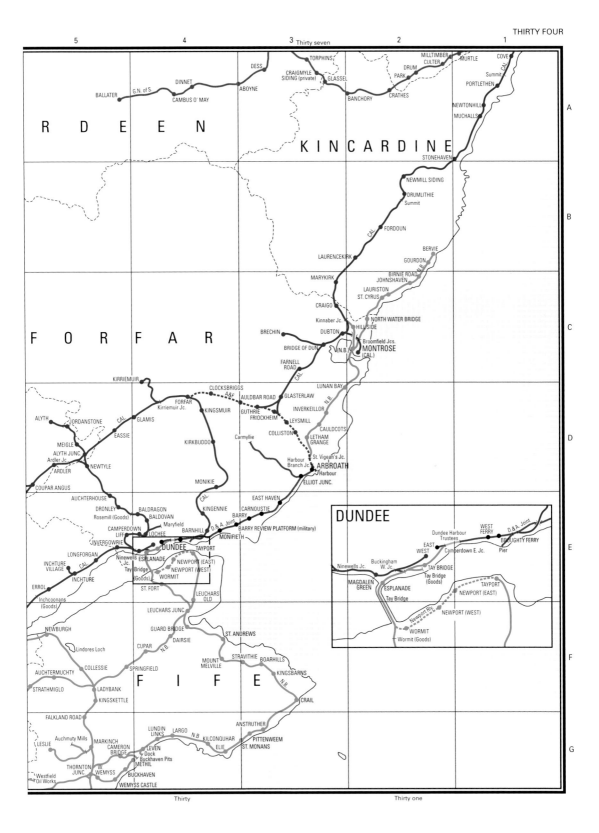

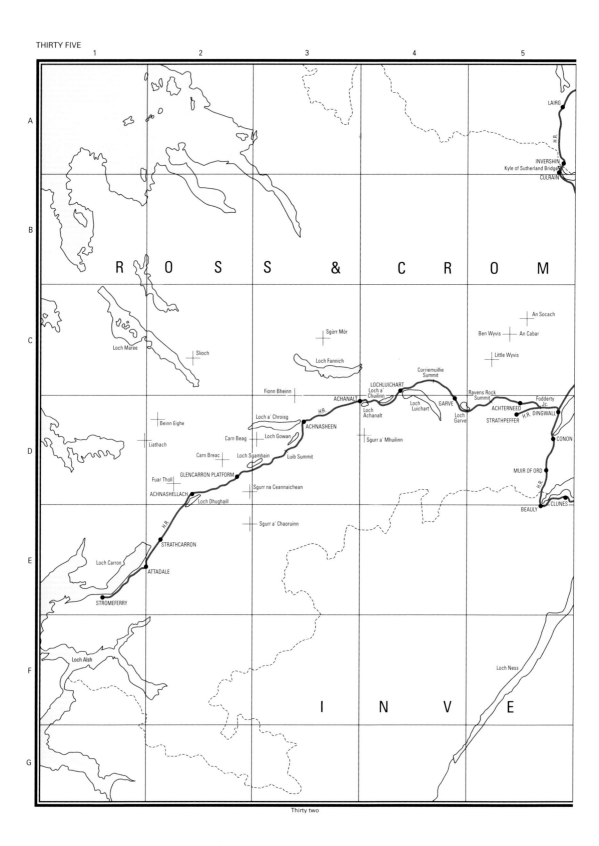

1   2   3   4   5

A

B

R   O   S   S   &   C   R   O   M

C

LAIRG

INVERSHIN
Kyle of Sutherland Bridge
CULRAIN

An Socach
Ben Wyvis — An Cabar

Little Wyvis

Sgùrr Mòr

Loch Maree

Slioch

Loch Fannich

Corriemuillie Summit

LOCHLUICHART
Loch a' Chuilinn
ACHANALT
Loch Achanalt
Loch Luichart
GARVE
Loch Garve
Ravens Rock Summit
ACHTERNEED
STRATHPEFFER
Fodderty Jc.
H.R. DINGWALL
CONON

Fionn Bheinn

Beinn Eighe

Liathach

Loch a' Chroisg
ACHNASHEEN
H.R.

Carn Beag
Loch Gowan

Carn Breac
Loch Sgamhain
Luib Summit

GLENCARRON PLATFORM

Sgurr a' Mhuilinn

MUIR OF ORD
H.R.

BEAULY
CLUNES

D

Fuar Tholl
ACHNASHELLACH
Loch Dhughaill

Sgurr na Ceannaichean

Sgurr a' Chaoruinn

H.R.
STRATHCARRON

Loch Carron
ATTADALE

STROMEFERRY

E

Loch Alsh

Loch Ness

I   N   V   E

F

G

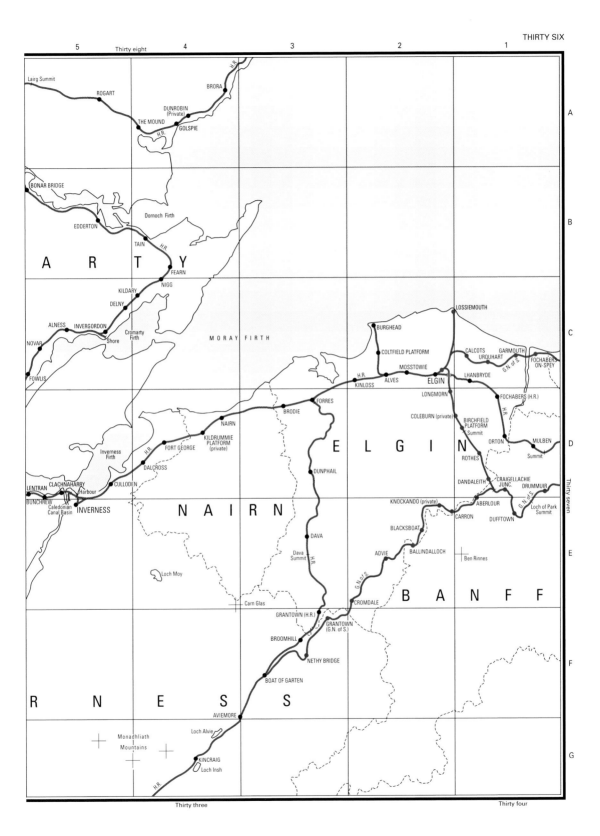

Lairg Summit
ROGART
BRORA
DUNROBIN (Private)
THE MOUND
GOLSPIE
H.R.

A

BONAR BRIDGE

EDDERTON
Dornoch Firth

TAIN
H.R.
FEARN
NIGG

A   R   T   Y

B

KILDARY
DELNY

ALNESS   INVERGORDON
NOVAR   Shore   Cromarty Firth

FOWLIS

MORAY   FIRTH

LOSSIEMOUTH
BURGHEAD
COLTFIELD PLATFORM
CALCOTS   GARMOUTH
URQUHART   FOCHABERS ON-SPEY
G.N. of S.
MOSSTOWIE
LHANBRYDE
H.R.   ALVES   ELGIN
KINLOSS
LONGMORN   FOCHABERS (H.R.)
COLEBURN (private)   H.R.
BIRCHFIELD PLATFORM
Summit   MULBEN
ORTON
ROTHES   Summit

C

FORRES
BRODIE

NAIRN
KILDRUMMIE PLATFORM (private)
FORT GEORGE
Inverness Firth
H.R.
DALCROSS

CULLODEN

DUNPHAIL

E   L   G   I   N

DANDALEITH
CRAIGELLACHIE JUNC.
DRUMMUIR
Thirty seven
ABERLOUR
G.N. of S.
Loch of Park Summit
CARRON   DUFFTOWN

LENTRAN   CLACHNAHARRY   Harbour
BUNCHREW
Caledonian Canal Basin   INVERNESS

N   A   I   R   N

KNOCKANDO (private)
BLACKSBOAT
DAVA

Dava Summit
H.R.
ADVIE   BALLINDALLOCH
Ben Rinnes

Loch Moy

B   A   N   F   F

Carn Glas
CROMDALE
G.N. of S.
GRANTOWN (H.R.)
GRANTOWN (G.N. of S.)
BROOMHILL
NETHY BRIDGE

R   N   E   S   S

BOAT OF GARTEN

AVIEMORE

Loch Alvie
Monadhliath Mountains
KINCRAIG
Loch Insh
H.R.

A

B

C

D

E

F

G

1 2 3 4 5

A

B

C

FINDOCHTY
PORTESSIE
(G.N.S.)
BUCKIE (H.R.)
BUCKPOOL
PORT
GORDON
ENZIE

PORTKNOCKIE
CULLEN
TOCHIENEAL
RATHVEN
GLASSAUGH
DRYBRIDGE
PLATFORM

PORTSOY
ORDENS
(private)
LADYSBRIDGE
TILLYNAUGHT
CORNHILL

BANFF
HARBOUR
MACDUFF
BANFF
BRI.

KING EDWARD

FRASERBURGH
PHILORTH (Private)
RATHEN
LONMAY
MORMOND

D

FORGIE
KEITH
H.R.
EARLSMILL
AUCHINDACHY
Towiemore (Goods)
ROTHIEMAY

KNOCK
GRANGE
Grange N. Jc.
Grange S. Jc.

GLENBARRY

PLAIDY
TURRIFF
AUCHTERLESS

STRICHEN
BRUCKLAY
MINTLAW
MAUD JUNC.
PITFOUR CURLING
PLATFORM (curling events)
AUCHNAGATT

LONGSIDE NEWSEAT
INVERUGIE
PETERHEAD
Harbour

G. N. of S.

Thirty six

HUNTLY

FYVIE
ROTHIE NORMAN

ARNAGE

A B E R D E E N

E

GARTLY
Summit
KENNETHMONT
WARDHOUSE
INSCH
OYNE
PITCAPLE

WARTLE

INVER-
AMSAY
OLD MELDRUM
FINGASK PLATFORM
LETHENTY

ELLON for CRUDEN
ESSLEMONT
LOGIERIEVE
UDNY

G. N. of S.

F

ALFORD
WHITEHOUSE
MONYMUSK
TILLYFOURIE

INVERURIE
Port Elphinstone
(Goods)
PARADISE SIDING
(workmen)
KEMNAY
KINTORE
KINALDIE

Newmachar
Summit
NEWMACHAR
PITMEDDEN
PARKHILL
DYCE
STONEYWOOD
BANKHEAD
BUXBURN
WOODSIDE
DON ST.
KITTYBREWSTER

G

LUMPHANAN
TORPHINS
DESS
CRAIGMYLE SIDING
(private)
GLASSEL
DINNET
ABOYNE
PARK
DRUM
MILLTIMBER
CULTER
MURTLE

HUTCHEON ST.
JOINT
Waterloo (Goods)
Ferryhill Jc.
ABERDEEN
RUTHRIESTON
CULTS
COVE
Summit
CAL.
PORTLETHEN

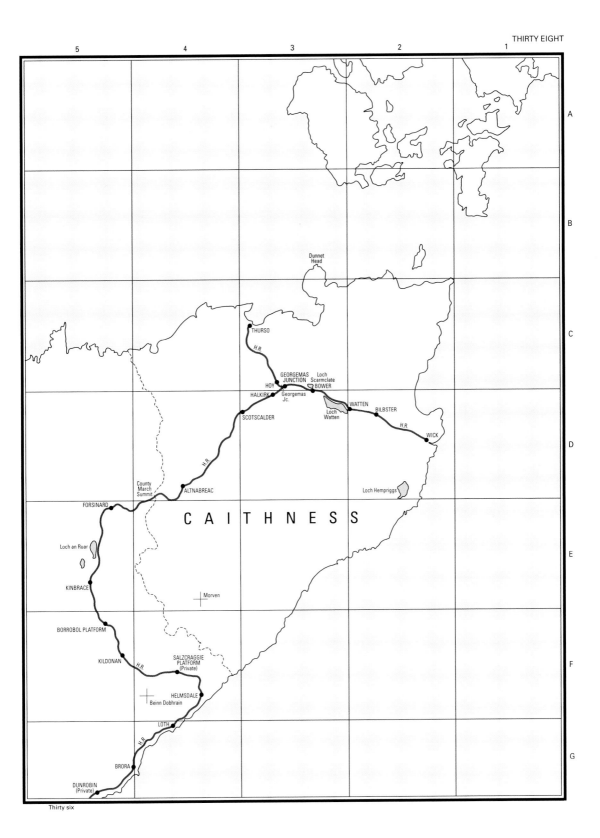

5   4   3   2   1

A

B

Dunnet
Head

C

THURSO
H.R.

GEORGEMAS   Loch
JUNCTION   Scarmclate
HOY   BOWER
HALKIRK   Georgemas
Jc.

SCOTSCALDER   Loch   WATTEN
Watten   BILBSTER

H.R.   H.R.
WICK

D

County
March
Summit   ALTNABREAC   Loch Hempriggs

FORSINARD

C A I T H N E S S

Loch an Ruar

E

KINBRACE   Morven

BORROBOL PLATFORM

KILDONAN   SALZCRAGGIE
H.R.   PLATFORM
(Private)

F

HELMSDALE
Beinn Dobhrain

LOTH

H.R.

G

BRORA

DUNROBIN
(Private)

1	Warwick Rd Jc.	11	FINCHLEY RD. (MID.)	28	WESTBOURNE PARK	45	Maiden Lane (Gds)
2	West Street Jc.	12	ST PAUL'S	29	ROYAL OAK	46	KINGS CROSS (SUBURBAN)
3	Smithfield G.W. Gds	13	MANSION HOUSE	30	Junction Rd Jc.	47	HAMMERSMITH GROVE RD.
4	Worship Str. (Goods)	14	CANNON ST. (MET./MET-DIS. Jt)	31	Highgate Rd Jc.	48	Upper Abbey Mills Jc.
5	Minories Jc.	15	THE MONUMENT	32	CHALK FARM (N.L.)	49	Spitalfields (Goods)
6	ALDGATE EAST	16	MARK LANE	33	Camden (Goods)	50	Spitalfields
7	Haydon Square L.N.W. (Goods)	17	ST MARY'S (WHITECHAPEL)	34	Hampstead Rd Jc.	51	Bishopsgate Jc.
8	Goodman's Yard G.E. (Goods)	18	Caledonian Rd. Coal (LNW)	35	Kentish Town Jc.	52	BISHOPSGATE (GE)
9	Mint Str. G.N. (Goods)	19	Caledonian Rd. Goods (GN)	36	CAMDEN TOWN (N.W.W./N.L.)	53	Borough Market Jc.
10	Mint Str MID. (Goods)	20	Earls Court Jc.	37	Maiden Lane Jc.	54	Metropolitan Jc.
		21	Thames Wharf	38	St Pancras Jc. (West)	55	WEST HAMPSTEAD
		22	West London Ext. Jc.	39	KENTISH TOWN (L.N.W.)	56	Primrose Hill Tun.
		23	Kensington Lillie Bri. (Gds)	40	St Pancras Jc.	57	MAIDEN LANE
		24	TURNHAM GREEN	41	North London Incline Jc.		
		25	CHISWICK PARK & ACTON GREEN	42	St Pancras (Goods)		
		26	WEST END LANE	43	HOLLOWAY		
		27	NOTTING HILL & LADBROKE GROVE	44	Copenhagen Tun.		

A L.B.S.C. & L.S.W. Joint
B WEST LONDON Joint
C WEST LONDON EXTENSION Joint
D HAMMERSMITH & CITY Joint
E EAST LONDON
F L.B.S.C. & S.E. Joint
G NORTH & STH. WESTERN JUNC.
H TOTTENHAM & HAMPSTEAD
J MET./MET-DIS. Jt

NOTE:
TO AVOID CONFUSION MET. & MET.-DISTRICT COVERED
SECTIONS ARE SHOWN AS SURFACE LINES

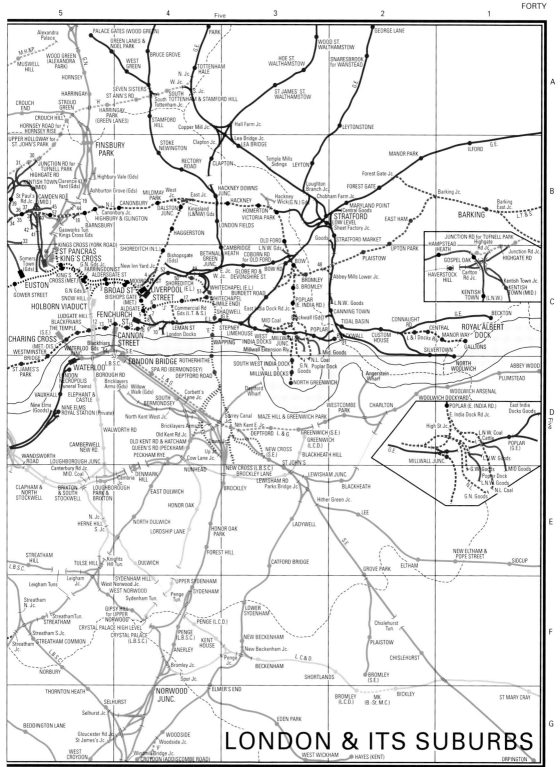

LONDON & ITS SUBURBS

1 Forty two 2 3 4 Twenty one 5

DERBY & NOTTINGHAM TO SHEFFIELD

SHEFFIELD VICTORIA
Park (Goods) ATTERCLIFFE RD.
Pond St (Goods) Woodburn Jc. DARNALL TREETON
MIDLAND WOODHOUSE MILL
HEELEY
Birley Col. WOODHOUSE WOODHOUSE MILL
MILL HOUSES & ECCLESALL
BEIGHTON
MID.
BEAUCHIEF & ABBEY DALE
KIVETON PARK
DORE & TOTLEY KILLAMARSH Kiveton Canal Siding
Norwood Col. Park Col. W. Jc. E. Jc.
Bradway Tun. SHIREOAKS WORKSOP
DRONFIELD S. Jc.
Springwell Pit ECKINGTON & M. S. & L.
UNSTON RENISHAW
Monkwood Col. Broomhouse Tun. WHITTINGTON STAVELEY CLOWN WHITWELL
Nesfield Col. NETHERTHORPE
SHEEPBRIDGE Seymour Jc. ELMTON & CRESWELL
MARKHAM Tapton Jc. COLLIERY (miners)
CHESTERFIELD
Brampton Bolsover LANGWITH
(Goods) (Gds.)
Sutton & Palterton
(Gds.) SHIREBROOK
Avenue Jc. GLAPWELL COLLIERY
SIDINGS (miners)
ROWSLEY for Lings Col.
CHATSWORTH LINGS COLLIERY PLEASLEY MANSFIELD
CLAY CROSS PLATFORM (miners) WOODHOUSE
Clay Cross Tun. Gds Pilsley Col.
DARLEY Butterwood Col. MANSFIELD
MID. STRETTON for TEVERSALL
MATLOCK BRIDGE ASHOVER
High Tor Tuns. DOE HILL WOODEND for SUTTON-IN-ASHFIELD BLIDWORTH
MATLOCK BATH TIBSHELF & HUCKNALL HUWTHWAITE MID.
Willersley Tun. NEWTON
Shirland Col. New Hucknall Col. FARNSFIELD
CROMFORD WESTHOUSES
& BLACKWELL
Lea Wood Tun. ALFRETON KIRKBY
Steeplehouse Cromford High Peak Jc. Alfreton Tun. PINXTON & Langton Col.
(Goods) L.N.W. Gds SELSTON Annesley G. N.
WHATSTANDWELL Wingfield Tun. PINXTON Col. NEWSTEAD
WIRKSWORTH BRIDGE WINGFIELD (G.N.) ANNESLEY MID.
Moorwoods Col. PYE BRIDGE PYE HILL LINBY
BUTTERLEY Riddings Jc. MID. G. N.
W. Jc. E. Jc. Ripley Spelter CODNOR PARK CODNOR PARK MID.
AMBERGATE S. Jc. Wks. & SELSTON G. N. HUCKNALL
RIPLEY Codnor Park Jc. Brinsley Jc. BUTLER'S HILL BESTWOOD
IDRIDGEHAY COLLIERY
BELPER MID. G. N.
SHOTTLE DENBY EASTWOOD & Watnall Col. BULWELL FOREST
HAZELWOOD KILBURN LANGLEY MILL LANGLEY MILL BULWELL DAYBROOK
Milford Tun. NEWTHORPE, GREASLEY Watnall Sidings Leen Valley SHERWOOD BURTON
DUFFIELD COXBENCH & SHIPLEY GATE KIMBERLEY (MID.) WATNALL Jc. JOYCE
Shipley (Nutbrook Col.) SHIPLEY KIMBERLEY (G. N.) BASFORD & ST ANN'S GEDLING &
LITTLE EATON Shipley GATE AWSWORTH BULWELL WELL CARLTON
Little Eaton G. N. Babbington BASFORD Nott. Sub. Rly. CARLTON &
Jc. ILKESTON JNC. (MID.) THORNEYWOOD GEDLING
BREADSALL TOWN G. N. LONDON N. Jc.
St Mary's Jc. WEST HALLAM TROWELL RADFORD Gds ROAD W. Jc.
St. Mary's Bridge Wharf NOTTINGHAM ROAD Gds LENTON MID. RACE Rectory
FRIAR GATE (G.N.) Gds. Cattle Sidings Jc. BRAMCOTE COURSE Jc.
DERBY Cattle G. N. (private) MID. NETHERFIELD
MICKLEOVER Chaddesden Sidings STANTON GATE NOTTINGHAM & COLWICK
G.N. L.N.W. Gds MID. SPONDON BEESTON MID.
Spondon Jc. BORROWASH STAPLEFORD & ATTENBOROUGH EDWALTON
PEAR TREE & NORMANTON DRAYCOTT SANDIACRE Toton
LONG EATON Sidings

Fifteen

Sixteen

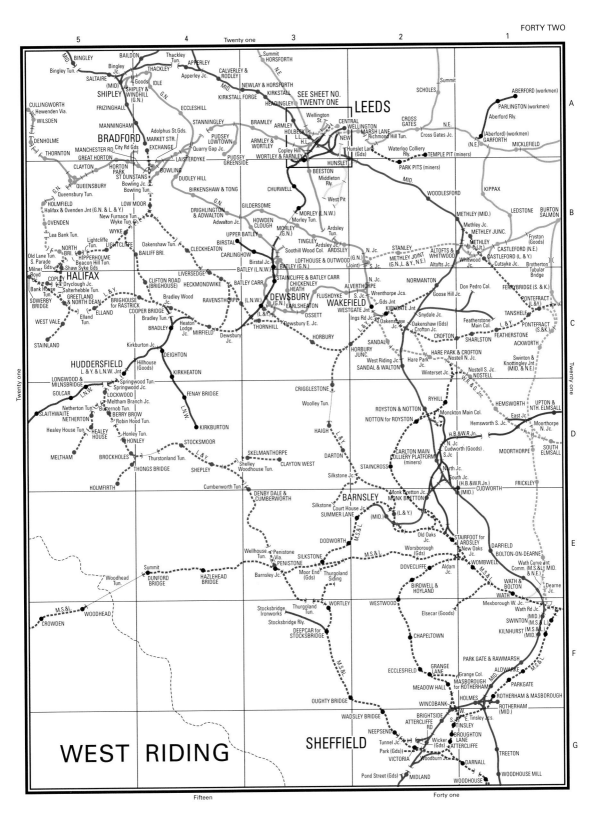

WEST RIDING

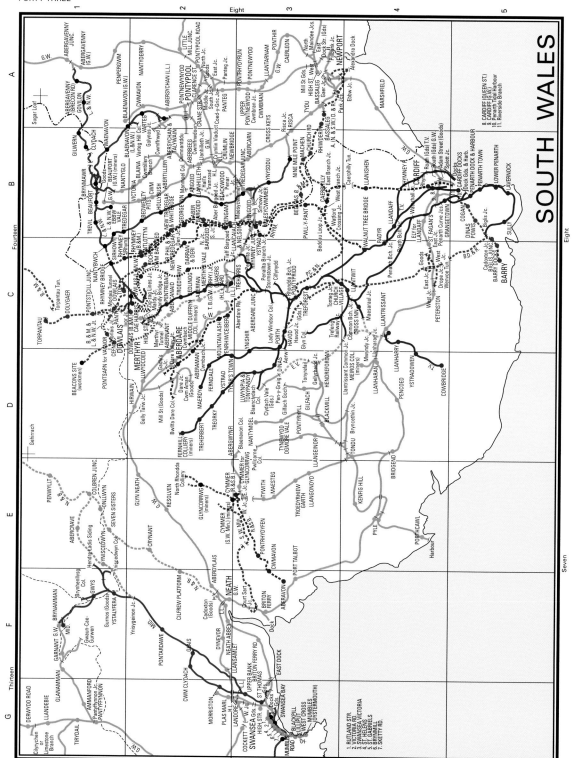

SOUTH WALES

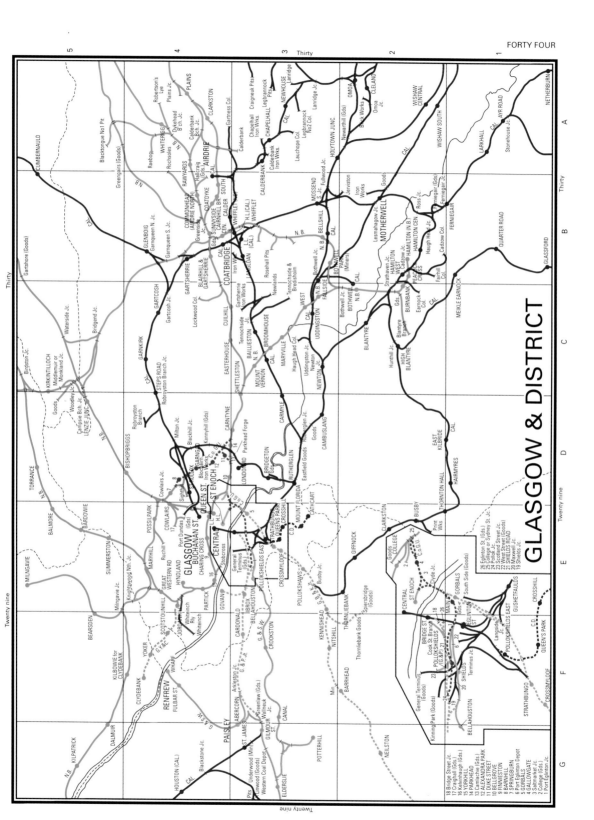

GLASGOW & DISTRICT

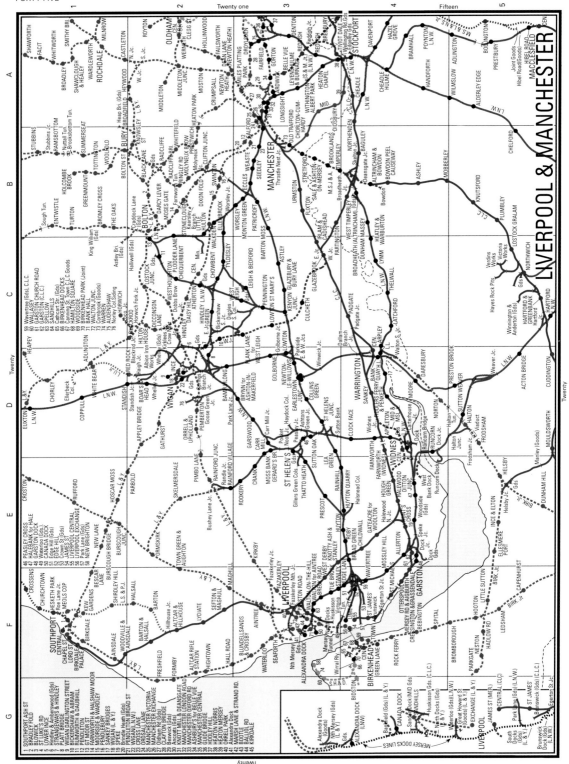

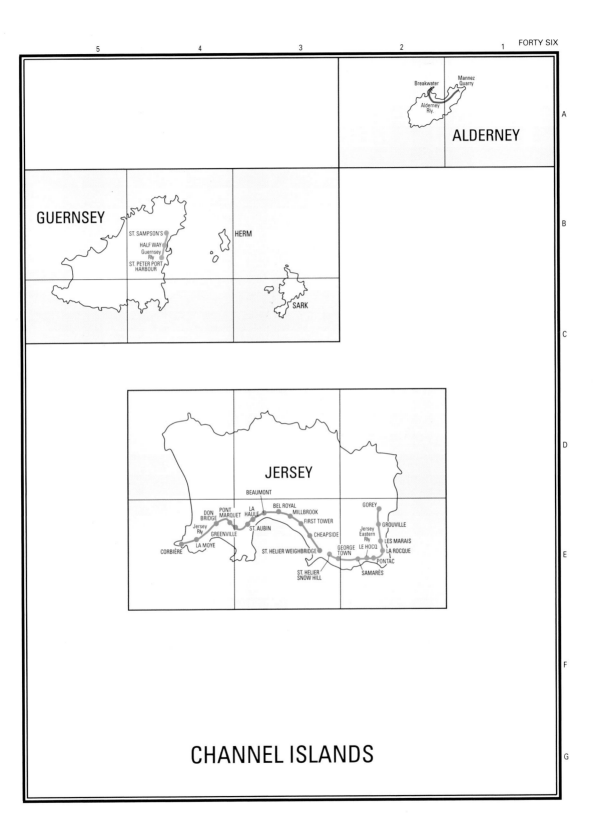

ALDERNEY

Breakwater
Mannez Quarry
Alderney Rly.

GUERNSEY

ST. SAMPSON'S
HALF WAY
Guernsey Rly
ST. PETER PORT HARBOUR

HERM

SARK

JERSEY

BEAUMONT
BEL ROYAL
GOREY
DON BRIDGE
PONT MARQUET
LA HAULE
MILLBROOK
FIRST TOWER
GROUVILLE
Jersey Rly
GREENVILLE
ST. AUBIN
CHEAPSIDE
Jersey Eastern Rly
LES MARAIS
LA MOYE
LE HOCQ
LA ROCQUE
CORBIÈRE
ST. HELIER WEIGHBRIDGE
GEORGE TOWN
PONTAC
ST. HELIER SNOW HILL
SAMARÈS

CHANNEL ISLANDS

A

B

C

D

E

F

G

5   4   3   2   1

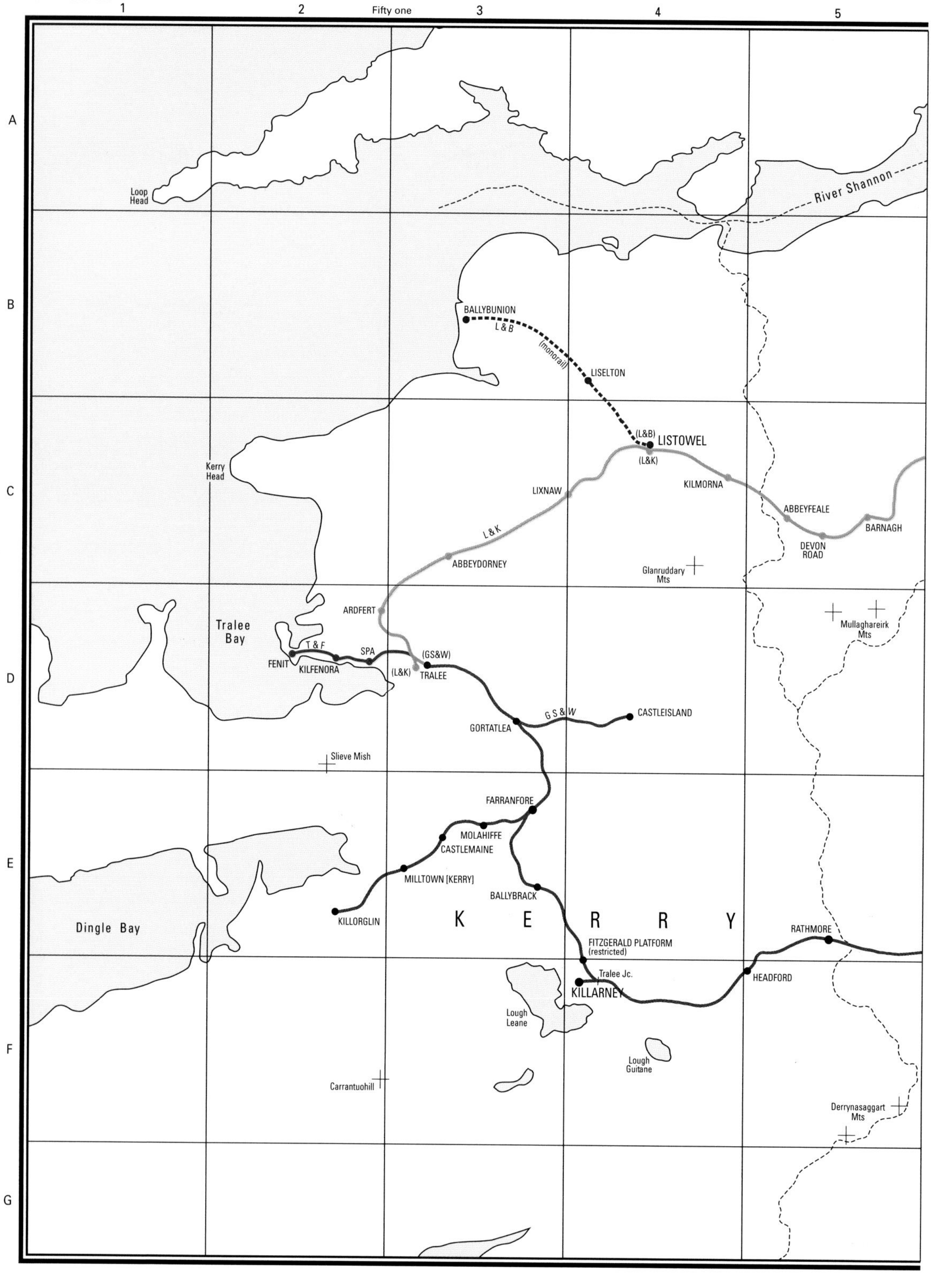

1   2   Fifty one   3   4   5

A

B

C

D

E

F

G

Loop
Head

River Shannon

BALLYBUNION
L & B
(monorail)
LISELTON
(L&B) LISTOWEL
(L&K)

Kerry
Head

LIXNAW
KILMORNA
ABBEYFEALE
BARNAGH
L & K
DEVON
ROAD
ABBEYDORNEY
Glanruddary
Mts

Mullaghareirk
Mts

ARDFERT

Tralee
Bay
T & F
SPA
(GS&W)
FENIT
KILFENORA
(L&K) TRALEE
GORTATLEA
G S & W
CASTLEISLAND

Slieve Mish

FARRANFORE

MOLAHIFFE
CASTLEMAINE

Dingle Bay

MILLTOWN [KERRY]
BALLYBRACK

K   E   R   R   Y

RATHMORE

KILLORGLIN

FITZGERALD PLATFORM
(restricted)

Tralee Jc.
KILLARNEY

HEADFORD

Lough
Leane

Carrantuohill

Lough
Guitane

Derrynasaggart
Mts

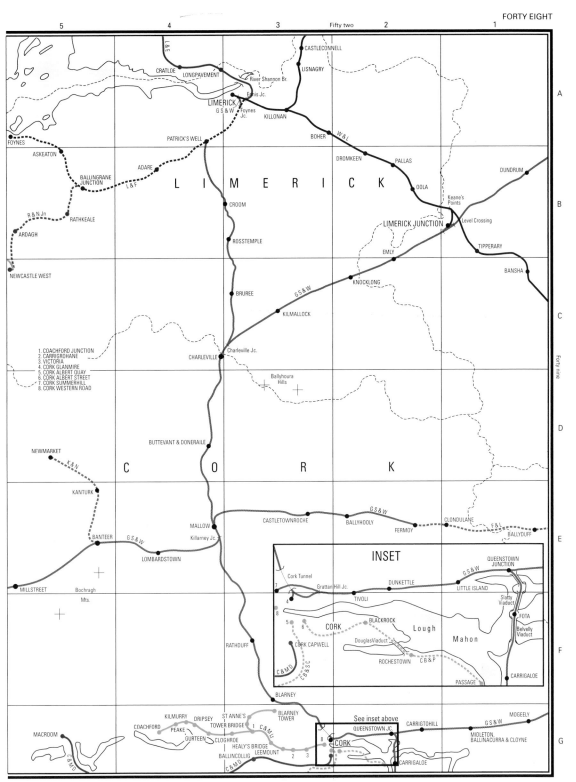

L & E
CASTLECONNELL
CRATLOE
LONGPAVEMENT
LISNAGRY
River Shannon Br.
Ennis Jc.
LIMERICK
G S & W
Foynes
Jc.
KILLONAN
FOYNES
PATRICK'S WELL
BOHER
W & L
ASKEATON
DROMKEEN
PALLAS
DUNDRUM
ADARE
L & F
BALLINGRANE
JUNCTION
L　I　M　E　R　I　C　K
OOLA
Keane's
Points
R & N Jn
RATHKEALE
CROOM
Level Crossing
LIMERICK JUNCTION
ARDAGH
ROSSTEMPLE
TIPPERARY
EMLY
BANSHA
NEWCASTLE WEST
BRUREE
G S & W
KNOCKLONG
KILMALLOCK
1. COACHFORD JUNCTION
2. CARRIGROHANE
3. VICTORIA
4. CORK GLANMIRE
5. CORK ALBERT QUAY
6. CORK ALBERT STREET
7. CORK SUMMERHILL
8. CORK WESTERN ROAD
Charleville Jc.
CHARLEVILLE
Ballyhoura
Hills
NEWMARKET
K & N
BUTTEVANT & DONERAILE
C　O　R　K
KANTURK
MALLOW
CASTLETOWNROCHE
BALLYHOOLY
G S & W
CLONDULANE
F & L
BANTEER
G S & W
Killarney Jc.
FERMOY
BALLYDUFF
LOMBARDSTOWN
MILLSTREET
Bochragh
Mts.

INSET

Cork Tunnel
7
Grattan Hill Jc.
DUNKETTLE
LITTLE ISLAND
QUEENSTOWN
JUNCTION
G S & W
4
TIVOLI
Slatty
Viaduct
8
5
6
CORK
BLACKROCK
Lough
FOTA
CORK CAPWELL
Mahon
Belvelly
Viaduct
DouglasViaduct
C & M D
C.B & S.C
ROCHESTOWN
C B & P
CARRIGALOE
RATHDUFF
PASSAGE

BLARNEY
See inset above
KILMURRY
DRIPSEY
ST ANNE'S
BLARNEY
TOWER
CARRIGTOHILL
MOGEELY
COACHFORD
TOWER BRIDGE
1
C & M L
QUEENSTOWN JC.
G S & W
PEAKE
GURTEEN
CLOGHROE
8
CORK
MIDLETON,
BALLINACURRA & CLOYNE
MACROOM
HEALY'S BRIDGE
LEEMOUNT
2
3
CARRIGALOE
C & M D
BALLINCOLLIG
C & M D

CONTINUATION BELOW
SEE INSET ON SHEET 50

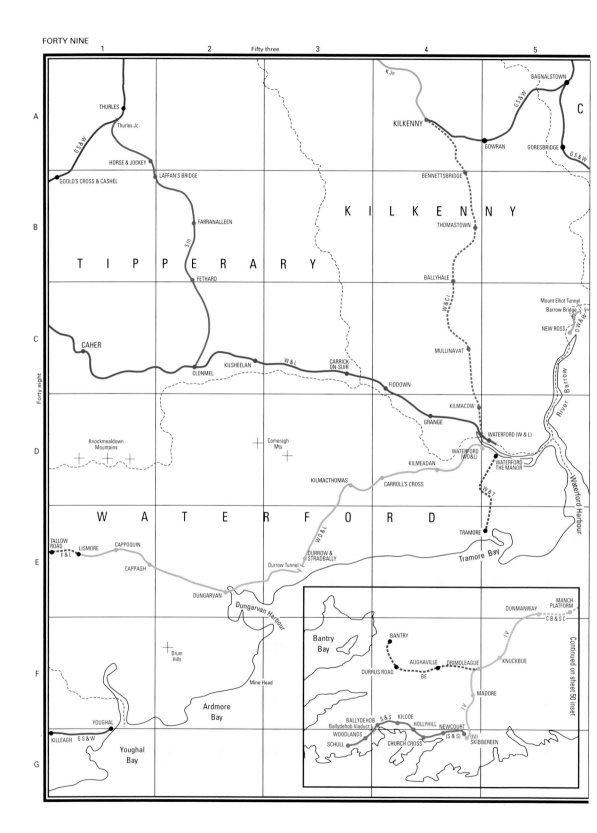

1 2 Fifty three 3 4 5

A

THURLES

Thurles Jc.

K Jn

KILKENNY

BAGNALSTOWN

GS&W

GOWRAN

GORESBRIDGE

GS&W

C

HORSE & JOCKEY

GS&W

LAFFAN'S BRIDGE

GOOLD'S CROSS & CASHEL

BENNETTSBRIDGE

B

FARRANALLEEN

Suir

THOMASTOWN

K I L K E N N Y

T I P P E R A R Y

FETHARD

BALLYHALE

Mount Elliot Tunnel

Barrow Bridge

W & C I

DW&W

NEW ROSS

C

CAHER

CLONMEL

KILSHEELAN

W & L

CARRICK-ON-SUIR

MULLINAVAT

Forty eight

FIDDOWN

River Barrow

KILMACOW

GRANGE

WATERFORD (W & L)

Knockmealdown
Mountains

Comeragh
Mts

KILMEADAN

WATERFORD
(WD&L)

WATERFORD
THE MANOR

Waterford Harbour

D

KILMACTHOMAS

CARROLL'S CROSS

W & T

W A T E R F O R D

WD&L

TALLOW
ROAD

F&L

LISMORE

CAPPOQUIN

DURROW &
STRADBALLY

TRAMORE

Tramore Bay

E

CAPPAGH

Durrow Tunnel

DUNGARVAN

Dungarvan Harbour

MANCH
PLATFORM

DUNMANWAY

CB&SC

Continued on sheet 50 inset

Drum
Hills

Bantry
Bay

BANTRY

AUGHAVILLE

DRIMOLEAGUE

KNUCKBUE

IV

F

Mine Head

DURRUS ROAD

BE

MADORE

IV

Ardmore
Bay

YOUGHAL

BALLYDEHOB

Ballydehob Viaduct

S & S

KILCOE

HOLLYHILL

NEWCOURT

KILLEAGH

GS&W

WOODLANDS

SCHULL

CHURCH CROSS

(S & S)

(IV)

SKIBBEREEN

Youghal
Bay

G

5   4   3   Fifty four   2   1

A

Tara Hill

ARLOW

Mt. Leinster

Slieveboy

GOREY

D W & W

CAMOLIN

BORRIS

Knockroe

FERNS

Cahore
Point

B

G S & W

Blackstairs
Mt.

WEXFORD

ENNISCORTHY

Enniscorthy
Tunnel

BALLYWILLIAM

EDERMINE FERRY

CHAPEL

PALACE EAST

D W & W

MACMINE JUNCTION

C

KILLURIN

Ferrycarrig Tunnel

WEXFORD

Wexford Harbour

WEXFORD

BAY

W & W

Rosslare Pier

Greenore
Point

D

Bannow Bay

Carnsore
Point

Forlorn
Point

See inset sheet 48

Hook
Head

Continued on sheet 49 inset

BALLINCOLLIG

CARRIGALOE

DOONISKEY

KILCREA

C & M D

KILUMNEY

WATERFALL

PASSAGE

QUEENSTOWN

RUSHBROOKE

E

CROOKSTOWN ROAD

Chetwynd
Viaduct

Gogginshill Tunnel

C B & S C

BALLINHASSIG

UPTON

KINSALE JUNCTION

CORK

INNISHANNON

BALLYMARTLE

HARBOUR

BALLINEEN

ENNISKEAN

CLONAKILTY
JUNC.

BANDON

DESERT

CASTLE
BERNARD

FARRANGALWAY

F

MANCH PLATFORM

BALLINASCARTY

KINSALE

C B & S C

CLONAKILTY

Continuation from
sheet 48

G

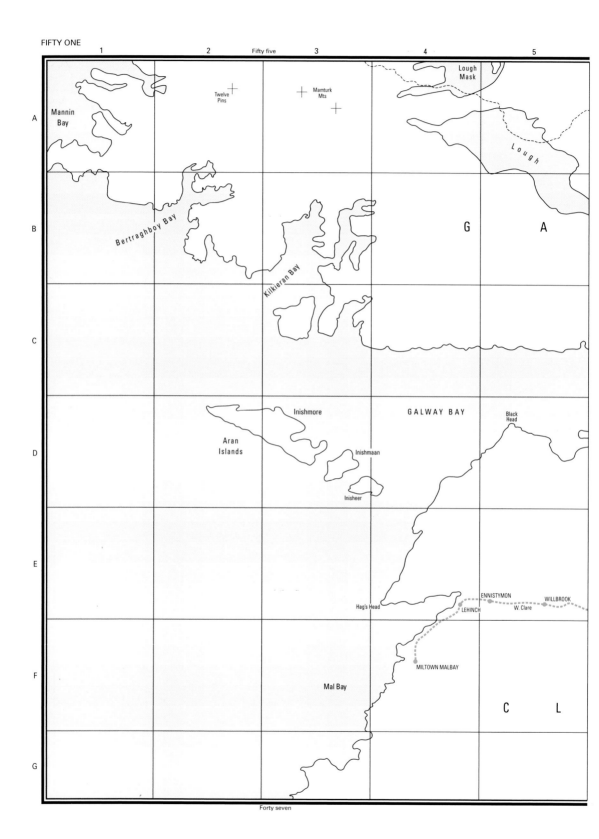

1   2   3   4   5

A

Mannin
Bay

Lough
Mask

Twelve
Pins

Mamturk
Mts

Lough

B

Bertraghboy Bay

G   A

Kilkieran Bay

C

D

Inishmore

GALWAY BAY

Black
Head

Aran
Islands

Inishmaan

Inisheer

E

Hag's Head

ENNISTYMON   WILLBROOK

LEHINCH   W. Clare

F

MILTOWN MALBAY

Mal Bay

C   L

G

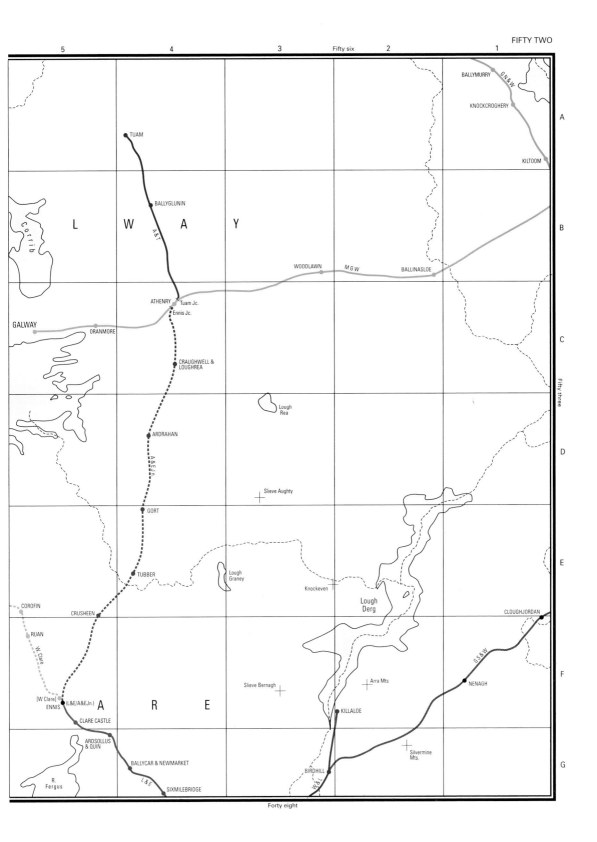

A

BALLYMURRY

G N & W

KNOCKCROGHERY

KILTOOM

TUAM

L   W   A   Y

BALLYGLUNIN

A & T

B

Corrib

WOODLAWN   M G W   BALLINASLOE

ATHENRY   Tuam Jc.

Ennis Jc.

GALWAY   ORANMORE

C

Fifty three

CRAUGHWELL & LOUGHREA

Lough Rea

ARDRAHAN

D

A & E Jn.

Slieve Aughty

GORT

E

TUBBER

Lough Graney

Knockeven

Lough Derg

CLOUGHJORDAN

COROFIN

CRUSHEEN

RUAN

W Clare

G S & W

F

Arra Mts

NENAGH

Slieve Bernagh

[W Clare]   (IL&E/A&EJn.)

ENNIS   A   R   E

KILLALOE

CLARE CASTLE

ARDSOLLUS & QUIN

Silvermine Mts.

BALLYCAR & NEWMARKET

G

R. Fergus

L & E

SIXMILEBRIDGE

BIRDHILL

W & L

1 Fifty seven 2 3 4 5

A

W E S T   M E A T H

CLONHUGH

Lough
Owel

Lough
Ree

MULLINGAR

M G W

KILLUCAN

HILL OF DOWN

CASTLETOWN

Lough
Ennell

ATHLONE (MGW)

East
Jc.

ATHLONE
[GS&W]

STREAMSTOWN JUNCTION

MOYVALLEY

B

BALLINAHOUN
(private)

MOATE

HORSELEAP

CARBERRY

PROSPECT [MGW]

EDENDERRY

C & Ba [GS&W]
Jc.

CLARA

Streamstown Jc.

FERBANE

K I L

BELMONT & CLOGHAN

K I N G ' S   C O U N T Y

TULLAMORE

C

C & Ba

GS & W

BANAGHER

GEASHILL

KILDARE

PARSONSTOWN

Portarlington Jc.

PORTARLINGTON

Cherryville
Jc.

D

MOUNTMELLICK

MONASTEREVAN

W & C I

Slieve Bloom Mountains

Q U E E N ' S

MARYBOROUGH

Conniberry Jc.

ATHY

E

ROSCREA

GS & W

C O U N T Y

GS & W

K Jn.

GS & W

GS & W

MOUNTRATH &
CASTLETOWN

ABBEYLEIX

MAGENEY

F

BALLYBROPHY

ATTANAGH

CARLOW

TEMPLEMORE

BALLYRAGGET

MILFORD

G

Fifty two

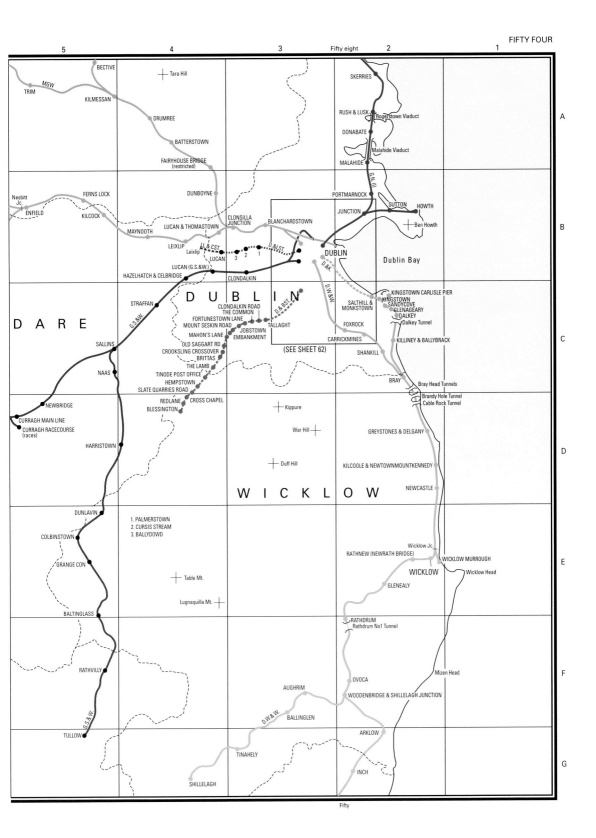

5   4   3   Fifty eight   2   1

BECTIVE

MGW
TRIM
KILMESSAN

Tara Hill

SKERRIES

RUSH & LUSK
Rogerstown Viaduct

DONABATE

A

DRUMREE

BATTERSTOWN

FAIRYHOUSE BRIDGE
(restricted)

Malahide Viaduct

MALAHIDE

G.N.(I)

Nesbitt
Jc.
ENFIELD

FERNS LOCK

KILCOCK

DUNBOYNE

PORTMARNOCK

JUNCTION

SUTTON   HOWTH

B

MAYNOOTH

CLONSILLA
JUNCTION   BLANCHARDSTOWN

LUCAN & THOMASTOWN

Ben Howth

LEIXLIP   LL & CST
Leixlip   D &LST
LUCAN   3   2   1
LUCAN (G.S.&W.)

DUBLIN

Dublin Bay

D.&K.

HAZELHATCH & CELBRIDGE   CLONDALKIN

STRAFFAN   D U B L I N

D.W.&W.

KINGSTOWN CARLISLE PIER
KINGSTOWN
SALTHILL &   SANDYCOVE
MONKSTOWN   GLENAGEARY
DALKEY
Dalkey Tunnel

D A R E

G.S.&W.

CLONDALKIN ROAD
THE COMMON
FORTUNESTOWN LANE   D & BST
MOUNT SESKIN ROAD   TALLAGHT
MAHON'S LANE   JOBSTOWN
OLD SAGGART RD   EMBANKMENT
SALLINS   CROOKSLING CROSSOVER
BRITTAS
NAAS   THE LAMB
TINODE POST OFFICE
HEMPSTOWN
SLATE QUARRIES ROAD

FOXROCK

KILLINEY & BALLYBRACK

C

(SEE SHEET 62)

CARRICKMINES

SHANKILL

NEWBRIDGE   REDLANE   CROSS CHAPEL
BLESSINGTON
CURRAGH MAIN LINE
CURRAGH RACECOURSE
(races)

BRAY   Bray Head Tunnels

Brandy Hole Tunnel
Cable Rock Tunnel

Kippure

GREYSTONES & DELGANY

HARRISTOWN

War Hill

KILCOOLE & NEWTOWNMOUNTKENNEDY

D

Duff Hill

NEWCASTLE

W I C K L O W

DUNLAVIN   1. PALMERSTOWN
2. CURSIS STREAM
3. BALLYDOWD

COLBINSTOWN

Wicklow Jc.
RATHNEW (NEWRATH BRIDGE)   WICKLOW MURROUGH

GRANGE CON   Table Mt.   WICKLOW   Wicklow Head   E

GLENEALY

Lugnaquilla Mt.

BALTINGLASS

RATHDRUM
Rathdrum No1 Tunnel

RATHVILLY   Mizen Head   F

AUGHRIM   OVOCA

G.S.&W.   WOODENBRIDGE & SHILLELAGH JUNCTION

D.W.&W.   BALLINGLEN

TULLOW   ARKLOW

TINAHELY

INCH   G

SHILLELAGH

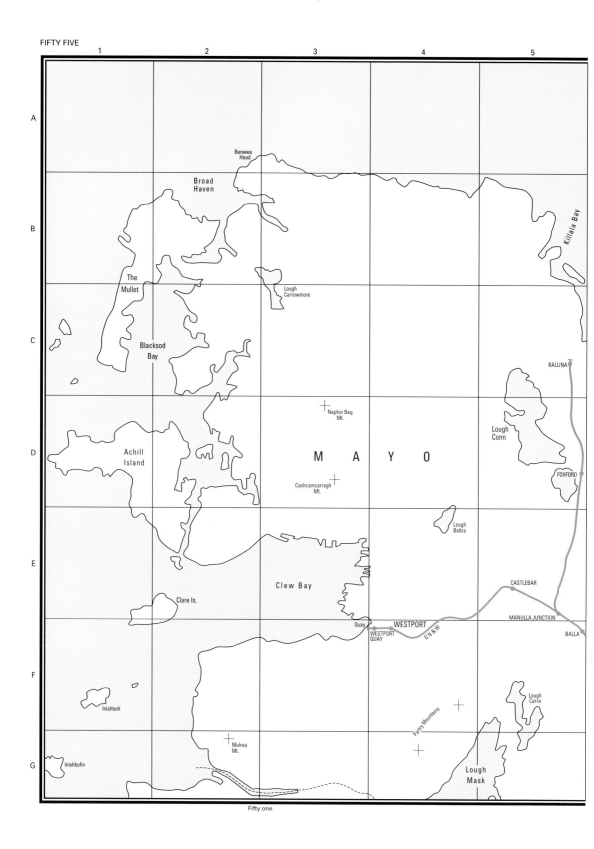

1   2   3   4   5

A

Benwee
Head

Broad
Haven

B

The
Mullet

Lough
Carrowmore

C

Blacksod
Bay

BALLINA

Nephin Beg
Mt.

Lough
Conn

D

Achill
Island

M A Y O

FOXFORD

Cashcamcarragh
Mt.

Lough
Beltra

E

Clew Bay

CASTLEBAR

Clare Is.

MANULLA JUNCTION

Quay   WESTPORT
WESTPORT
QUAY   G N & W   BALLA

F

Inishturk

Lough
Carra

Partry Mountains

Mulrea
Mt.

G

Inishbofin

Lough
Mask

Killala Bay

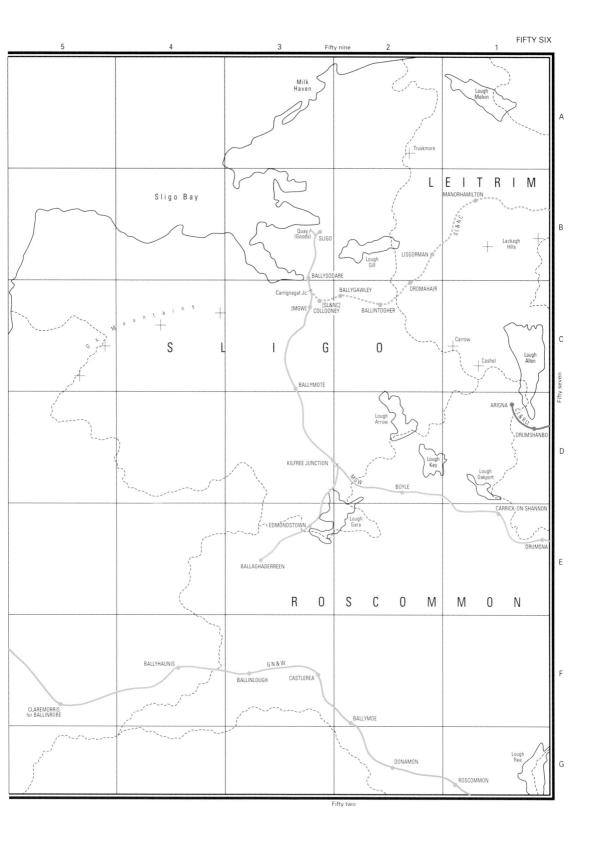

5 4 3 Fifty nine 2 1

A

Milk
Haven

Lough
Melvin

LEITRIM

Sligo Bay

MANORHAMILTON

Truskmore

SL & NC

B

Lackagh
Hills

Quay
(Goods)
SLIGO

Lough
Gill

LISGORMAN

BALLYSODARE

Carrignagat Jc.
[MGW]

BALLYGAWLEY
[SL&NC]
COLLOONEY BALLINTOGHER

DROMAHAIR

Carrow

Lough
Allen

C

S L I G O

Cashel

Ox Mountains

BALLYMOTE

ARIGNA

Lough
Arrow

C & R Lt

DRUMSHANBO

Fifty seven

D

KILFREE JUNCTION

Lough
Key

Lough
Oakport

MGW

BOYLE

CARRICK-ON-SHANNON

EDMONDSTOWN

Lough
Gara

DRUMSNA

BALLAGHADERREEN

E

R O S C O M M O N

BALLYHAUNIS

G N & W

BALLINLOUGH CASTLEREA

F

CLAREMORRIS
for BALLINROBE

BALLYMOE

Lough
Ree

DONAMON

G

ROSCOMMON

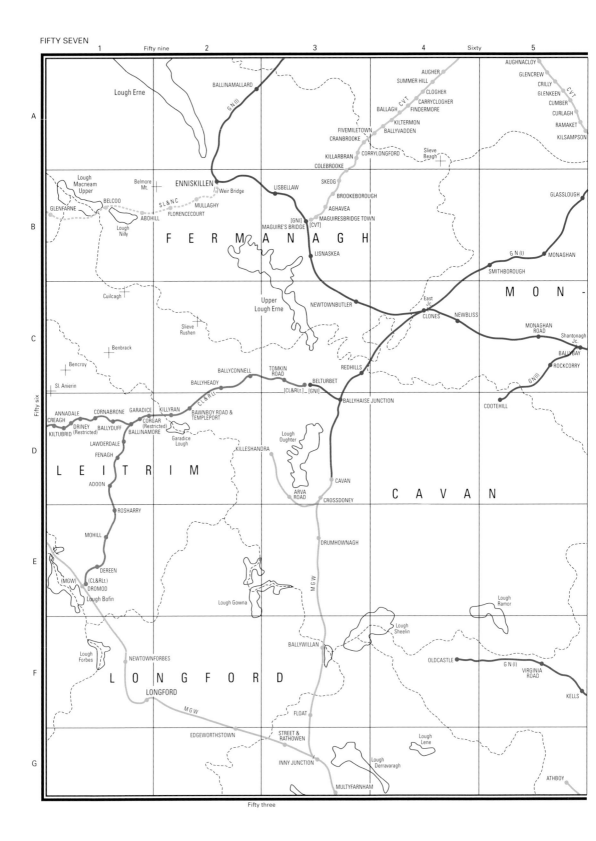

Lough Erne

AUGHNACLOY
GLENCREW
CRILLY
GLENKEEN
CUMBER
CURLAGH
RAMAKET
KILSAMPSON

CVT

GN III

BALLINAMALLARD

AUGHER
SUMMER HILL
CLOGHER
CARRYCLOGHER
FINDERMORE

BALLAGH
KILTERMON
BALLYVADDEN

CVT

A

FIVEMILETOWN
CRANBROOKE
CORRYLONGFORD

Slieve
Beagh

KILLARBRAN
COLEBROOKE

Lough
Macneam
Upper

Belmore
Mt.

ENNISKILLEN

Weir Bridge

LISBELLAW

SKEOG

BROOKEBOROUGH

GLASSLOUGH

BELCOO
GLENFARNE

SL&NC

MULLAGHY
FLORENCECOURT

AGHAVEA
MAGUIRESBRIDGE TOWN

GN (I)

MONAGHAN

B

ABOHILL
Lough
Nilly

MAGUIRE'S BRIDGE
[GNI]
[CVT]

LISNASKEA

SMITHBOROUGH

MON-

F E R M A N A G H

Cuilcagh

Upper
Lough Erne

NEWTOWNBUTLER

East
Jc.
CLONES

NEWBLISS

MONAGHAN
ROAD

Shantonagh
Jc.

BALLYBAY

C

Benbrack

Slieve
Rushen

REDHILLS

ROCKCORRY

Bencroy

BALLYCONNELL

TOMKIN
ROAD

BELTURBET

GN (I)

COOTEHILL

Sl. Anierin

BALLYHEADY

[CL&RLt.] [GNI]

Fifty six

CREAGH
ANNADALE
KILTUBRID
DRINEY
(Restricted)
CORNABRONE
BALLYDUFF

GARADICE
CORGAR
(Restricted)
BALLINAMORE

KILLYRAN

BAWNBOY ROAD &
TEMPLEPORT

CL & RLt.

BALLYHAISE JUNCTION

LAWDERDALE
FENAGH

Garadice
Lough

KILLESHANDRA

Lough
Oughter

D

L E I T R I M

ADOON

CAVAN

ROSHARRY

ARVA
ROAD

CROSSDONEY

C A V A N

MOHILL

DRUMHOWNAGH

E

DEREEN
(MGW)
(CL&RLt.)
DROMOD
Lough Bofin

M G W

Lough Gowna

Lough
Ramor

Lough
Sheelin

BALLYWILLAN

OLDCASTLE

Lough
Forbes

NEWTOWNFORBES

GN (I)
VIRGINIA
ROAD

F

L O N G F O R D

LONGFORD

M G W

FLOAT

KELLS

EDGEWORTHSTOWN

STREET &
RATHOWEN

Lough
Lene

Lough
Derravaragh

G

INNY JUNCTION

ATHBOY

MULTYFARNHAM

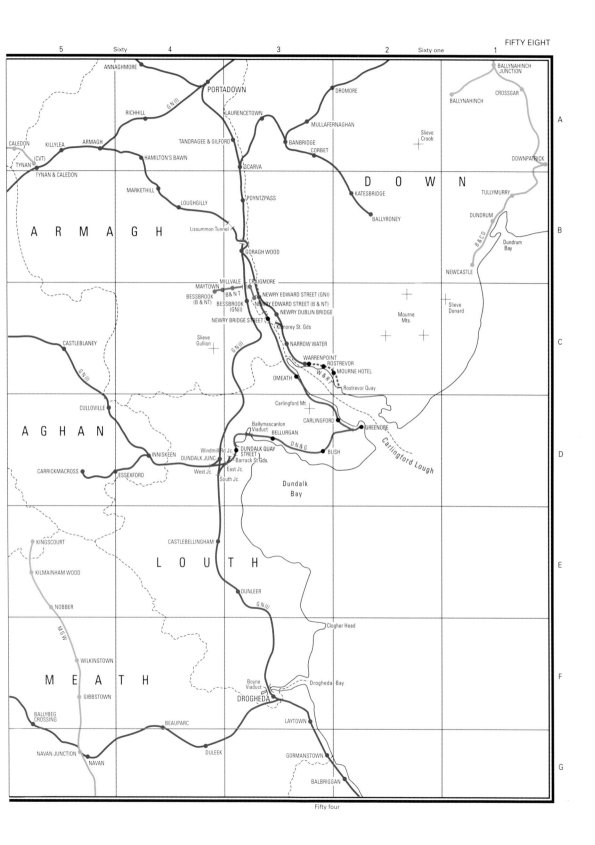

ANNAGHMORE

PORTADOWN

DROMORE

BALLYNAHINCH
JUNCTION

CROSSGAR

BALLYNAHINCH

A

RICHHILL

GN(I)

LAURENCETOWN

MULLAFERNAGHAN

Slieve
Croob

CALEDON

KILLYLEA

ARMAGH

TANDRAGEE & GILFORD

BANBRIDGE

CORBET

DOWNPATRICK

(CVT)

TYNAN

HAMILTON'S BAWN

SCARVA

D O W N

TYNAN & CALEDON

TULLYMURRY

MARKETHILL

POYNTZPASS

KATESBRIDGE

DUNDRUM

B&CO

A R M A G H

LOUGHGILLY

Lissummon Tunnel

BALLYRONEY

Dundrum
Bay

B

GORAGH WOOD

NEWCASTLE

MAYTOWN

MILLVALE

CRAIGMORE

BESSBROOK
(B & NT)

B & NT

NEWRY EDWARD STREET (GNI)

Slieve
Donard

BESSBROOK
(GN(I))

NEWRY EDWARD STREET (B & NT)

Mourne
Mts.

NEWRY DUBLIN BRIDGE

NEWRY BRIDGE STREET

Kilmorey St. Gds

CASTLEBLANEY

GN(I)

NARROW WATER

C

Slieve
Gullion

WARRENPOINT

ROSTREVOR

GN(I)

OMEATH

W & R

MOURNE HOTEL

Rostrevor Quay

CULLOVILLE

Carlingford Mt.

AGHAN

CARLINGFORD

GREENORE

INNISKEEN

Ballymascanlon
Viaduct

BELLURGAN

DN&G

BUSH

Carlingford Lough

CARRICKMACROSS

ESSEXFORD

Windmill Rd Jc.

DUNDALK QUAY
STREET

Barrack St Gds.

DUNDALK JUNC.

West Jc.

East Jc.

South Jc.

Dundalk
Bay

D

KINGSCOURT

L O U T H

CASTLEBELLINGHAM

KILMAINHAM WOOD

E

NOBBER

DUNLEER

GN(I)

Clogher Head

MGW

WILKINSTOWN

M E A T H

Boyne
Viaduct

Drogheda Bay

F

GIBBSTOWN

DROGHEDA

BALLYBEG
CROSSING

BEAUPARC

LAYTOWN

NAVAN JUNCTION

DULEEK

GORMANSTOWN

NAVAN

G

BALBRIGGAN

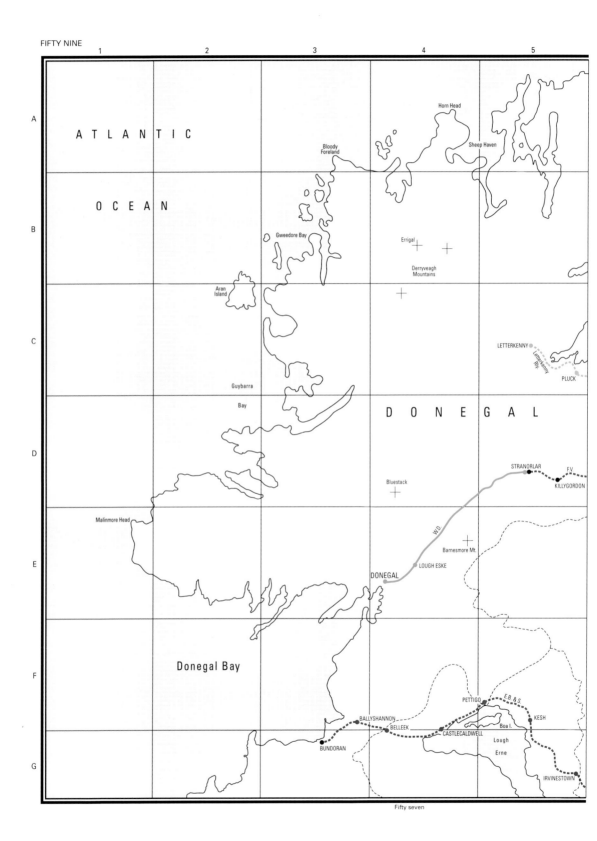

1 2 3 4 5

A

ATLANTIC

Horn Head

Bloody
Foreland

Sheep Haven

OCEAN

B

Gweedore Bay

Errigal

Derryveagh
Mountains

Aran
Island

LETTERKENNY

Letterkenny Rly.

C

Guybarra

PLUCK

Bay

DONEGAL

D

STRANORLAR

F.V.

Bluestack

KILLYGORDON

Malinmore Head

W.D.

Barnesmore Mt.

E

LOUGH ESKE

DONEGAL

Donegal Bay

F

PETTIGO

F.B. & S.

BALLYSHANNON

KESH

BELLEEK

Boa I.

CASTLECALDWELL

Lough

BUNDORAN

Erne

G

IRVINESTOWN

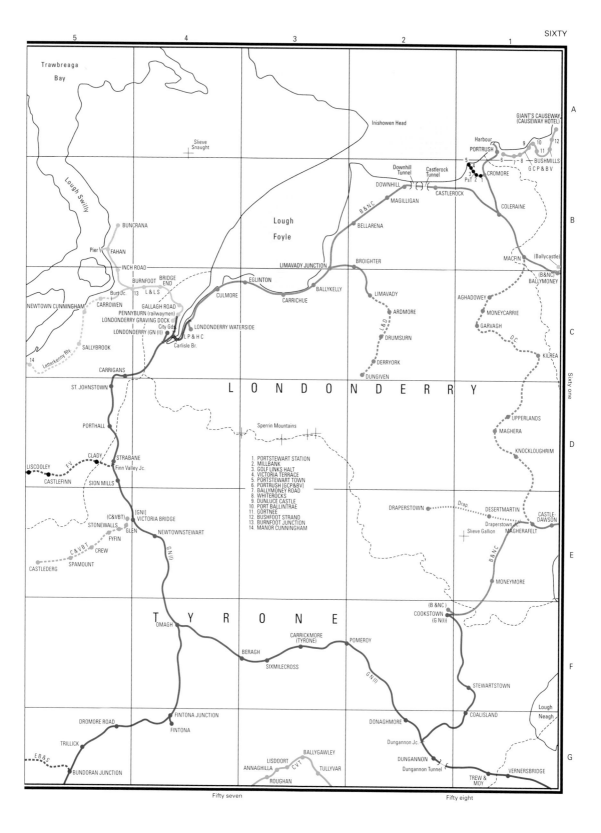

Trawbreaga Bay

Lough Swilly

Slieve Snaught

Inishowen Head

Lough Foyle

Giant's Causeway (Causeway Hotel)

Harbour

PORTRUSH

9 10 12
11
6 8
BUSHMILLS
GCP&BV

PsT 2 1
5
3
CROMORE

Downhill Tunnel
Castlerock Tunnel

DOWNHILL

CASTLEROCK

COLERAINE

B&NC

MAGILLIGAN

BELLARENA

MACFIN   (Ballycastle)

(B&NC)
BALLYMONEY

BUNCRANA

Pier
FAHAN

INCH ROAD

BURNFOOT
BRIDGE END

Burt Jc. 13 L&LS

BROIGHTER

LIMAVADY JUNCTION

EGLINTON

BALLYKELLY

AGHADOWEY

MONEYCARRIE

GARVAGH

KILREA

NEWTOWN CUNNINGHAM

CARROWEN

PENNYBURN (railwaymen)
LONDONDERRY GRAVING DOCK

GALLAGH ROAD

CULMORE

CARRICHUE

LIMAVADY

ARDMORE

L&D

DRUMSURN

DERRYORK

DUNGIVEN

City Gds
LONDONDERRY (GN (I))
LP&HC
Carlisle Br.

LONDONDERRY WATERSIDE

SALLYBROOK

14
Letterkenny Rly

CARRIGANS

ST. JOHNSTOWN

L O N D O N D E R R Y

Sixty one

UPPERLANDS

MAGHERA

KNOCKLOUGHRIM

PORTHALL

Sperrin Mountains

1. PORTSTEWART STATION
2. MILLBANK
3. GOLF LINKS HALT
4. VICTORIA TERRACE
5. PORTSTEWART TOWN
6. PORTRUSH (GCP&BV)
7. BALLYMONEY ROAD
8. WHITEROCKS
9. DUNLUCE CASTLE
10. PORT BALLINTRAE
11. GORTNEE
12. BUSHFOOT STRAND
13. BURNFOOT JUNCTION
14. MANOR CUNNINGHAM

DRAPERSTOWN

Drap.

DESERTMARTIN

CASTLE-DAWSON

LISCOOLEY

CASTLEFINN

CLADY

F V

Finn Valley Jc.

STRABANE

SION MILLS

Draperstown Jc.
Slieve Gallion

MAGHERAFELT

B&NC

(C&VBT)
STONEWALLS

GLEN

[GNI]
VICTORIA BRIDGE

NEWTOWNSTEWART

MONEYMORE

FYFIN

C&VBT

CREW

SPAMOUNT

CASTLEDERG

GN(I)

(B&NC)
COOKSTOWN
(GN(I))

T Y R O N E

OMAGH

CARRICKMORE (TYRONE)

POMEROY

BERAGH

SIXMILECROSS

GN(I)

STEWARTSTOWN

Lough Neagh

DROMORE ROAD

FINTONA JUNCTION

FINTONA

TRILLICK

E.B&S

BUNDORAN JUNCTION

BALLYGAWLEY

LISDOORT
ANNAGHILLA
C.V.T
TULLYVAR

ROUGHAN

COALISLAND

DONAGHMORE

Dungannon Jc.

DUNGANNON

Dungannon Tunnel

VERNERSBRIDGE

TREW & MOY

1   2   3   4   5

N O R T H

Rathlin Island

Fair Head

BALLYCASTLE

CAPECASTLE   Capecastle Tun¹

Ballycastle   ARMOY   Knocklayd

STRANOCUM

DERVOCK

Red Bay

DUNLOY

B & NC   KILLAGAN

GLARRYFORD

Trostan   Retreat

PARKMORE

Cargan

CROSS ROADS

KNOCKANALLY

CLOUGH ROAD

RATHKENNY

BALLYCLOUGHAN

BALLYGARVEY

CULLYBACKEY

A N T R I M

(n.g.)   BALLYMENA

Slemish

HARRYVILLE

COLLIN HALT   BALLYNASHEE

MOORFIELDS   B & NC

KELLSWATER   KELLS

Lough Beg

Agnews Hill

LARNE HARBOUR [n.g.]   Larne Lough

LARNE [n.g.]   LARNE HARBOUR

HEADWOOD   LARNE

BALLYBOLEY   GLYNN

JUNCTION   MAGHERAMORNE

BALLYNURE   C & L

(n.g.)   BALLYCLARE   BALLYCARRY

WHITEHEAD

LISNALINCHY   Whitehead Tunnel

TOOME BRIDGE   COOKSTOWN JUNCTION

RANDALSTOWN   DOAGH [n.g.]   KILROOT

Randalstown Viaduct   ANTRIM JUNCTION   DOAGH   CARRICKFERGUS

ANTRIM (GN[I])   Kingsbog Jc.   Harbour   Belfast Lough

B & NC   TEMPLEPATRICK   CARRICKFERGUS JUNCTION   Copeland Is.

DUNADRY   BALLYCLARE JUNC.   JORDANSTOWN

CARNALEA   BANGOR

ALDERGROVE   WHITEABBEY   HELEN'S BAY   DONAGHADEE

CRAIGAVAD

CRUMLIN   WHITEHOUSE   CULTRA   GROOMSPORT ROAD

Divis Mt.   YORK RD.   MARINO   HOLYWOOD

GLENAVY   BELFAST   QUEENS QUAY   DUNDONALD   NEWTOWNARDS

GREAT VICTORIA STREET   KNOCK

Lough Neagh   BALMORAL   COMBER

Portmore Lough   DUNMURRY   (SEE INSET ABOVE)

BALLINDERRY   LAMBEG

BROOKMOUNT   Knockmore Jc.   B & C D

GN (I)   LISBURN   BALLYGOWAN   Strangford Lough

MOIRA

LURGAN   HILLSBOROUGH   SAINTFIELD

C H A N N E L

Sixty

Twenty five

Inset (Belfast):

WHITEHOUSE   HOLYWOOD

GREENCASTLE   Belfast Lough

B & NC   B & CO

TILLYSBURN

Dufferin Dock (Gds)   Clarendon Dock (Goods)   SYDENHAM

BELFAST YORK ROAD   Abercorn Basin (Goods)

Donegal Quay (Goods)   BLOOMFIELD

BELFAST QUEEN'S QUAY   Ballymacarrett Jc.

Queen's Bridge (Goods)   KNOCK

BELFAST GREAT VICTORIA STREET

Grosvenor Street (Goods)   Ulster Jc.   Lisburn Rd. Tunnel

GN (I)

BALMORAL

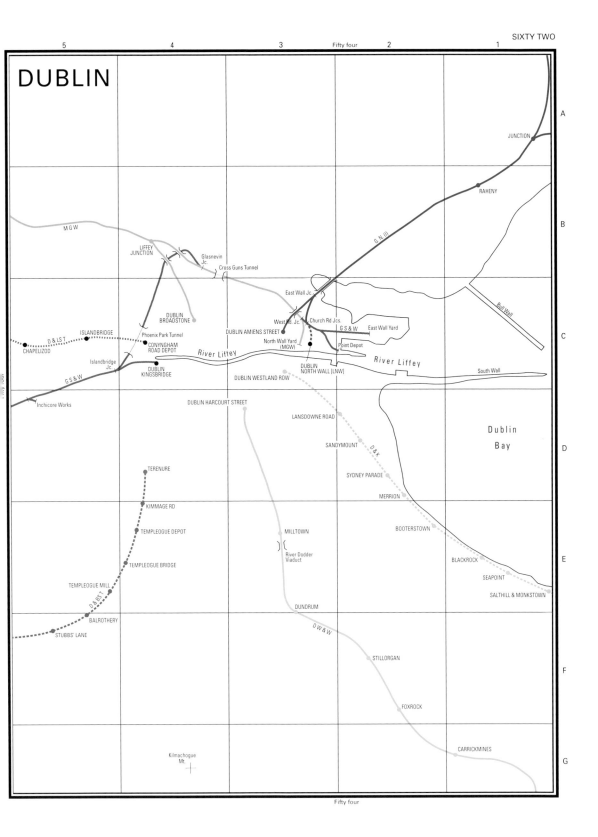

STATION OPENINGS, CLOSURES AND RENAMINGS DURING 1890

Station	day	month
Harryville (B&NC) Closed	1	January
Pevensey (LB&SC) Renamed Pevensey & Westham	1	January
Farnworth (L&NW) Renamed Farnworth & Bold	2	January
Halling (SE) Opened	1	March
Bradford (Mid) (later Forster Square) Opened	2	March
Bradford Market Street (Mid) Closed	2	March
Comeley Park (NB) Closed	5	March
Dalmeny (NB) Closed	5	March
Dunfermline Lower (NB) Opened	5	March
Forth Bridge (NB) Opened (Renamed Dalmeny 28 April)	5	March
North Queensferry (NB (Forth Br)) Opened	5	March
North Queensferry (NB) Closed	5	March
Port Edgar (NB) Closed	5	March
South Queensferry (NB) Closed	5	March
Blacon (MS&L) Opened	31	March
Liverpool Road (MS&L) Opened	31	March
Saughall (MS&L) Opened	31	March
Buckley (WM&CQ) Closed (Re-opened 1893)	31	March
Buckley Junc (WM&CQ) Opened	31	March
Connah's Quay (WM&CQ) Opened	31	March
Hawarden (WM&CQ) Opened	31	March
Ynysybwl (TV) Opened		March
Tattyknuckle (ClVyT) Opened	8	April
Forth Bridge (NB) Renamed Dalmeny	28	April
Brampton Junc (NE) Renamed Brampton	30	April
Ashbury (L&SW) Renamed Ashbury & North Lew		April
Bainton (NE) Opened	1	May
Duffield Gate (NE) Closed	1	May
Enthorpe (NE) Opened	1	May
Middleton-on-the-Wolds (NE) Opened	1	May
Southburn (NE) Opened	1	May
Brampton Town (Bramp.) Closed (Re-opened 1913)	1	May
Clock House (SE) Opened	1	May
Craiglockhart (NB) Closed (Re-opened 1891)	1	May
Drumchapel (NB) Opened	1	May
Lochburn (NB) Opened	1	May
Exhibition (Cal) Opened (Closed 3 November 1890)	1	May
Blenheim & Woodstock (GW) Opened	19	May
Woodstock Road (GW) Renamed Kidlington for Blenheim	19	May
Yaxley (GN) Opened	19	May
Kensal Green (L&NW) Renamed Kensal Rise	24	May
Park Street (L&NW) Closed	24	May
Park Street & Frogmore (L&NW) Opened	24	May
Ardrossan Pier (L&A) Opened	30	May
Biglis Junc (Barry) Renamed Cadoxton	1	June
Horeham Rd for Waldron (LB&SC) Renamed Horeham Rd & Waldron	1	June
Cowdenbeath (NB) Renamed Cowdenbeath Old	1	June
Aberdour (NB) Opened	2	June
Cowdenbeath New (NB) Opened	2	June
Dunfermline (NB) Renamed Dunfermline Upper	2	June
Glenfarg (NB) Opened	2	June
Inveresk Junc (NB) Renamed Inveresk	2	June
Turnhouse (NB) Opened	2	June
Lenzie Junc (NB) Renamed Lenzie		June
Beer Alston (PD&SWJn) Opened	2	June
Beer Ferris (PD&SWJn) Opened	2	June
Brentor (PD&SWJn) Opened	2	June
Ford (PD&SWJn) Opened	2	June
St. Budeaux for Saltash (PD&SWJn) Opened	2	June
Tavistock (PD&SWJn) Opened	2	June
Crosshill & Codnor (Mid.) Opened	2	June
Heanor (Mid) Opened	2	June
Irvine (Cal) Opened	2	June
Bidston (SH&D) Closed (Re-opened 1896)		June
Halifax (L&Y) Renamed Halifax Old		June
Heversham (Furn.) Opened	1	July
Long Parish (L&SW) Renamed Longparish	1	July
Overseal & Moira (A&N) Closed	1	July

Station	day	month
Blaengwynfi (R&SB) Opened	2	July
Blaenrhondda (R&SB) Opened	14	July
Bisley Camp (L&SW) Opened	14	July
Bridgwater (L&SW) Opened	21	July
Cossington (L&SW) Opened	21	July
Edington Road (S&DJ) Renamed Edington Junc	21	July
Sevenoaks Tubs Hill (SE) Renamed Sevenoaks Tubs Hill & Riverhead		July
Thorne Falcon (GW) Renamed Thorne		July
Woodkirk (GN) Opened	1	August
Kirtlington (GW) Renamed Bletchington	11	August
Bolsover (Mid) Opened	1	September
Palterton & Sutton (Mid) Opened	1	September
Rowthorn & Hardwick (Mid) Opened	1	September
Clifton (BP&P) Renamed Hotwells	1	September
Croydon Central (LB&SC) Closed	1	September
Tanhouse Lane (Mid/MS&L) Opened	1	September
Halifax St. Paul's (HHL) Opened	5	September
Pellon (HHL) Opened	5	September
Colyton Town (L&SW) Renamed Colyton		September
Apperley (Mid) Renamed Apperley & Rawdon	1	October
Darley (Mid.) Renamed Darley Dale	1	October
Thorpe (Mid) Renamed Thorpe-on-the-Hill	1	October
Ocker Hill (L&NW) Closed (Re-opened 1895)	1	November
Princes End (L&NW) Closed (Re-opened 1895)	1	November
Chell Halt (NS) Opened	3	November
Havod (TV) Renamed Hafod (later Trehafod)		November
Attymon Junc. (MGW) Opened	1	December
Dunsandle (MGW) Opened	1	December
Loughrea (MGW) Opened	1	December
Ilkeston Junc. (Mid) Renamed Ilkeston Junc. & Cossall	1	December
Elephant & Castle (C&SL) Opened	18	December
Great Dover Street (C&SL) Opened	18	December
Kennington (C&SL) Opened (Renamed Kennington New Road, December 1890)	18	December
King William Street (C&SL) Opened	18	December
Stockwell (C&SL) Opened	18	December
The Oval (C&SL) Opened	18	December
Stanmore (L&NW) Opened	18	December
Ballinascarthy (T&CL) Opened	20	December
Skeaf (T&CL) Opened	20	December
Timoleague (T&CL) Opened	20	December
Gracehill (Ballycastle) Opened		December
Stanstead (GE) Renamed Stansted		December
Lucan & Leixlip Tramway Opened		
Aintree Cinder Lane (L&Y) Opened		
Ballineen (CB&SC) Closed		
Ballineen & Enniskean (CB&SC) Opened		
Castle Bernard (CB&SC) Closed		
Enniskean (CB&SC) Closed		
Manch Platform (CB&SC) Closed		
Prospect (GS&W) Renamed Ballycumber		
Foaty (GS&W) Renamed Fota		
Bathing Beach (Fairbourne) Opened		
Ferry (Fairbourne) Opened		
Golf Links (Fairbourne) Opened		
Penrhyn Bridge (Fairbourne) Opened		
Penrhyn Point (Fairbourne) Opened		
Chester (Birk.) Renamed Chester General		
Cogie Hill Crossing (G&KE) Renamed Cogie Hill Halt		
Cwm Colliers' Platform (GW) Opened		
Exhibition (NB) Opened (Closed 1 January 1891)		
Kinross Junc (NB) Resited		
Falmer (LB&SC) Resited		
Harold's Moor (Oystermouth) Closed		
Haughley Road (GE) Renamed Haughley		
Meldon Quarry Staff Halt (L&SW) Opened		
Neill's Hill (B&CD) Opened		
North Shields (NE) Resited		
Tunnel Pit Workmen's Platform (Mid) Opened		

INDEX

Station, junction, tunnel, viaduct, etc	Railway	Reference	Station, junction, tunnel, viaduct, etc	Railway	Reference
ALNESS	HR	36 C5	ARDLEIGH	GE	12 E4
ALNWICK	NE	31 F5	ARDLER	CAL.	34 D5
ALRESFORD	GE	12 E4	Ardler Jc.	CAL.	34 D5
ALRESFORD	L&SW	4 C3	ARDMORE	L&D	60 C2
ALREWAS	L&NW	15 E5	ARDRAHAN	A&EJn	52 D4
ALSAGER RODE HEATH	NS	15 C3	ARDROSSAN	G&SW	29 D3
ALSTON	NE	27 D2	ARDROSSAN	L&A	29 D3
ALTCAR & HILLHOUSE	CLC	45 F2	ARDROSSAN PIER	G&SW	29 D3
ALTCAR RIFLE STATION	L&Y	45 F2	ARDROSSAN SOUTH BEACH	G&SW	29 D3
ALTHORNE	GE	12 G5	ARDSLEY	GN	42 B3
ALTHORP PARK	L&NW	10 B3	Ardsley Jc.	GN	42 B3
ALTHORPE	MS&L	22 F5	Ardsley Tunnel	GN	42 B3
ALTNABREAC	HR	38 D4	ARDSOLLUS & QUIN	L&E	52 C5
ALTOFTS & WHITWOOD	MID.	42 B1	ARDWICK	L&NW	45 A3
Altofts Jc.	MID./NE	42 B2	ARDWICK	MS&L	45 A3
ALTON	L&SW	4 C2	ARENIG	B&F	19 F4
ALTON	NS	15 C4	ARGOED	L&NW	43 B2
ALTRINCHAM & BOWDON	MSJ&A	45 B4	ARIGNA	CL&RLt	56 D1
ALVA	NB	30 A5	ARKHOLME for KIRKBY LONSDALE	FUR. & MID. Jt	24 B2
ALVECHURCH	MID.	9 A4	Arkleston Jc.	G&PJt/G&SW	44 F3
ALVERSTONE	IoWC	4 F3	ARKLOW	DW&W	54 G2
ALVERTHORPE	GN	42 C3	ARKSEY	GN	21 F2
ALVES	HR	36 C2	Arlecdon	C&WJn	26 E3
ALVESCOT	E Glos.	10 E5	ARLESEY & SHEFFORD ROAD	GN	11 D2
ALYTH	CAL.	34 D5	ARLEY	GW	9 A2
ALYTH JUNCTION	CAL.	34 D5	ARLEY & FILLONGLEY	MID.	16 G5
AMBERGATE	MID.	41 E2	ARMADALE	NB	30 C4
Ambergate East, South & West Jcs.	MID.	41 E2	Armadale Cols.	NB	30 C4
AMBERLEY	LB&SC	5 F1	ARMAGH	GN(I)	58 A5
AMBLE	NE	31 F5	ARMATHWAITE	MID.	27 D1
Amble Branch Jc.	NE	31 G5	Armathwaite Tunnel	MID.	27 D1
AMISFIELD	CAL.	26 A3	ARMITAGE	L&NW	15 E5
AMLWCH	L&NW	19 C1	ARMLEY	MID.	21 B1
AMMANFORD	GW	43 G1	ARMLEY & WORTLEY	GN	42 A3
AMOTHERBY	NE	22 B5	ARMOY	Ballycastle	61 B1
AMPLEFORTH	NE	21 B5	ARNAGE	GNoS	37 E4
AMPTHILL	MID.	11 D1	Arne	Furzebrook	3 F4
Ampthill Tunnel	MID.	11 D1	ARNSIDE	FUR.	24 A3
ANCASTER	GN	16 C1	ARRAM	NE	22 D4
Ancoats (Goods)	MID.	45 A3 (f30)	ARTHINGTON	NE	21 D3
ANDOVER JUNCTION	L&SW	4 C4	ARTHOG	CAM.	13 A5
ANDOVER TOWN	L&SW	4 C4	ARUNDEL	LB&SC	5 F1
ANDOVERSFORD	Banbury & Chelt. Dir.	9 D4	Arundel Jc.	LB&SC	5 F1
ANERLEY	LB&SC	40 F4	ARVA ROAD	MGW	57 D3
ANGEL ROAD	GE	5 A3	ASCOT & SUNNINGHILL	L&SW	5 B1
Angerstein Wharf	SE	40 D2	ASCOTT-UNDER-WYCHWOOD	GW	10 D5
ANGERTON	NB	27 A4	ASFORDBY (late KIRBY)	MID.	16 E3
ANGMERING	LB&SC	5 F2	Asfordby Tunnel	MID.	16 E3
ANNADALE	CL&RLt	57 D1	ASH GREEN	L&SW	5 C1
ANNAGHILLA	CVT	60 G3	Ash Jc.	L&SW/SE	5 C1
ANNAGHMORE	GN(I)	58 A4	ASH JUNCTION	SE	5 C1
ANNAN	CAL.	26 B2	ASHBOURNE	NS	15 C5
ANNAN	G&SW	26 B2	ASHBURTON	BT&SD	2 C4
ANNBANK	G&SW	29 E4	Ashburton Grove (Goods)	GN	40 B5
ANNESLEY Col.	MID.	41 E4	Ashburton Jc.	GW/BT&SD	2 D4
Annesley Col.	GN	41 E4	ASHBURY	L&SW	1 B5
ANNITSFORD	NE	27 B5	ASHBURY'S for BELLE VUE	MS&L	45 A3 (f34)
ANSDELL	L&Y & L&NWJt	24 E4	ASHBY	MID.	16 E5
Ansley Hall Col.	MID.	16 F5	ASHCHURCH	MID.	9 D3
ANSTRUTHER	NB	34 G3	ASHCOTT	S&D Jt.	8 E2
ANTRIM	GN(I)	61 E2	ASHEY	IoWC	4 F3
ANTRIM JUNCTION	B&NC	61 E2	ASHEY RACECOURSE	IoWC	4 F3
Apedale Col.	NS	15 C3	ASHFORD	L&SW	5 B2
Apethorne Jc.	S&MJt	21 G1	ASHFORD	LC&D	6 D4
APPERLEY	MID.	42 A4	ASHFORD	SE	6 D4
Apperley Jc.	MID.	42 A4	ASHINGTON	NE	27 A5
APPLEBY	MID.	27 E2	ASHLEY	CLC	45 B4
APPLEBY	MS&L	22 E4	ASHLEY & WESTON	L&NW	16 G2
APPLEBY	NE	27 E2	ASHLEY HILL	GW	3 F1
APPLEDORE	SE	6 E4	Ashley Hill Jc.	GW/MID./BP&P	3 F1
Applehurst Jc.	NE/WR&GJt	21 F5	ASHPERTON	GW	9 C2
APPLETON	L&NW	45 D4	ASHTEAD	E&L Jt.	5 C2
APPLEY BRIDGE	L&Y	45 D2	ASHTON	GW	2 C3
AQUARIUM	VE	5 F3	ASHTON CHARLESTOWN	L&Y	21 A2
ARBROATH	D&AJt	34 D3	ASHTON HALL	L&NW	24 C3
Arbroath Harbour	A&F	34 D3	Ashton Moss Jc.	L&NW	21 A2
Arbroath Harbour Branch Jc.	A&F/D&AJt	34 D3	ASHTON OLDHAM ROAD	OA&G	21 A2
Archcliffe Jc.	SE/SE & LC&D Jt.	6 D2	Ashton Oldham Road (Goods)	L&NW	21 A2
ARDAGH	R&NJn	48 B5	ASHTON PARK PARADE	MS&L	21 A2
ARDDLEEN	CAM.	14 A2	Ashtons Green Jc.	L&NW	45 D3
Ardeer	L&A	29 E3	ASHTON-UNDER-HILL	MID.	9 C4
ARDFERT	L&K	47 D2	ASHURST	LB&SC	5 D4
ARDINGLY	LB&SC	5 E3	ASHWATER	L&SW	1 B5

Station, junction, tunnel, viaduct, etc	Railway	Reference	Station, junction, tunnel, viaduct, etc	Railway	Reference
ASHWELL	MID.	16 E2	AYR ROAD	CAL.	44 A1
ASHWELL	R&H	11 D2	AYSGARTH	NE	27 G4
ASHWELLTHORPE	GE	18 F3	AYTON	NB	31 C3
Ashwood Basin	Pensnett	15 G3			
ASKAM	FUR.	24 A5	Babbington	MID.	41 F3
ASKEATON	L&F	48 B5	BACKWORTH	NE	28 B5
ASKERN	L&Y	21 E5	BACTON ROAD	Golden Valley	14 F1
Askern Jc.	GN/L&Y	21 F5	BACUP	L&Y	24 E1
Askham Tunnel	GN	16 A2	Baddesley Col.	MID.	16 F5
ASKRIGG	NE	27 G3	BAGGROW	M&C	26 D2
ASLOCKTON	N&GR&C	16 C2	BAGILLT	L&NW	20 D5
ASPATRIA	M&C	26 D3	BAGNALSTOWN	GS&W	49 A5
ASTLEY	L&NW	45 C3	BAGSHOT	L&SW	4 B1
Astley Bridge (Goods)	L&Y	45 C1	BAGULEY	CLC	45 B4
ASTON	L&NW	13 B4	BAGWORTH	MID.	16 E4
ASTON ROWANT	GW	10 F3	BAILDON	MID.	42 A4
ASWARBY & SCREDINGTON	GN	17 D1	BAILEY GATE	S&D Jt.	3 E4
ATHBOY	MGW	57 G5	BAILIFF BRIDGE	L&Y	42 B4
ATHELNEY	GW	8 F3	BAILLIESTON	CAL.	44 C3
ATHENRY	MGW	52 C4	BAKER STREET	MET.	39 C5
ATHERSTONE	L&NW	16 F5	BAKEWELL	MID.	15 B5
ATHERTON	L&NW	45 C2	BALA	B&F	19 F4
Atherton (Goods)	L&NW	45 C2	BALA JUNCTION	C&B/B&F	19 F4
ATHERTON CENTRAL	L&Y	45 C2	BALADO	NB	33 G5
ATHLONE	GS&W	53 B1	BALBRIGGAN	GN(I)	58 G2
ATHLONE	MGW	53 B1	Balby Jc.	GN/MS&L	21 G2
Athlone East Jc.	MGW/GS&W	53 B1	BALCOMBE	LB&SC	5 E3
ATHY	GS&W	53 E5	Balcombe Tunnel	LB&SC	5 E3
ATTADALE	HR	35 E2	BALDERSBY	NE	21 A3
ATTANAGH	KJn	53 F3	Balderton (Goods)	GW	20 E4
ATTENBOROUGH	MID.	41 G4	BALDOCK	R&H	11 E2
ATTERCLIFFE	MS&L	42 G2	BALDOVAN	CAL.	34 E4
ATTERCLIFFE ROAD	MID.	42 G2	BALDRAGON	CAL.	34 E4
ATTLEBOROUGH	GE	18 F4	BALERNO	CAL.	30 C3
ATTLEBRIDGE	E&M	18 E3	Balerno Goods	CAL.	30 C3
AUCHENDINNY	NB	30 C2	Balerno Jc.	CAL.	30 B2
AUCHENGRAY	CAL.	30 D4	BALFRON	F&CJn	29 A4
AUCHENHEATH	CAL.	30 D5	BALGOWAN	CAL.	33 F4
AUCHENMADE	L&A	29 D3	BALHAM	LB&SC	39 E5
AUCHINCRUIVE	G&SW	29 F3	Balham Jc.	LB&SC	39 E5
AUCHINDACHY	GNoS	37 D1	BALLA	GN&W	55 F5
AUCHINLECK	G&SW	29 F5	BALLABEG	IoM	23 C2
Auchmuty Mills	NB	34 G5	BALLAGH	CVT	57 A4
AUCHNAGATT	GNoS	37 D4	BALLAGHADERREEN	MGW	56 E3
AUCHTERARDER	CAL.	33 F4	BALLASALLA	IoM	23 C2
AUCHTERHOUSE	CAL.	34 E5	BALLATER	GNoS	34 A5
AUCHTERLESS	GNoS	37 D3	Ballathie (Goods)	CAL.	33 E5
AUCHTERMUCHTY	NB	34 F5	BALLAUGH	MN	23 A2
AUDENSHAW	L&NW	45 A3 (f75)	BALLINA	GN&W	55 C5
Audenshaw Jc. W.	OA&G	21 A2	BALLINAHOUN	GS&W	53 B1
AUDLEM	N&MD	20 F2	BALLINAMALLARD	GN(I)	57 A2
AUDLEY	NS	15 C3	BALLINAMORE	CL&RLt	57 D1
AUDLEY END	GE	11 E4	BALLINASCARTY	CB&SC	50 F5
AUGHAVILLE	BE	49 F4	BALLINASLOE	MGW	52 B2
AUGHER	CVT	57 A4	BALLINCOLLIG	C&MD	48 G3
AUGHNACLOY	CVT	57 A5	BALLINDALLOCH	GNoS	36 E2
AUGHRIM	DW&W	54 F3	BALLINDERRY	GN(I)	61 G2
AULDBAR ROAD	A&F	34 D3	BALLINEEN	CB&SC	50 F5
AULDGIRTH	G&SW	26 A4	BALLINGLEN	DW&W	54 F3
AUTHORPE	GN	17 A3	BALLINGRANE JUNCTION	L&F	48 B5
Avenue Jc.	MID.	41 C2	BALLINHASSIG	CB&SC	50 E3
AVIEMORE	HR	36 F4	BALLINLOUGH	GN&W	56 F3
AVON LODGE	L&SW	4 E5	BALLINLUIG	HR	33 D4
AVONBRIDGE	NB	30 B4	BALLINTOGHER	SL&NC	56 C2
AVONMOUTH	GW	8 C2	BALLIOL ROAD	L&NW	45 F3 (f44)
Avonmouth Dock Goods	BP&P	8 C2	BALLOCH	NB	29 B3
AVONMOUTH DOCK Joint	BP&P	8 C2	BALLOCH PIER	NB	29 B3
AWRE JUNCTION	GW	8 A1	BALLYBAY	GN(I)	57 C5
AWSWORTH	GN	41 F3	BALLYBEG CROSSING	GN(I)	58 F5
AXBRIDGE	GW	8 E3	BALLYBOLEY JUNCTION	B&NC	61 D3
AXMINSTER	L&SW	2 B1	BALLYBRACK	GS&W	47 E3
AYCLIFFE	NE	28 E5	BALLYBROPHY	GS&W	53 F2
AYLESBURY	L&NW	10 E2	BALLYBUNION	L&B	47 B3
AYLESBURY Joint	GW/A&B	10 E2	BALLYCAR & NEWMARKET	L&E	52 G4
AYLESFORD	SE	6 C5	BALLYCARRY	C&L	61 E4
AYLSHAM	GE	18 D3	BALLYCASTLE	Ballycastle	61 A1
AYLSHAM TOWN	E&M	18 D3	BALLYCLARE	B&NC	61 E3
AYNHO	GW	10 D4	BALLYCLARE (narrow gauge)	B&NC	61 E3
AYOT	GN	11 F2	BALLYCLARE JUNCTION	B&NC	61 E3
AYR	G&SW	29 F3	BALLYCLOUGHAN	B&NC	61 D2
Ayr (Goods)	G&SW	29 F3	BALLYCONNELL	CL&RLt	57 C2
Ayr New Harbour	G&SW	29 F3	BALLYDEHOB	S&SLt	49 F4
Ayr Old Harbour	G&SW	29 F3	Ballydehob Viaduct	S&SLt	49 G4

Station, junction, tunnel, viaduct, etc	Railway	Reference
BALLYDOWD	D&LST	54 B3 (f3)
BALLYDUFF	CL&RLt	57 D1
BALLYDUFF	F&L	48 E1
BALLYGARVEY	B&NC	61 D1
BALLYGAWLEY	CVT	60 G3
BALLYGAWLEY	SL&NC	56 C2
BALLYGLUNIN	A&T	52 B4
BALLYGOWAN	B&CD	61 G4
BALLYHAISE JUNCTION	GN(I)	57 D3
BALLYHALE	W&CI	49 B4
BALLYHAUNIS	GN&W	56 F4
BALLYHEADY	CL&RLt	57 C2
BALLYHOOLY	GS&W	48 E2
BALLYKELLY	B&NC	60 C3
Ballymacarrett Jc.	B&CD	61 B4
BALLYMARTLE	CB&SC	50 F3
Ballymascanlon Viaduct	DN&G	58 D3
BALLYMENA	B&NC	61 D1
BALLYMENA (narrow gauge)	B&NC	61 D1
BALLYMOE	GN&W	56 F2
BALLYMONEY	B&NC	60 C1
BALLYMONEY	Ballycastle	60 B1
BALLYMONEY ROAD	GCP&BV	60 A1 (f7)
BALLYMOTE	MGW	56 C3
BALLYMURRY	GN&W	52 A1
BALLYNAHINCH	B&CD	58 A1
BALLYNAHINCH JUNCTION	B&CD	58 A1
BALLYNASHEE	B&NC	61 D3
BALLYNURE	B&NC	61 E3
BALLYRAGGET	KJn	53 G3
BALLYRONEY	GN(I)	58 B2
BALLYSHANNON	EB&S	59 F3
BALLYSODARE	MGW	56 B3
BALLYVADDEN	CVT	57 A4
BALLYWILLAN	MGW	57 F3
BALLYWILLIAM	GS&W	50 B5
BALMORAL	GN(I)	61 B4
BALMORE	NB	44 E5
Balmule	NB	30 A3
BALNE	NE	21 E5
Balne Moor (Goods)	HB&WRJn	21 E5
BALROTHERY	D&BST	62 F5
BALTINGLASS	GS&W	54 E5
BAMBER BRIDGE	L&Y	24 E3
BAMFURLONG	L&NW	45 D2
BAMPTON	E Glos.	10 E5
BAMPTON	T&ND	7 G5
BANAGHER	C&Ba	53 C1
BANBRIDGE	GN(I)	58 A3
BANBURY	GW	10 C4
BANBURY	L&NW	10 C4
BANCHORY	GNoS	34 A2
BANDON	CB&SC	50 F4
BANFF BRIDGE	GNoS	37 C2
BANFF HARBOUR	GNoS	37 C2
BANGOR	B&CD	61 F4
BANGOR	L&NW	19 D2
Bangor Tunnel	L&NW	19 D2
BANK HALL	L&Y	45 F3 (f71)
Bank House Tunnel	L&Y	42 C5
Bankend	CAL.	30 E5
Bankfield Goods	L&Y	45 G4
BANKHEAD	CAL.	30 D4
BANKHEAD	GNoS	37 F4
BANKNOCK	K&B	30 B5
BANKS	WLancs	24 E4
BANNOCKBURN	CAL.	30 A5
BANSHA	W&L	48 C1
BANSTEAD	LB&SC	5 C3
BANTEER	GS&W	48 E5
BANTRY	BE	49 F4
BARASSIE	G&SW	29 E3
BARBER'S BRIDGE	Newent	9 D2
BARBON	L&NW	24 A2
BARCOMBE	LB&SC	5 F4
BARCOMBE MILLS	LB&SC	5 F4
BARDNEY	GN	17 B1
BARDON HILL	MID.	16 E4
BARDON MILL	NE	27 B2
BARDOWIE	NB	44 E5
BARDSEY	NE	21 D3
BARE LANE	L&NW	24 B3
Bare Lane Jc.	L&NW	24 B3
BARGOED	Rhym.	43 B2
Bargoed North Jc.	Rhym.	43 B2
Bargoed South Jc.	Rhym./B&M	43 B2
BARHAM	SE	6 C2
BARKING	LT&S	40 B1
Barking East Jc.	LT&S	40 B1
Barking Jc.	LT&S	40 B1
BARKSTONE	GN	16 C1
BARLASTON	NS	15 D3
Barlby Jc.	NE	21 D5
BARMBY	HB&WRJn	21 E5
BARMING	LC&D	6 C5
BARMOUTH	CAM.	13 A5
Barmouth Bridge	CAM.	13 A5
BARMOUTH JUNCTION	CAM.	13 A5
BARNACK	S&E	17 F1
BARNAGH	L&K	47 C5
BARNARD CASTLE	NE	27 E4
BARNBY DUN	MS&L	21 F5
BARNES	L&SW	39 E4
BARNETBY	MS&L	22 F3
BARNHAM	GE	12 B5
BARNHAM JUNCTION	LB&SC	5 F1
BARNHILL	CAL.	34 E4
BARNHILL	CoGU	44 D4 (f8)
BARNOLDSWICK	Barnoldswick	21 A1
BARNSBURY	NL	40 B5
BARNSLEY	L&Y	42 E2
BARNSLEY	MID.	42 E2
Barnsley Jc.	MS&L	42 E3
BARNSTAPLE	Devon & Somerset	7 F3
BARNSTAPLE JUNCTION	L&SW	7 F3
BARNSTAPLE TOWN	L&SW	7 F3
BARNSTON	GN&L&NWJt	16 D2
BARNT GREEN	MID.	9 A4
BARNWELL	L&NW	11 A1
BARNWELL JUNCTION	GE	11 C3
Baron Wood Tunnels	MID.	27 D1
Barr Road Jc.	GN/N&GR&C	16 D1
BARRAS	NE	27 F3
BARRASFORD	NB	27 B3
BARRHEAD	GB&KJt	44 F2
Barrhead (Mineral)	GB&KJt	44 F3
BARRHILL	A&W	25 A3
BARRMILL	GB&KJt	29 D3
Barrow (Goods)	FUR.	24 B5
Barrow Bridge	DW&W	49 C5
BARROW CENTRAL	FUR.	24 B5
BARROW for TARVIN	CLC	20 D3
BARROW HAVEN	MS&L	22 E3
BARROW RAMSDEN DOCK	FUR.	24 B5
BARROW-ON-SOAR	MID.	16 E3
Barrs Court Jc.	S&HJt/GW	9 C1
BARRY	BD&R	43 C5
BARRY	D&AJt	34 E3
BARRY DOCKS	BD&R	43 C5
BARRY REVIEW PLATFORM	D&AJt	34 E4
BARTLOW	GE	11 D4
BARTON	LS&PJc	45 F2
BARTON	MS&L	22 E4
BARTON & BROUGHTON	L&NW	24 D3
BARTON & HALSALL	CLC	45 F2
BARTON & WALTON	MID.	15 E5
Barton (Goods)	M&D	27 F5
BARTON HILL	NE	22 B5
Barton Jc.	S&HJt/GW	9 C1
BARTON MOSS	L&NW	45 B3
Barton Quarries	M&D	27 F5
BARTON-LE-STREET	NE	22 B5
BASCHURCH	GW	20 G4
BASFORD	MID.	41 F4
BASFORD & BULWELL	GN	41 F4
BASINGSTOKE	GW	4 B2
BASINGSTOKE	L&SW	4 B2
BASON BRIDGE	S&D Jt.	8 E3
BASSALEG	B&M	43 A3
BASSALEG	GW	43 A3
BASSENTHWAITE LAKE	CK&P	26 E2
BATH	GW	3 A3
BATH	MID.	3 A3
BATHAMPTON	GW	3 A3
BATHGATE (LOWER)	NB	30 C4
BATHGATE (UPPER)	E&B	30 C4

Station, junction, tunnel, viaduct, etc	Railway	Reference	Station, junction, tunnel, viaduct, etc	Railway	Reference
BATLEY	GN	42 B3	BELLAHOUSTON	G&SW	44 G1
BATLEY	L&NW	42 B3	BELLARENA	B&NC	60 B2
BATLEY CARR	GN	42 C3	BELLE VUE	S&MJt	45 A3
BATTERSBY JUNCTION	NE	28 F4	BELLEEK	EB&S	59 G4
BATTERSEA	WLEJt	39 E3	BELLGROVE	NB	44 D4 (f10)
BATTERSEA PARK	LB&SC	39 E4	BELLINGHAM	NB	27 A3
BATTERSEA PARK ROAD	LC&D	39 E4	BELLSHILL	CAL.	44 B3
Battersea Pier Jc.	LB&SC/LC&D	39 E4	BELLSHILL	NB	44 B3
Battersea Wharf (Goods)	LB&SC	39 E4	BELLURGAN	DN&G	58 D3
BATTERSTOWN	MGW	54 A4	BELMONT	LB&SC	5 C3
BATTLE	SE	6 F5	BELMONT & CLOGHAN	C&Ba	53 C1
BATTLESBRIDGE	GE	6 A5	Belmont Tunnel	L&NW	19 D2
Batty Moss Viaduct	MID.	24 A1	BELPER	MID.	41 F2
BAWNBOY ROAD & TEMPLEPORT	CL&RLt	57 D2	BELSES	NB	31 E1
BAWTRY	GN	21 G5	Belston Jc.	G&SW	29 F4
BAXENDEN	L&Y	24 E1	BELTON	GE	18 F1
Baxenden Summit	L&Y	24 E1	BELTURBET	CL&RLt	57 C3
BAY HORSE	L&NW	24 C3	BELTURBET	GN(I)	57 C3
BAYNARDS	LB&SC	5 D2	BELVEDERE	SE	5 B4
BAYSWATER	MET.	39 C5	Belvelly Viaduct	GS&W	48 F1
Beacon Hill Tunnel	L&Y	42 B5	Belvoir Jc.	N&GR&C/GN	16 D2
BEACONS SITE	Cardiff Corp.	43 D1	BEMBRIDGE	BHI&RC	4 F2
Beag	NP&F	13 G2	BEMPTON	NE	22 B3
BEAL	NE	31 D4	BEN RHYDDING	O&IJt	21 C2
BEALINGS	GE	12 D3	BENFLEET	LT&S	6 A5
BEARLEY	GW	9 B5	BENGEWORTH	MID.	9 C4
BEARSDEN	NB	44 F5	Benhar Cols.	NB	30 C4
BEARSTED	LC&D	6 C5	BENNETTSBRIDGE	W&CI	49 B4
BEATTOCK	CAL.	30 G3	BENSHAM	NE	28 B2
Beattock Summit	CAL.	30 F4	BENTHAM	MID.	24 B2
BEAUCHIEF & ABBEY DALE	MID.	41 A2	BENTLEY	GE	12 D4
BEAUFORT	GW	43 B1	BENTLEY	L&SW	4 C1
BEAUFORT	L&NW	43 B1	BENTLEY	MID.	15 F4
BEAULY	HR	35 E5	BENTON	NE	27 B5
BEAUMONT	Jersey	46 E3	BENTS	NB	30 C4
BEAUPARC	GN(I)	58 F4	BERAGH	GN(I)	60 F3
BEBINGTON	BIRK. Jt.	45 F4	BERKELEY	MID.	9 F2
BEBSIDE	NE	27 A5	BERKELEY ROAD	MID.	9 F2
BECCLES	GE	12 A2	BERKHAMSTED	L&NW	10 E1
Beccles Swing Bridge	GE	12 A2	BERKSWELL	L&NW	9 A5
BECKENHAM	LC&D	40 F3	BERNEY ARMS	GE	18 F1
BECKERMET	WC&EJt	26 F3	BERRINGTON	GW	15 F1
BECKFOOT	R&E	26 F2	BERRINGTON & EYE	S&HJt	9 B1
BECKFORD	MID.	9 C4	BERRY BROW	L&Y	42 D5
Beckhole	NE	28 F2	BERVIE	NB	34 B2
BECKINGHAM	GN&GEJt.	22 G5	BERWICK	LB&SC	5 F4
BECKTON	GE	40 C1	BERWICK	NE/NB	31 C3
BECTIVE	MGW	54 A5	BERWYN	LI&C	20 F5
BEDALE	NE	21 A3	BESCAR LANE	L&Y	45 F1
Beddau Loop Jc.	Rhym.	43 B3	BESCOT	L&NW	13 A3
BEDDINGTON LANE	LB&SC	40 G5	Bescot East & West Jcs.	L&NW	13 A2
BEDFORD	L&NW	11 D1	Bescot South Jc.	L&NW	13 A3
BEDFORD	MID.	11 D1	BESSBROOK	B&NT	58 C4
BEDLINGTON	NE	27 A5	BESSBROOK	GN(I)	58 C3
BEDLINOG	TBJt.	43 C2	BESTWOOD COLLIERY	GN	41 E4
BEDMINSTER	GW	3 G1	Beswick (Goods)	L&Y	45 A3 (f29)
Bedminster Jc.	GW	3 G1	BETCHWORTH	SE	5 C2
BEDWAS	B&M	43 B3	Betchworth Tunnel	LB&SC	5 D2
BEDWELLTY PITS	L&NW	43 B2	BETHESDA	L&NW	19 D2
BEDWORTH	L&NW	16 G5	Bethnal Green East & West Jcs.	GE	40 C4
BEDWYN	GW	4 A5	BETHNAL GREEN JUNCTION	GE	40 C4
BEECHBURN	NE	27 D5	BETLEY ROAD	L&NW	20 E2
BEESTON	GN	42 B3	BETTISFIELD	CAM.	20 F3
BEESTON	MID.	41 G4	BETTWS GARMON	NWNG	19 E2
BEESTON CASTLE & TARPORLEY	L&NW	20 E3	BETTWS-Y-COED	L&NW	19 E4
BEIGHTON	MS&L	41 A3	BEVERLEY	NE	22 D3
BEITH	G&SW	29 D3	Beverley Jc.	NE	22 D4
BEITH	GB&KJt	29 D3	BEWDLEY	GW	9 A3
BEKESBOURNE	LC&D	6 C2	BEXHILL	LB&SC	6 F5
BEL ROYAL	Jersey	46 E3	BEXLEY	SE	5 B4
Belah Viaduct	NE	27 F3	BICESTER	L&NW	10 D3
BELCOO	SL&NC	57 B1	BICKERSHAW & ABRAM	WJn	45 C2 (f10)
Belfast Abercorn Basin (Goods)	B&CD/GN(I)	61 B4	Bickershaw East & South Jcs.	L&NW	45 C2
Belfast Clarendon Dock (Goods)	GN(I)	61 A4	BICKLEIGH	GW	2 D5
Belfast Donegal Quay (Goods)	GN(I)	61 B4	BICKLEY	MK(B-StMC)	40 G2
Belfast Dufferin Dock (Goods)	GN(I)	61 A4	Biddulph Jc.	NS	15 B3
BELFAST GREAT VICTORIA STREET	GN(I)	61 B4	BIDEFORD	L&SW	7 F3
Belfast Grosvenor Street (Goods)	GN(I)	61 B4	BIDFORD	ER&SuAJn	9 B5
Belfast Queen's Bridge (Goods)	GN(I)	61 B4	BIDSTON	SH&D	45 G4
BELFAST QUEEN'S QUAY	B&CD	61 B4	BIGGAR	CAL.	30 E3
BELFAST YORK ROAD	B&NC	61 A4	BIGGLESWADE	GN	11 D2
BELFORD	NE	31 E4	Biglis Jc.	BD&R/TV	43 B5
BELL BUSK	MID.	21 C1	BIGLIS JUNCTION	BD&R	43 B5

Station, junction, tunnel, viaduct, etc	Railway	Reference
Bignall Hill Col.	NS	15 C3 (f8)
BIGSWEIR	Wye Valley	8 A2
BILBSTER	HR	38 D2
BILLERICAY	GE	5 A5
BILLING	L&NW	10 B2
BILLINGBOROUGH & HORBLING	GN	17 D1
BILLINGHAM JUNCTION	NE	28 E4
BILLINGSHURST	LB&SC	5 E2
Bilson (Goods)	GW	8 A1
Bilson Jc.	GW/S&WJt	8 A1
BILSTON (MAIN LINE)	GW	13 A2
BILSTON (WEST MIDLAND)	GW	13 A1
BILTON	NE	31 F5
Bilton Road Jc.	NE	21 C3
Bincombe Summit	GW	3 F3
Bincombe Tunnels	GW	3 F3
BINEGAR	S&D Jt.	3 B3
BINGHAM	N&GR&C	16 C3
BINGHAM ROAD	GN/L&NWJt	16 D3
BINGLEY	MID.	42 A5
Bingley Jc.	MID.	42 A5
Bingley Tunnel	MID.	42 A5
BINTON	ER&SuAJn	9 B5
Birch Coppice Col.	MID.	16 F5
BIRCH VALE	S&MJt	21 G1
BIRCHFIELD PLATFORM	GNoS	36 D1
BIRCHILLS	L&NW	15 F4
BIRCHINGTON-ON-SEA	LC&D	6 B2
BIRDBROOK	CV&H	11 D5
BIRDHILL	W&L	52 G3
BIRDINGBURY	L&NW	10 A4
Birdston Jc.	NB	44 C5
BIRDWELL & HOYLAND	MS&L	42 E2
BIRKDALE	L&Y	45 F1
BIRKDALE PALACE	CLC	45 F1
Birkenhead Canning Street Town (Goods)	CLC	45 F4 (f67)
Birkenhead Cathcart Street (Goods)	BIRK. Jt.	45 F4 (f65)
BIRKENHEAD CENTRAL	MER.	45 F4
BIRKENHEAD DOCKS	Wirral	45 F4 (f66)
BIRKENHEAD PARK (Joint)	MER./Wirral	45 F4 (f70)
BIRKENHEAD TOWN	BIRK. Jt.	45 F4
BIRKENHEAD WOODSIDE	BIRK. Jt.	45 F4 (f69)
BIRKENSHAW & TONG	GN	42 B4
Birkett Tunnel	MID.	27 F2
Birley Col.	MS&L	41 A2
Birmingham Camp Hill (Goods)	MID.	13 C4
BIRMINGHAM CURZON STREET	L&NW	13 C4
Birmingham Lawley Street (Goods)	MID.	13 C4
BIRMINGHAM NEW STREET	L&NW/MID.	13 C4
BIRMINGHAM SNOW HILL	GW	13 C4
Birmingham Worcester Wharf	MID.	13 C3
BIRNIE ROAD	NB	34 C2
BIRSTAL	L&NW	42 B4
Birstal Jc.	L&NW/GN	42 B3
BIRSTWITH	NE	21 C3
BIRTLEY	NE	27 C5
BISHOP AUCKLAND	NE	27 E5
BISHOPBRIGGS	NB	44 D4
Bishopley	NE	27 D4
BISHOP'S CASTLE	BC	14 C1
BISHOPS COURT	MN	23 B2
BISHOP'S LYDEARD	West Somerset	8 F4
BISHOP'S NYMPTON & MOLLAND	Devon & Somerset	7 F5
BISHOP'S STORTFORD	GE	11 E3
BISHOP'S WALTHAM	L&SW	4 D3
BISHOPSBOURNE	SE	6 C2
BISHOPSGATE	GE	40 C4 (f52)
BISHOPSGATE	MET.	40 C4
Bishopsgate (Goods)	GE	40 C4
Bishopsgate Jc.	EL/GE	40 C4 (f50)
BISHOPSTONE	LB&SC	5 G4
BISHOPTON	CAL.	29 C4
BISPHAM	L&Y & L&NWJt	24 D4
Bitterley	Ludlow & Clee Hill	9 A1
BITTERNE ROAD	L&SW	4 E4
BITTON	MID.	8 D1
BLABY	L&NW	16 F4
BLACK BANK	GE	11 A4
BLACK BULL (BRINDLEY FORD)	NS	15 C3
Black Carr Jc.	GN/GN&GEJt.	21 G2
BLACK DOG SIDING	Calne	3 A5
BLACK DYKES	NB	26 C3
BLACK LANE	L&Y	45 B2
Blackbraes	NB	30 B4
BLACKBURN	L&Y	24 D2
BLACKFORD	CAL.	33 F4
BLACKFORD HILL	NB	30 G2
BLACKFRIARS	MET.-DIS.	40 C5
Blackfriars (Goods)	LC&D	40 C5
BLACKHALL	NB	30 C4
BLACKHEATH	SE	40 E2
BLACKHEATH HILL	LC&D	40 D3
Blackhill Jc.	CAL.	44 D4
Blackhouse Jc.	G&SW	29 F3
BLACKMILL	GW	43 D3
BLACKPILL	Oy.	43 G3
BLACKPOOL CENTRAL	L&Y & L&NWJt	24 D4
BLACKPOOL TALBOT ROAD	L&Y & L&NWJt	24 D4
BLACKROCK	CB&P	48 F2
BLACKROCK	D&K	62 E1
BLACKROD	L&Y	45 C2
Blackrod Jc.	L&Y	45 C2
BLACKSBOAT	GNoS	36 E2
BLACKSTON JUNCTION	NB	30 B4
Blackstone Jc.	CAL.	44 G4
Blacktongue No. 1 Pit	NB	44 A5
BLACKWALL	GE	40 C2
Blackwall (Goods)	GE	40 C3
BLACKWATER	IoWC	4 F3
BLACKWATER	SE	4 B1
BLACKWELL	MID.	9 A4
BLACKWOOD	CAL.	30 D5
BLACKWOOD	L&NW	43 B2
Blackwood Quarry	CAL.	30 E5
BLAENAU FESTINIOG	B&F	19 F3
BLAENAU FESTINIOG	Fest.	19 F3
BLAENAU FESTINIOG	L&NW	19 F3
BLAENAVON	GW	43 A1
BLAENAVON	L&NW	43 A1
Blaenavon Col.	GW	43 D3
Blaenclydach Col.	EV	43 D3
Blaenclydach Col.	TV	43 D3
BLAINA	GW	43 B2
BLAIR ATHOLE	HR	33 C3
BLAIRADAM	NB	30 A3
BLAIRGOWRIE	CAL.	33 D5
BLAIRHILL & GARTSHERRIE	NB	44 B4
Blairinbathie	NB	30 A3
BLAKE HALL	GE	11 G4
BLAKE STREET	L&NW	15 F5
Blakeney (Goods)	FoDC	8 A1
BLAKESLEY	E&WJn.	10 C3
BLAKEY JUNCTION	NE	28 F3
BLANCHARDSTOWN	MGW	54 B3
BLANDFORD	S&D Jt.	3 E4
BLANEFIELD	BV	29 B4
BLANKNEY & METHERINGHAM	GN&GEJt.	17 B1
BLANTYRE	CAL.	44 C2
Blantyre Branch	NB	44 C2
BLARNEY	GS&W	48 F3
BLARNEY TOWER	C&MLt	48 G3
BLAYDON	NE	28 A3
Blaydon East Jc.	NE	28 A3
Blea Moor Summit	MID.	24 A1
Blea Moor Tunnel	MID.	24 A1
BLEADON & UPHILL	GW	8 D3
BLEASBY	MID.	16 C3
BLEDLOW	GW	10 E2
BLENCOW	CK&P	26 E1
BLESSINGTON	D&BST	54 D4
Bletchingley Tunnel	SE	5 D3
BLETCHLEY	L&NW	10 D2
BLIDWORTH	MID.	41 D5
BLISWORTH	L&NW	10 B3
BLISWORTH	N&BJn.	10 B3
Blochairn Iron Works	CAL.	44 D4
BLOCKLEY	GW	9 C5
BLOOMFIELD	B&CD	61 B5
Bloomfield Basins	L&NW	13 B1
BLOWICK	L&Y	45 F1 (f3)
BLOXHAM	Banbury & Chelt. Dir.	10 C4
BLOXWICH	L&NW	15 F4
BLUE ANCHOR	Minehead	8 E5
BLUESTONE	E&M	18 D3
BLUNDELLSANDS & CROSBY	L&Y	45 F3
BLUNHAM	L&NW	11 D1

Station, junction, tunnel, viaduct, etc	Railway	Reference
BLUNTISHAM	E&StI	11 B3
BLYTH	NE	28 A5
BLYTH BRIDGE	NS	15 C4
BLYTHBURGH	Southwold	12 B2
BLYTON for CORRINGHAM	MS&L	22 G5
BOARHILLS	NB	34 F3
BOAR'S HEAD	L&NW	45 D2
BOAT OF GARTEN	HR	36 F3
BODFARI	M&DJn.	19 D5
BODMIN	GW	1 D3
Bodmin	L&SW	1 D3
BODMIN ROAD	GW	1 D3
BODORGAN	L&NW	19 D1
Bodorgan Tunnels	L&NW	19 D1
BOGNOR	LB&SC	5 G1
BOGSIDE	G&SW	29 E3
BOGSIDE	NB	30 A4
BOGSTON	CAL.	29 B3
BOHER	W&L	48 A3
Boldon (Goods)	NE	28 C5
Bolham Jc.	T&ND/GW	7 G5
BOLLINGTON	MS&L/NSJt	45 A5
Bollo Lane Jc.	L&SW/N&SWJn	39 D3
Bolsover (Goods)	MID.	41 C3
BOLTON	L&Y	45 B2
BOLTON ABBEY	MID.	21 C1
BOLTON GREAT MOOR STREET	L&NW	45 C2 (f13)
BOLTON PERCY	NE	21 D4
BOLTON-LE-SANDS	L&NW	24 B3
BOLTON-ON-DEARNE	S&KJt	42 E1
BOLT'S DOWN	W&R	27 D4
BONAR BRIDGE	HR	36 B5
BONCATH	W&C	13 F3
Bond End	MID.	15 D5
BO'NESS	NB	30 B4
BONNINGTON	NB	30 F2
Bonnington North & South Jcs.	NB	30 F2
Bonnington Road Goods	NB	30 F2
BONNYBRIDGE	CAL.	30 B5
BONNYBRIDGE	NB	30 B5
BONNYBRIDGE CENTRAL	K&B	30 B5
BONNYRIGG	NB	30 C2
Bonnywater Jc.	CAL./K&B	30 B5
BONTNEWYDD	GW	14 A5
Bonville's Court Col.	P&T	7 D3
BOOKHAM	L&SW	5 C2
BOOSBECK	NE	28 E3
BOOT	R&E	26 F2
BOOTERSTOWN	D&K	62 E2
Bootham Jc.	NE	21 A4
BOOTLE	FUR.	26 G3
BOOTLE	L&Y	45 F3 (f43)
Bopeep Jc.	LB&SC/SE	6 F5
Bopeep Tunnel	SE	6 F5
Border Counties Jc.	NB/NE	27 B3
BORDESLEY	GW	13 C4
Bordesley Jc.	GW	13 C4
Borough Market Jc.	SE	40 C4 (f53)
BOROUGH ROAD	LC&D	40 D5
BOROUGHBRIDGE	NE	21 B4
BORRIS	GS&W	50 A5
BORROBOL PLATFORM	HR	38 F5
BORROWASH	MID.	41 G2
BORTH	CAM.	13 C5
BORWICK	FUR. & MID. Jt	24 B3
Boscarne Jc.	GW/L&SW	1 D3
BOSCOMBE	L&SW	4 F5
BOSHAM	LB&SC	4 E1
BOSLEY	NS	15 B3
BOSTON	GN	17 C3
Boston Docks	GN	17 C3
BOSTON ROAD	MET.-DIS.	39 D2
BOTHWELL	CAL.	44 B2
BOTHWELL	NB	44 C2
Bothwell Jc.	CAL.	44 B3
Bothwell Jc.	NB	44 C2
BOTHWELL PARK	NB	44 B3
BOTLEY	L&SW	4 E3
BOTTESFORD	N&GR&C	16 D2
Bottesford East Jc.	N&GR&C/GN&L&NWJt	16 D2
Bottesford North Jc.	GN	16 C2
Bottesford South Jc.	GN&L&NWJt	16 D2
Bottesford West Jc.	N&GR&C/GN	16 C2
BOTTISHAM	GE	11 C4
BOUGHROOD	Mid-Wales	14 F3
Boultham Jc.	GN&GEJt.	16 A1
BOURN	GN	17 E1
BOURNE END	GW	10 G2
BOURNEMOUTH EAST	L&SW	3 F5
BOURNEMOUTH WEST	L&SW	3 F5
BOURNVILLE & STIRCHLEY STREET	MID.	9 A4
BOURTON-ON-THE-WATER	GW	9 D5
BOVEY	GW	2 C4
BOW	NL	40 C3
BOW (DEVON)	L&SW	2 B4
BOW ROAD	GE	40 C3
BOW STREET	CAM.	13 C5
Bowdon	MSJ&A	45 B4
BOWDON PEEL CAUSEWAY	CLC	45 B4
BOWER	HR	38 C3
BOWES	NE	27 F4
BOWES PARK	GN	5 A3
BOWHOUSE	NB	30 B4
BOWLAND	NB	30 D1
BOWLING	GN	42 B4
BOWLING	NB	29 B4
Bowling Jc.	L&Y/GN	42 B4
Bowling Tunnel	L&Y	42 B4
BOWNESS	SJ	26 C2
BOX	GW	3 A4
BOX HILL	SE	5 C2
Box Tunnel	GW	3 A4
BOXHILL & BURFORD BRIDGE	LB&SC	5 C2
BOXMOOR	L&NW	11 F1
BOYCES BRIDGE	GE (Wisbech Tmy.)	17 F4
BOYLE	MGW	56 D2
Boyne Viaduct	GN(I)	58 F3
BRACEBOROUGH SPA	GN	17 E1
Bracebridge (Goods)	GN	16 B1
BRACKLEY	L&NW	10 C4
BRACKNELL	L&SW	4 A1
BRADBURY	NE	28 E5
BRADFIELD	GE	12 E4
BRADFORD	GW	3 B4
Bradford Adolphus Street (Goods)	GN	42 B4
Bradford City Road (Goods)	GN	42 A4
BRADFORD EXCHANGE	L&Y	42 A4
Bradford Jc.	GW	3 B4
BRADFORD MARKET STREET	MID.	42 A4
BRADING	IoW	4 F3
BRADLEY	L&NW	42 C4
BRADLEY & MOXLEY	GW	13 A2
BRADLEY FOLD	L&Y	45 B2 (f2)
Bradley Tunnel	L&NW	42 C4
Bradley Wood Jc.	L&Y/L&NW	42 C4
Bradway Tunnel	MID.	41 B2
BRADWELL	L&NW	10 C2
BRAFFERTON	NE	21 B4
BRAIDWOOD	CAL.	30 D5
BRAINTREE	GE	11 E5
Braintree (Goods)	GE	11 E5
BRAITHWAITE	CK&P	26 E2
BRAMBER	LB&SC	5 F2
BRAMCOTE	MID.	41 G4
BRAMFORD	GE	12 D4
BRAMHALL	L&NW	45 A4
Bramhope Tunnel	NE	21 D3
BRAMLEY	GN	42 A3
BRAMLEY & WONERSH	LB&SC	5 D1
Bramley Siding	GW	4 B2
BRAMPFORD SPEKE	GW	2 B3
BRAMPTON	GE	12 B2
Brampton (Goods)	MID.	41 C2
BRAMPTON JUNCTION	NE	27 C1
BRAMPTON TOWN	Brampton	27 C1
BRAMWITH	WR&GJt	21 F5
BRANCEPETH	NE	27 D5
BRANDON	GE	11 A5
BRANDON	NE	27 D5
BRANDON & WOLSTON	L&NW	10 A5
Brandy Bridge Jc.	TV/GW&TVJt.	43 C2
Brandy Hole Tunnel	DW&W	54 D2
BRANSFORD ROAD	GW	9 B3
Bransford Road Jc.	GW	9 B3
BRANSTON	MID.	15 E5
BRANSTON & HEIGHINGTON	GN&GEJt.	16 B1

Station, junction, tunnel, viaduct, etc	Railway	Reference
BRANTHWAITE	WC&EJt	26 E3
BRASTED	SE	5 C4
BRAUGHING	GE	11 E3
BRAUNTON	L&SW	7 F3
BRAY	DW&W	54 C2
Bray Head Tunnels	DW&W	54 C2
BRAYSTONES	FUR.	26 F3
BRAYTON	M&C	26 D2
BREADSALL	GN	41 G2
Breakwater Jc.	CAL.	30 F3
BREAMORE	L&SW	4 D5
BRECHIN	CAL.	34 C3
BRECK ROAD	L&NW	45 F3
BRECON	B&M	14 F3
Brecon Watton (Goods)	B&M	14 G3
BREDBURY	S&MJt	21 G1
BREDON	MID.	9 C3
BREICH	CAL.	30 C4
BRENDON HILL	West Somerset Mineral	8 F5
BRENT	GW	2 D4
Brent Jc.	L&NW	39 C3
Brent Jc.	MID.	39 B4
BRENT KNOLL	GW	8 E3
BRENTFORD	GW	39 D2
BRENTFORD	L&SW	39 D2
BRENTWOOD & WARLEY	GE	5 A5
Bretby	MID.	16 E5
BRETTELL LANE	GW	15 G3
Breydon Jc.	GE	18 F1
BRICKET WOOD	L&NW	11 G1
Bricklayers Arms (Goods)	SE	40 D4
Bricklayers Arms Jc.	LB&SC	40 D4
BRIDESTOWE	L&SW	2 B5
BRIDGE	SE	6 C3
BRIDGE END	L&LS	60 C4
BRIDGE END	WM&CQ	20 E4
BRIDGE OF ALLAN	CAL.	30 A5
BRIDGE OF DEE	G&SW	26 C5
BRIDGE OF DUN	CAL.	34 C3
BRIDGE OF EARN	NB	33 F5
BRIDGE OF WEIR	G&SW	29 C3
Bridge Street Jc.	CAL./G&PJt	44 F2 (f18)
BRIDGEFOOT	WC&EJt	26 E3
BRIDGEND	GW	43 D4
Bridgend Jc.	NB	44 C5
Bridgeness	NB	30 B4
BRIDGES	Cornwall Minerals	1 D3
BRIDGETON	CAL.	44 D3
Bridgeton (Goods)	CAL.	44 D3
BRIDGNORTH	GW	15 F2
BRIDGWATER	GW	8 F3
Bridgwater Docks	GW	8 F3
BRIDLINGTON	NE	22 B3
BRIDPORT	Bridport	3 F2
BRIERFIELD	L&Y	24 D1
BRIERLEY HILL	GW	15 G3
BRIGG	MS&L	22 F4
BRIGHAM	L&NW	26 E3
BRIGHOUSE for RASTRICK	L&Y	42 C4
BRIGHTLINGSEA	W&B	12 F4
BRIGHTON CENTRAL	LB&SC	5 F3
BRIGHTON ROAD	MID.	13 D4
BRIGHTSIDE	MID.	42 G2
BRILL	O&AT	10 E3
BRIMSCOMBE near CHALFORD	GW	9 F3
BRIMSDOWN	GE	11 G3
Brindle Heath (Goods)	L&Y	45 B3 (f20)
BRINKBURN	NB	31 G4
BRINKLOW	L&NW	10 A4
BRINSCALL	LUJt	24 E2
Brinsley Jc.	GN	41 E3
BRISLINGTON	GW	8 D1
Brislington Tunnel	GW	8 C1
Bristol Lower Yard (Goods)	MID.	3 G1
Bristol Pylle Hill (Goods)	GW	3 G1
Bristol Temple Meads (Goods)	GW	3 G1
BRISTOL TEMPLE MEADS Joint	GW/MID.	3 G1
BRITANNIA	L&Y	24 E1
Britannia Tubular Bridge	L&NW	19 D2
BRITON FERRY	GW	43 F3
Briton Ferry Dock	GW	43 F3
BRITON FERRY ROAD	GW	43 F3
BRITTAS	D&BST	54 C4
BRIXHAM	GW	2 D3
BRIXTON & SOUTH STOCKWELL	LC&D	40 E5
Brixton (Coal)	MID.	40 E5
BRIXWORTH	L&NW	10 A2
BROAD CLYST	L&SW	2 B3
BROAD GREEN	L&NW	45 E4
BROAD STREET	NL	40 C4
Broad Street (Goods)	L&NW	40 C4
BROADFIELD	L&Y	45 A2
BROADHEATH (ALTRINCHAM)	L&NW	45 B4
Broadheath (Altrincham) (Goods)	L&NW	45 B4
Broadheath Jc.	L&NW	45 B4
BROADLEY	L&Y	45 A1
BROADSTAIRS	LC&D	6 B1
BROADSTONE JUNCTION	L&SW	3 F5
BROADWAY	Abbotsbury	3 F3
BROCK	L&NW	24 D3
BROCKENHURST	L&SW	4 E4
BROCKHOLES	L&Y	42 D5
BROCKHURST	L&SW	4 E3
BROCKLESBY	MS&L	22 E3
BROCKLEY	LB&SC	40 E3
BROCKLEY LANE	LC&D	40 E3
BROCKLEY WHINS	NE	28 C5
BRODIE	HR	36 D3
BROIGHTER	B&NC	60 B2
BROMBOROUGH	BIRK. Jt.	45 F5
BROMFIELD	S&HJt	9 A1
BROMLEY	LC&D	40 G2
BROMLEY	LT&S	40 C3
BROMLEY	SE	40 F2
BROMLEY CROSS	L&Y	45 B1
Bromley Jc.	LB&SC/LC&D	40 F4
BROMPTON	NE	28 G5
BROMPTON (GLOUCESTER ROAD)	MET.	39 D5
BROMPTON (GLOUCESTER ROAD)	MET.-DIS.	39 D5
BROMSGROVE	MID.	9 A4
Bromshall (Goods)	NS	15 D4
BROMYARD	GW	9 B2
BRONDESBURY	L&NW	39 B4
BRONWYDD ARMS	GW	13 G4
BROOKEBOROUGH	CVT	57 B3
BROOKLAND	Lydd	6 E4
BROOKLANDS	MSJ&A	45 B3
BROOKMOUNT	GN(I)	61 G2
Brooksbottom Tunnel	L&Y	45 B1
BROOKSBY	MID.	16 E3
BROOKWOOD	L&SW	5 C1
BROOKWOOD NECROPOLIS N. & S.	London Necropolis Co.	5 C1
BROOM JUNCTION	MID.	9 B4
BROOME	L&NW	14 C1
BROOMFIELD	SJ	26 D2
Broomfield Jcs.	CAL./NB	34 C2
BROOMFLEET	NE	22 E5
BROOMHILL	HR	36 F3
BROOMHILL	NE	31 G5
BROOMHOUSE	NB	44 C3
Broomhouse Tunnel	MID.	41 B2
BROOMIEKNOWE	NB	30 C2
BROOMIELAW	NE	27 E4
BROOMLEE	NB	30 D3
BRORA	HR	38 G5
Brotherton Tubular Bridge	NE	42 B1
BROTTON	NE	28 E3
BROUGH	NE	22 E4
BROUGHTON	CAL.	30 E3
BROUGHTON	FUR.	24 A5
BROUGHTON ASTLEY	MID.	16 G4
BROUGHTON CROSS	L&NW	26 E3
BROUGHTON HALL	L&NW	20 D4
BROUGHTON LANE	MS&L	42 G2
BROUGHTY FERRY	D&AJt	34 E1
Broughty Ferry Pier	D&AJt	34 E1
BROWNHILLS	L&NW	15 F4
BROWNHILLS	MID.	15 F4
Brownqueen Tunnel	GW	1 D3
BROXBOURNE & HODDESDON	GE	11 F3
Broxbourne Jc.	GE	11 F3
Broxburn (Goods)	NB	30 B3
BROXTON	L&NW	20 E3
BRUCE GROVE	GE	40 A4
BRUCKLAY	GNoS	37 D4
BRUNDALL	GE	18 F2

Station, junction, tunnel, viaduct, etc	Railway	Reference	Station, junction, tunnel, viaduct, etc	Railway	Reference
CAERSWS	CAM.	14 C3	CARDENDEN	NB	30 A2
CAERWYS	M&DJn.	20 D5	CARDIFF	GW	43 B4 (f9)
CAHER	W&L	49 C1	CARDIFF	Rhym.	43 B4
CAIRNHILL BRIDGE	NB	44 B4	CARDIFF (QUEEN STREET)	TV	43 B4 (f8)
CAISTER	E&M	18 E1	Cardiff Adam Street (Goods)	Rhym.	43 B4
CALBOURNE & SHALFLEET	FY&N	4 F4	Cardiff Docks	GW	43 B5
CALCOTS	GNoS	36 C1	Cardiff Docks	Rhym.	43 B5
CALDARVAN	F&CJn	29 B4	CARDIFF DOCKS	TV	43 B5
CALDER	CAL.	44 B4	Cardiff Docks	TV	43 B5
CALDERBANK	CAL.	44 A3	Cardiff Riverside Branch	GW	43 B4 (f11)
Calderbank	NB	44 A3	CARDIGAN	W&C	13 E2
Calderbank Branch Jc.	NB	44 A4	Cardigan Jc.	GW/P&T	7 A1
Calderbank Iron Works	CAL.	44 A3	CARDINGTON	MID.	11 D1
CALDERCRUIX	NB	30 C5	CARDONALD	G&PJt	44 F3
Caldew Jc.	CAL./GTC	26 D1	CARDRONA	NB	30 D2
Caldon Low	NS	15 C4	CARDROSS	NB	29 B3
CALDWELL	GB&KJt	29 D4	Cargan	B&NC	61 C2
CALEDON	CVT	58 A5	CARGILL	CAL.	33 E5
Caledonian Road (Coal)	L&NW	40 B5 (f18)	CARGO FLEET	NE	28 E4
Caledonian Road (Goods)	GN	40 B5 (f19)	CARHAM	NE	31 D2
CALLANDER	CAL.	33 G2	CARISBROOKE	FY&N	4 F3
CALNE	Calne	3 A5	CARK-IN-CARTMEL	FUR.	24 B4
Calstock Quay	E.Corn. Min.	1 C5	CARLIN HOW	NE	28 E3
CALTHWAITE	L&NW	27 D1	CARLINGFORD	DN&G	58 D2
CALVELEY	L&NW	20 E3	CARLINGHOW	L&NW	42 B3
CALVERLEY & RODLEY	MID.	42 A4	Carlisle (Cattle)	L&NW	26 D1
CAM	MID.	9 F2	Carlisle (Goods)	CAL.	26 D1
CAMBERLEY & YORK TOWN			Carlisle (Goods)	L&NW	26 D1
for SANDHURST	L&SW	4 B1	Carlisle Bridge	LP&HC	60 C4
CAMBERWELL NEW ROAD	LC&D	40 D5	Carlisle Canal (Goods)	NB	26 D2
CAMBORNE	GW	1 E5	CARLISLE CITADEL (JOINT)	CSJC	26 D1
Cambria Jc.	LB&SC/LC&D	40 E4	Carlisle Crown Street (Goods)	M&C	26 D1
CAMBRIDGE	GE	11 C3	Carlisle Dentonholme (Goods)	DJt	26 D2
CAMBRIDGE HEATH	GE	40 C4	Carlisle London Road (Goods)	NE	26 D1
CAMBUS	NB	30 A5	Carlisle Petterill (Goods)	MID.	26 D1
CAMBUS O' MAY	GNoS	34 A4	CARLOW	GS&W	53 F5
CAMBUSLANG	CAL.	44 D3	CARLTON	HB&WRJn	21 E5
Cambuslang (Goods)	CAL.	44 D3	CARLTON	NE	28 E5
Camden (Goods)	L&NW	40 B5 (f33)	CARLTON & GEDLING	MID.	41 F5
CAMDEN ROAD	MID.	40 B5	CARLTON COLVILLE	GE	12 A1
CAMDEN TOWN	L&NW/NL	40 B5 (f36)	CARLTON MAIN COLLIERY PLATFORM	MID.	42 D2
CAMERON BRIDGE	NB	34 G5	Carlton Road Jc.	MID.	40 C1
CAMERTON	GW	8 D1	CARLTON-ON-TRENT	GN	16 B2
CAMERTON	L&NW	26 E3	CARLUKE	CAL.	30 D5
CAMERTON COLLIERY HALT	C&WJn	26 D3	CARMARTHEN	GW	13 G4
Camlachie (Goods)	NB	44 D3 (f13)	CARMARTHEN JUNCTION	GW	7 A2
CAMOLIN	DW&W	50 A3	CARMYLE	CAL.	44 D3
CAMP HILL & BALSALL HEATH	MID.	13 C4	Carmyllie	D&AJt	34 D3
Camp Hill Jc.	MID.	13 C4	CARN BREA	GW	1 E5
CAMPDEN	GW	9 C5	CARNABY	NE	22 B3
Campden Tunnel	GW	9 C5	CARNALEA	B&CD	61 F4
CAMPERDOWN	CAL.	34 E4	CARNARVON	L&NW	19 D2
Camperdown East Jc.	D&AJt/DHT/NB	34 E2	CARNFORTH	L&NW/FUR. & MID. Jt	24 B3
Camps	CAL.	30 C3	CARNO	CAM.	14 B4
Camps	NB	30 C3	CARNOUSTIE	D&AJt	34 E3
Campsie Branch Jc.	NB	44 D5	CARNTYNE	NB	44 D3
CAMPSIE GLEN	BV	29 B5	CARNWATH	CAL.	30 D4
CANADA DOCK	L&NW	45 G4	CARR MILL	L&NW	45 D3
Canal Jc.	L&NW/NE	21 B2	Carr Mill Jc.	L&NW	45 D3
Canal Jc.	NB/NE	26 D2	CARRICHUE	B&NC	60 C3
Canal Siding	MS&L	41 A4	CARRICKFERGUS	C&L	61 E4
CANNING TOWN	GE	40 C2	Carrickfergus Harbour	B&NC	61 E3
Canning Town (Goods)	L&NW	40 C2	CARRICKFERGUS JUNCTION	B&NC	61 E3
CANNOCK	L&NW	15 E4	CARRICKMACROSS	GN(I)	58 D5
CANNON STREET	MET.-DIS./MET.Jt	40 C5 (f14)	CARRICKMINES	DW&W	62 G1
CANNON STREET	SE	40 C4	CARRICKMORE (TYRONE)	GN(I)	60 F7
CANOBIE	NB	26 B1	CARRICK-ON-SHANNON	MGW	56 E1
CANONBURY	NL	40 B4	CARRICK-ON-SUIR	W&L	49 C3
Canonbury Jc.	NL/GN	40 B5	CARRIGALOE	GS&W	48 F1
CANTERBURY	LC&D	6 C3	CARRIGANS	GN(I)	60 C5
CANTERBURY	SE	6 C3	Carrignagat Jc.	MGW/SL&NC	56 C3
Canterbury Road Jc.	LC&D	40 E5	CARRIGROHANE	C&MLt	48 G3 (f2)
CANTLEY	GE	18 F2	CARRIGTOHILL	GS&W	48 G2
CAPECASTLE	Ballycastle	61 B1	CARROG	LI&C	20 F5
Capecastle Tunnel	Ballycastle	61 B1	CARROLL'S CROSS	WD&L	49 D4
CAPEL	GE	12 D4	CARRON	GNoS	36 E2
CAPENHURST	BIRK. Jt.	45 F5	CARRONBRIDGE	G&SW	30 G4
CAPPAGH	WD&L	49 E1	CARROWEN	Letterkenny	60 C5
CAPPOQUIN	WD&L	49 E1	CARRYCLOGHER	CVT	57 A4
CARBERRY	MGW	53 B5	CARSHALTON	LB&SC	5 C3
CARBIS BAY	GW	1 E4	CARSTAIRS	CAL.	30 D4
Carbus	Cornwall Minerals	1 D2	Carterhouse Jc.	L&NW	45 D4
CARCROFT & ADWICK-LE-STREET	WR&GJt	21 F4	CARTSDYKE	CAL.	29 B3

Station, junction, tunnel, viaduct, etc	Railway	Reference
CARVILLE	NE	28 B5 (f3)
CASSILLIS	G&SW	29 F3
CASTLE ASHBY & EARL'S BARTON	L&NW	10 B2
CASTLE BERNARD	CB&SC	50 F4
CASTLE BROMWICH	MID.	15 G5
CASTLE CARY	GW	3 C3
CASTLE DONINGTON	MID.	16 D4
CASTLE DOUGLAS	G&SW	26 C5
Castle Douglas Branch Jc.	G&SW	26 B4
CASTLE EDEN	NE	28 D5
CASTLE EDEN COLLIERY	NE	28 D5
CASTLE HILL (EALING DEAN)	GW	39 C2
Castle Hill Tunnel	L&Y	21 E1
CASTLE HOWARD	NE	22 B5
Castle Jc.	NE	28 A1
CASTLE KENNEDY	P&WJt	25 C2
CASTLEBAR	GN&W	55 E5
CASTLEBELLINGHAM	GN(I)	58 E4
CASTLEBLANEY	GN(I)	58 C5
CASTLECALDWELL	EB&S	59 F4
CASTLECARY	NB	30 B5
CASTLECONNELL	W&L	48 A3
CASTLEDAWSON	B&NC	60 E1
CASTLEDERG	C&VBT	60 E5
CASTLEFINN	FV	60 D5
CASTLEFORD	L&Y	42 B1
CASTLEFORD	NE	42 B1
Castlehill (Goods)	NB	30 D5
CASTLEISLAND	GS&W	47 D4
CASTLEMAINE	GS&W	47 E3
CASTLEREA	GN&W	56 F3
CASTLEROCK	B&NC	60 B2
Castlerock Tunnel	B&NC	60 B2
CASTLETHORPE	L&NW	10 C2
CASTLETON	L&Y	45 A1
CASTLETON	NE	28 F3
Castleton North, South & West Jcs.	L&Y	45 A2
CASTLETOWN	IoM	23 C2
CASTLETOWN	MGW	53 A3
CASTLETOWNROCHE	GS&W	48 E3
CASTOR	L&NW	11 A1
CATERHAM	SE	5 C3
CATFIELD	E&M	18 E2
CATFORD BRIDGE	SE	40 E3
CATHCART	CD	44 E3
CATON	MID.	24 B3
CATTAL	NE	21 C4
CATTERICK BRIDGE	NE	27 F5
Cattewater Harbour	L&SW	1 A2
Cattle Sidings Jc.	MID.	41 G2
CATTON ROAD	NE	27 C3
CAULDCOTS	NB	34 D3
CAUSELAND	L&L	1 D4
CAUSEWAYEND	NB	30 B4
CAUSEWAYHEAD	NB	30 A5
CAVAN	MGW	57 D3
CAVENDISH	GE	11 D5
CAWSTON	GE	18 E3
CAYTHORPE	GN	16 C1
CAYTON	NE	22 A3
CEFN	B&M & L&NW Jt.	43 C1
CEFN	GW	20 F4
CEFN-Y-BEDD	WM&CQ	20 E4
Cemetery Jcs.	NE	28 D4
CEMMES	Mawddwy	14 B4
CEMMES ROAD	CAM.	14 B5
CERNEY & ASHTON KEYNES	M&SWJn.	9 F4
Ceryst	Van	14 C4
CHACEWATER	GW	1 E1
Chaddesden Sidings	MID.	41 G2
CHADWELL HEATH	GE	5 A4
CHALFONT ROAD	MET.	10 F1
CHALK FARM	L&NW	39 B5
CHALK FARM	NL	39 B5 (f32)
Challoch Jc.	P&WJt/A&W	25 C3
CHALLOW	GW	10 F5
Chaloners Whin Jc.	NE	21 A4
CHANDLER'S FORD	L&SW	4 D4
CHAPEL	DW&W	50 C5
CHAPEL-EN-LE-FRITH	L&NW	15 A4
CHAPEL-EN-LE-FRITH	MID.	15 A4
CHAPELHALL	CAL.	44 A3
Chapelhall Iron Works	CAL.	44 A3

Station, junction, tunnel, viaduct, etc	Railway	Reference
CHAPELIZOD	D&LST	62 C5
CHAPELTON	L&SW	7 F3
CHAPELTOWN	MS&L	42 F2
CHAPPEL	CSVS&H	12 E5
CHARD JOINT	GW/L&SW	3 E1
CHARD JUNCTION	L&SW	3 E1
CHARD TOWN	L&SW	3 E1
CHARFIELD for WOTTON-UNDER-EDGE	MID.	9 F2
CHARING	LC&D	6 C4
CHARING CROSS	MET.-DIS.	40 C5
CHARING CROSS	NB	44 E4
CHARING CROSS	SE	40 D5
CHARLBURY	GW	10 D5
Charlestown	NB	30 B3
CHARLEVILLE	GS&W	48 C4
Charleville Jc.	GS&W	48 C3
CHARLTON	SE	40 D2
CHARLTON KINGS	Banbury & Chelt. Dir.	9 D4
Charlton Tunnel	LC&D	6 D2
CHARTHAM	SE	6 C3
CHARTLEY	GN	15 D4
Chasetown	CC&W	15 E4
CHATBURN	L&Y	24 D1
CHATHAM	LC&D	6 B5
Chatham Dockyard	LC&D	6 B5
Chatham Tunnel	LC&D	6 B5
CHATHILL	NE	31 E5
CHATTERIS	GN&GEJt.	11 A3
CHATTERLEY	NS	15 C3
CHEADLE	CLC	45 A4
CHEADLE	L&NW	45 A4
CHEADLE HULME	L&NW	45 A4
CHEAM	LB&SC	5 C3
CHEAPSIDE	Jersey	46 E3
CHECKER HOUSE	MS&L	16 A3
CHEDDAR	GW	8 E2
CHEDDINGTON	L&NW	10 E1
CHEDDLETON	NS	15 C4
Cheddleton Jc.	NS	15 C4
Chee Tor Tunnels	MID.	15 A5
Cheesewring Quarry	L&C	1 C4
CHELFORD	L&NW	45 B5
CHELLASTON	MID.	16 D5
CHELMSFORD	GE	11 F5
CHELSEA	WLEJt	39 D5
Chelsea Basin	WLEJt	39 D5
Chelsea Basin Jc.	WLEJt	39 D5
CHELSFIELD	SE	5 C4
CHELTENHAM	GW	9 D4
CHELTENHAM	MID.	9 D3
CHELTENHAM HIGH STREET	MID.	9 D4
CHEPSTOW	GW	8 B2
Chepstow Tubular Bridge	GW	8 B2
CHEQUERBENT	L&NW	45 C2
CHERRY BURTON	NE	22 D4
CHERRY TREE	L&Y	24 E2
Cherryville Jc.	GS&W	53 D5
CHERTSEY	L&SW	5 B1
CHESHAM	MET.	10 F1
CHESHUNT	GE	11 G3
CHESTER Joint	L&NW/GW	20 D4
Chester Line Jc.	L&NW	20 E2
CHESTER NORTHGATE	CLC	20 D4
CHESTER ROAD	L&NW	15 F5
CHESTER TICKET PLATFORM	BIRK. Jt.	20 D4
CHESTERFIELD	MID.	41 C2
CHESTER-LE-STREET	NE	27 C5
Chetwynd Viaduct	CB&SC	50 E3
CHEVINGTON	NE	31 G5
CHICHESTER	LB&SC	4 E1
CHICKENLEY HEATH	GN	42 C3
CHIGWELL LANE	GE	11 G3
CHILCOMPTON	S&D Jt.	3 B3
Chilcompton Tunnel	S&D Jt.	3 B3
CHILD'S HILL & CRICKLEWOOD	MID.	39 B4
CHILDWALL	CLC	45 E4
CHILHAM	SE	6 C3
CHILTERN GREEN	MID.	11 F1
CHILVERS COTON	L&NW	16 G5
CHILWORTH & ALBURY	SE	5 D1
CHINGFORD	GE	5 A4
CHINLEY	MID.	15 A4
CHINNOR	GW	10 F2

Station, junction, tunnel, viaduct, etc	Railway	Reference	Station, junction, tunnel, viaduct, etc	Railway	Reference
CHIPPENHAM	GW	3 A4	CLAYGATE	L&SW	5 C2
Chippenham Jc.	E&N/GE	11 C4	CLAYPOLE	GN	16 C2
CHIPPING NORTON	GW	10 D5	CLAYTON	GN	42 B5
CHIPPING NORTON JUNCTION	GW	9 D5	CLAYTON BRIDGE	L&Y	45 A3 (f28)
Chirk	GVT	20 F4	Clayton Tunnel	LB&SC	5 F3
CHIRK	GW	20 F4	CLAYTON WEST	L&Y	42 D3
Chirk Viaduct	GW	20 F4	CLEADON LANE	NE	28 C5
Chirmorie Summit	A&W	25 B3	CLEATOR MOOR	C&WJn	26 F3
CHIRNSIDE	NB	31 C3	CLEATOR MOOR	WC&EJt	26 F3
CHISELDON	M&SWJn	9 G5	Cleator Moor (Goods)	WC&EJt	26 F3
CHISLEHURST	SE	40 F2	CLECKHEATON	L&Y	42 B4
Chislehurst Tunnel	SE	40 F2	Clee Hill	Ludlow & Clee Hill	9 A1
CHISWICK & GROVE PARK	L&SW	39 D3	CLEETHORPES	MS&L	22 F2
Chiswick Jc.	L&SW	39 D3	CLEEVE	MID.	9 D3
CHISWICK PARK & ACTON GREEN	MET.-DIS.	39 D3 (f25)	CLEGHORN	CAL.	30 D4
CHITTISHAM	GE	11 B4	CLELAND	CAL.	44 A2
Chobham Farm Jc.	GE	40 B3	CLENCHWARTON	E&M	17 E4
CHOLLERFORD	NB	27 B3	CLEOBURY MORTIMER	GW	9 A2
CHOLLERTON	NB	27 B3	Cleuch (Lower)	CAL.	30 D4
CHOPPINGTON	NE	27 A5	CLEVEDON	GW	8 D3
CHORLEY	L&Y	45 D1	CLEVELEYS	L&Y & L&NWJt	24 D4
CHORLEY WOOD	MET.	10 F1	CLIBURN	NE	27 E1
CHORLTON-CUM-HARDY	MID.	45 B3	CLIFF COMMON	NE	21 D5
CHOWBENT	L&NW	45 C2	CLIFFE	SE	6 B5
CHRISTCHURCH	L&SW	4 F5	CLIFFORD	Golden Valley	14 E2
Christleton Tunnel	L&NW	20 D3	CLIFTON	BP&P	3 G1
CHRISTON BANK	NE	31 E5	CLIFTON	NE	27 E1
CHUDLEIGH	GW	2 C3	CLIFTON	NS	15 C5
CHURCH	L&Y	24 E1	CLIFTON & LOWTHER	L&NW	27 E1
CHURCH CROSS	S&SLt	49 G4	CLIFTON BRIDGE	GW	3 G1
CHURCH FENTON	NE	21 D4	CLIFTON DOWN	BP&P	3 F1
CHURCH ROAD	B&M	43 B3	CLIFTON JUNCTION	L&Y	45 B2
CHURCH ROAD	MID.	13 C3	Clifton Maybank (Goods)	GW	3 E2
Church Road Jcs.	GN(I)/GS&W/L&NW	62 C3	Clifton Maybank Jc.	GW	3 D2
CHURCH SIDING	O&AT	10 E3	CLIFTON MILL	L&NW	10 A4
CHURCH STRETTON	S&HJt	14 B1	CLIFTON ROAD (BRIGHOUSE)	L&Y	42 C4
CHURCH VILLAGE	TV	43 C3	Climpy	CAL.	30 C4
CHURCHDOWN	GW/MID.	9 D3	CLIPSTON & OXENDON	L&NW	16 G3
CHURCHILL & BLAKEDOWN	GW	9 A3	CLITHEROE	L&Y	24 D1
CHURCHTOWN	WLancs	45 F1	CLOCK FACE	L&NW	45 D4
CHURN	DN&S	10 G4	CLOCKSBRIGGS	A&F	34 D4
CHURSTON	GW	2 D3	CLOGHER	CVT	57 A4
CHURWELL	L&NW	42 B3	CLOGHROE	C&MLt	48 G3
CHWILOG	L&NW	19 F1	CLONAKILTY	CB&SC	50 G5
CILFREW PLATFORM	N&B	43 F2	CLONAKILTY JUNCTION	CB&SC	50 F4
Cilfynydd	TV	43 C3	CLONDALKIN	GS&W	54 B3
CILMERY	L&NW	14 E3	CLONDALKIN ROAD	D&BST	54 C3
Cilyrychen or Limestone Branch	GW	43 G1	CLONDULANE	F&L	48 E1
CINDERFORD	S&WJt	8 A1	CLONES	GN(I)	57 C4
CIRENCESTER	GW	9 E4	Clones East Jc.	GN(I)	57 C4
CIRENCESTER	M&SWJn.	9 F4	CLONHUGH	MGW	53 A3
CLACHNAHARRY	HR	36 D5	CLONMEL	W&L	49 C2
CLACKMANNAN	NB	30 A4	CLONSILLA JUNCTION	MGW	54 B3
CLACTON-ON-SEA	GE	12 F3	CLOSEBURN	G&SW	26 A4
CLADY	FV	60 D5	Cloud Hill	MID.	16 E4
CLANDON & RIPLEY	L&SW	5 C1	CLOUGH FOLD	L&Y	24 E1
CLAPHAM	MID.	24 B1	CLOUGH ROAD	B&NC	61 C2
CLAPHAM & NORTH STOCKWELL	LC&D	40 E5	CLOUGHJORDAN	GS&W	52 F1
CLAPHAM JUNCTION	L&SW	39 F2	CLOUGHTON	Sc&Wby	28 G1
CLAPHAM JUNCTION	LB&SC	39 F2	CLOVENFORDS	NB	30 E1
CLAPHAM JUNCTION	WLEJt	39 F3	CLOWN	MID.	41 B4
CLAPTON	GE	40 B4	CLUNES	HR	35 D5
Clapton Jc.	GE	40 B4	CLUTTON	GW	8 D1
CLARA	GS&W	53 B2	CLYDACH	L&NW	43 B1
CLARA	MGW	53 B2	Clydach Vale (Goods)	EV	43 D3
Clara & Banagher Jc.	GS&W/C&Ba	53 B2	Clyde Jc.	CoGU	44 E2
CLARBESTON ROAD	GW	13 G1	CLYDEBANK	GY&C	44 F4
Clarborough Jc.	MS&L	16 A2	CLYNDERWEN	GW	13 G2
Clarborough Tunnel	MS&L	16 A2	COACHFORD	C&MLt	48 G4
CLARE	GE	11 D5	COACHFORD JUNCTION	C&MLt	48 G3 (f1)
CLARE CASTLE	L&E	52 F5	Coal Yard Jc.	L&NW/WLEJt	39 F3
CLAREMORRIS for BALLINROBE	GN&W	56 F5	COALBROOKDALE	GW	15 F2
Clarence Yard (Goods)	GN	40 B5	Coalburn	CAL.	30 E5
CLARENCE YARD, GOSPORT	L&SW	4 E2 (f2)	COALEY	MID.	9 F2
CLARKSTON	CAL.	44 E2	COALISLAND	GN(I)	60 G1
CLARKSTON	NB	44 A4	Coalpit Heath Col.	MID.	8 C1
CLATFORD	L&SW	4 C4	COALPORT	GW	15 F2
CLAVERDON	GW	9 B5	COALPORT	L&NW	15 F2
CLAY CROSS	MID.	41 C2	COALVILLE	MID.	16 E4
Clay Cross (Goods)	MID.	41 D2	COALVILLE EAST	CF	16 E4
Clay Cross Tunnel	MID.	41 D2	COANWOOD	NE	27 C2
CLAYDON	GE	12 D4	COATBRIDGE	CAL.	44 B4
CLAYDON	L&NW	10 D3	COATBRIDGE CENTRAL	NB	44 B4

Station, junction, tunnel, viaduct, etc	Railway	Reference	Station, junction, tunnel, viaduct, etc	Railway	Reference
COATBRIDGE SUNNYSIDE	NB	44 B4	CONGLETON	NS	15 B3
COATDYKE	NB	44 B4	Congleton Brunswick Street (Goods)	NS	15 B3
COBBINSHAW	CAL.	30 C4	CONGRESBURY	GW	8 D3
COBHAM	L&SW	5 C2	CONISBOROUGH	MS&L	21 F4
COBORN ROAD for OLD FORD	GE	40 C3	CONISHEAD PRIORY	FUR.	24 B4
COBRIDGE	NS	15 C3	CONISTON LAKE	FUR.	26 G1
COCKBURNSPATH	NB	31 B2	CONNAH'S QUAY	L&NW	20 D4
COCKERHAM CROSSING	G&KE	24 C3	Connah's Quay (Goods)	Buckley	20 D4
COCKERMOUTH	CK&P	26 E3	CONNEL FERRY	C&O	32 E4
COCKETT	GW	43 G3	Conniberry Jc.	KJn/W&CI	53 E4
COCKFIELD	GE	12 C5	CONON	HR	35 D5
COCKFIELD	NE	27 E4	CONONLEY	MID.	21 C1
COCKING	LB&SC	4 D1	CONSETT & BLACKHILL	NE	27 C4
Cockley Brake Jc.	L&NW/N&BJn.	10 C4	CONSTABLE BURTON	NE	21 A2
CODFORD	GW	3 C5	CONWAY	L&NW	19 D3
CODNOR PARK	MID.	41 E3	Conway Tubular Bridge	L&NW	19 D3
CODNOR PARK & SELSTON	GN	41 E3	CONWIL	GW	13 G4
Codnor Park Jc.	MID./GN	41 E3	CONYNGHAM ROAD DEPOT	D&LST	62 C4
CODSALL	GW	15 F3	Cook Street Branch	G&SW	44 F2
Coed Poeth (Goods)	GW	20 E4	COOKHAM	GW	10 G2
Coed Talon	L&NW	20 E4	COOKSBRIDGE	LB&SC	5 F4
Coed-y-Gric Jc.	GW	43 A2	COOKSTOWN	B&NC	60 F2
COGAN	BD&R	43 B5	COOKSTOWN	GN(I)	60 F2
COGIE HILL CROSSING	G&KE	24 C3	COOKSTOWN JUNCTION	B&NC	61 E1
COLBINSTOWN	GS&W	54 E5	COOMBE	L&L	1 D4
COLBREN JUNCTION	N&B	43 E1	COOMBE & MALDEN	L&SW	39 F3
COLBY	IoM	23 C2	Coombe & Malden Goods	L&SW	39 F3
COLCHESTER	GE	12 E4	COOMBE LANE	LB&SC/SE Joint	5 C3
Colchester East Gate Jc.	CSVS&H/GE	12 E4	COOPER BRIDGE	L&Y	42 C4
COLD NORTON	GE	12 G5	COOTEHILL	GN(I)	57 D5
COLDHAM	GE	17 F3	Copenhagen Tunnel	GN	40 B5 (f44)
COLDSTREAM	NE	31 D3	COPGROVE	NE	21 B3
COLE	S&D Jt.	3 C3	COPLEY	L&Y	42 C5
COLE GREEN	GN	11 F2	Copley Hill (Goods)	L&NW	21 C2
COLEBROOKE	CVT	57 A3	COPMANTHORPE	NE	21 C5
COLEBURN	GNoS	36 D1	Copper Mill Jc.	GE	40 A4
COLEFORD	GW	8 A2	COPPLESTONE	L&SW	2 A4
COLEFORD	S&WJt	8 A2	COPPULL	L&NW	45 D1
Coleford Jc.	L&SW	2 B4	Copyhold Jc.	LB&SC	5 E3
COLEFORD JUNCTION PLATFORM	S&WJt	8 A1	CORBET	GN(I)	58 A3
Coleorton Col.	MID.	16 E4	Corbett's Lane Jc.	LB&SC/SE	40 D4
COLERAINE	B&NC	60 B1	CORBIERE	Jersey	46 E4
COLESHILL	MID.	15 G5	CORBRIDGE	NE	27 C4
COLFIN	P&WJt	25 C2	Corbridge Tunnel	NE	27 C4
COLINTON	CAL.	30 C2	CORBY	GN	16 D1
COLLEGE	NB	44 E2	Corby Tunnel	MID.	16 G2
College (Goods)	G&SW	44 E2 (f2)	CORFE CASTLE	L&SW	3 G5
College (Goods)	NB	44 E2	Corfe Mullen Jc.	S&D Jt.	3 F5
College or Sydney Street Jc.	NB/CoGU	44 E2 (f25)	CORGAR	CL&RLt	57 D1
COLLESSIE	NB	34 F5	CORK ALBERT QUAY	CB&SC	48 F3 (f5)
COLLIN HALT	B&NC	61 D2	CORK ALBERT STREET	CB&P	48 F3 (f6)
COLLINGBOURNE	M&SWJn.	4 B5	CORK CAPWELL	C&MD	48 F3
COLLINGHAM	MID.	16 B2	CORK GLANMIRE	GS&W	48 F3 (f4)
COLLINGHAM BRIDGE	NE	21 C4	CORK SUMMERHILL	GS&W	48 E3 (f7)
COLLINS GREEN	L&NW	45 D3	Cork Tunnel	GS&W	48 E3
COLLISTON	A&F	34 D3	CORK WESTERN ROAD	C&MLt	48 F3 (f8)
COLLOONEY	MGW	56 C3	CORNABRONE	CL&RLt	57 D1
COLLOONEY	SL&NC	56 C3	Cornbrook (Goods)	CLC	45 B3 (f73)
COLNBROOK	GW	5 B1	CORNHILL	GNoS	37 C2
COLNE	CV&H	12 E5	CORNHOLME	L&Y	24 E1
COLNE	L&Y/MID.	21 B1	Cornwall Jc.	GW	1 A2
COLTFIELD PLATFORM	HR	36 C2	CORNWOOD	GW	2 D5
COLTISHALL	GE	18 E3	COROFIN	WClare	52 E5
COLWALL	GW	9 C2	CORPUSTY & SAXTHORPE	E&M	18 D4
COLWICH	L&NW	15 E4	Corriemuillie Summit	HR	35 C4
Colwich East Jc.	L&NW	15 E4	CORRIS	Corris	14 B5
Colwich West Jc.	L&NW/NS	15 E4	CORRYLONGFORD	CVT	57 A3
COLWYN BAY	L&NW	19 D4	CORSEHILL	CAL.	26 B2
COLYFORD	L&SW	2 B1	CORSHAM	GW	3 A4
COLYTON TOWN	L&SW	2 B1	CORSTORPHINE	NB	30 B3
COLZIUM	K&B	30 B5	CORWEN	C&B	19 F5
Combe Down Tunnel	S&D Jt.	3 B3	CORYTON	GW	1 C5
COMBE ROW	West Somerset Mineral	8 F5	COSHAM	L&SW & LB&SC Jt.	4 E2
COMBER	B&CD	61 F4	Cosham Jc.	L&SW & LB&SC Jt.	4 E2
COMELEY PARK	NB	30 A3	COTEHILL	MID.	27 C1
Commercial Road (Goods)	LT&S	40 C4	COTHAM	GN	16 C2
Common Branch Jc.	TV	43 C4	COTHERSTONE	NE	27 E4
COMMONDALE SIDING	NE	28 F3	Coton Hill (Goods)	GW	15 E1
COMMONDYKE	G&SW	29 F5	COTTAM	MS&L	16 A2
COMMONHEAD (AIRDRIE NORTH)	NB	44 B4	COTTINGHAM	NE	22 D3
COMPTON	DN&S	10 G4	Cottingham Jc.	NE	22 D3
CONDER GREEN	L&NW	24 C3	COUGHTON	MID.	9 B4
CONDOVER	S&HJt	15 F1	COULSDON	SE	5 C3

Station, junction, tunnel, viaduct, etc	Railway	Reference	Station, junction, tunnel, viaduct, etc	Railway	Reference
COULTER	CAL.	30 E4	CROFT BANK	W&F	17 B4
COUNDEN ROAD	L&NW	10 A5	Croft Coal Depot	NE	28 F5
COUNDON	NE	27 E5	CROFTHEAD	NB	30 C4
COUNTER DRAIN	E&M	17 E2	CROFTON	L&Y	42 C2
COUNTESTHORPE	MID.	16 F3	CROFTON	M&C	26 C2
County March Summit	HR	38 D4	Crofton Jc.	L&Y/WR&GJt	42 C2
COUNTY SCHOOL	GE	18 E4	Crofty	GW	1 E5
COUPAR ANGUS	CAL.	34 D5	CROMDALE	GNoS	36 E2
Court House Jc.	MS&L/MID.	42 E2	CROMER	GE	18 D3
Court Sart Jc.	GW/SWMin.	43 F3	CROMER BEACH	E&M	18 D3
COVE	CAL.	37 G4	CROMFORD	MID.	41 D1
COVENTRY	L&NW	10 A5	Cromford (Goods)	L&NW	41 E1
COW BANK	W&F	17 B4	CROMORE	B&NC	60 B1
Cow Lane Jc.	LB&SC/LC&D	40 D4	Cromwell Curve North & East Jcs.	MET.-DIS.	39 D5
COWBIT	GN&GEJt.	17 E2	CRONBERRY	G&SW	29 F5
COWBRIDGE	TV	43 D4	CROOK	NE	27 D5
COWDEN	LB&SC	5 D4	CROOK OF DEVON	NB	30 A4
COWDENBEATH	NB	30 A3	CROOKSLING CROSSOVER	D&BST	54 C4
COWES	IoWC	4 F3	CROOKSTON	G&SW	44 F3
COWLAIRS	NB	44 E4	CROOKSTOWN ROAD	C&MD	50 E4
Cowlairs Jc.	NB	44 D4	CROOM	GS&W	48 B3
Cowley Bridge Jc.	GW/L&SW	2 B3	CROPREDY	GW	10 C4
COWTON	NE	28 F5	CROSBY	IoM	23 B2
COXBENCH	MID.	41 F2	CROSBY GARRETT	MID.	27 F2
COXGREEN	NE	28 C5	CROSS CHAPEL	D&BST	54 D4
COXHOE	NE	28 D5	CROSS GATES	NE	42 A2
COXHOE BRIDGE	NE	28 D5	Cross Gates Jc.	NE	42 A2
COXWOLD	NE	21 A4	Cross Guns Tunnel	MGW	62 B4
Craddock Lane (Goods)	L&Y	45 B2	Cross Hands	L&MM	7 A3
CRADLEY	GW	15 G4	CROSS INN	TV	43 C4
CRADOC	N&B	14 F3	CROSS KEYS	GW	43 B3
CRAIGAVAD	B&CD	61 F4	CROSS LANE	L&NW	45 B3 (f23)
CRAIGELLACHIE JUNCTION	GNoS	36 D1	CROSS ROADS	B&NC	61 C2
CRAIGENDORAN	NB	29 B3	CROSSDONEY	MGW	57 D3
Craighall (Goods)	NB	44 E4 (f17)	CROSSENS	WLancs	45 F1
CRAIGLEITH	CAL.	30 F3	Crossfield (Goods)	WC&EJt	26 F3
CRAIGLOCKHART	NB	30 G2	CROSSGAR	B&CD	58 A1
CRAIGMORE	B&NT	58 C3	CROSSGATES	NB	30 A3
CRAIGMYLE SIDING	GNoS	34 A3	CROSSHILL	CD	44 E1
Craigneuk Pits	CAL.	44 A3	CROSSHOUSE	G&SW	29 E4
CRAIGO	CAL.	34 C3	CROSSMICHAEL	P&WJt	26 B5
CRAIL	NB	34 F3	CROSSMYLOOF	GB&KJt	44 F1
CRAKEHALL	NE	21 A3	CROSTON	L&Y	45 E1
CRAMLINGTON	NE	27 B5	CROUCH END	GN	40 A5
CRANBROOKE	CVT	57 A3	CROUCH HILL	T&HJn	40 A5
Crane Street Jc.	L&NW/MID.	15 E3	Crow Nest Jc.	L&Y	45 C2
CRANFORD	KT&H	10 A1	CROW PARK	GN	16 B2
CRANK	L&NW	45 E3	CROWBOROUGH	LB&SC	5 E5
CRANLEIGH	LB&SC	5 D2	CROWCOMBE	West Somerset	8 F4
CRANMORE	GW	3 C3	CROWDEN	MS&L	42 F5
Cransley	MID.	10 A2	Crowhurst Jc.	LB&SC/SE Joint	5 D4
CRATHES	GNoS	34 A2	CROWLE	MS&L	22 F5
CRATLOE	L&E	48 A4	Crows Nest Lead Mine	Snailbeach Dist.	14 B1
CRAUGHWELL & LOUGHREA	A&EJn	52 C4	Crowthorn Jc.	L&NW/OA&G	21 A2
CRAVEN ARMS & STOKESAY	S&HJt	14 C1	CROXALL	MID.	15 E5
CRAWLEY	LB&SC	5 D3	CROXDALE	NE	27 D5
CRAY	N&B	14 G4	CROY	NB	30 B5
CRAYFORD	SE	5 B4	CROYDON (ADDISCOMBE ROAD)	SE	40 G4
CREAGH	CL&RLt	57 D1	CROYDON CENTRAL	LB&SC	5 C3
CREDENHILL	MID.	14 F1	Cruckmeole Jc.	S&WpJt.	14 A1
CREDITON	L&SW	2 B4	CRUDGINGTON	GW	15 E2
Creech Jc.	GW	8 F4	CRUMLIN	GN(I)	61 F2
CREETOWN	P&WJt	25 C4	CRUMLIN HIGH LEVEL	GW	43 B2
CRESSAGE	GW	15 F1	CRUMLIN LOW LEVEL	GW	43 B2
Cressbrook Tunnel	MID.	15 A5	Crumlin Viaduct	GW	43 B2
CRESSINGTON & GRASSENDALE	CLC	45 F4	CRUMPSALL	L&Y	45 A2
CRESSWELL	NS	15 D4	CRUSHEEN	A&EJn	52 E5
CREW	C&VBT	60 E5	CRYMMYCH ARMS	W&C	13 F2
Crew Jc.	CAL.	30 F3	CRYNANT	N&B	43 E2
CREWE	L&NW	20 E2	CRYSTAL PALACE	LB&SC	40 F4
CREWKERNE	L&SW	3 E1	CRYSTAL PALACE HIGH LEVEL	LC&D	40 F4
CRIANLARICH	C&O	32 F1	CUDDINGTON	CLC	45 D5
CRICCIETH	CAM.	19 F2	CUDWORTH	HB&WRJn	42 D1
Crick Tunnel	L&NW	10 A3	CUDWORTH	MID.	42 E1
CRICKLADE	M&SWJn	9 F5	Cudworth (Goods)	HB&WRJn	42 D2
CRIEFF	CAL.	33 F3	Cudworth North & South Jcs.	HB&WRJn	42 D2
CRIEFF JUNCTION	CAL.	33 F4	Cudworth North & South Jcs.	MID.	42 D2
CRIGGLESTONE	L&Y	42 D3	CUILHILL	NB	44 C3
CRILLY	CVT	57 A5	CULCHETH	WJn	45 C3
Crimple Jc.	NE	21 C3	CULGAITH	MID.	27 E1
Crimple Tunnel	NE	21 C3	Culgaith Tunnel	MID.	27 E1
CROFT	L&NW	16 F4	CULHAM	GW	10 F4
CROFT	NE	28 F5	CULKERTON	GW	9 F3

Station, junction, tunnel, viaduct, etc	Railway	Reference
CULLEN	GNoS	37 C1
CULLERCOATS	NE	28 B5
CULLINGWORTH	GN	42 A5
CULLODEN	HR	36 D5
CULLOMPTON	GW	2 A2
CULLOVILLE	GN(I)	58 D5
CULLYBACKEY	B&NC	61 D1
CULMORE	B&NC	60 C4
CULMSTOCK	GW	2 A2
CULRAIN	HR	35 A5
CULTER	GNoS	37 G3
CULTRA	B&CD	61 F4
CULTS	GNoS	37 G4
Culver Jc.	LB&SC	5 F4
CUMBER	CVT	57 A5
CUMBERNAULD	CAL.	44 B5
Cumberworth Tunnel	L&Y	42 D3
CUMMERSDALE	M&C	26 C1
CUMMERTREES	G&SW	26 B3
CUMNOCK	G&SW	29 F5
CUMWHINTON	MID.	26 C1
CUNNINGHAMHEAD	G&SW	29 D3
CUPAR	NB	34 F4
CURLAGH	CVT	57 A5
CURLING POND HALT	CAL.	33 F3
CURRAGH MAIN LINE	GS&W	54 D5
CURRAGH RACECOURSE	GS&W	54 D5
CURRIE	CAL.	30 C3
CURRIE HILL	CAL.	30 C3
Currock Jc.	M&C	26 D2
CURSIS STREAM	D&LST	54 B3 (f2)
CURTHWAITE	M&C	26 C1
Curzon Street Jc.	L&NW/MID.	13 C4
CUSTOM HOUSE	GE	40 C2
Cutsyke Jc.	L&Y/NE	42 B1
CUXTON	SE	6 B5
CWM	GW	43 B2
Cwm Aman (Goods)	GW	43 D2
CWM BARGOED	TBJt.	43 C2
Cwm Blawd	L&MM	7 A3
Cwm Branch	L&NW	19 D5
CWM CLYDACH	MID.	43 F2
Cwm Trwgl	GJ&P	19 E2
CWMAVON	GW	43 A2
CWMAVON	R&SB	43 F3
Cwmbach	Aberdare	43 C2
Cwmbach Jc.	Aberdare	43 C2
CWMBRAN	GW	43 A3
Cwmbran Jc.	GW	43 A3
Cwmffrwdoer	GW	43 A2
Cwmffrwyd	GW	43 B2
Cwmmawr	BP&GV	7 A3
Cwmnantddu	GW	43 B2
Cwmtillery Branch	GW	43 B2
CWM-Y-GLO	L&NW	19 E2
CYMMER	R&SB	43 E3
CYMMER	SWMin.	43 E2
Cymmer East Jc.	GW/R&SB	43 E3
CYMMER for GLYNCORRWG	GW	43 E3
Cymmer West Jc.	GW/SWMin.	43 E3
CYNGHORDY	L&NW	14 F5
Cynheidre	L&MM	7 A3
CYNWYD	C&B	19 F5
DACRE	NE	21 B2
Dafen	GW	7 B3
DAGENHAM	LT&S	5 A4
DAGGENS ROAD	L&SW	3 E5
DAILLY	G&SW	29 G3
Dainton Summit	GW	2 D4
Dainton Tunnel	GW	2 D3
DAIRSIE	NB	34 F4
Dairy Coates Jc.	NE	22 A2
DAISY BANK	GW	13 A1
DAISY HILL	L&Y	45 C2
DAISYFIELD	L&Y	24 D2
DALBEATTIE	G&SW	26 C4
DALCROSS	HR	36 D4
Dalderse (Goods)	NB	30 B4
DALGUISE	HR	33 D4
DALHOUSIE	NB	30 C2
DALKEITH	NB	30 C2
DALKEY	D&K	54 C2
Dalkey Tunnel	DW&W	54 C2
Dallam Branch Jc.	L&NW	45 D4
DALMALLY	C&O	32 F2
DALMELLINGTON	G&SW	29 G4
DALMENY	NB	30 B3
Dalmonach	F&CJn	29 B4
DALMUIR	NB	44 G5
DALNASPIDAL	HR	33 C2
DALREOCH	NB	29 B3
DALRY	G&SW	29 D3
Dalry Jc.	CAL.	30 G2
Dalry Jc.	G&SW	29 D3
DALRYMPLE	G&SW	29 F3
Dalrymple Jc.	G&SW	29 F3
DALSTON	M&C	26 C1
Dalston East & West Jcs.	NL	40 B4
DALSTON JUNCTION	NL	40 B4
DALTON	FUR.	24 B5
DALTON JUNCTION	NE	28 F5
DALWHINNIE	HR	33 B2
DAMEMS	MID.	21 D1
DANBY	NE	28 F3
DANBY WISKE	NE	28 G5
DANDALEITH	GNoS	36 D1
DARCY LEVER	L&Y	45 B2
Dare Jc.	GW	43 D2
Dare Valley Jc.	Aberdare/GW	43 D2
DARESBURY	BIRK. Jt.	45 D4
DARFIELD	MID.	42 E1
DARLASTON & JAMES BRIDGE	L&NW	13 A2
DARLEY	MID.	41 D1
DARLEY	NE	21 C2
DARLINGTON BANK TOP	NE	28 F5
DARLINGTON NORTH ROAD	NE	28 E5
DARNALL	MS&L	42 G1
DARRAN & DERI	Rhym.	43 C2
DARSHAM	GE	12 B2
DARTFORD	SE	5 B5
DARTON	L&Y	42 D3
DARWEN	L&Y	24 E2
DATCHET	L&SW	5 B1
DAUNTSEY	GW	9 G4
DAVA	HR	36 E3
Dava Summit	HR	36 E3
DAVENPORT	L&NW	45 A4
DAVENTRY	L&NW	10 B3
DAWLISH	GW	2 C3
DAYBROOK	GN	41 F5
DDUALLT	Fest.	19 F3
DEADWATER	NB	31 G1
DEAL	SE	6 C1
Deal Jc.	LC&D	6 D2
DEAN	L&SW	4 D5
DEAN LANE (NEWTON HEATH)	L&Y	45 A2
Deansgate Jc.	MSJ&A/CLC	45 B4
Deanshanger	WSS&D	10 C2
DEARHAM	M&C	26 D3
DEARHAM BRIDGE	M&C	26 D3
Dearne Jc.	S&KJt	42 E1
Dee Viaduct	GW	20 F4
DEEPCAR for STOCKSBRIDGE	MS&L	42 F3
DEEPDALE	L&Y & L&NWJt	24 D3
DEEPFIELDS	L&NW	13 A1
DEFFORD	MID.	9 C3
DEGANWY	L&NW	19 C3
DEIGHTON	L&NW	42 C4
DELAMERE	CLC	20 D3
DELNY	HR	36 C5
DELPH	L&NW	21 F1
DENBIGH	L&NW	19 D5
DENBY	MID.	41 F2
DENBY DALE & CUMBERWORTH	L&Y	42 D3
DENHOLME	GN	42 A5
DENMARK HILL	LB&SC	40 E4
DENNY	CAL.	30 B5
Denny West Jc.	CAL.	30 B5
DENNYLOANHEAD	K&B	30 B5
DENSTONE CROSSING	NS	15 C5
DENT	MID.	24 A1
DENTON	L&NW	45 A3
Denton Jc.	L&NW	21 B2
DENVER	GE	17 F4
DEPTFORD	L&G	40 D3

Station, junction, tunnel, viaduct, etc	Railway	Reference	Station, junction, tunnel, viaduct, etc	Railway	Reference
DEPTFORD ROAD	EL	40 D4	DODWORTH	MS&L	42 E3
Deptford Wharf	LB&SC	40 D3	DOE HILL	MID.	41 D3
DERBY	MID.	41 G2	DOGDYKE	GN	17 C2
Derby (Cattle)	GN	41 G1	DOLAU	L&NW	14 D3
Derby (Cattle)	MID.	41 G2	DOLDOWLOD	Mid-Wales	14 D4
Derby (Goods)	L&NW	41 G2	DOLGARROG	L&NW	19 D3
DERBY FRIAR GATE	GN	41 G1	DOLGELLY	GW	14 A5
Derby Friar Gate (Goods)	GN	41 G2	DOLGOCH	Talyllyn	13 B5
DERBY NOTTINGHAM ROAD	MID.	41 G2	DOLLAR	NB	30 A4
DERBY ROAD	GE	12 D3	DOLPHINTON	CAL.	30 D3
Derby St. Mary's Bridge Wharf	MID.	41 G2	DOLPHINTON	NB	30 D3
DEREEN	CL&RLt	57 E1	DOLWEN	CAM.	14 C3
DEREHAM	GE	18 E4	DOLWYDDELEN	L&NW	19 E3
Deri Jc.	B&M/Rhym.	43 C2	DOLYGAER	B&M	43 C1
DERRY ORMOND	M&M	13 E5	DOLYHIR	K&E	14 E2
DERRYORK	L&D	60 C2	Dolywern	GVT	20 F5
DERSINGHAM	H&WN	17 D5	DON BRIDGE	Jersey	46 E4
DERVOCK	Ballycastle	61 B1	Don Pedro Col.	MID.	42 C1
DERWEN	L&NW	19 E5	DON STREET	GNoS	37 F4
Derwent Iron Works	C&WJn	26 E4	DONABATE	GN(I)	54 A2
Derwenthaugh (Goods)	NE	28 A2	DONAGHADEE	B&CD	61 F5
DERWYDD ROAD	GW	43 G1	DONAGHMORE	GN(I)	60 G2
DESBOROUGH for ROTHWELL	MID.	16 G2	DONAMON	GN&W	56 G2
Desborough Summit	MID.	16 G2	DONCASTER	GN	21 G2
DESERT	CB&SC	50 F4	Doncaster Cherry Tree Lane (Goods)	MID.	21 G2
DESERTMARTIN	Drap.	60 E1	Doncaster Marsh Gate (Goods)	MS&L	21 G2
DESFORD	MID.	16 F4	Doncaster North Jc.	GN/MS&L	21 G2
DESS	GNoS	37 G2	Doncaster South Jc.	GN/MS&L	21 G2
Deviation Jc.	NE	28 F2	DONEGAL	WD	59 E4
DEVIZES	GW	3 B5	DONINGTON ROAD	GN&GEJt.	17 D2
DEVON ROAD	L&K	47 C5	DONINGTON-ON-BAIN	GN	17 A2
DEVONPORT	GW	1 A1	DONISTHORPE	A&NJt	16 E5
DEVONPORT	L&SW	1 A1	DONNINGTON	L&NW	15 E2
Devonport (Goods)	L&SW	1 A1	DOONISKEY	C&MD	50 E4
Devonport Jc.	GW/L&SW	1 A1	DORCHESTER	GW	3 F3
Devonshire Tunnel	S&D Jt.	3 B3	DORCHESTER	L&SW	3 F3
DEVYNOCK	N&B	14 F4	Dorchester (Goods)	L&SW	3 F3
DEW SIDING	Golden Valley	14 F2	Dorchester Jc.	GW	3 F3
DEWSBURY	GN	42 C3	DORE & TOTLEY	MID.	41 A1
DEWSBURY	L&NW	42 C3	DORKING	LB&SC	5 C2
DEWSBURY	L&Y	42 C3	DORKING	SE	5 C2
Dewsbury East Jc.	L&Y	42 C3	DORMANS	LB&SC	5 D4
Dewsbury Jc.	L&Y/L&NW	42 C4	DORNOCK	G&SW	26 B2
DICCONSON LANE	L&Y	45 C2	DORRINGTON	S&HJt	15 F1
DIDCOT	GW	10 F4	DORSTONE	Golden Valley	14 F1
Didcot East Jc.	GW/DN&S	10 F4	DOUBLEBOIS	GW	1 D4
Didcot North & West Jcs.	GW	10 F4	DOUGLAS	CAL.	30 E5
DIDSBURY	MID.	45 A3	DOUGLAS	IoM	23 C3
DIGBY	GN&GEJt.	17 C1	Douglas Viaduct	CB&P	48 F2
DIGGLE	L&NW	21 F1	DOUNE	CAL.	33 G3
Diggle Jc.	L&NW	21 F1	Doura Main Col.	G&SW	29 D3
Diggles South Col.	L&NW	45 C3	DOUSLAND	Princetown	2 C5
Diglake Jc.	NS	15 C3	DOVE HOLES	L&NW	15 A4
Dinas	Fest.	19 F3	Dove Holes Tunnel	MID.	15 A4
DINAS	TV	43 D3	Dove Jc.	NS/GN	15 D5
DINAS JUNCTION	L&NW	19 E2	DOVECLIFFE	MS&L	42 E2
DINAS JUNCTION	NWNG	19 E2	DOVENBY	M&C	26 D3
DINAS MAWDDWY	Mawddwy	14 A4	DOVER ADMIRALTY PIER	SE	6 D2
DINAS POWIS	BD&R	43 B5	DOVER PRIORY	LC&D	6 D2
DINGESTOW	GW	8 A2	DOVER TOWN	SE	6 D2
DINGWALL	HR	35 D5	DOVER TOWN & HARBOUR	LC&D	6 D2
DINMORE	S&HJt	9 B1	DOVERCOURT	GE	12 E3
Dinmore Tunnel	S&HJt	9 B1	DOWLAIS	B&M	43 C2
DINNET	GNoS	34 A4	DOWLAIS	L&NW	43 C2
Dinorwic Quarries	Padarn	19 E2	DOWLAIS CAE HARRIS	TBJt.	43 C2
DINSDALE	NE	28 F5	DOWLAIS TOP	B&M	43 C1
DINTING	MS&L	21 G1	DOWNHAM	GE	17 F4
Dinting Viaduct	MS&L	21 G1	DOWNHILL	B&NC	60 B2
DINTON	L&SW	3 C5	Downhill Tunnel	B&NC	60 B2
DINWOODIE	CAL.	26 A3	DOWNPATRICK	B&CD	58 A1
DIRLETON	NB	31 B1	DOWNTON	L&SW	4 D5
DISLEY	L&NW	15 A4	Dragon Jc.	NE	21 C3
DISS	GE	12 B4	DRAPERSTOWN	Drap.	60 E2
DISTINGTON	C&WJn/WC&EJt	26 E3	Draperstown Jc.	B&NC/Drap.	60 E1
DITCHFORD	L&NW	10 A1	DRAX	HB&WRJn	21 E5
DITCHINGHAM	GE	12 A2	DRAYCOTT	GW	8 E2
DITTON JUNCTION	L&NW	45 E4	DRAYCOTT	MID.	41 G3
DIXON FOLD	L&Y	45 B2	DRAYTON	E&M	18 E3
DOAGH	B&NC	61 E3	DRAYTON	LB&SC	4 E1
DOAGH (narrow gauge)	B&NC	61 E2	Drayton Jc.	L&NW/GN&L&NWJt	16 F2
Dobbs Brow Jc.	L&Y	45 C2	DREGHORN	G&SW	29 E3
DOCKING	H&WN	17 D5	DREM	NB	30 B1
Dr. Days Bridge Jc.	GW	3 G1	DRIFFIELD	NE	22 C4

Station, junction, tunnel, viaduct, etc	Railway	Reference	Station, junction, tunnel, viaduct, etc	Railway	Reference
DRIGG	FUR.	26 G3	Dundalk East Jc.	GN(I)	58 D3
DRIGHLINGTON & ADWALTON	GN	42 B4	DUNDALK JUNCTION	GN(I)	58 D4
DRIMOLEAGUE	IV	49 F4	DUNDALK QUAY STREET	DN&G	58 D3
DRINEY	CL&RLt	57 D1	Dundalk South & West Jcs.	GN(I)	58 D4
Drinnick Mill	Cornwall Minerals	1 D2	DUNDEE EAST	D&AJt	34 E2
DRIPSEY	C&MLt	48 G4	DUNDEE ESPLANADE	NB	34 E2
DROGHEDA	GN(I)	58 E3	DUNDEE TAY BRIDGE	NB	34 E2
DROITWICH	GW	9 B3	Dundee Tay Bridge (Goods)	NB	34 E2
Droitwich Road (Goods)	MID.	9 B3	DUNDEE WEST	CAL.	34 E2
DROMAHAIR	SL&NC	56 C2	DUNDONALD	B&CD	61 F4
DROMKEEN	W&L	48 B2	DUNDRUM	B&CD	58 B1
DROMOD	CL&RLt	57 E1	DUNDRUM	DW&W	62 E3
DROMOD	MGW	57 E1	DUNDRUM	GS&W	48 B1
DROMORE	GN(I)	58 A3	DUNFERMLINE	NB	30 A3
DROMORE	P&WJt	25 C5	DUNFORD BRIDGE	MS&L	42 E4
DROMORE ROAD	GN(I)	60 G5	DUNGANNON	GN(I)	60 G2
Dromore Summit	P&WJt	25 C5	Dungannon Jc.	GN(I)	60 G2
DRONFIELD	MID.	41 B2	Dungannon Tunnel	GN(I)	60 G2
DRONGAN	G&SW	29 F4	DUNGARVAN	WD&L	49 E2
DRONLEY	CAL.	34 E5	DUNGENESS	Lydd	6 E3
Drope Jc.	BD&R	43 C4	DUNGIVEN	L&D	60 C2
DROYLSDEN	L&Y/L&NW	21 A2	DUNHAM	GE	18 E5
DRUM	GNoS	34 A2	DUNHAM HILL	BIRK. Jt.	45 E5
DRUMBURGH	NB	26 C2	DUNHAM MASSEY	L&NW	45 B4
DRUMHOWNAGH	MGW	57 E3	Dunhampstead (Goods)	MID.	9 B3
DRUMLITHIE	CAL.	34 B2	DUNKELD	HR	33 D4
Drumlithie Summit	CAL.	34 B2	DUNKETTLE	GS&W	48 E2
DRUMMUIR	GNoS	36 D1	DUNLAVIN	GS&W	54 E5
Drumochter Summit	HR	33 B2	DUNLEER	GN(I)	58 E3
DRUMREE	MGW	54 A4	DUNLOP	GB&KJt	29 D4
DRUMSHANBO	CL&RLt	56 D1	DUNLOY	B&NC	61 C1
DRUMSHORELAND	E&B	30 B3	DUNLUCE CASTLE	GCP&BV	60 A1 (f9)
DRUMSNA	MGW	56 E1	DUNMANWAY	CB&SC	49 E5
DRUMSURN	L&D	60 C2	Dunmore Jc.	CAL.	30 A5
DRWS-Y-NANT	GW	19 G4	DUNMOW	GE	11 E4
DRYBRIDGE	K&T	29 E3	DUNMURRY	GN(I)	61 F3
DRYBRIDGE PLATFORM	HR	37 C1	DUNNING	CAL.	33 F4
DRYBROOK ROAD	S&WJt	8 A1	DUNPHAIL	HR	36 D3
Dryclough Jc.	L&Y	42 C5	DUNRAGIT	P&WJt	25 C2
DRYMEN	F&CJn	29 B4	DUNROBIN	HR	36 A4
DRYSLLWYN	L&NW	13 G5	DUNS	NB	31 C2
Dubbs Jc.	G&SW	29 D3	DUNSLAND CROSS	L&SW	1 A5
DUBLIN AMIENS STREET	GN(I)	62 C3	DUNSTABLE	L&NW	10 D1
DUBLIN BROADSTONE	MGW	62 C4	DUNSTABLE CHURCH STREET	GN	11 E1
Dublin East Wall Yard	GS&W	62 C2	DUNSTALL PARK	GW	15 E3
DUBLIN HARCOURT STREET	DW&W	62 D3	DUNSTER	Minehead	8 E5
DUBLIN KINGSBRIDGE	GS&W	62 C4	DUNSYRE	CAL.	30 D3
DUBLIN NORTH WALL	L&NW	62 C3	DUNTON GREEN	SE	5 C4
Dublin North Wall Yard	MGW	62 C3	DUNVANT	L&NW	7 B3
Dublin Point Depot	GS&W	62 C2	DURHAM	NE	27 D5
DUBLIN WESTLAND ROW	D&K	62 C3	Durham (Goods)	NE	28 D5
DUBTON	CAL.	34 C3	Durham Ox Jc.	GN/MS&L	16 A1
DUDBRIDGE	MID.	9 E3 (f2)	DURROW & STRADBALLY	WD&L	49 E3
Dudding Hill (Goods)	MID.	39 B4	Durrow Tunnel	WD&L	49 E3
DUDDINGSTON & CRAIGMILLAR	NB	30 G1	DURRUS ROAD	BE	49 F4
DUDLEY	GW	13 B1	DURSLEY	MID.	9 F2
DUDLEY	L&NW	13 B1	DURSTON	GW	8 F3
DUDLEY HILL	GN	42 B4	DYCE	GNoS	37 F4
DUDLEY PORT (HIGH LEVEL)	L&NW	13 B2	DYFFRYN	CAM.	19 G2
DUDLEY PORT (LOW LEVEL)	L&NW	13 B2	Dykehead Branch Jc.	NB	44 A4
DUDLEY SOUTHSIDE & NETHERTON	GW	13 B1	DYMOCK	Newent	9 D2
DUFFIELD	MID.	41 F2	DYNEVOR	GW	43 F2
DUFFIELD GATE	NE	21 D5	DYSART	NB	30 A2
DUFFTOWN	GNoS	36 E1	Dyserth (Goods)	L&NW	19 C5
DUFFWS	Fest.	19 F3			
DUKE STREET	CoGU	44 D4 (f11)	EAGLESCLIFFE	NE	28 E5
DUKINFIELD	MS&L	21 A2	EALING BROADWAY	GW	39 C2
DULEEK	GN(I)	58 G4	EALING BROADWAY	MET.-DIS.	39 C2
DULLATUR	NB	30 B5	EALING COMMON & WEST ACTON	MET.-DIS.	39 C3
DULLINGHAM	GE	11 C4	Eamont Bridge Jc.	L&NW/NE	27 E1
DULVERTON	Devon & Somerset	7 F5	EARBY	MID.	21 B1
DULWICH	LC&D	40 E4	EARDINGTON	GW	15 G2
DUMBARTON	NB	29 B3	EARDISLEY	MID.	14 E2
DUMFRIES	G&SW	26 B3	EARITH BRIDGE	E&Stl	11 B3
DUMFRIES HOUSE	G&SW	29 F4	EARLESTOWN JUNCTION	L&NW	45 D3
DUNADRY	B&NC	61 E2	EARLEY	SE	4 A2
DUNBALL	GW	8 E3	EARLS COURT	MET.-DIS.	39 D5
DUNBAR	NB	31 B1	Earls Court Jc.	MET.-DIS./WLJt	39 D4 (f20)
DUNBLANE	CAL.	33 G3	EARLSFIELD & SUMMERS TOWN	L&SW	39 E5
DUNBOYNE	MGW	54 B4	EARLSHEATON	GN	42 C3
DUNBRIDGE	L&SW	4 D4	EARLSMILL	GNoS	37 D1
DUNCHURCH	L&NW	10 A4	EARLSTON	NB	31 D1
Dundalk Barrack Street (Goods)	GN(I)	58 D3	EARLSWOOD	LB&SC	5 D3

Station, junction, tunnel, viaduct, etc	Railway	Reference	Station, junction, tunnel, viaduct, etc	Railway	Reference
Earnock Col.	CAL.	44 C2	EDWALTON	MID.	41 G5
EARSHAM	GE	12 A2	EFFINGHAM JUNCTION	L&SW	5 C2
EARSWICK	NE	21 A5	Egerton Street Jc.	CLC/MD&HB	45 G5
EASINGTON	NE	28 E3	Egerton Street Tunnel	CLC	45 F4
EASSIE	CAL.	34 D5	EGGESFORD	L&SW	2 A5
EAST ANSTEY	Devon & Somerset	7 F5	Egginton East & West Jcs.	NS/GN	16 D5
EAST BARKWITH	GN	17 A2	EGGINTON JUNCTION	GN/NS	16 D5
East Calder (Goods)	NB	30 C3	EGHAM	L&SW	5 B1
East Cannock Jc.	L&NW	15 E4	EGLINTON	B&NC	60 C3
EAST CROYDON	LB&SC	5 C3	Eglinton Street (Goods)	G&SW	44 F2 (f26)
EAST DULWICH	LB&SC	40 E4	EGREMONT	WC&EJt	26 F3
EAST FARLEIGH	SE	6 C5	EGTON BRIDGE	NE	28 F2
EAST FINCHLEY	GN	39 A5	Elbowend Jc.	NB	30 B3
EAST FORTUNE	NB	31 B1	ELDERSLIE	G&SW	44 G3
EAST GRANGE	NB	30 A4	ELEPHANT & CASTLE	LC&D	40 D5
EAST GRINSTEAD HIGH LEVEL	LB&SC	5 D4	ELFORD & HASELOUR	MID.	15 E5
EAST GRINSTEAD LOW LEVEL	LB&SC	5 D4	ELGIN	GNoS	36 C2
EAST HAM	LT&S	40 B2	ELGIN	HR	36 C2
EAST HAVEN	D&AJt	34 E3	Elgin Jc.	NB	30 A3
EAST HORNDON	LT&S	5 A5	ELHAM	SE	6 D2
East India Dock Road Jc.	NL	40 D1	ELIE	NB	34 G4
East India Docks (Goods)	GE	40 D1	ELLAND	L&Y	42 C5
EAST KILBRIDE	CAL.	44 D2	Elland Tunnel	L&Y	42 C5
EAST LINTON	NB	31 B1	ELLENBROOK	L&NW	45 B2
EAST NORTON	GN&L&NWJt	16 F2	Ellerbeck Col.	LUJt	45 D1
EAST PUTNEY	L&SW	39 E4	ELLERBY	NE	22 D3
East Rosedale (Goods)	NE	28 F3	ELLESMERE	CAM.	20 F4
EAST RUDHAM	E&M	18 D5	ELLESMERE PORT	BIRK. Jt.	45 E5
EAST STREET	Bridport	3 F1	ELLINGHAM	GE	12 A2
East Suffolk Jc.	GE	12 D3	ELLIOT JUNCTION	D&AJt	34 D3
EAST VILLE	GN	17 C3	ELLON for CRUDEN	GNoS	37 E4
East Wall Jc.	GN(I)	62 C3	ELM BRIDGE	GE (Wisbech Tmy.)	17 F4
East Wheal Rose	Cornwall Minerals	1 D1	ELMER'S END	SE	40 G4
EAST WINCH	GE	17 E5	ELMESTHORPE	L&NW	16 F4
EASTBOURNE	LB&SC	5 G5	ELMSWELL	GE	12 C4
EASTER ROAD	NB	30 F2	ELMTON & CRESWELL	MID.	41 B4
EASTERHOUSE	NB	44 C4	ELRINGTON	NE	27 C3
Eastfield (Goods)	CAL.	44 D3	Elsecar (Goods)	MS&L	42 F2
EASTLEIGH & BISHOPSTOKE	L&SW	4 D3	ELSENHAM	GE	11 E4
Eastleigh South Jc.	L&SW	4 D3	Elsenham Summit	GE	11 E4
EASTON COURT	S&HJt	9 A1	ELSHAM	MS&L	22 F4
EASTON LODGE	GE	11 E4	ELSLACK	MID.	21 C1
EASTRINGTON	HB&WRJn	22 D5	ELSTED	L&SW	4 D1
EASTRINGTON	NE	22 D5	ELSTREE & BOREHAM WOOD	MID.	5 A2
Eastwell	GN	16 D2	Elstree Tunnel	MID.	5 A2
EASTWOOD	L&Y	21 E1	ELSWICK	NE	28 A2
EASTWOOD & LANGLEY MILL	GN	41 F3	ELTHAM	SE	40 E2
EATON	BC	14 C1	ELTON	L&NW	11 A1
Eaton	GN	16 D2	ELTON & ORSTON	N&GR&C	16 C2
Ebbw Jc.	GW	43 A4	ELVANFOOT	CAL.	30 F4
EBBW VALE	GW	43 B1	ELY	GE	11 B4
EBBW VALE	L&NW	43 B1	Ely Dock Jc.	GE/E&N	11 B4
EBCHESTER	NE	27 C4	ELY for LLANDAFF	GW	43 B4
ECCLEFECHAN	CAL.	26 B2	EMBANKMENT	D&BST	54 C3
ECCLES	L&NW	45 B3	EMBLETON	CK&P	26 E2
ECCLES ROAD	GE	12 A4	EMBSAY	MID.	21 C1
ECCLESFIELD	MS&L	42 F2	EMLY	GS&W	48 C2
ECCLESHILL	GN	42 A4	EMNETH	GE	17 F4
ECKINGTON	MID.	9 C3	EMSWORTH	LB&SC	4 E2
ECKINGTON & RENISHAW	MID.	41 B3	Enbourne Jc.	GW/DN&S	4 A3
EDDERTON	HR	36 B5	ENDON	NS	15 C4
EDDLESTON	NB	30 D2	ENFIELD	GN	5 A3
EDEN PARK	SE	40 G3	ENFIELD	MGW	54 B5
Eden Valley Jc.	L&NW/NE	27 E1	ENFIELD LOCK	GE	11 G3
EDENBRIDGE	LB&SC	5 D4	ENFIELD TOWN	GE	5 A3
EDENBRIDGE	SE	5 D4	Engine Shed Jc.	MID.	21 C2
EDENDERRY	MGW	53 B5	ENNIS	L&E/A&EJn	52 F5
EDERMINE FERRY	DW&W	50 C4	ENNIS	WClare	52 F5
EDGE HILL	L&NW	45 F4 (f52)	Ennis Jc.	MGW/A&EJn	52 C4
Edge Hill (Goods)	L&NW	45 F4 (f51)	Ennis Jc.	W&L/L&E	48 A3
EDGE LANE	L&NW	45 F4	ENNISCORTHY	DW&W	50 B4
EDGEWORTHSTOWN	MGW	57 G2	Enniscorthy Tunnel	DW&W	50 B4
EDGWARE	GN	5 A2	ENNISKEAN	CB&SC	50 F5
EDGWARE ROAD	MET.	39 C5	ENNISKILLEN	GN(I)	57 B2
Edinburgh Lothian Road (Goods)	CAL.	30 G2	ENNISTYMON	WClare	51 E5
EDINBURGH PRINCES STREET	CAL.	30 F2	ENTWISTLE	L&Y	45 B1
Edinburgh Scotland Street (Goods)	NB	30 F2	ENZIE	HR	37 C1
Edinburgh St. Leonard's (Goods)	NB	30 G2	EPPING	GE	11 G3
EDINBURGH WAVERLEY	NB	30 F2	EPSOM	LB&SC	5 C3
EDINGTON ROAD	S&D Jt.	8 E3	EPSOM (Joint)	E&L Jt.	5 C2
EDLINGHAM	NE	31 F4	EPSOM DOWNS	LB&SC	5 C3
EDMONDSTOWN	MGW	56 E3	ERDINGTON	L&NW	15 F5
EDROM	NB	31 C2	ERIDGE	LB&SC	5 D5

Station, junction, tunnel, viaduct, etc	Railway	Reference
FIDDOWN	W&L	49 C4
Fighting Cocks (Goods)	NE	28 F5
FILEY	NE	22 A3
FILLEIGH	Devon & Somerset	7 F4
FILTON	GW	8 C1
FINCHLEY	GN	39 A5
FINCHLEY ROAD	MID.	39 B5 (f11)
FINCHLEY ROAD & FROGNAL	L&NW	39 B5
FINCHLEY ROAD (SOUTH HAMPSTEAD)	MET.	39 B5
FINDERMORE	CVT	57 A4
FINDOCHTY	GNoS	37 C1
FINEDON	MID.	10 A2
FINGASK PLATFORM	GNoS	37 E3
FINGHALL LANE	NE	21 A2
Finn Valley Jc.	GN(I)/FV	60 D5
FINNIESTON	NB	44 E4 (f9)
FINNINGHAM	GE	12 C4
FINNINGLEY	GN&GEJt.	21 F5
FINSBURY PARK	GN	40 B5
FINTONA	GN(I)	60 G4
FINTONA JUNCTION	GN(I)	60 G4
FIRSBY	GN	17 B3
Firsby South Jc.	GN	17 B3
FIRST TOWER	Jersey	46 E3
FISH PONDS	MID.	8 C1
Fisherrow	NB	30 B2
Fisherton Tunnel	L&SW	4 C5
FISKERTON	MID.	16 C3
FITTLEWORTH	LB&SC	5 E1
FITZGERALD PLATFORM	GS&W	47 E4
FIVE MILE HOUSE	GN	17 B1
FIVE WAYS	MID.	13 C3
Five Ways Col.	L&NW	15 E4
FIVEMILETOWN	CVT	57 A4
FLADBURY	GW	9 C4
FLAG STATION	GW	19 F4
FLAMBOROUGH	NE	22 B2
FLAX BOURTON	GW	8 D2
FLAXTON	NE	21 B5
FLEET	E&M	17 E3
FLEET	L&SW	4 B1
Fleet Jc.	GE	18 F1
FLEETWOOD	L&Y & L&NWJt	24 C4
Fletton (Goods)	GN	17 G2
FLIMBY	L&NW	26 D3
FLINT	L&NW	20 D5
FLITWICK	MID.	11 E1
FLIXTON	CLC	45 B3
FLOAT	MGW	57 F3
FLORDON	GE	18 F3
FLORENCECOURT	SL&NC	57 B2
FLORISTON	CAL.	26 C1
FLUSHDYKE	GN	42 C3
FOCHABERS	HR	36 D1
FOCHABERS-ON-SPEY	GNoS	36 C1
FOCHRIW	B&M	43 C2
Fodderty Jc.	HR	35 D5
FOGGATHORPE	NE	22 D5
FOLESHILL	L&NW	10 A5
FOLKESTONE	SE	6 D2
FOLKESTONE HARBOUR	SE	6 D2
FONTBURN	NB	31 G4
Foord Viaduct	SE	6 D2
Forcett Depot	Forcett	27 F5
Forcett Jc.	NE/Forcett	27 E5
FORD BRIDGE	S&HJt	9 B1
FORD GREEN & SMALLTHORNE	NS	15 C3
FORD JUNCTION	LB&SC	5 F1
FORDEN	CAM.	14 B2
FORDHAM	E&N	11 B4
FORDINGBRIDGE	L&SW	4 D5
FORDOUN	CAL.	34 B2
FOREST GATE	GE	40 B2
Forest Gate Jc.	GE/LT&S	40 B2
FOREST HALL	NE	27 B5
FOREST HILL	LB&SC	40 E4
FOREST ROW	LB&SC	5 D4
FORFAR	CAL.	34 D4
FORGANDENNY	CAL.	33 F5
FORGE MILLS for COLESHILL	MID.	15 F5
FORGE VALLEY	NE	22 A4
FORGIE	HR	37 D1
Forks Jc.	M&C	26 D1
FORMBY	L&Y	45 G2
FORNCETT	GE	18 F3
FORRES	HR	36 D3
FORRESTFIELD	NB	30 C5
FORSINARD	HR	38 E5
FORT GEORGE	HR	36 D4
FORT MATILDA	CAL.	29 B3
Fort Pitt Tunnel	LC&D	6 B5
FORTEVIOT	CAL.	33 F4
Fortisset Col.	NB	30 C5
FORTUNESTOWN LANE	D&BST	54 C3
FORYD	L&NW	19 C5
Foryd Jc.	L&NW	19 C5
Foryd Pier	L&NW	19 C5
Foss Islands (Goods)	NE	21 A4
FOTA	GS&W	48 F1
FOULRIDGE	MID.	21 B1
FOULSHAM	GE	18 E4
FOUNTAINHALL	NB	30 D1
FOUR ASHES	L&NW	15 E3
FOUR CROSSES	CAM.	14 A2
FOUR OAKS	L&NW	15 F5
FOURSTONES	NE	27 B3
FOWEY	Cornwall Minerals	1 D3
FOWLIS	HR	36 C5
FOXDALE	MN	23 B2
FOXFIELD	FUR.	24 A5
FOXFORD	GN&W	55 D5
Foxhall Jc.	GW	10 F4
FOXROCK	DW&W	62 F2
FOXTON	GE	11 D3
FOYNES	L&F	48 A5
Foynes Jc.	GS&W/L&F	48 A3
FRAMLINGHAM	GE	12 C3
FRANKTON	CAM.	20 F4
FRANSHAM	GE	18 E5
FRANT	SE	5 D5
FRASERBURGH	GNoS	37 C4
FRATTON	L&SW & LB&SC Jt.	4 E2
FREMINGTON	L&SW	7 F3
FRENCH DROVE	GN&GEJt.	17 F3
FRESHFIELD	L&Y	45 G2
FRESHFORD	GW	3 B4
FRESHWATER	FY&N	4 F4
Friary Jc.	GW/L&SW	1 A2
FRICKLEY	S&KJt	42 D1
Friden (Goods)	L&NW	15 B5
FRIEZLAND	L&NW	21 F1
FRIMLEY	L&SW	4 B1
FRINTON-ON-SEA	GE	12 F3
FRIOCKHEIM	A&F	34 D3
FRISBY	MID.	16 E3
FRIZINGHALL	MID.	42 A5
FRIZINGTON	WC&EJt	26 F3
FROCESTER	MID.	9 E3
FRODINGHAM & SCUNTHORPE	MS&L	22 F4
FRODSHAM	BIRK. Jt.	45 D5
Frodsham Jc.	BIRK. Jt./L&NW	45 D5
Frodsham Viaduct	BIRK. Jt.	45 D5
FROGHALL	NS	15 C4
Froghall (Goods)	NS	15 C4
FROME	GW	3 C3
FRONGOCH	B&F	19 F4
FROSTERLEY	NE	27 D4
Fry's Bottom Col.	GW	8 D1
Fryston (Goods)	NE	42 B1
FULBOURNE	GE	11 C4
FULLERTON JUNCTION	L&SW	4 C4
Fullwood Jc.	CAL.	44 B3
FULWELL & HAMPTON HILL	L&SW	39 F1
FULWELL & WESTBURY	L&NW	10 D3
FULWOOD	L&Y & L&NWJt	24 D3
FURNESS ABBEY	FUR.	24 B5
FURNESS VALE	L&NW	15 A4
FUSHIEBRIDGE	NB	30 C2
FYFIN	C&VBT	60 E5
FYLING HALL	Sc&Wby	28 F1
FYVIE	GNoS	37 E3
Gadly's Jc.	GW	43 D2
Gaer Jc.	GW	43 A3
GAERWEN	L&NW	19 D2
GAILES	G&SW	29 E3

Station, junction, tunnel, viaduct, etc	Railway	Reference
GAILEY	L&NW	15 E3
GAINFORD	NE	27 E5
GAINSBOROUGH	GN&GEJt.	22 G5
GAINSBOROUGH	MS&L	22 G5
Gainsborough North & South Jcs.	MS&L/GN&GEJt.	22 G5
GAISGILL	NE	27 F2
GALASHIELS	NB	30 E1
GALGATE	L&NW	24 C3
GALLAGH ROAD	L&LS	60 C4
GALSTON	G&SW	29 E4
Galton Jc.	L&NW/GW	13 B2
GALWAY	MGW	52 C5
GAMLINGAY	L&NW	11 D2
Gannow Jc.	L&Y	24 D1
GANTON	NE	22 A4
GARADICE	CL&RLt	57 D1
Garawhistle Col.	CAL.	30 E5
GARFORTH	Aberford	42 A1
GARFORTH	NE	42 A1
GARGRAVE	MID.	21 C1
GARGUNNOCK	F&CJn	29 A5
GARLIESTOWN	P&WJt	25 D4
GARMOUTH	GNoS	36 C1
GARNANT	GW	43 F1
GARNEDDWEN	Corris	14 A5
GARNGAD	CoGU	44 D4
GARNKIRK	CAL.	44 C4
Garnqueen North Jc.	CAL.	44 B4
Garnqueen South Jc.	CAL./NB	44 B4
GARSTANG	G&KE	24 C3
GARSTANG & CATTERALL	L&NW	24 D3
GARSTON	CLC	45 E4 (f62)
GARSTON CHURCH ROAD	L&NW	45 E4 (f61)
GARSTON DOCK	L&NW	45 E4 (f48)
Garston Dock (Goods)	L&NW	45 E4
Garston Dock Jc.	L&NW	45 E4
GARSWOOD	L&NW	45 D3
GARTCOSH	CAL.	44 C4
Gartcosh Jc.	CAL.	44 C4
GARTH	L&NW	14 E4
Garth & Van Road	Van	14 C4
GARTLY	GNoS	37 E1
GARTMORE	S&A	29 A4
GARTNESS	F&CJn	29 B4
Gartness Col.	CAL.	44 A4
GARTON	NE	22 C4
GARTSHERRIE	CAL.	44 B4
Gartsherrie Iron Works	CAL.	44 C3
Gartshore (Goods)	NB	44 B5
GARVAGH	DC	60 C1
GARVE	HR	35 D4
GASCOIGNE WOOD JUNCTION	NE	21 D4
Gask	NB	30 A3
Gasworks Tunnel	GN	40 B5
GATEACRE for WOOLTON	CLC	45 E4
GATEHEAD	K&T	29 E4
GATESHEAD EAST	NE	28 A1
GATESHEAD WEST	NE	28 A1
GATESIDE	NB	33 F5
GATHURST	L&Y	45 D2
GAVELL	NB	29 B5
GAYTON ROAD	E&M	17 E5
GEASHILL	GS&W	53 C4
GEDDINGTON	MID.	16 G2
GEDLING & CARLTON	GN	41 F5
GEDNEY	E&M	17 E3
Geldard Jc.	NE/GN	21 B2
GELDESTON	GE	12 A2
Gelly Tarw Jc.	GW	43 D2
Gellyrhaidd Jc.	EV/GW	43 D3
GEORGE INN	Rhym.	43 B2
GEORGE LANE	GE	40 A2
GEORGE TOWN	JE	46 E3
Georgemas Jc.	HR	38 C3
GEORGEMAS JUNCTION	HR	38 C3
GERARD'S BRIDGE	L&NW	45 D3
GIANT'S CAUSEWAY (CAUSEWAY HOTEL)	GCP&BV	60 A1
GIBBSTOWN	MGW	58 F5
GIFFEN	L&A	29 D3
GIFFNOCK	CAL.	44 E2
GIGGLESWICK	MID.	24 B1
GILDERSOME	GN	42 B3
GILFACH	GW	43 D3

Station, junction, tunnel, viaduct, etc	Railway	Reference
Gilfach Goch	GW	43 D3
Gillers Green Cols.	L&NW	45 E3
Gillfoot (Goods)	WC&EJt	26 F3
GILLING	NE	21 A5
GILLINGHAM	L&SW	3 D4
Gillingham Tunnel	LC&D	6 B5
GILLOW HEATH	NS	15 B3
GILMERTON	NB	30 C2
GILNOCKIE	NB	26 B1
GILSLAND	NE	27 B1
GILWERN	L&NW	43 B1
GIPSY HILL for UPPER NORWOOD	LB&SC	40 F4
GIRVAN NEW	A&W	29 G2
GIRVAN OLD	G&SW	29 G2
GISBURN	L&Y	24 C1
Gisburn Tunnel	L&Y	24 C1
GLAIS	MID.	43 F2
GLAISDALE	NE	28 F2
GLAMIS	CAL.	34 D4
GLAN CONWAY	L&NW	19 D4
GLANAMMAN	GW	43 F1
GLANDOVEY	CAM.	14 B5
GLANDOVEY JUNCTION	CAM.	14 B5
GLANRHYD	GW & L&NW Jt.	14 G5
GLANTON	NE	31 F4
GLAPWELL COLLIERY SIDINGS	MID.	41 C3
GLARRYFORD	B&NC	61 C1
GLASBURY	MID.	14 F2
GLASGOW BRIDGE STREET	CAL.	44 F2
GLASGOW BUCHANAN STREET	CAL.	44 E4
GLASGOW CENTRAL	CAL.	44 E4
GLASGOW EGLINTON STREET	CAL.	44 F1
GLASGOW GALLOWGATE	CoGU	44 E2 (f4)
Glasgow General Terminus (Goods)	CAL.	44 F2
GLASGOW LONDON ROAD	CAL.	44 D3
GLASGOW MAIN STREET	CoGU	44 E2
GLASGOW QUEEN STREET HIGH LEVEL	NB	44 E4
GLASGOW QUEEN STREET LOW LEVEL	NB	44 E4
Glasgow South Side (Goods)	CAL.	44 E1
Glasgow South Side (Goods)	GB&KJt	44 E1
GLASGOW ST. ENOCH	G&SW	44 E2
Glasgow West Street (Goods)	CAL.	44 F1 (f22)
Glasnevin Jc.	MGW/GS&W	62 B4
GLASSAUGH	GNoS	37 C2
GLASSEL	GNoS	34 A3
GLASSFORD	CAL.	44 B1
GLASSLOUGH	GN(I)	57 B5
GLASSON	NB	26 C2
GLASSON DOCK	L&NW	24 C3
GLASTERLAW	CAL.	34 D3
Glaston Tunnel	MID.	16 F1
GLASTONBURY & STREET	S&D Jt.	8 E2
GLAZEBROOK	CLC	45 C3
Glazebrook East Jc.	CLC	45 C3
Glazebrook West Jc.	CLC/WJn	45 C3
GLAZEBURY & BURY LANE	L&NW	45 C3
GLEMSFORD	GE	12 D5
GLEN	C&VBT	60 E5
GLEN	MID.	16 F3
GLENAGEARY	D&K	54 C2
GLENAVY	GN(I)	61 F2
GLENBARRY	GNoS	37 D2
GLENBOIG	CAL.	44 B4
GLENBUCK	CAL.	30 E5
GLENCARRON PLATFORM	HR	35 D2
GLENCARSE	CAL.	33 F5
GLENCORSE	NB	30 C2
GLENCREW	CVT	57 A5
Glencruitten Summit	C&O	32 F4
Glendon Jc.	MID.	10 A2
GLENEALY	DW&W	54 E2
GLENFARNE	SL&NC	57 B1
GLENFIELD	MID.	16 F4
Glenfield Tunnel	MID.	16 F4
GLENGARNOCK	L&A	29 D3
GLENGARNOCK & KILBIRNIE	G&SW	29 D3
GLENKEEN	CVT	57 A5
GLENLUCE	P&WJt	25 C3
GLENOGLEHEAD	C&O	33 E2
Glenoglehead Summit	C&O	33 E2
GLENWHILLY	A&W	25 B3
GLOBE ROAD & DEVONSHIRE STREET	GE	40 C3
GLOGUE	W&C	13 F3

Station, junction, tunnel, viaduct, etc	Railway	Reference
GLOSSOP	MS&L	21 G1
GLOUCESTER	GW	9 D3
GLOUCESTER	MID.	9 E3
Gloucester Docks	GW	9 E3
Gloucester Docks	MID.	9 E3
Gloucester Road Jc.	LB&SC	40 G4
Glyn Col.	TV	43 C3
GLYN NEATH	GW	43 E2
Glynceiriog	GVT	20 F5
GLYNCORRWG	SWMin.	43 E2
GLYNDE	LB&SC	5 F4
GLYNDYFRDWY	Ll&C	20 F5
GLYNN	C&L	61 D3
GNOSALL	L&NW	15 E3
GOATHLAND MILL	NE	28 F2
Goathorn Pier	Goathorn	3 F5
GOBOWEN	GW	20 F4
Gobowen Jc.	GW	20 F4
GOB-Y-DIEGAN	MN	23 B2
GODALMING NEW	L&SW	5 D1
GODALMING OLD	L&SW	5 D1
GODLEY JUNCTION	CLC/MS&L	21 G1 (f5)
GODMANCHESTER	GN&GE	11 B2
GODNOW BRIDGE	MS&L	22 F5
GODSTONE	SE	5 D3
GOGAR	NB	30 B3
Gogginshill Tunnel	CB&SC	50 E3
GOLBORNE	L&NW	45 D3
Golborne Jc.	L&NW	45 D3
GOLCAR	L&NW	42 D5
GOLDEN GROVE	L&NW	13 G5
GOLDENHILL	NS	15 C3
GOLDSBOROUGH	NE	21 C4
GOLF LINKS HALT	PsT	60 B1 (f3)
GOLSPIE	HR	36 A4
Golynos Jc.	L&NW/GW	43 A2
GOMSHALL & SHERE	SE	5 D2
Goodman's Yard (Goods)	GE	40 C4 (f8)
GOOLD'S CROSS & CASHEL	GS&W	49 B1
GOOLE	NE	22 E5
Goole Docks	L&Y	22 E5
Goole Swing Bridge	NE	22 E5
Goose Green Jc.	L&NW	45 D2
Goose Hill Jc.	MID./L&Y	42 C2
GORAGH WOOD	GN(I)	58 B3
GORBALS	GB&KJt	44 E1
GORDON	NB	31 D1
GOREBRIDGE	NB	30 C2
GORESBRIDGE	GS&W	49 A5
GOREY	DW&W	50 A3
GOREY	JE	46 E2
GORGIE	NB	30 G3
GORING	GW	10 G3
GORING	LB&SC	5 F2
GORMANSTOWN	GN(I)	58 G3
GORSEINON	L&NW	7 B3
GORT	A&EJn	52 E4
GORTATLEA	GS&W	47 D3
GORTNEE	GCP&BV	60 A1 (f11)
GORTON	MS&L	45 A3
GOSBERTON	GN&GEJt.	17 D2
GOSFORTH	NE	27 B5
GOSPEL OAK	L&NW	40 C1
GOSPEL OAK	T&HJc	40 C1
GOSPORT	L&SW	4 E2 (f1)
GOSPORT ROAD	L&SW	4 E3
GOURDON	NB	34 B2
GOUROCK	CAL.	29 B3
GOVAN	G&PJt	44 E4
GOVILON	L&NW	43 A1
Gowdall Jc.	HB&WRJn	21 E5
GOWER STREET	MET.	40 C5
GOWERTON	GW	7 B3
GOWERTON	L&NW	7 B3
GOWRAN	GS&W	49 A5
GOXHILL	MS&L	22 E3
GOXHILL	NE	22 D3
GRAFHAM	KT&H	11 B1
GRAFTON & BURBAGE	M&SWJn.	4 B5
Grafton Jc.	GW/M&SWJn.	4 B5
GRAHAMSTON (FALKIRK)	NB	30 B4
GRAMPOUND ROAD	GW	1 E2
GRANDBOROUGH ROAD	A&B	10 D3

Station, junction, tunnel, viaduct, etc	Railway	Reference
GRANDTULLY	HR	33 D4
Grane Road (Goods)	L&Y	24 E1
GRANGE	FUR.	24 B3
GRANGE	GNoS	37 D1
GRANGE	W&L	49 D4
Grange Col.	MS&L	42 F2
GRANGE CON	GS&W	54 E5
GRANGE COURT	GW	9 E2
GRANGE LANE	MS&L	42 F2
Grange North & South Jcs.	GNoS	37 D1
GRANGE ROAD for CRAWLEY DOWN & TURNER'S HILL	LB&SC	5 D3
GRANGEMOUTH	CAL.	30 B4
Grangemouth Harbour	CAL.	30 B4
GRANGETOWN	TV	43 B4
GRANTHAM	GN	16 D1
Grantham Canal Yard	N&GR&C	16 D1
GRANTON	NB	30 F2
Granton (Goods)	CAL.	30 F2
Granton Jc.	CAL.	30 G2
GRANTON ROAD	CAL.	30 F2
Granton Western Breakwater	CAL.	30 F3
GRANTOWN	GNoS	36 F3
GRANTOWN	HR	36 F3
GRANT'S HOUSE	NB	31 C2
Grassmoor Jc.	GE/GN&GEJt.	17 F3
GRATELEY	L&SW	4 C5
Grattan Hill Jc.	GS&W	48 E3
GRAVELLY HILL	L&NW	13 B4
Graveney (Goods)	LC&D	6 C3
GRAVESEND	SE	5 B5
GRAVESEND WEST STREET	LC&D	5 B5
GRAYRIGG	L&NW	27 G1
GRAYS	LT&S	5 B5
GREAT ALNE	GW	9 B5
GREAT AYTON	NE	28 F4
GREAT BARR	L&NW	13 B3
GREAT BENTLEY	GE	12 E4
GREAT BRIDGE	GW	13 B2
GREAT BRIDGE	L&NW	13 B2
GREAT BRIDGEFORD	L&NW	15 D3
Great Broughton (Goods)	C&WJn	26 D3
GREAT CHESTERFORD	GE	11 D4
GREAT COATES	MS&L	22 F2
GREAT DALBY	GN&L&NWJt	16 E2
GREAT GRIMSBY	MS&L	22 F2
GREAT HARWOOD	L&Y	24 D1
Great Harwood Jc.	L&Y	24 D2
GREAT HAYWOOD	NS	15 E4
GREAT HORTON	GN	42 A5
GREAT LINFORD	L&NW	10 C2
GREAT MALVERN	GW	9 C3
GREAT MARLOW	Gt. Marlow	10 G2
GREAT ORMESBY	E&M	18 E1
GREAT PONTON	GN	16 D1
GREAT WESTERN ROAD	NB	44 E4
GREATHAM	NE	28 E4
GREEN LANE	MER.	45 F4
Green Lane Jc.	GW	39 C1
GREEN LANES & NOEL PARK	GE	40 A5
GREEN ROAD	FUR.	24 A5
Greenbank	CAL.	30 D4
GREENCASTLE	B&NC	61 A4
GREENFIELD	L&NW	21 F1
Greengairs (Goods)	NB	44 A5
GREENHEAD	NE	27 B2
GREENHILL	CAL.	30 B5
GREENHITHE	SE	5 B5
GREENLAW	NB	31 D2
GREENLOANING	CAL.	33 G3
GREENMOUNT	L&Y	45 B1
GREENOCK CATHCART STREET	CAL.	29 B3
GREENOCK LYNEDOCH STREET	G&SW	29 B3
GREENOCK PRINCES PIER	G&SW	29 B3
GREENOCK WEST	CAL.	29 B3
GREENODD	FUR.	24 A4
Greenodd Jc.	FUR.	24 A4
GREENORE	DN&G	58 D2
Greenside Jc.	NB	44 B4
GREENVILLE	Jersey	46 E3
GREENWICH	LC&D	40 D3
GREENWICH	SE	40 D3
GREETLAND & NORTH DEAN	L&Y	42 C5

Station, junction, tunnel, viaduct, etc	Railway	Reference
Greetwell Jcs.	GN&GEJt./GN	16 B1
GRESFORD	GW	20 E4
GRESLEY	MID.	16 E5
GRETNA	CAL.	26 B1
GRETNA	NB	26 B1
GRETNA GREEN	G&SW	26 B1
Gretna Jc.	CAL./G&SW	26 B1
GRETTON	MID.	16 F1
Greyfield Col.	GW	8 D1
GREYSTONES & DELGANY	DW&W	54 D2
Griff Col.	L&NW	16 G5
GRIFFITHS CROSSING	L&NW	19 D2
GRIMOLDBY	L&EC	17 A3
GRIMSARGH	L&Y & L&NWJt	24 D2
GRIMSARGH	Whit.	24 D2
Grimsby Alexandra Dock	MS&L	22 F2
GRIMSBY DOCKS	MS&L	22 F2
Grimsby Docks (Goods)	GN	22 F2
Grimsby Docks (Goods)	MS&L	22 F2
GRIMSBY PIER	MS&L	22 F2
GRIMSTON	MID.	16 E3
GRIMSTON ROAD	E&M	17 E5
Grimston Tunnel	MID.	16 E3
GRIMSTONE & FRAMPTON	GW	3 F3
GRINDLEY	GN	15 D4
GRISTHORPE	NE	22 A3
GROESLON	L&NW	19 E2
Grogley Jc.	L&SW	1 C2
GROOMBRIDGE	LB&SC	5 D4
GROOMSPORT ROAD	B&CD	61 F4
GROSMONT	NE	28 F2
GROSVENOR ROAD	LC&D	39 D5
GROSVENOR ROAD & BATTERSEA PIER	LB&SC	39 D5
GROTTON	L&NW	21 F1
GROUVILLE	JE	46 E2
GROVE BRIDGE	Wantage	10 F5
GROVE FERRY	SE	6 C2
Grove Jc.	LB&SC/SE	5 D5
GROVE PARK	SE	40 E2
Grove Rake Lead Mine	W&R	27 D3
Grove Tunnel	SE	5 D5
GUARD BRIDGE	NB	34 F4
GUAY	HR	33 D4
GUESTWICK	E&M	18 D4
GUIDE BRIDGE	MS&L	21 A2
Guide Bridge Goods	L&NW	21 A2
GUILDFORD	L&SW	5 C1
GUISBOROUGH	NE	28 E3
GUISELEY	MID.	21 D2
Gunhouse Wharf	MS&L	22 F5
GUNNERSBURY	L&SW	39 D3
Gunnersbury Jc.	L&SW	39 D3
GUNNESS & BURRINGHAM	MS&L	22 F5
GUNTON	GE	18 D3
GUPWORTHY	West Somerset Mineral	8 F5
Gurnos (Goods)	MID.	43 F1
GURTEEN	C&MLt	48 G4
GUSHETFAULDS	CAL.	44 E1
Guston Tunnel	SE & LC&D Jt.	6 D2
GUTHRIE	A&F	34 D3
GUYHIRNE	GN&GEJt.	17 F3
Gwaun-Cae-Gurwen	GW	43 F1
GWERSYLLT & WHEATSHEAF	WM&CQ	20 E4
GWINEAR ROAD	GW	1 E4
GWYDDELWERN	L&NW	19 F5
GWYS	MID.	43 F1
HABROUGH	MS&L	22 E3
HACKBRIDGE	LB&SC	39 G5
HACKNEY	NL	40 B3
HACKNEY DOWNS JUNCTION	GE	40 B4
Hackney Wick (Goods)	GN	40 B3
HADDENHAM	E&Stl	11 B3
HADDINGTON	NB	30 B1
HADDISCOE	GE	18 F2
Haddon Tunnel	MID.	15 B5
HADFIELD	MS&L	21 G1
HADHAM	GE	11 F3
HADLEIGH	GE	12 D4
HADLEY	L&NW	15 E2
Hadley North & South Tunnels	GN	11 G2
HADLEY WOOD	GN	11 G2
HADLOW ROAD	BIRK. Jt.	45 F5

Station, junction, tunnel, viaduct, etc	Railway	Reference
HADNALL	L&NW	15 E1
Haggerleases	NE	27 E5
HAGGERSTON	NL	40 B4
HAGLEY	GW	9 A3
HAGLEY ROAD	Harborne	13 C3
HAIGH	L&Y	42 D3
Haigh Jc.	L&NW/LUJt	45 D2
HAILSHAM	LB&SC	5 F5
HAIRMYRES	CAL.	44 D1
HALBEATH	NB	30 A3
HALE END	GE	5 A4
HALEBANK for HALE	L&NW	45 E4 (f47)
HALESOWEN	GW	15 G4
Halesowen Jc.	MID./Halesowen	9 A4
HALESWORTH	GE	12 B2
HALESWORTH	Southwold	12 B2
HALEWOOD	CLC	45 E4
Halewood North Jc.	CLC	45 E4
HALF WAY	Guernsey	46 B4
HALIFAX	L&Y	42 B5
Halifax Shaw Syke (Goods)	L&Y	42 C5
Halifax South Parade (Goods)	GN	42 B5
HALKIRK	HR	38 D3
Hall Farm Jc.	GE	40 A3
HALL ROAD	L&Y	45 F2
Hall Royd Jc.	L&Y	21 E1
HALLATON	GN&L&NWJt	16 F2
Hallaton Jc.	GN&L&NWJt	16 F2
HALLATROW	GW	8 D1
Hallcraig	CAL.	30 D5
Hallcraig (Goods)	NB	44 B4
HALLILOO PLATFORM	SE	5 C3
HALLINGTON	GN	17 A2
Halliwell (Goods)	L&Y	45 C2
HALMEREND	NS	15 C3
HALSALL	LS&PJc	45 F2
Halsnead Col.	L&NW	45 E4
HALSTEAD	CV&H	11 E5
HALSTEAD for KNOCKHOLT	SE	5 C4
HALTON	BIRK. Jt.	45 D5
HALTON (LANCS)	MID.	24 B3
HALTON HOLGATE	S&F	17 B3
Halton Jc.	L&NW	45 D5
Halton Tunnel	BIRK. Jt.	45 D5
HALTWHISTLE	NE	27 B2
Haltwhistle Tunnel	NE	27 C2
HALWILL JUNCTION	L&SW	1 B5
HAM STREET	SE	6 D4
HAMBLETON	NE	21 D5
HAMILTON	NB	44 B2
HAMILTON CENTRAL	CAL.	44 B2
HAMILTON SQUARE	MER.	45 F4 (f68)
HAMILTON WEST	CAL.	44 B2
HAMILTON'S BAWN	GN(I)	58 A4
HAMMERSMITH	H&CJt	39 D4
HAMMERSMITH	MET.-DIS.	39 D4
HAMMERSMITH & CHISWICK	N&SWJn	39 D3
HAMMERSMITH GROVE ROAD	L&SW	39 D4 (f47)
Hammersmith Jc.	N&SWJn	39 D3
HAMMERTON	NE	21 C4
HAMMERWICH	L&NW	15 E4
HAMPOLE	WR&GJt	21 F4
HAMPSTEAD HEATH	L&NW	40 C1
HAMPSTEAD NORRIS	DN&S	4 A3
Hampstead Road Jc.	L&NW/NL	40 B5 (f34)
Hampstead Tunnel	L&NW	39 B5
HAMPSTHWAITE	NE	21 C3
HAMPTON	L&SW	39 F1
HAMPTON	MID.	15 G5
HAMPTON COURT for MOULSEY	L&SW	39 G2
Hampton Court Jc.	L&SW	39 G2
HAMPTON LOADE	GW	15 G2
HAMPTON WICK	L&SW	39 F2
HAMPTON-IN-ARDEN	L&NW	9 A5
HAMWORTHY	L&SW	3 F5
HAMWORTHY JUNCTION	L&SW	3 F5
HANDBOROUGH	GW	10 E4
HANDFORTH	L&NW	45 A4
HANDSWORTH & SMETHWICK	GW	13 B3
Handsworth Jc.	GW	13 B3
Handsworth Jc.	L&NW	13 B3
HANDSWORTH WOOD	L&NW	13 B3
HANLEY	NS	15 C3

Station, junction, tunnel, viaduct, etc	Railway	Reference
HANNINGTON	GW	9 F5
HANWELL	GW	39 C2
HANWOOD	S&WpJt	14 A1
HAPTON	L&Y	24 D1
HARBORNE	Harborne	13 C3
Harborne Jc.	L&NW/Harborne	13 C3
Harbour Tunnel	LC&D	6 D2
HARBURN	CAL.	30 C3
HARBY & STATHERN	GN&L&NWJt	16 D2
Hardengreen Jc.	NB	30 C2
Hardham Jc.	LB&SC	5 F1
HARDINGHAM	GE	18 F4
Hardwick Road (Goods)	E&M	17 E5
HARE PARK & CROFTON	WR&GJt	42 C2
Hare Park Jc.	WR&GJt	42 C2
HARECASTLE	NS	15 C3
HARESFIELD	MID.	9 E3
HARKER	NB	26 C1
HARLECH	CAM.	19 F2
HARLESTON	GE	12 B3
HARLING ROAD	GE	12 A4
HARLINGTON for TODDINGTON	MID.	11 E1
HARLOW	GE	11 F3
HARMSTON	GN	16 B1
HAROLD WOOD	GE	5 A5
HARPENDEN	GN	11 F1
HARPENDEN	MID.	11 F1
Harpenden Jc.	MID.	11 F1
HARPERLEY	NE	27 D4
Harpur Hill (Goods)	L&NW	15 B4
HARRIETSHAM	LC&D	6 C4
HARRINGAY	GN	40 A5
HARRINGAY PARK (GREEN LANES)	T&HJn	40 A5
HARRINGTON	L&NW	26 E3
HARRINGWORTH	MID.	16 F1
HARRISTOWN	GS&W	54 D4
HARROGATE	NE	21 C3
Harrogate Goods	NE	21 C3
HARROW	L&NW	39 A2
HARROW	MET.	39 A2
HARRYVILLE	B&NC	61 D1
HARSTON	GE	11 D3
HART	NE	28 D4
HARTFIELD	LB&SC	5 D4
HARTFORD	L&NW	45 C5
HARTFORD & GREENBANK	CLC	45 C5
Hartford Jc.	CLC/L&NW	45 C5
HARTLEBURY	GW	9 A3
HARTLEPOOL	NE	28 D4
Hartlepool Docks	NE	28 D4
HARTLEY	NE	28 B5
HARTON ROAD	Wenlock	15 G1
HART'S HILL & WOODSIDE	GW	15 G4
HARTWOOD	CAL.	30 C5
HARVINGTON	MID.	9 C4
HARWICH TOWN	GE	12 E3
HASLEMERE	L&SW	4 C1
HASLINGDEN	L&Y	24 E1
HASSENDEAN	NB	31 F1
Hassockrig Pit	NB	30 C5
HASSOCKS	LB&SC	5 F3
HASSOP for CHATSWORTH	MID.	15 B5
HASTINGS (Joint)	SE/LB&SC	6 F5
Hastings Tunnel	SE	6 F5
HASWELL	NE	28 D5
HATCH	GW	8 G3
HATFIELD	GN	11 F2
HATFIELD PEVEREL	GE	11 F5
HATHERN	MID.	16 D4
HATTON	GW	9 B5
Haugh Head Col.	CAL.	44 C3
Haugh Head Jc.	CAL.	44 B2
HAUGHLEY ROAD	GE	12 C4
HAUGHTON	L&NW	15 E3
HAVANT	LB&SC	4 E2
HAVEN STREET	IoWC	4 F3
HAVERFORDWEST	GW	7 C2
HAVERHILL	CV&H	11 D5
HAVERHILL	GE	11 D5
HAVERSTOCK HILL	MID.	40 C1
Haverstock Hill Tunnel	MID.	39 B5
HAVERTHWAITE	FUR.	24 A4
HAVERTON HILL	NE	28 E4
HAVOD	TV	43 C3
Havod Jc.	TV/BD&R	43 C3
Hawcoat Quarry	FUR.	24 B5
HAWES	NE/MID.	27 G3
HAWES JUNCTION	MID.	27 G2
HAWICK	NB	31 F1
HAWKESBURY LANE	L&NW	16 G5
Hawkhill Jc.	G&SW	29 F3
HAWORTH	MID.	21 D1
HAWSKER	Sc&Wby	28 F2
HAWTHORNDEN	NB	30 C2
HAXBY	NE	21 C5
HAXEY & EPWORTH	GN&GEJt.	22 F5
HAY	MID.	14 F2
HAYBURN WYKE	Sc&Wby	28 G1
Haydock Col.	L&NW	45 D3
HAYDON BRIDGE	NE	27 B3
Haydon Square (Goods)	L&NW	40 C4 (f7)
HAYDONS ROAD	LB&SC/L&SWJt	39 F5
HAYES	GW	5 B2
HAYES (KENT)	SE	40 G2
Hayes Rock Pits	CLC	45 C5
HAYFIELD	S&MJt	21 G1
HAYLE	GW	1 E4
Hayle Wharves	GW	1 E4
HAYMARKET	NB	30 G2
HAYWARDS HEATH	LB&SC	5 E3
Haywards Heath Tunnel	LB&SC	5 E3
HAYWOOD	CAL.	30 C4
HAZEL GROVE	L&NW	45 A4
HAZELHATCH & CELBRIDGE	GS&W	54 B4
HAZELWOOD	MID.	41 F1
HAZLEHEAD BRIDGE	MS&L	42 E4
HEACHAM	H&WN	17 D5
HEADCORN	SE	6 D5
HEADFORD	GS&W	47 F5
HEADINGLEY	NE	42 A3
HEADS NOOK	NE	27 C1
Headstone Tunnel	MID.	15 B5
HEADWOOD	B&NC	61 D3
HEALEY HOUSE	L&Y	42 D5
Healey House Tunnel	L&Y	42 D5
HEALING	MS&L	22 F2
HEALY'S BRIDGE	C&MLt	48 G3
Heap Bridge (Goods)	L&Y	45 A1
HEAPEY	LUJt	45 D1
HEATH TOWN	MID.	15 E3
Heath Town Jc.	MID./L&NW	15 E3
HEATHER	A&NJt	16 E5
HEATHFIELD	GW	2 C4
HEATHFIELD & CROSS IN HAND	LB&SC	5 E5
HEATLEY & WARBURTON	L&NW	45 C4
HEATON	NE	28 A1
HEATON CHAPEL	L&NW	45 A3
Heaton Lodge Jc.	L&Y/L&NW	42 C4
HEATON MERSEY	MID.	45 A4 (f39)
HEATON NORRIS	L&NW	45 A3 (f38)
HEATON PARK	L&Y	45 B2
HEBBURN	NE	28 B5
HEBDEN BRIDGE	L&Y	21 E1
HECK	NE	21 E5
HECKINGTON	GN	17 C2
HECKMONDWIKE	L&Y	42 C4
HEDDON-ON-THE-WALL	NE	27 B5
HEDGELEY	NE	31 F4
HEDNESFORD	L&NW	15 E4
Hednesford Col.	CC&W	15 E4
HEDON	NE	22 E3
HEELEY	MID.	41 A2
HEIGHINGTON	NE	27 E5
Heights Quarry	W&R	27 D3
HELE & BRADNINCH	GW	2 A3
HELEN'S BAY	B&CD	61 F4
HELENSBURGH	NB	29 B3
HELLESDON	E&M	18 E3
HELLIFIELD	MID.	24 C1
HELLINGLY	LB&SC	5 F5
Helm Tunnel	MID.	27 F2
HELMDON	N&BJn.	10 C3
HELMSDALE	HR	38 F4
HELMSHORE	L&Y	24 E1
HELMSLEY	NE	21 A5
HELPRINGHAM	GN&GEJt.	17 D1

Station, junction, tunnel, viaduct, etc	Railway	Reference	Station, junction, tunnel, viaduct, etc	Railway	Reference
HELPSTON for MARKET DEEPING	MID.	17 F1	HIGHLANDMAN	CAL.	33 F3
HELSBY	BIRK. Jt.	45 E5	HIGHLEY	GW	15 G2
Helsby (Goods)	CLC	45 E5	HIGHTOWN	L&Y	45 F2
Helsby Jc.	BIRK. Jt./CLC	45 E5	HIGHWORTH	GW	9 F5
HELSTON	Helston	1 F5	Highworth Jc.	GW	9 G5
HEMEL HEMPSTED	MID.	11 F1	HILDENBOROUGH	SE	5 D5
Hemerdon Bank	GW	2 D5	HILGAY FEN	GE	17 F4
HEMINGBROUGH	NE	21 D5	HILL OF DOWN	MGW	53 A5
HEMPSTOWN	D&BST	54 C4	Hillhouse (Goods)	L&NW	42 C4
HEMSBY	E&M	18 E1	Hillhouse Jc.	CLC/LS&PJc	45 F2
HEMSWORTH	WR&GJt	42 D1	HILLINGTON	E&M	17 E5
Hemsworth East Jc.	HB&WRJn	42 D1	HILLSBOROUGH	GN(I)	61 G2
Hemsworth South Jc.	WR&GJt/HB&WRJn	42 D1	HILLSIDE	NB	34 C2
HEMYOCK	GW	2 A2	HILTON HOUSE	L&Y	45 C2
Hendon	L'derry	28 C5	Hilton Jc.	CAL./NB	33 F5
HENDON	MID.	39 A4	Himley Park	Pensnett	15 F3
Hendre Ladis Siding	MID.	43 E1	Hincaster Jc.	FUR./L&NW	24 A3
HENDREFORGAN	GW	43 D3	HINCKLEY	L&NW	16 F4
HENFIELD	LB&SC	5 F2	Hinckley Summit	L&NW	16 F4
HENGOED	Rhym.	43 B3	HINDERWELL	NE	28 E2
HENLEY	GW	10 G2	HINDLEY	L&Y	45 C2
HENLOW	MID.	11 E1	Hindley & Amberswood (Goods)	L&NW	45 C2 (f6)
HENSALL	L&Y	21 E5	HINDLEY GREEN	L&NW	45 C2
Hensall Jc.	L&Y/HB&WRJn	21 E5	Hindlow (Goods)	L&NW	15 B5
HENSTRIDGE	S&D Jt.	3 D3	HINDOLVESTONE	E&M	18 D4
HENWICK	GW	9 B3	HINTON	MID.	9 C4
HEPSCOTT	NE	27 A5	HINTON ADMIRAL for HIGHCLIFFE-ON-SEA	L&SW	4 F5
HEREFORD BARRS COURT	S&HJt	9 C1	HIPPERHOLME	L&Y	42 B5
HEREFORD BARTON	GW	9 C1	HIRWAIN	GW	43 D2
Hereford Moorfields (Gds)	MID.	9 C1	HISTON	GE	11 C3
HERIOT	NB	30 C1	HITCHIN	GN	11 E2
HERMITAGE	DN&S	4 A3	Hitchin (Goods)	MID.	11 E2
HERNE	L&SW	4 E5	Hither Green Jc.	SE	40 E3
HERNE BAY & HAMPTON-ON-SEA	LC&D	6 B2	HIXON	NS	15 D4
HERNE HILL	LC&D	40 E5	HOCKLEY	GE	6 A5
Herne Hill North & South Jcs.	LC&D	40 E5	HOCKLEY	GW	13 C3
HERTFORD	GE	11 F2	Hodbarrow	FUR.	24 A5
HERTFORD COWBRIDGE	GN	11 F2	Hoddlesden (Goods)	L&Y	24 E2
HERTINGFORDBURY	GN	11 F2	HODNET	GW	15 D2
HESKETH BANK	WLancs	24 E3	HOE STREET, WALTHAMSTOW	GE	40 A3
HESKETH PARK	WLancs	45 F1	Hoggersgate Jc.	NE	28 D5
HESLERTON	NE	22 A4	HOGHTON	L&Y	24 E2
HESSAY	NE	21 C4	HOLBEACH	E&M	17 E3
HESSLE	NE	22 E4	HOLBECK HIGH LEVEL	GN	21 C2
Hessle Jc.	NE	22 A2	HOLBECK LOW LEVEL	MID.	21 C2
Hessle Road Jc.	NE	22 A1	HOLBORN VIADUCT	LC&D	40 C5
HEST BANK	L&NW	24 B3	HOLCOMBE BROOK	L&Y	45 B1
HESTON HOUNSLOW	MET.-DIS.	39 D1	Holgate Bridge Jc.	NE	21 A4
HESWALL	BIRK. Jt.	20 C5	HOLGATE EXCURSION PLATFORM	NE	21 A4
HETHERSETT	GE	18 F3	HOLKHAM	H&WN	18 C5
HETTON	NE	28 D5	HOLLAND ARMS	L&NW	19 D1
HEVER	LB&SC	5 D4	HOLLINGBOURNE	LC&D	6 C5
Hewenden Viaduct	GN	42 A5	HOLLINS	Longdendale	21 F1 (f2)
Hewish Summit	L&SW	3 E1	Hollins (Goods)	L&Y	24 E2
HEXHAM	NE	27 B3	HOLLINWOOD	L&Y	45 A2
Hexthorpe Jc.	MS&L	21 G2	HOLLOWAY	GN	40 B5 (f43)
HEYFORD	GW	10 D4	Holloway (Cattle)	GN	40 B5
HEYTESBURY	GW	3 C4	HOLLYBUSH	G&SW	29 F4
HEYWOOD	L&Y	45 A2	HOLLYBUSH	L&NW	43 B2
HIGH BARNET	GN	5 A3	HOLLYHILL	S&SLt	49 F4
HIGH BLAITHWAITE	M&C	26 D2	HOLME	GN	11 A2
HIGH BLANTYRE	CAL.	44 C2	HOLME	L&Y	24 D1
HIGH FIELD	NE	22 D5	HOLME (YORKS)	NE	22 D5
HIGH HARRINGTON	C&WJn	26 E3	HOLME HALE	W&S	18 F5
HIGH LANE	MS&L/NSJt	15 A4	HOLME LACY	GW	9 C1
High Level Bridge	NE	28 A1	HOLMES	MID.	42 F1
High Peak Jc.	MID./L&NW	41 E2	HOLMES CHAPEL	L&NW	15 B3
HIGH SHIELDS	NE	28 B5	HOLMFIELD	H&OJt	42 B5
High Tor Tunnels	MID.	41 D1	HOLMFIRTH	L&Y	42 D5
HIGH WYCOMBE	GW	10 F2	HOLMSLEY	L&SW	4 E5
HIGHAM	GE	11 C5	HOLMWOOD	LB&SC	5 D2
HIGHAM	SE	6 B5	HOLSWORTHY	L&SW	1 A4
HIGHAM FERRERS & IRTHLINGBOROUGH	L&NW	10 A1	HOLT	E&M	18 D4
Higham Tunnel	SE	6 B5	HOLT JUNCTION	GW	3 B4
HIGHAM-ON-THE-HILL	A&NJt	16 F5	HOLTBY	NE	21 C5
HIGHBRIDGE	GW	8 E3	HOLTON	MS&L	22 F3
HIGHBRIDGE	S&D Jt.	8 E3	HOLTON-LE-CLAY	GN	22 F2
HIGHBURY & ISLINGTON	NL	40 B5	Holwell (Goods)	MID.	16 E3
Highbury Vale (Goods)	GN	40 B5	HOLYHEAD	L&NW	19 A1
HIGHCLERE	DN&S	4 B3	HOLYHEAD ADMIRALTY PIER	L&NW	19 A1
HIGHGATE	GN	39 A5	HOLYTOWN JUNCTION	CAL.	44 A3
HIGHGATE ROAD	T&HJn	40 C1	HOLYWELL	L&NW	20 D5
Highgate Road Jc.	T&HJn/MID.	40 C1	Holywell (Goods)	NE	28 B5

Station, junction, tunnel, viaduct, etc	Railway	Reference	Station, junction, tunnel, viaduct, etc	Railway	Reference
HOLYWOOD	B&CD	61 A5	HUCKNALL	GN	41 E4
HOLYWOOD	G&SW	26 A4	HUCKNALL	MID.	41 E4
HOMERSFIELD	GE	12 A3	HUDDERSFIELD	L&Y/L&NW Jt	42 C5
HOMERTON	NL	40 B3	HUGGLESCOTE	A&NJt	16 E4
HONEYBOURNE	GW	9 C5	Hull Albert Dock	NE	22 A1
HONING	E&M	18 D2	HULL ALEXANDRA DOCK	HB&WRJn	22 A1
HONINGTON	GN	16 C1	HULL BEVERLEY ROAD	HB&WRJn	22 A1
HONITON	L&SW	2 B2	HULL BOTANIC GARDENS	NE	22 A1
Honiton Summit	L&SW	2 A2	Hull Burleigh Street (Goods)	HB&WRJn	22 A1
Honiton Tunnel	L&SW	2 A1	HULL CANNON STREET	HB&WRJn	22 A1
HONLEY	L&Y	42 D5	Hull Kingston Street (Goods)	NE	22 A1
Honley Tunnel	L&Y	42 D5	Hull Neptune Street (Goods)	HB&WRJn	22 A1
HONOR OAK	LC&D	40 E4	HULL PARAGON	NE	22 A1
HONOR OAK PARK	LB&SC	40 E4	Hull Sculcoates (Goods)	HB&WRJn	22 A1
Hoo Jc.	SE	6 B5	Hull Victoria Dock	NE	22 A1
HOOK	L&SW	4 B2	HUMBERSTONE	GN	16 F3
HOOK NORTON	Banbury & Chelt. Dir.	10 D5	HUMBERSTONE ROAD	MID.	16 F3
HOOLE	WLancs	24 E3	HUNCOAT	L&Y	24 D1
HOOLEY HILL	L&NW	21 A2	HUNDRED END	WLancs	24 E3
HOOTON	BIRK. Jt.	45 F5	HUNGERFORD	GW	4 A4
HOPE	L&NW	20 E4	HUNMANBY	NE	22 B3
HOPE EXCHANGE	L&NW	20 E4	HUNNINGTON	Halesowen	9 A4
HOPE EXCHANGE	WM&CQ	20 E4	Hunsbury Hill Tunnel	L&NW	10 B3
HOPTON HEATH	L&NW	14 C1	HUNSTANTON	H&WN	17 D5
HORBURY	L&Y	42 C3	Hunthill Jc.	CAL.	44 C2
HORBURY JUNCTION	L&Y	42 C2	HUNTINGDON	GN	11 B2
HORDERLEY	BC	14 C1	HUNTINGDON Joint	GN&GEJt./KT&H	11 B2
Horeb	L&MM	7 A3	HUNTLY	GNoS	37 E1
HOREHAM ROAD for WALDRON	LB&SC	5 F5	HUNT'S CROSS	CLC	45 E4
HORLEY	LB&SC	5 D3	HUNWICK	NE	27 D5
HORNBY	MID.	24 B2	Hurdlow (Goods)	L&NW	15 B5
HORNCASTLE	H'castle	17 B2	HURLFORD	G&SW	29 E4
HORNCHURCH	LT&S	5 A5	Hurst Green Jc.	LB&SC/SE Joint	5 C4
HORNINGLOW	NS	15 C5	HURSTBOURNE	L&SW	4 B4
Horninglow Jc.	MID.	15 D5	HURWORTH BURN	NE	28 D5
HORNSEA	NE	22 C2	Huskisson (Goods)	CLC	45 G4
HORNSEA BRIDGE	NE	22 C2	HUSTHWAITE GATE	NE	21 B4
HORNSEY	GN	40 A5	HUTCHEON STREET	GNoS	37 G4
HORNSEY ROAD for HORNSEY RISE	T&HJn	40 A5	HUTTON CRANSWICK	NE	22 C4
HORRABRIDGE	GW	1 C5	HUTTON GATE	NE	28 F3
HORRINGFORD	IoWC	4 F3	HUTTON JUNCTION	NE	28 E3
Horrocksford	L&Y	24 D1	HUTTONS AMBO	NE	22 B5
Horrocksford Jc.	L&Y	24 D1	HUYTON	L&NW	45 E4
HORSE & JOCKEY	S(I)	49 A1	HUYTON QUARRY	L&NW	45 E4
HORSEBRIDGE	L&SW	4 C4	HYDE	S&MJt	21 G1
HORSEHAY	W&SJc	15 F2	HYDE JUNCTION	S&MJt	21 G1
HORSELEAP	MGW	53 B2	HYKEHAM	MID.	16 B1
Horsfall Tunnel	L&Y	21 E1	HYLTON	NE	28 C5
HORSFORTH	NE	42 A3	Hylton Lane (Goods)	NE	28 C5
Horsforth Summit	NE	42 A3	HYNDLAND	NB	44 E4
HORSHAM	LB&SC	5 E2	HYTHE	CSVS&H	12 E4
HORSLEY & OCKHAM & RIPLEY	L&SW	5 C2	HYTHE	SE	6 D3
Horsley Fields Jc.	L&NW/GW	13 B2			
HORSTED KEYNES	LB&SC	5 E3	IBROX	G&PJt	44 E3
HORTON	MID.	24 B1	ICKNIELD PORT ROAD	Harborne	13 C3
HORTON KIRBY BOYS HOME	LC&D	5 B5	IDLE	GN	42 A4
HORTON PARK	GN	42 B5	IDRIDGEHAY	MID.	41 E1
HORWICH	L&Y	45 C1	ILDERTON	NE	31 E4
Horwich Fork Jc.	L&Y	45 C2	ILFORD	GE	40 B1
Horwich Locomotive Works Jc.	L&Y	45 C1	ILFRACOMBE	L&SW	7 E3
HOSCAR MOSS	L&Y	45 E1	ILKESTON	GN	41 F3
HOTHFIELD	LC&D	6 D4	ILKESTON JUNCTION	MID.	41 F3
HOUGH GREEN	CLC	45 E4	ILKESTON TOWN	MID.	41 F3
HOUGHAM	GN	16 C1	ILKLEY	MID.	21 C2
HOUNSLOW & WHITTON	L&SW	39 E1	ILKLEY	O&IJt	21 C2
HOUNSLOW BARRACKS	MET.-DIS.	39 D1	ILMINSTER	GW	3 D1
Hounslow Jc.	L&SW	39 E1	INCE	L&Y	45 D2
HOUSTON	CAL.	44 G4	INCE & ELTON	BIRK. Jt.	45 E5
HOUSTON (CROSSLEE)	G&SW	29 C4	INCH	DW&W	54 G2
HOVINGHAM	NE	21 A5	INCH ROAD	L&LS	60 C5
HOW MILL	NE	27 C1	Inchcoonans (Goods)	CAL.	34 E5
Howbeach Col.	FoDC	8 A1	INCHES	CAL.	30 E5
HOWDEN	HB&WRJn	22 E5	Inchicore Works	GS&W	62 D5
HOWDEN	NE	22 D5	INCHTURE	CAL.	34 E5
HOWDEN CLOUGH	GN	42 B3	INCHTURE VILLAGE	CAL.	34 E5
HOWDON-ON-TYNE	NE	28 B5	INCLINE TOP	NE	28 F4
HOWICK	WLancs	24 E3	INGATESTONE	GE	11 G4
HOWSHAM	MS&L	22 F3	INGERSBY	GN	16 F3
HOWTH	GN(I)	54 B2	INGESTRE	GN	15 D4
HOWWOOD	G&SW	29 C4	INGHAM	GE	12 B5
HOY	HR	38 C3	INGLEBY	NE	28 F4
HOYLAKE	SH&D	20 C5	INGLETON	L&NW	24 B2
HUBBERT'S BRIDGE	GN	17 C2	INGLETON	MID.	24 B2

Station, junction, tunnel, viaduct, etc	Railway	Reference	Station, junction, tunnel, viaduct, etc	Railway	Reference
Ingliston	CAL.	30 B5	Kearsley Branch	L&Y	45 B2
Ingrave Summit	GE	5 A5	KEARSNEY	LC&D	6 D2
INGROW	GN	21 D1	KEELE	NS	15 C3
INGROW	MID.	21 D1	KEGWORTH	MID.	16 D4
Ings Road Jc.	GN/L&Y	42 C2	KEIGHLEY	MID.	21 D1
INNERLEITHEN	NB	30 E2	Keighley Goods	GN	21 D1
INNERPEFFRAY	CAL.	33 F4	KEITH	GNoS	37 D1
INNERWICK	NB	31 B2	KEITH	HR	37 D1
INNISHANNON	CB&SC	50 F4	KELLS	B&NC	61 D2
INNISKEEN	GN(I)	58 D4	KELLS	GN(I)	57 F5
INNY JUNCTION	MGW	57 G3	KELLSWATER	B&NC	61 D1
INSCH	GNoS	37 E2	KELMARSH	L&NW	10 A2
INSTOW	L&SW	7 F3	KELSO	NB	31 E2
Inver Tunnel	HR	33 D4	Kelso Jc.	NB	31 E1
INVERAMSAY	GNoS	37 E3	KELSTON for SALTFORD	MID.	8 D1
INVERESK JUNCTION	NB	30 B2	Kelton Fell	R&KF	26 E3
INVERGORDON	HR	36 C5	KELTY	NB	30 A3
Invergordon Shore	HR	36 C5	KELVEDON	GE	12 F5
INVERGOWRIE	CAL.	34 E5	Kelvinhaugh (Goods)	NB	44 E4 (f16)
INVERKEILLOR	NB	34 D3	KEMBLE	GW	9 F4
INVERKEITHING	NB	30 B3	KEMNAY	GNoS	37 F3
INVERKIP	G&WB	29 C2	KEMP TOWN	LB&SC	5 F3
INVERNESS	HR	36 E5	KEMPTON PARK	L&SW	39 F1
Inverness Caledonian Canal Basin	HR	36 E5	KEMSING	LC&D	5 C5
Inverness Harbour	HR	36 D5	KENDAL	L&NW	27 G1
INVERSHIN	HR	35 A5	Kendal (Goods)	L&NW	27 G1
INVERUGIE	GNoS	37 D5	KENFIG HILL	GW	43 E4
INVERURIE	GNoS	37 F3	KENILWORTH	L&NW	10 A5
IPSWICH	GE	12 D3	Kenilworth Jc.	L&NW	10 A5
Ipswich Docks	GE	12 D3	KENLEY	SE	5 C3
IRCHESTER for RUSHDEN &			KENNET	GE	11 C5
HIGHAM FERRERS	MID.	10 B1	KENNETHMONT	GNoS	37 E2
IRLAM & CADISHEAD	CLC	45 C3	Kennington Jc.	GW	10 E4
IRON ACTON	MID.	8 C1	KENNISHEAD	GB&KJt	44 E3
IRONBRIDGE & BROSELEY	GW	15 F2	Kennyhill (Goods)	CAL.	44 D4
IRTON ROAD	R&E	26 F3	KENSAL GREEN	L&NW	39 B4
IRVINE	G&SW	29 E3	Kensal Green Jc.	L&NW	39 B4
Irvine Harbour	G&SW	29 E3	Kensal Green Tunnels	L&NW	39 C4
IRVINESTOWN	EB&S	59 G5	KENSINGTON ADDISON ROAD	WLJt	39 D4
ISFIELD	LB&SC	5 F4	KENSINGTON HIGH STREET	MET.	39 D5
ISHAM & BURTON LATIMER	MID.	10 A2	KENSINGTON HIGH STREET	MET.-DIS.	39 D5
ISLANDBRIDGE	D&LST	62 C5	Kensington High Street (Coal)	MID.	39 D5
Islandbridge Jc.	GS&W	62 C5	Kensington Lillie Bridge (Goods)	WLEJt	39 D4 (f23)
ISLEHAM	GE	11 B4	KENT HOUSE	LC&D	40 F4
ISLEWORTH & SPRING GROVE	L&SW	39 D2	KENTISH TOWN	L&NW	40 C1
ISLIP	L&NW	10 E4	KENTISH TOWN	MID.	40 C1
ITCHEN ABBAS	L&SW	4 C3	Kentish Town Jc.	L&NW/NL	40 B5 (f35)
Itchingfield Jc.	LB&SC	5 E2	Kentish Town Jc.	MID.	40 C1
Ivor Jc.	B&M/L&NW	43 C2	KENT'S BANK	FUR.	24 B4
IVYBRIDGE	GW	2 D5	KENYON JUNCTION	L&NW	45 C3
			KERNE BRIDGE	R&M	9 D1
Jamage Jc.	NS	15 C3	KERRY	CAM.	14 C2
JAMES STREET	MER.	45 G5	KERSHOPE FOOT	NB	27 A1
JAMESTOWN	F&CJn	29 B3	KESH	EB&S	59 F5
JARROW	NE	28 B5	KESWICK	CK&P	26 E2
Jawcraig	NB	30 B5	KETLEY	W&SJc	15 E2
JEDBURGH	NB	31 E1	Ketley Jc.	GW/W&SJc	15 E2
JEDFOOT BRIDGE	NB	31 E1	KETTERING	MID.	10 A2
JERVAULX	NE	21 A2	Kettering Jc.	MID./KT&H	10 A2
Jerviston	CAL.	44 B2	KETTLENESS	NE	28 E2
JESMOND	NE	28 A1	KETTON	MID.	16 F1
Joan Croft Jc.	NE	21 F5	KEW BRIDGE	L&SW	39 D3
JOBSTOWN	D&BST	54 C3	Kew East Jc.	L&SW/N&SWJn	39 D3
JOHN O' GAUNT	GN&L&NWJt	16 E2	KEW GARDENS	L&SW	39 D3
JOHNSHAVEN	NB	34 C2	KEW GARDENS	LS&PJc	45 F1
JOHNSTON	GW	7 C1	KEYHAM ADMIRALTY PLATFORM	GW	1 A1
JOHNSTONE	G&SW	29 C4	KEYINGHAM	NE	22 E2
JOHNSTONE NORTH	G&SW	29 C4	KEYMER JUNCTION	LB&SC	5 E3
JOPPA	NB	30 G1	KEYNSHAM	GW	8 D1
JORDANHILL	NB	44 E4	KIBWORTH	MID.	16 F3
JORDANSTONE	CAL.	34 D5	Kibworth Summit	MID.	16 F3
JORDANSTOWN	B&NC	61 E3	KIDDERMINSTER	GW	9 A3
JUNCTION	GN(I)	62 A1	KIDSGROVE	NS	15 C3
JUNCTION ROAD	NB	30 F2	KIDWELLY	GW	7 A2
JUNCTION ROAD for TUFNELL PARK	T&HJn	40 B1	Kidwelly Quay	BP&GV	7 A2
Junction Road Jc.	T&HJn/MID.	40 C1	KIELDER	NB	27 A2
JUNIPER GREEN	CAL.	30 C3	KILBIRNIE	L&A	29 D3
			KILBOWIE for CLYDEBANK	NB	44 F4
KANTURK	K&N	48 E5	KILBURN	MID.	41 F2
KATESBRIDGE	GN(I)	58 B2	KILBURN & BRONDESBURY	MET.	39 B4
Keadby	MS&L	22 F5	KILBURN & MAIDA VALE	L&NW	39 B5
Keadby Swing Bridge	MS&L	22 F5	KILCOCK	MGW	54 B5
Keane's Points	W&L	48 B1	KILCOE	S&SLt	49 F4

Station, junction, tunnel, viaduct, etc	Railway	Reference
KILCONQUHAR	NB	34 G4
KILCOOLE & NEWTONMOUNTKENNEDY	DW&W	54 D2
KILCREA	C&MD	50 E4
KILDALE	NE	28 F3
KILDARE	GS&W	53 D5
KILDARY	HR	36 C4
KILDONAN	HR	38 F5
KILDRUMMIE PLATFORM	HR	36 D4
KILDWICK & CROSSHILLS	MID.	21 C1
KILFENORA	T&F	47 D2
KILFREE JUNCTION	MGW	56 D3
KILGERRAN	W&C	13 F3
KILGETTY & BEGELLY	P&T	7 D3
KILKENNY	W&CI	49 A4
KILKERRAN	G&SW	29 G3
KILLAGAN	B&NC	61 C1
KILLALOE	W&L	52 F2
KILLAMARSH	MID.	41 A3
KILLARBRAN	CVT	57 A3
KILLARNEY	GS&W	47 F4
Killarney Jc.	GS&W	48 E4
KILLAY	L&NW	7 B3
KILLEAGH	GS&W	49 G1
KILLEARN NEW	S&A	29 B4
KILLEARN OLD	BV	29 B4
KILLESHANDRA	MGW	57 D3
KILLIECRANKIE	HR	33 C4
Killiecrankie Tunnel	HR	33 C4
KILLIN	Killin	33 E2
KILLIN JUNCTION	C&O	33 E1
KILLINEY & BALLYBRACK	DW&W	54 C2
KILLINGWORTH	NE	27 B5
KILLOCHAN	G&SW	29 G3
KILLONAN	W&L	48 A3
KILLORGLIN	GS&W	47 E2
KILLUCAN	MGW	53 A4
KILLURIN	DW&W	50 C4
KILLYGORDON	FV	59 D5
KILLYLEA	GN(I)	58 A5
KILLYRAN	CL&RLt	57 D2
KILLYWHAN	G&SW	26 B4
KILMACOW	W&CI	49 D4
KILMACTHOMAS	WD&L	49 D3
KILMAINHAM WOOD	MGW	58 E5
KILMALCOLM	G&SW	29 C3
KILMALLOCK	GS&W	48 C3
KILMARNOCK	G&SW	29 E4
Kilmarnock (Goods)	GB&KJt	29 E4
KILMAURS	GB&KJt	29 D4
KILMEADAN	WD&L	49 D4
KILMESSAN	MGW	54 A5
KILMORNA	L&K	47 C4
KILMURRY	C&MLt	48 G4
KILNHURST	MID.	42 F1
KILNHURST	MS&L	42 F1
Kilnknowe Jc.	NB	30 E1
Kilnwick Gate (Goods)	NE	22 C4
KILPATRICK	NB	44 G5
KILREA	DC	60 C1
KILROOT	C&L	61 E4
KILSAMPSON	CVT	57 A5
KILSBY & CRICK	L&NW	10 A4
Kilsby Tunnel	L&NW	10 A4
KILSHEELAN	W&L	49 C2
KILSYTH	NB	29 B5
KILSYTH NEW	K&B	29 B5
KILTERMON	CVT	57 A4
Kilton Viaduct	NE	28 E3
Kiltonthorpe	NE	28 E3
KILTOOM	GN&W	52 A1
KILTUBRID	CL&RLt	57 D1
KILUMNEY	C&MD	50 E3
KILWINNING	G&SW	29 D3
KILWINNING	L&A	29 D3
KIMBERLEY	GE	18 F4
KIMBERLEY	GN	41 F4
KIMBERLEY	MID.	41 F4
KIMBOLTON	KT&H	11 B1
Kimbridge Jc.	L&SW	4 D4
KIMMAGE ROAD	D&BST	62 E4
KINALDIE	GNoS	37 F3
KINBRACE	HR	38 E5
KINBUCK	CAL.	33 G3
KINCARDINE	NB	30 A4
KINCRAIG	HR	36 G4
KINETON	E&WJn.	10 B5
KINFAUNS	CAL.	33 F5
KING EDWARD	GNoS	37 C3
King William (Goods)	L&Y	45 B1
KINGENNIE	CAL.	34 E4
KINGHORN	NB	30 A2
KING'S CLIFFE	L&NW	16 F1
KING'S CROSS	GN	40 C5
KING'S CROSS	MET.	40 C5
King's Cross (Goods)	GN	40 B5
KING'S CROSS (SUBURBAN)	GN	40 C5 (f46)
KING'S CROSS (YORK ROAD)	GN	40 C5
King's Ferry Bridge	LC&D	6 B4
KINGS HEATH	MID.	9 A4
KING'S LANGLEY	L&NW	11 G1
KING'S NORTON	MID.	9 A4
KING'S SUTTON	GW	10 C4
KINGSBARNS	NB	34 F3
Kingsbog Jc.	B&NC	61 E3
KINGSBRIDGE ROAD	GW	2 D5
KINGSBURY	MID.	15 F5
KINGSBURY & NEASDEN	MET.	39 B4
KINGSCOTE for TURNER'S HILL	LB&SC	5 D3
KINGSCOURT	MGW	58 E5
KINGSHOUSE	C&O	33 F2
KINGSKERSWELL	GW	2 D3
KINGSKETTLE	NB	34 F5
KINGSKNOWE	CAL.	30 B2
KINGSLAND	Lm&K	14 D1
Kingsland (Goods)	L&NW	40 B4
KINGSMUIR	CAL.	34 D4
KINGSTON (HIGH LEVEL)	L&SW	39 F2
KINGSTON (NEW)	L&SW	39 F2
Kingston-on-Sea (Goods)	LB&SC	5 F3
KINGSTOWN	D&K	54 C2
KINGSTOWN CARLISLE PIER	D&K	54 C2
KINGSWEAR	GW	2 D3
Kingswinford Branch	GW	15 G3
KINGSWOOD	GW	9 A5
Kingswood Jc.	MID.	3 G2
Kingswood Summit	HR	33 E5
Kingswood Tunnel	HR	33 E5
KINGTHORPE	GN	17 B1
KINGTON	Lm&K	14 E2
KINGUSSIE	HR	33 A2
KINLOSS	HR	36 C2
Kinnaber Jc.	CAL./NB	34 C3
KINNERSLEY	MID.	14 E1
Kinning Park (Goods)	CAL.	44 F2
KINROSS JUNCTION	NB	33 G5
KINSALE	CB&SC	50 F3
KINSALE JUNCTION	CB&SC	50 F3
KINTBURY	GW	4 A4
KINTORE	GNoS	37 F3
KIPLING COTES	NE	22 D4
KIPPAX	NE	42 B1
KIPPEN	F&CJn	29 A5
KIRBY CROSS	GE	12 E3
KIRBY MOORSIDE	NE	21 A5
KIRBY MUXLOE	MID.	16 F4
KIRK MICHAEL	MN	23 B2
KIRK SMEATON	HB&WRJn	21 E4
KIRKANDREWS	NB	26 C1
KIRKBANK	NB	31 E2
KIRKBRIDE	NB	26 C2
KIRKBUDDO	CAL.	34 D4
KIRKBURTON	L&NW	42 D4
Kirkburton Jc.	L&NW	42 C4
KIRKBY	FUR.	24 A5
KIRKBY	L&Y	45 E3
KIRKBY	MID.	41 E4
KIRKBY LONSDALE	L&NW	24 A2
KIRKBY STEPHEN	MID.	27 F2
KIRKBY STEPHEN	NE	27 F2
KIRKBY THORE	NE	27 E2
KIRKCALDY	NB	30 A2
Kirkcaldy Harbour	NB	30 A2
KIRKCONNEL	G&SW	30 F5
KIRKCOWAN	P&WJt	25 C3
KIRKCUDBRIGHT	G&SW	26 C5
KIRKDALE	L&Y	45 F3 (f45)

Station, junction, tunnel, viaduct, etc	Railway	Reference
KIRKGUNZEON	G&SW	26 B4
KIRKHAM	L&Y & L&NWJt	24 D3
KIRKHAM ABBEY	NE	22 B5
KIRKHEATON	L&NW	42 C4
KIRKINNER	P&WJt	25 C4
KIRKINTILLOCH	NB	44 C5
Kirkintilloch (Goods)	NB	44 D5
Kirklees Jc.	L&NW	45 D2
KIRKLINGTON & EDINGLEY	MID.	16 B3
KIRKLISTON	NB	30 B3
KIRKNEWTON	NE	31 E3
KIRKPATRICK	CAL.	26 B2
KIRKSTALL	MID.	42 A3
KIRKSTALL FORGE	MID.	42 A3
KIRKSTEAD	GN	17 B2
KIRRIEMUIR	CAL.	34 C4
Kirriemuir Jc.	CAL.	34 D4
KIRTLEBRIDGE	CAL.	26 B2
KIRTLINGTON	GW	10 E4
KIRTON	GN	17 D3
KIRTON LINDSEY	MS&L	22 F4
Kirton Tunnel	MS&L	22 F4
Kit Hill	E.Corn. Min.	1 C5
KITTYBREWSTER	GNoS	37 F4
KIVETON PARK	MS&L	41 A4
Kiveton Park Col.	MID.	41 A4
KNAPTON	NE	22 B4
KNARESBOROUGH	NE	21 C3
KNEBWORTH	GN	11 F2
KNIGHTON	L&NW	14 D2
Knighton North & South Jcs.	MID.	16 F3
Knighton Tunnel	MID.	16 F3
Knight's Hill Tunnel	LB&SC	40 E5
Knightswood North Jc.	NB	44 E4
KNIGHTWICK	GW	9 B2
KNITSLEY	NE	27 C5
KNOCK	B&CD	61 B5
KNOCK	GNoS	37 D1
KNOCKANALLY	B&NC	61 C2
KNOCKANDO	GNoS	36 E2
KNOCKCROGHERY	GN&W	52 A1
KNOCKLONG	GS&W	48 C2
KNOCKLOUGHRIM	DC	60 D1
Knockmore Jc.	GN(I)	61 G2
KNOTT MILL & DEANSGATE	MSJ&A	45 A3 (f31)
KNOTTINGLEY	L&Y/GN	21 E4
KNOTTY ASH & STANLEY	CLC	45 E3
KNOWE'S GATE	NB	27 A4
KNOWLE	GW	9 A5
KNUCKBUE	IV	49 F5
KNUCKLAS	L&NW	14 D2
KNUTSFORD	CLC	45 B5
Kyle of Sutherland Bridge	HR	35 A5
LA HAULE	Jersey	46 E3
LA MOYE	Jersey	46 E4
LA ROCQUE	JE	46 E2
Ladmanlow (Goods)	L&NW	15 B4
Lady Windsor Col.	TV	43 C3
LADYBANK	NB	34 F5
LADYLANDS SIDING	F&CJn	29 A5
LADYSBRIDGE	GNoS	37 C2
LADYWELL	SE	40 E3
LAFFAN'S BRIDGE	S(I)	49 B1
LAINDON	LT&S	5 A5
Laira Jc.	GW	1 A2
LAIRG	HR	35 A5
Lairg Summit	HR	36 A5
LAISTERDYKE	GN	42 A4
LAKENHEATH	GE	11 A5
LAMANCHA	NB	30 D2
LAMBEG	GN(I)	61 G3
LAMBLEY	NE	27 C2
LAMESLEY	NE	27 C5
LAMINGTON	CAL.	30 E4
LAMPETER	M&M	13 E5
LAMPHEY	P&T	7 D2
LAMPORT	L&NW	10 A2
LANARK	CAL.	30 D4
LANCASTER CASTLE	L&NW	24 C3
LANCASTER GREEN AYRE	MID.	24 B3
LANCHESTER	NE	27 D5
LANCING	LB&SC	5 F2

Station, junction, tunnel, viaduct, etc	Railway	Reference
Landor Street Jc.	MID.	13 C4
LANDORE HIGH LEVEL	GW	43 G3
LANDORE LOW LEVEL	GW	43 G3
Landore West Jc.	GW	43 G3
LANGBANK	CAL.	29 C3
LANGFORD	GE	12 F5
LANGHAM HILL	West Somerset Mineral	8 F5
LANGHO	L&Y	24 D2
LANGHOLM	NB	26 A1
LANGLEY	GW	5 B1
LANGLEY	NE	27 C3
LANGLEY GREEN	GW	13 C2
LANGLEY MILL & EASTWOOD	MID.	41 F3
LANGLOAN	CAL.	44 B3
Langloan Iron Works	CAL.	44 B3
LANGPORT	GW	8 F3
LANGRICK	GN	17 C2
Langside Jc.	GB&KJt/CAL.	44 F1
LANGSTON	Hayling	4 E2
LANGTON	MID.	16 F3
Langton Col.	MID.	41 E3
LANGWATHBY	MID.	27 D1
LANGWITH	MID.	41 C4
LANGWORTH for WRAGBY	MS&L	17 A1
Lanridge	CAL.	44 A3
Lanridge Jc.	CAL.	44 A3
Lansdowne Jc.	GW/Banbury & Chelt. Dir.	9 D3
LANSDOWNE ROAD	D&K	62 D2
LAPFORD	L&SW	2 A4
LARBERT	CAL.	30 B5
LARGO	NB	34 G4
LARGS	G&SW	29 C2
LARKHALL	CAL.	44 A1
LARNE	C&L	61 D3
LARNE (narrow gauge)	B&NC	61 D3
LARNE HARBOUR	C&L	61 D4
LARNE HARBOUR (narrow gauge)	B&NC	61 D3
LARTINGTON	NE	27 E4
LASSWADE	NB	30 C2
LATCHFORD	L&NW	45 C4
Latchmere Main Jc.	WLEJt	39 E3
Latchmere S.W. Jc.	WLEJt	39 E3
LATIMER ROAD	H&CJt	39 C4
Lauchope Col.	CAL.	44 A3
LAUNCESTON	GW	1 B4
LAUNCESTON	L&SW	1 B4
LAUNTON	L&NW	10 D3
LAURENCEKIRK	CAL.	34 B2
LAURENCETOWN	GN(I)	58 A3
LAURISTON	NB	34 C2
LAVANT	LB&SC	4 E1
Lavender Hill Jc.	L&SW/LC&D	39 E3
LAVENHAM	GE	12 D5
LAVERNOCK	TV	43 B5
LAW JUNCTION	CAL.	30 D5
LAWDERDALE	CL&RLt	57 D1
LAWLEY BANK	W&SJc	15 E2
LAWRENCE HILL	GW	3 G1
Lawrence Hill Jc.	MID.	3 G1
LAYTOWN	GN(I)	58 F3
LAZONBY	MID.	27 D1
Lazonby Tunnel	MID.	27 D1
LE HOCQ	JE	46 E2
LEA	GN&GEJt.	16 A2
Lea Bank Tunnel	H&OJt	42 B5
LEA BRIDGE	GE	40 B3
Lea Bridge Jc.	GE	40 B3
LEA GREEN	L&NW	45 D3
LEA ROAD	L&Y & L&NWJt	24 D3
Lea Wood Tunnel	MID.	41 E1
LEADBURN	NB	30 C2
LEADENHAM	GN	16 C1
LEAGRAVE	MID.	11 E1
LEALHOLM	NE	28 F3
LEAMINGTON	GW	10 B5
LEAMINGTON AVENUE	L&NW	10 B5
LEAMSIDE	NE	28 D5
LEATHERHEAD	E&L Jt.	5 C2
LEATHERHEAD	LB&SC	5 C2
LEATON	GW	15 E1
LECHLADE	E Glos.	9 F5
LECKHAMPTON	Banbury & Chelt. Dir.	9 D4
LEDBURY	GW	9 C2

Station, junction, tunnel, viaduct, etc	Railway	Reference	Station, junction, tunnel, viaduct, etc	Railway	Reference
LEDSHAM	BIRK. Jt.	45 F5	LICHFIELD TRENT VALLEY LOW LEVEL	L&NW	15 E5
LEDSTONE	NE	42 B1	Lickey Incline	MID.	9 A4
LEE	SE	40 E2	Lickey Incline Summit	MID.	9 A4
Lee Moor	Lee Moor	2 D5	LIDFORD	GW	1 C5
LEEBOTWOOD	S&HJt	14 B1	LIDFORD	L&SW	1 C5
LEEDS CENTRAL	GN/L&Y/L&NW/NE	21 B2	LIDLINGTON	L&NW	10 C1
Leeds Hunslet Lane (Goods)	MID.	21 C2	LIFF	CAL.	34 E5
Leeds Jc.	MID./NE	21 C2	LIFFEY JUNCTION	MGW	62 B4
LEEDS MARSH LANE	NE	42 A2	LIFFORD	MID.	9 A4
LEEDS NEW	L&NW/NE	21 B2	LIFTON	GW	1 B5
LEEDS WELLINGTON	MID.	21 B2	LIGHTCLIFFE	L&Y	42 B5
Leeds Wellington Street (Goods)	GN	21 B2	Lightcliffe Tunnel	L&Y	42 B5
Leeds Wellington Street (Goods)	L&Y/L&NW	21 B2	LILBOURNE	L&NW	10 A4
Leeds Wellington Street (Goods)	NE	21 B2	Lilliehill Jc.	NB	30 A3
Leeds Whitehall Road	L&Y/L&NW	21 C2	LILLIPUT	Oy.	43 G3
LEEGATE	M&C	26 D2	LIMAVADY	B&NC	60 C2
LEEK	NS	15 B4	LIMAVADY JUNCTION	B&NC	60 B3
LEEMING LANE	NE	21 A3	Limefield Jc.	CAL.	30 C4
LEEMOUNT	C&MLt	48 G3	LIMEHOUSE	GE	40 C3
Leen Valley Jc.	GN	41 F4	LIMERICK	W&L	48 A3
LEES	L&NW	21 F1	LIMERICK JUNCTION	GS&W	48 B1
LEGBOURNE ROAD	GN	17 A3	Limestone Branch (see Cilyrychen or Limestone Branch)		
Legbrannock No. 2 Col.	CAL.	44 A3	LIMPLEY STOKE	GW	3 B3
Legbrannock Pits	CAL.	44 A3	LINBY	GN	41 E4
LEHINCH	WClare	51 E4	LINBY	MID.	41 E4
Leicester (Goods)	L&NW	16 F3	LINCOLN	GN	16 A1
LEICESTER BELGRAVE ROAD	GN	16 F3	LINCOLN	MID.	16 A1
LEICESTER CAMPBELL STREET	MID.	16 F3	LINDAL	FUR.	24 B4
LEICESTER WEST BRIDGE	MID.	16 F3	LINDEAN	NB	30 E1
LEIGH	LT&S	6 A5	Linefoot (Goods)	C&WJn	26 D3
LEIGH	NS	15 D4	LINGFIELD	LB&SC	5 D4
LEIGH & BEDFORD	L&NW	45 C3	Lings Col.	MID.	41 C3
Leigh & Bedford (Goods)	L&NW	45 C3	LINGS COLLIERY PLATFORM	MID.	41 C3
LEIGH COURT	GW	9 B3	LINGWOOD	GE	18 F2
Leigham Jc.	LB&SC	40 E5	LINLEY	GW	15 F2
Leigham Tunnels	LB&SC	40 E5/40 F5	LINLITHGOW	NB	30 B4
LEIGHTON	L&NW	10 D1	Linslade Tunnels	L&NW	10 D1
LEISTON	GE	12 C2	LINTON	GE	11 D4
LEITH	CAL.	30 F2	LINTZ GREEN	NE	27 C5
LEITH WALK	NB	30 F2	Linwood	G&SW	29 C4
Leith Walk Goods	NB	30 F2	Linwood (Goods)	CAL.	44 G3
Leixlip	LL&CST	54 B4	Linwood Pits	CAL.	44 G3
LEIXLIP	MGW	54 B4	LIPHOOK	L&SW	4 D1
LELANT	GW	1 E4	LISBELLAW	GN(I)	57 B3
LEMAN STREET	GE	40 C4	LISBURN	GN(I)	61 G3
LEMINGTON	NE	28 A3	Lisburn Road Tunnel	GN(I)	61 B4
LENHAM	LC&D	6 C4	LISCOOLEY	FV	60 D5
LENNOXTOWN	BV	29 B5	LISDOORT	CVT	60 G3
LENTON	MID.	41 G4	LISELTON	L&B	47 B4
LENTRAN	HR	36 D5	LISGORMAN	SL&NC	56 B2
LENWADE	E&M	18 E4	LISKEARD	GW	1 D4
LENZIE JUNCTION	NB	44 D5	LISMORE	F&L	49 E1
LEOMINSTER	S&HJt	9 B1	LISNAGRY	W&L	48 A3
LES MARAIS	JE	46 E2	LISNALINCHY	B&NC	61 E3
LESLIE	NB	34 G5	LISNASKEA	GN(I)	57 B3
LESMAHAGOW	CAL.	30 D5	LISS	L&SW	4 D1
Lesmahagow Jc.	CAL.	44 B2	Lissens (Goods)	L&A	29 D3
LETHAM GRANGE	NB	34 D3	Lissummon Tunnel	GN(I)	58 B3
Lethans	NB	30 A3	LISTOWEL	L&B	47 C4
LETHENTY	GNoS	37 E3	LISTOWEL	L&K	47 C4
LETTERKENNY	Letterkenny	59 C5	LITCHFIELD	DN&S	4 B3
LEUCHARS JUNCTION	NB	34 F4	Litchfield Tunnel	L&SW	4 B3
LEUCHARS OLD	NB	34 E4	LITTLE BYTHAM	GN	16 E1
LEVEN	NB	34 G4	LITTLE EATON	MID.	41 F2
Leven Dock	NB	34 G4	Little Eaton Jc.	MID.	41 F2
Leven Jc.	FUR.	24 A4	LITTLE HULTON	L&NW	45 B2
LEVENSHULME & BURNAGE	L&NW	45 A3	Little Hulton Mineral	L&NW	45 C2
LEVERTON	MS&L	16 A2	LITTLE ISLAND	GS&W	48 E1
LEVISHAM	NE	28 G2	LITTLE KIMBLE	GW	10 E2
LEWES	LB&SC	5 F4	LITTLE MILL	NE	31 F5
LEWES ROAD	LB&SC	5 F3	LITTLE MILL JUNCTION	GW	43 A2
LEWISHAM JUNCTION	SE	40 E3	LITTLE SALKELD	MID.	27 D1
LEWISHAM ROAD	LC&D	40 E3	LITTLE STEEPING	GN	17 B3
LEYBURN	NE	21 A2	LITTLE SUTTON	BIRK. Jt.	45 F5
LEYCETT	NS	15 C3	LITTLE WEIGHTON	HB&WRJn	22 D4
LEYLAND	L&Y & L&NWJt	24 E3	LITTLEBOROUGH	L&Y	21 E1
LEYSMILL	A&F	34 D3	Littlegill Col.	CAL.	30 D5
LEYTON	GE	40 B3	LITTLEHAMPTON	LB&SC	5 G1
LEYTONSTONE	GE	40 A2	Littlehampton Jc.	LB&SC	5 F1
LEZAYRE	MN	23 A3	LITTLEMORE	GW	10 E4
LHANBRYDE	HR	36 C1	LITTLEPORT	GE	11 A4
LICHFIELD CITY	L&NW	15 E5	LITTLETON & BADSEY	GW	9 C4
LICHFIELD TRENT VALLEY HIGH LEVEL	L&NW	15 E5	LITTLEWORTH	GN	17 E2

Station, junction, tunnel, viaduct, etc	Railway	Reference	Station, junction, tunnel, viaduct, etc	Railway	Reference
Litton Tunnel	MID.	15 A5	LLANWRDA	GW & L&NW Jt.	14 F5
LIVERPOOL CENTRAL	CLC	45 G5	LLANWRTYD WELLS	L&NW	14 E4
Liverpool Crown Street (Goods)	L&NW	45 F4 (f53)	LLANYBYTHER	M&M	13 F5
LIVERPOOL EXCHANGE	L&Y	45 G5	Llanycefn	NP&F	13 G2
Liverpool Great Howard Street (Goods)	L&Y	45 G5	LLANYMYNECH	CAM.	14 A2
LIVERPOOL LIME STREET	L&NW	45 F4	LLIWDY	Corris	14 B5
Liverpool North Docks (Goods)	L&Y	45 G5	LLONG	L&NW	20 E5
Liverpool South Docks (Goods)	L&Y	45 G5	LLWYDCOED	GW	43 D2
LIVERPOOL STREET	GE	40 C4	LLWYNGWERN	Corris	14 B5
Liverpool Waterloo (Goods)	L&NW	45 G5	LLWYNGWRIL	CAM.	13 A5
LIVERSEDGE	L&Y	42 C4	LLWYNPIA & TONYPANDY	TV	43 D3
LIVINGSTONE	E&B	30 C4	LLYNCLYS	CAM.	20 G4
LIXNAW	L&K	47 C3	LLYSFAEN	L&NW	19 D4
LLANARTHNEY	L&NW	13 G5	LOANHEAD	NB	30 C2
LLANBEDR & PENSARN	CAM.	19 G2	LOCH AWE	C&O	32 F2
LLANBERIS	L&NW	19 E2	LOCH LEVEN	NB	33 G5
LLANBISTER ROAD	L&NW	14 D2	Loch of Park Summit	GNoS	36 E1
LLANBRYNMAIR	CAM.	14 B4	LOCH SKERROW	P&WJt.	25 B5
LLANCAIACH & NELSON	GW	43 C3	LOCH TAY (KILLIN PIER)	Killin	33 E2
LLANDAFF	TV	43 B4	LOCHANHEAD	G&SW	26 B4
LLANDEBIE	GW	43 G1	LOCHARBRIGGS	CAL.	26 B3
Llandegai Tunnel	L&NW	19 D2	LOCHEARNHEAD	C&O	33 F2
LLANDENNY	GW	8 A3	LOCHEE	CAL.	34 E4
LLANDERFEL	C&B	19 F5	Lochend Jc.	NB	30 F1
Llanderfel Tunnel	C&B	19 F5	LOCHGELLY	NB	30 A3
LLANDILO	GW	13 G5	LOCHLUICHART	HR	35 C4
LLANDILO BRIDGE	L&NW	13 G5	LOCHMABEN	CAL.	26 A3
LLANDINAM	CAM.	14 C3	Lochmill (Goods)	NB	30 B4
LLANDOVERY	GW & L&NW Jt.	14 F5	LOCHWINNOCH	G&SW	29 C3
LLANDRILLO	C&B	19 F5	LOCKERBIE	CAL.	26 A3
LLANDRINDOD WELLS	L&NW	14 D3	LOCKINGTON	NE	22 C4
LLANDUDNO	L&NW	19 C3	LOCKWOOD	L&Y	42 D5
LLANDUDNO JUNCTION	L&NW	19 D4	Lockwood Col.	NB	44 C4
LLANDULAS	L&NW	19 D4	LODGE HILL	GW	8 E2
LLANDYSSIL	GW	13 F4	LOFTHOUSE & OUTWOOD	GN	42 B2
LLANELLY	GW	7 B3	LOFTHOUSE & OUTWOOD	MJt.	42 B2
Llanelly Dock (Goods)	GW	7 B3	Lofthouse North & South Jcs.	GN/MJt	42 B2
Llanelly Docks	L&MM	7 B3	LOFTUS	NE	28 E3
Llanelly Victoria Road (Goods)	L&MM	7 B3	Logan Jc.	G&SW	29 F5
LLANERCHYMEDD	L&NW	19 C1	LOGIERIEVE	GNoS	37 E4
LLANFAIR	L&NW	19 D2	LOGIN	W&C	13 G2
LLANFAIRFECHAN	L&NW	19 D3	LOMBARDSTOWN	GS&W	48 E4
LLANFALTEG	W&C	13 G2	LONDESBOROUGH	NE	22 D5
LLANFECHAIN	CAM.	14 A2	LONDON BRIDGE	LB&SC	40 D4
LLANFIHANGEL	CAM.	13 C5	LONDON BRIDGE	SE	40 C4
LLANFIHANGEL	GW	14 G2	London Docks (Goods)	GE	40 C4
LLANFYLLIN	CAM.	14 A3	LONDON FIELDS	GE	40 B4
LLANFYRNACH	W&C	13 F3	LONDON NECROPOLIS	L&SW	40 D5
LLANGADOCK	GW & L&NW Jt.	14 F5	LONDON ROAD	L&SW	5 C1
LLANGAMMARCH WELLS	L&NW	14 E4	LONDON ROAD	LB&SC	5 F3
LLANGEFNI	L&NW	19 D1	LONDONDERRY	GN(I)	60 C4
LLANGEINOR	GW	43 D3	Londonderry City (Goods)	LP&HC	60 C4
LLANGENNECH	GW	7 B3	LONDONDERRY GRAVING DOCK	L&LS	60 C4
LLANGLYDWEN	W&C	13 G2	LONDONDERRY WATERSIDE	B&NC	60 C4
LLANGOLLEN	VoL	20 F5	LONG BUCKBY	L&NW	10 B3
LLANGONOYD	GW	43 E3	LONG CLAWSON & HOSE	GN&L&NWJt	16 D2
LLANGUNLLO	L&NW	14 D2	LONG EATON	MID.	41 G3
LLANGWYLLOG	L&NW	19 C1	Long Eaton Jc.	MID.	16 D4
LLANGYBI	L&NW	19 F1	LONG MARSTON	GW	9 C5
LLANGYBI	M&M	13 E5	LONG MARTON	MID.	27 E2
LLANHARAN	GW	43 D4	LONG MELFORD	CSVS&H	12 D5
Llanharan Jc.	GW	43 D4	LONG PARISH	L&SW	4 C4
LLANHARRY	TV	43 C4	LONG PRESTON	MID.	24 C1
LLANHILLETH	GW	43 B2	LONG STANTON	GE	11 C3
Llanhilleth Jc.	GW	43 B2	Long Stow Siding (Goods)	KT&H	11 B1
LLANIDLOES	CAM.	14 C4	LONG SUTTON	E&M	17 E3
LLANILAR	M&M	13 D5	Longcliffe (Goods)	L&NW	15 C5
LLANISHEN	Rhym.	43 B4	LONGDON ROAD for ILMINGTON	GW	9 C5
LLANMORLAIS	L&NW	7 B3	LONGFORD	MGW	57 F1
LLANPUMPSAINT	GW	13 F4	LONGFORD & EXHALL	L&NW	16 G5
LLANRHAIADR	L&NW	19 E5	LONGFORGAN	CAL.	34 E5
LLANRHYSTYD ROAD	M&M	13 C5	Longhedge Jc.	LC&D/WLEJt	39 E3
LLANRWST & TREFRIW	L&NW	19 E4	LONGHIRST	NE	27 A5
LLANSAMLET	GW	43 F2	LONGHOPE	GW	9 D2
LLANSANTFFRAID	CAM.	14 A2	LONGHOUGHTON	NE	31 F5
LLANTARNAM	GW	43 A3	LONGMORN	GNoS	36 D2
LLANTRISSANT	GW	43 C4	LONGNIDDRY	NB	30 B1
LLANTRISSANT	TV	43 C4	LONGPAVEMENT	L&E	48 A4
Llantrissant Common Jc.	EV/TV	43 C4	LONGPORT	NS	15 C3
LLANTWIT	TV	43 C4	LONGRIDGE	L&Y & L&NWJt	24 D2
LLANUWCHLLYN	GW	19 G4	Longridge Quarries	L&NW	24 D2
LLANWERN	GW	8 B3	LONGRIGGEND	NB	30 C5
LLANWNDA	L&NW	19 E2	LONGSIDE	GNoS	37 D5

Station, junction, tunnel, viaduct, etc	Railway	Reference	Station, junction, tunnel, viaduct, etc	Railway	Reference
MANCHESTER CENTRAL	CLC	45 A3 (f35)	Martello Tunnel	SE	6 D2
MANCHESTER EXCHANGE	L&NW	45 A3 (f26)	MARTHAM	E&M	18 E1
Manchester Line Jc.	L&NW	20 E2	MARTIN MILL	SE & LC&D Jt.	6 D1
MANCHESTER LONDON ROAD	L&NW	45 A3 (f32)	MARTOCK	GW	3 D2
MANCHESTER LONDON ROAD	MSJ&A	45 A3 (f32)	MARTON	L&NW	10 A5
Manchester Oldham Road (Goods)	L&Y	45 A3 (f27)	MARYBOROUGH	GS&W	53 E4
MANCHESTER OXFORD ROAD	MSJ&A	45 A3 (f33)	Maryfield	CAL.	34 E4
MANCHESTER ROAD	GN	42 B4	MARYHILL	NB	44 E4
MANCHESTER VICTORIA	L&Y	45 A3 (f25)	MARYKIRK	CAL.	34 C3
MANEA	GE	11 A3	MARYLAND POINT	GE	40 B2
MANGOTSFIELD	MID.	8 C1	MARYPORT	M&C	26 D3
Manley (Goods)	CLC	45 E5	Maryport Docks	L&NW	26 D3
Manmoel Col.	Hall's Tm.	43 B2	Maryport Docks Branch Jc.	L&NW	26 D3
Mannez Quarry	Alderney	46 A1	MARYTAVY	GW	1 C5
MANNINGHAM	MID.	42 A4	MARYVILLE	NB	44 C3
MANNINGTREE	GE	12 E4	MASBOROUGH for ROTHERHAM	MID.	42 F1
Manningtree East & North Jcs.	GE	12 E4	MASBURY	S&D Jt.	3 C2
MANOD	B&F	19 F3	Masbury Summit	S&D Jt.	3 B2
MANOR CUNNINGHAM	Letterkenny	60 C5 (f14)	MASHAM	NE	21 A3
MANOR PARK	GE	40 B2	MASSINGHAM	E&M	18 E5
MANORBIER	P&T	7 D2	MATLOCK BATH	MID.	41 D1
MANORHAMILTON	SL&NC	56 B1	MATLOCK BRIDGE	MID.	41 D1
MANORS	NE	28 A1	MAUCHLINE for CATRINE	G&SW	29 E4
MANSFIELD	MID.	41 D4	MAUD JUNCTION	GNoS	37 D4
MANSFIELD WOODHOUSE	MID.	41 D4	Mauds Bridge (Goods)	MS&L	22 F5
MANSION HOUSE	MET.-DIS.	40 C5 (f13)	MAWCARSE	NB	33 G5
MANTON for UPPINGHAM	MID.	16 F2	MAXTON	NB	31 E1
Manton Tunnel	MID.	16 F2	Maxwell Jc.	CAL.	44 F1 (f20)
MANUEL HIGH LEVEL	NB	30 B4	MAXWELLTOWN	G&SW	26 B4
MANUEL LOW LEVEL	NB	30 B4	MAYBOLE	G&SW	29 F3
MANULLA JUNCTION	GN&W	55 E5	MAYFIELD	LB&SC	5 E5
MARAZION ROAD	GW	1 F4	Mayfield Branch	G&SW	29 E4
MARCH	GE	17 F3	MAYNOOTH	MGW	54 B4
March North, South & West Jcs.	GE	17 F3	MAYTOWN	B&NT	58 C4
MARCHINGTON	NS	15 D5	MAZE HILL & GREENWICH PARK	SE	40 D3
MARCHMONT	NB	31 D2	MEADOW HALL	MS&L	42 F2
MARDEN	SE	6 D5	MEALSGATE	M&C	26 D2
MARDEN PARK	LB&SC/SE Joint	5 C3	MEASHAM	A&NJt	16 E5
MARDOCK	GE	11 F3	MEDBOURNE	GN&L&NWJt	16 F2
Mardy Jc.	GW/GW&TVJt.	43 C2	MEDGE HALL	MS&L	22 F5
Marefield North & South Jcs.	GN&L&NWJt/GN	16 F2	Medina Wharf	IoWC	4 F3
Marefield West Jc.	GN	16 F2	Medomsley Col.	NE	27 C4
MARFLEET	NE	22 D3	MEDSTEAD	L&SW	4 C2
MARGATE	SE	6 B1	MEIGLE	CAL.	34 D5
MARGATE & CLIFTONVILLE	LC&D	6 B1	MEIKLE EARNOCK	CAL.	44 B1
MARGATE EAST	LC&D	6 B1	MEIROS COLLIERY	GW	43 D4
MARINO	B&CD	61 F3	Melangoose Mill	Cornwall Minerals	1 D2
MARISHES ROAD	NE	22 A5	MELBOURNE	MID.	16 D5
MARK LANE	MET.-DIS./MET.Jt	40 C4 (f16)	MELDON	NB	27 A5
MARKET BOSWORTH	A&NJt	16 F5	Meldon Jc.	L&SW	2 B5
MARKET DRAYTON	GW	20 F2	MELDRETH & MELBOURN	R&H	11 D3
Market Drayton Jc.	L&NW/N&MD	20 E2	Meliden (Goods)	L&NW	19 C5
Market Drayton Jc.	S&WnJt/GW	15 E2	MELKSHAM	GW	3 A4
MARKET HARBOROUGH	L&NW	16 G2	MELLING	FUR. & MID. Jt	24 B2
MARKET HARBOROUGH	MID.	16 G2	MELLIS	GE	12 B4
MARKET RASEN	MS&L	22 G3	MELLS	GW	3 B3
MARKET WEIGHTON	NE	22 D5	MELMERBY	NE	21 A3
MARKETHILL	GN(I)	58 B4	MELROSE	NB	31 E1
MARKHAM COLLIERY	MID.	41 B3	MELTHAM	L&Y	42 D5
MARKINCH	NB	34 G5	Meltham Branch Jc.	L&Y	42 D5
MARKS TEY	GE	12 E5	MELTON	GE	12 D3
MARLBOROUGH	M&SWJn.	4 A5	MELTON CONSTABLE	E&M	18 D4
MARLBOROUGH	Marl.	4 A5	Melton Jc.	MID.	16 E2
MARLBOROUGH ROAD	MET.	39 B5	MELTON MOWBRAY	MID.	16 E2
MARLESFORD	GE	12 C2	MELTON MOWBRAY (Joint)	GN&L&NWJt	16 E2
Marley Tunnel	GW	2 D4	MENAI BRIDGE	L&NW	19 D2
MARPLE	S&MJt	21 G1	MENHENIOT	GW	1 D4
MARRON JUNCTION	L&NW	26 E3	MENSTON	MID.	21 D2
MARSDEN	L&NW	21 F1	MENSTRIE	NB	30 A5
MARSDEN	SSM&WC	28 B5	MENTHORPE GATE	NE	21 D5
MARSH BROOK	S&HJt	14 C1	MEOLS	SH&D	20 C5
Marsh Farm Jc.	S&HJt/Wenlock	14 C1	MEOLS COP	LS&PJc	45 F1
MARSH GIBBON & POUNDON	L&NW	10 D3	MEOPHAM	LC&D	5 B5
Marsh Jc.	GE	18 F1	MERCHISTON	CAL.	30 G2
MARSH LANE & STRAND ROAD	L&Y	45 F3 (f42)	MERRION	D&K	62 D2
MARSH MILLS	GW	2 D5	Merrybent Jc.	NE/M&D	27 E5
MARSHFIELD	GW	43 A4	MERSEY ROAD & AIGBURTH	CLC	45 F4
MARSKE	NE	28 E3	MERSTHAM	SE	5 C3
MARSTON	GW	3 D2	Merstham Tunnel	SE	5 C3
MARSTON	NE	21 C4	MERSTONE	IoWC	4 F3
MARSTON GATE	L&NW	10 E2	MERTHYR HIGH STREET	GW	43 C2
MARSTON GREEN	L&NW	15 G5	Merthyr Tunnel	GW	43 C2
Marston Jc.	NS	15 D5	MERTHYR VALE	TV	43 C2

Station, junction, tunnel, viaduct, etc	Railway	Reference
MERTON ABBEY	LB&SC/L&SWJt	39 F5
MERTON PARK	L&SW	39 F4
MERTON PARK	LB&SC/L&SWJt	39 F4
METHIL	NB	30 A2
METHLEY	MID.	42 B1
METHLEY	MJt	42 B1
Methley Jc.	MID./L&Y	42 B1
METHLEY JUNCTION	L&Y	42 B1
METHVEN	CAL.	33 E4
METHVEN JUNCTION	CAL.	33 E4
Metropolitan Jc.	SE	40 D5 (f54)
MEXBOROUGH	MS&L	21 F4
Mexborough West Jc.	MS&L/S&KJt	42 F1
MICHELDEVER	L&SW	4 C3
MICKLE TRAFFORD	BIRK. Jt.	20 D3
MICKLE TRAFFORD	CLC	20 D3
MICKLEFIELD	NE	42 A1
Mickleham Tunnel	LB&SC	5 C2
MICKLEHURST	L&NW	21 F1
MICKLEOVER	GN	41 G1
MICKLETON	NE	27 E4
MICKLEY	NE	27 C4
MIDCALDER	CAL.	30 C3
Midcalder Jc.	CAL.	30 C3
MIDDLE DROVE	GE	17 F4
MIDDLE DUFFRYN COLLIERY	GW	43 C2
Middle Hill Tunnel	GW	3 A4
Middlemuir or Monkland Jc.	NB	44 C5
MIDDLESBROUGH	NE	28 E4
MIDDLETON	GE	17 E5
MIDDLETON	L&Y	45 A2
Middleton	Ludlow & Clee Hill	9 A1
MIDDLETON	NB	27 A4
MIDDLETON	NE	27 E3
MIDDLETON (WESTMORLAND)	L&NW	24 A2
MIDDLETON JUNCTION	L&Y	45 A2
MIDDLETOWN	S&WpJt	14 A2
MIDDLEWICH	L&NW	20 D2
MIDDLEWOOD	L&NW	15 A4
MIDDLEWOOD	MS&L/NSJt	15 A4
MIDFORD	S&D Jt.	3 B3
MIDGE HALL	L&Y	24 E3
MIDGHAM	GW	4 A3
MIDHURST	L&SW	4 D1
MIDHURST	LB&SC	4 D1
MIDLETON, BALLINACURRA & CLOYNE	GS&W	48 G1
MIDSOMER NORTON	S&D Jt.	3 B3
MILBORNE PORT	L&SW	3 D3
MILCOTE	GW	9 B5
MILDENHALL	GE	11 B5
MILDMAY PARK	NL	40 B4
Mileage Yard (Goods & Coal)	GW	39 C1
MILES PLATTING	L&Y	45 A3
MILFORD	GS&W	53 G5
MILFORD	L&SW	5 D1
MILFORD	Milford	7 D1
MILFORD & BROCTON	L&NW	15 E4
Milford Jc.	L&SW	4 D5
MILFORD JUNCTION	NE	21 D4
Milford Tunnel	MID.	41 F2
MILKWALL	S&WJt	8 A2
MILL HILL	GN	5 A3
MILL HILL	IoWC	4 F3
MILL HILL	L&Y	24 E2
MILL HILL	MID.	5 A2
MILL HILL PARK	MET.-DIS.	39 D3
MILL HOUSES & ECCLESALL	MID.	41 A2
Mill Street (Goods)	GW	43 D2
MILLBANK	PsT	60 B1 (f2)
MILLBROOK	Jersey	46 E3
MILLBROOK	L&SW	4 E4
MILLBROOK for AMPTHILL	L&NW	10 C1
MILLERHILL	NB	30 B2
MILLER'S DALE for TIDESWELL	MID.	15 A5
Miller's Dale Jc.	MID.	15 A5
MILLFIELD	NE	28 C5
MILLIKEN PARK	G&SW	29 C4
MILLISLE	P&WJt	25 D4
Millom (Goods)	FUR.	24 A5
MILLOM (HOLBORN HILL)	FUR.	24 A5
MILLSTREET	GS&W	48 E5
MILLTIMBER	GNoS	37 G3
MILLTOWN	DW&W	62 E3
MILLTOWN (KERRY)	GS&W	47 E3
MILLVALE	B&NT	58 C3
MILLWALL DOCKS	Millwall Ex.	40 D3
MILLWALL JUNCTION	GE	40 D1
Millwood Jc.	FUR.	24 B5
Millwood Tunnel	L&Y	21 E1
MILNATHORT	NB	33 G5
Milner Royd Jc.	L&Y	42 C5
Milner Wood Jc.	MID/O&IJt	21 C2
MILNGAVIE	NB	44 E5
Milngavie Jc.	NB	44 E5
MILNROW	L&Y	45 A1
MILNTHORPE	L&NW	24 A3
MILTON	L&SW	4 F5
MILTON	NB	29 B5
MILTON	NS	15 C3
Milton Jc.	CAL.	44 D4
MILTOWN MALBAY	WClare	51 F4
MILVERTON	Devon & Somerset	8 F4
MINDRUM	NE	31 E3
MINEHEAD	Minehead	8 E5
Minera	GW	20 E5
MINETY	GW	9 F4
MINFFORDD	CAM.	19 F2
MINFFORDD	Fest.	19 F2
Minions	L&C	1 C4
Minories Jc.	MET./MET.-DIS.	40 C4 (f5)
MINSHULL VERNON	L&NW	20 E2
Minster East & West Jcs.	SE	6 C2
MINSTER JUNCTION	SE	6 C2
MINSTERLEY	S&WpJt.	14 B1
Mint Street (Goods)	GE	40 C4 (f10)
Mint Street (Goods)	GN	40 C4 (f9)
MINTLAW	GNoS	37 D4
Mirehouse Jc.	FUR.	26 E4
MIRFIELD	L&Y	42 C4
MISTERTON	GN&GEJt.	22 G5
MISTLEY	GE	12 E4
MITCHAM	LB&SC	39 G5
MITCHAM JUNCTION	LB&SC	39 G5
MITCHELDEAN ROAD	GW	9 D2
Mitre Bridge (Goods)	L&NW	39 C4
Mitre Bridge Jc.	L&NW	39 C4
MOAT LANE JUNCTION	CAM.	14 C3
MOATE	MGW	53 B2
MOBBERLEY	CLC	45 B4
MOCHDRE & PABO	L&NW	19 D4
MOFFAT	CAL.	30 G3
MOGEELY	GS&W	48 G1
MOHILL	CL&RLt	57 E1
MOIRA	GN(I)	61 G2
MOIRA	MID.	16 E5
MOLAHIFFE	GS&W	47 E3
MOLD	L&NW	20 D5
Mold Jc.	L&NW	20 D4
MOLLINGTON	BIRK. Jt.	20 D4
MOLYNEUX BROW	L&Y	45 B2
Molyneux Jc.	L&Y/L&NW	45 B2
MONAGHAN	GN(I)	57 B5
MONAGHAN ROAD	GN(I)	57 C5
MONASTEREVAN	GS&W	53 D5
Monckton Main Col.	MS&L/HB&WRJn/MID.	42 D2
Moncrieff Tunnel	CAL.	33 F5
MONEYCARRIE	DC	60 C1
MONEYMORE	B&NC	60 E1
MONIFIETH	D&AJt	34 E4
MONIKIE	CAL.	34 D4
MONK BRETTON	MID.	42 E2
Monk Bretton Jc.	MID./HB&WRJn	42 E2
MONK FRYSTON	NE	21 D4
Monkland Jc. (see Middlemuir or Monkland Jc.)		
MONKSEATON	NE	28 B5
MONKTON	G&SW	29 E3
MONKWEARMOUTH	NE	28 C5
Monkwood Col.	MID.	41 B2
MONMORE GREEN	L&NW	15 E3
MONMOUTH MAY HILL	R&M	8 A2
MONMOUTH TROY	GW	8 A2
MONSAL DALE	MID.	15 A5
MONTACUTE	GW	3 D2
MONTGOMERY	CAM.	14 B2
MONTGREENAN	G&SW	29 D3
MONTON GREEN	L&NW	45 B3

Station, junction, tunnel, viaduct, etc	Railway	Reference	Station, junction, tunnel, viaduct, etc	Railway	Reference
MONTPELIER	BP&P	3 F1	MOUNT VERNON	NB	44 C3
MONTROSE	CAL.	34 C2	MOUNTAIN ASH	Aberdare	43 C2
MONTROSE	NB	34 C2	MOUNTAIN ASH	GW	43 C2
MONUMENT LANE	L&NW	13 C3	Mountain Branch	GW	7 A3
MONYMUSK	GNoS	37 F2	Mountfield Tunnel	SE	6 E5
Moor End (Goods)	MS&L	42 E3	MOUNTMELLICK	W&CI	53 D3
MOOR ROW	WC&EJt	26 F3	MOUNTRATH & CASTLETOWN	GS&W	53 E3
Moorcock Tunnel	MID.	27 G3	MOURNE HOTEL	W&RT	58 C2
MOORE	L&NW	45 D4	MOW COP	NS	15 B3
MOORFIELDS	B&NC	61 D2	MOYVALLEY	MGW	53 B5
MOORGATE STREET	MET.	40 C4	MUCH WENLOCK	MW&SJ	15 F2
MOORHAMPTON	MID.	14 E1	MUCHALLS	CAL.	34 A1
MOORSIDE & WARDLEY	L&Y	45 B2 (f15)	MUIR OF ORD	HR	35 D5
MOORSWATER	L&C	1 D4	MUIRKIRK	G&SW	29 E5
MOORTHORPE	S&KJt	42 D1	MULBEN	HR	36 D1
Moorthorpe North Jc.	S&KJt	42 D1	MULLAFERNAGHAN	GN(I)	58 A3
MOORTOWN	MS&L	22 F3	MULLAGHY	SL&NC	57 B2
Moorwoods Col.	MID.	41 E3	MULLINAVAT	W&CI	49 C4
MORCHARD ROAD	L&SW	2 A4	MULLINGAR	MGW	53 A3
MORDEN	LB&SC	39 F5	MULTYFARNHAM	MGW	57 G3
MOREBATH	Devon & Somerset	8 F5	MUMBLES (OYSTERMOUTH)	Oy.	43 G3
Morebath Jc.	Devon & Somerset/T&ND	7 F5	MUMBLES ROAD	L&NW	43 G3
MORECAMBE	L&NW	24 B3	MUMBLES ROAD	Oy.	43 G3
MORECAMBE	MID.	24 B3	MUMBY ROAD	S&W	17 A4
MORECAMBE HARBOUR	MID.	24 B3	MUNCASTER	R&E	26 G3
Morecambe North & South Jcs.	L&NW	24 B3	MURRAYFIELD	CAL.	30 F2
MORESBY PARKS	C&WJn	26 E3	MURROW	E&M	17 F3
MORETON	L&SW	3 F3	MURROW	GN&GEJt.	17 F3
MORETON	SH&D	20 C5	MURTHLY	HR	33 E5
MORETONHAMPSTEAD	GW	2 B4	MURTHWAITE	R&E	26 G3
MORETON-IN-MARSH	GW	9 D5	MURTLE	GNoS	37 G4
MORETON-ON-LUGG	S&HJt	9 C1	MURTON JUNCTION	NE	28 C5
Morlais Jc.	B&M & L&NW Jt.	43 C1	MUSGRAVE	NE	27 F2
Morlais Tunnel	L&NW	43 C1	MUSSELBURGH	NB	30 B2
MORLEY	GN	42 B3	MUSWELL HILL	MH&P	40 A5
MORLEY	L&NW	42 B3	MUTHILL	CAL.	33 F4
Morley Tunnel	L&NW	42 B3	MUTLEY	GW	1 A2
MORMOND	GNoS	37 C4	Mwyndy Jc.	EV	43 C4
MORNINGSIDE	CAL.	30 C5	Mynydd-y-Garreg	GV	7 A2
MORNINGSIDE	NB	30 C5	Myrtle Hill Jc.	GW	13 G4
MORNINGSIDE ROAD	NB	30 G2	MYTHOLMROYD	L&Y	21 E1
MORPETH	NE	27 A5			
MORRISTON	GW	43 G2	N&SW Jc.	L&NW/N&SWJn	39 C4
MORRISTON	MID.	43 G2	NAAS	GS&W	54 C5
MORTHOE	L&SW	7 E3	NABURN	NE	21 C5
Morthoe Summit	L&SW	7 E3	Naburn Swing Bridge	NE	21 C5
MORTIMER	GW	4 A2	NAFFERTON	NE	22 C3
MORTLAKE & EAST SHEEN	L&SW	39 E3	NAILSEA	GW	8 D2
MORTON PINKNEY	E&WJn.	10 C4	NAILSWORTH	MID.	9 F3
MORTON ROAD	GN	17 E1	NAIRN	HR	36 D4
MOSELEY	MID.	15 G4	NANCEGOLLAN	Helston	1 F5
MOSES GATE	L&Y	45 B2	NANNERCH	M&DJn.	20 D5
MOSS	NE	21 E5	NANTCLWYD	L&NW	19 E5
MOSS & PENTRE	WM&CQ	20 E4	NANTGAREDIG	L&NW	13 G4
Moss (Goods)	GW	20 E4	NANTLLE	L&NW	19 E2
MOSS BANK	L&NW	45 D3	Nantmawr	PS&NW	14 A2
Moss Bay Iron Works	C&WJn	26 E4	NANTWICH	L&NW	20 E2
MOSS SIDE	L&Y & L&NWJt	24 D4	NANTYBWCH	L&NW	43 C1
Mossdale Head Tunnel	MID.	27 G3	NANTYDERRY	GW	43 A2
MOSSEND	CAL.	44 B3	NANTYGLO	GW	43 B1
Mossend South Jc.	CAL.	44 B3	NANTYMOEL	GW	43 D3
MOSSLEY	L&NW	21 F1	NARBERTH	P&T	7 C3
MOSSLEY HILL	L&NW	45 F4	NARBOROUGH	GE	17 E5
MOSSTOWIE	HR	36 C2	NARBOROUGH	L&NW	16 F4
MOSTON	L&Y	45 A2	NARROW WATER	GN(I)	58 C3
MOSTYN	L&NW	20 C5	NASSINGTON	L&NW	11 A1
MOTHERWELL	CAL.	44 B2	NAVAN	GN(I)	58 G5
Motherwell (Goods)	CAL.	44 B2	NAVAN JUNCTION	MGW	58 G5
Motherwell Iron Works	CAL.	44 B2	NAVENBY	GN	16 B1
MOTTISFONT	L&SW	4 D4	NAWORTH	NE	27 C1
MOTTRAM & BROADBOTTOM	MS&L	21 G1	NAWTON	NE	21 A5
Mottram Viaduct	MS&L	21 G1	NEATH	GW	43 F2
Mouldron West	CAL.	30 C4	NEATH ABBEY	GW	43 F2
MOULDSWORTH	CLC	45 D5	NEATH LOW LEVEL	GW	43 F2
MOULSFORD	GW	10 G4	NEEDHAM	GE	12 C4
MOULTON	E&M	17 E3	Needingworth Jc.	GN&GEJt./GE/E&StI	11 B3
MOULTON	NE	27 F5	NEEN SOLLERS	GW	9 A2
Mount Elliot Tunnel	DW&W	49 C5	NEEPSEND	MS&L	42 G2
MOUNT FLORIDA	CD	44 E3	NEILSTON	GB&KJt	44 G2
MOUNT MELVILLE	NB	34 F4	NELSON	L&Y	24 D1
Mount Pleasant Tunnel	SE	6 F5	NENAGH	GS&W	52 F1
MOUNT SESKIN ROAD	D&BST	54 C3	Nesbitt Jc.	MGW	54 B5
MOUNT VERNON	CAL.	44 C3	Nesfield Col.	MID.	41 B2

Station, junction, tunnel, viaduct, etc	Railway	Reference	Station, junction, tunnel, viaduct, etc	Railway	Reference
NESTON	BIRK. Jt.	45 F5	NEWHAVEN HARBOUR	LB&SC	5 G4
NETHERBURN	CAL.	44 A1	NEWHAVEN HARBOUR (BOAT STA.)	LB&SC	5 G4
NETHERCLEUGH	CAL.	26 A3	NEWHAVEN TOWN	LB&SC	5 F4
NETHERFIELD & COLWICK	N&GR&C	41 F5	NEWHOUSE	CAL.	44 A3
Netherfield & Colwick (Goods)	GN	41 F5	NEWICK & CHAILEY	LB&SC	5 E4
Netherfield & Colwick North Jc.	GN	41 F5	NEWINGTON	LC&D	6 B4
Netherfield & Colwick West Jc.	N&GR&C/GN	41 F5	NEWINGTON	NB	30 G2
Netherseal Col.	MID.	16 E5	NEWLAND	GW	8 A2
NETHERTHORPE	MID.	41 B3	Newlands	CAL.	44 C3
NETHERTON	L&Y	42 D5	NEWLAY & HORSFORTH	MID.	42 A3
NETHERTON	NE	27 A5	NEWMACHAR	GNoS	37 F4
Netherton (Goods)	NB	30 A3	Newmachar Summit	GNoS	37 F4
Netherton Tunnel	L&Y	42 D5	NEWMAINS	CAL.	30 C5
NETHERTOWN	FUR.	26 F3	NEWMARKET	GE	11 C4
NETHY BRIDGE	GNoS	36 F3	NEWMARKET	K&N	48 C5
NETLEY	L&SW	4 E3	NEWMARKET WARREN HILL	GE	11 C4
NEW BARNET	GN	5 A3	NEWMILL SIDING	CAL.	34 B2
NEW BECKENHAM	SE	40 F3	NEWMILNS	G&SW	29 E4
New Beckenham Jc.	SE	40 F3	NEWNHAM	GW	9 E2
NEW BIGGIN	MID.	27 E2	NEWNHAM BRIDGE	GW	9 A2
NEW BRIGHTON	SH&D	45 F3 (f58)	NEWPARK	CAL.	30 C3
NEW BROMPTON (GILLINGHAM)	LC&D	6 B5	NEWPORT	GE	11 E4
NEW CLEE	MS&L	22 F2	NEWPORT	HB&WRJn	22 D5
NEW CROSS	LB&SC	40 D3	NEWPORT	IoWC	4 F3
NEW CROSS	SE	40 D3	NEWPORT	L&NW	15 E2
New Cross Up Jc.	LB&SC/EL	40 D4	NEWPORT	NE	28 E4
NEW CUMNOCK	G&SW	29 F5	NEWPORT (EAST)	Newport	34 E1
NEW ELTHAM & POPE STREET	SE	40 E1	NEWPORT (WEST)	Newport	34 F2
New England Sidings	GN	17 F2	Newport Dock Street (Goods)	GW	43 A3
New Furnace Tunnel	L&Y	42 B4	NEWPORT HIGH STREET	GW	43 A3
NEW GALLOWAY	P&WJt	26 B5	Newport Mill Street (Goods)	GW	43 A3
NEW HAILES	NB	30 B2	NEWPORT PAGNELL	L&NW	10 C2
New Hayes	CC&W	15 E4	NEWQUAY	Cornwall Minerals	1 D1
NEW HEY	L&Y	21 F1	Newquay Harbour	Cornwall Minerals	1 D1
NEW HOLLAND	MS&L	22 E3	NEWRY BRIDGE STREET	DN&G	58 C3
New Holland Dock	MS&L	22 E3	NEWRY DUBLIN BRIDGE	GN(I)	58 C3
NEW HOLLAND PIER	MS&L	22 E3	NEWRY EDWARD STREET	B&NT	58 C3
New Hucknall Col.	MID.	41 D3	NEWRY EDWARD STREET	GN(I)	58 C3
New Inn Yard Jc.	NL/L&NW	40 C4	Newry Kilmorey Street (Goods)	GN(I)	58 C3
NEW LANE	L&Y	45 E1	NEWSEAT	GNoS	37 D5
NEW LUCE	A&W	25 C3	NEWSHAM	NE	28 B5
NEW MILFORD	GW	7 D2	NEWSHOLME	L&Y	24 C1
NEW MILL END	GN	11 F1	NEWSTEAD	GN	41 E4
NEW MILLS	L&NW	15 A4	NEWSTEAD	MID.	41 E4
NEW MILLS	S&MJt	15 A4	NEWTHORPE, GREASLEY & SHIPLEY GATE	GN	41 F3
New Oaks Jc.	MS&L	42 E1	NEWTON	CAL.	44 C3
NEW QUAY ROAD	M&M	13 F4	NEWTON ABBOT	GW	2 C3
NEW RADNOR	K&E	14 E2	NEWTON for HYDE	MS&L	21 G1 (f4)
New Rhosydd Quarry	PC&BT	19 F3	NEWTON HEATH	L&Y	45 A4
NEW ROMNEY & LITTLESTONE-ON-SEA	Lydd	6 E3	Newton Jc.	CAL.	44 C3
NEW ROSS	DW&W	49 C5	NEWTON KYME	NE	21 C4
NEW SOUTHGATE for COLNEY HATCH	GN	5 A3	NEWTON ROAD	L&NW	13 B3
NEW TREDEGAR & WHITEROSE	B&M	43 B2	NEWTON STEWART	P&WJt	25 B4
New Wandsworth (Coal)	LB&SC	39 F2	NEWTONHILL	CAL.	34 A1
NEWARK	GN	16 C2	NEWTON-LE-WILLOWS	L&NW	45 D3
NEWARK	MID.	16 C2	NEWTONMORE	HR	33 A2
Newarthill (Goods)	CAL.	44 A2	NEWTON-ON-AYR	G&SW	29 F3
NEWBIGGIN-BY-THE-SEA	NE	28 A5	NEWTOWN	CAM.	14 C3
NEWBIGGING	CAL.	30 D4	NEWTOWN CUNNINGHAM	Letterkenny	60 C5
NEWBLISS	GN(I)	57 C4	NEWTOWNARDS	B&CD	61 F4
Newbold Wharf	GW	9 C5	NEWTOWNBUTLER	GN(I)	57 C3
NEWBRIDGE	GS&W	54 D5	NEWTOWNFORBES	MGW	57 F1
NEWBRIDGE	GW	43 B2	NEWTOWNSTEWART	GN(I)	60 E4
NEWBRIDGE-ON-WYE	Mid-Wales	14 E3	NEWTYLE	CAL.	34 D5
NEWBURGH	NB	34 F5	NIDD BRIDGE	NE	21 C3
NEWBURN	NE	28 A3	Niddrie	NB	30 B2
NEWBURY	GW	4 A3	Niddrie West Jc.	NB	30 G1
NEWCASTLE	B&CD	58 B1	NIGG	HR	36 C4
NEWCASTLE	DW&W	54 D2	Nine Elms (Goods)	L&SW	40 D5
NEWCASTLE NEW BRIDGE STREET	NE	28 A1	NINE ELMS ROYAL STATION	L&SW	40 D5
Newcastle New Bridge Street Depot	NE	28 A1	NINE MILE POINT	L&NW	43 B3
Newcastle Quayside	NE	28 A1	Ninewells Jc.	CAL.	34 E3
NEWCASTLE WEST	R&NJn	48 C5	NINGWOOD	FY&N	4 F4
NEWCASTLE-ON-TYNE CENTRAL	NE	28 A1	NISBET	NB	31 E2
Newcastle-on-Tyne Forth	NE	28 A2	NITSHILL	GB&KJt	44 F3
NEWCASTLETON	NB	27 A1	NOBBER	MGW	58 E5
NEWCASTLE-UNDER-LYME	NS	15 C3	NOCTON & DUNSTON	GN&GEJt.	17 B1
NEWCHURCH	IoWC	4 F3	NORBITON	L&SW	39 F3
NEWCOURT	S&SLt	49 G4	NORBURY	LB&SC	40 F5
NEWENT	Newent	9 D2	NORBURY	NS	15 C5
NEWHAM	NE	31 E5	Norden	Goathorn	3 G4
Newham (Goods)	GW	1 E1	NORHAM	NE	31 D3
NEWHAVEN	CAL.	30 F2	Norley Col. Siding	L&NW	45 D2 (f76)

Station, junction, tunnel, viaduct, etc	Railway	Reference
NORMACOT	NS	15 C3
Normanby	NE	28 E4
NORMANTON	MID.	42 C2
NORTH BERWICK	NB	31 B1
NORTH BRIDGE	H&OJt	42 B5
NORTH CAMP & ASH VALE	L&SW	4 B1
NORTH CAVE	HB&WRJn	22 D4
NORTH DROVE	E&M	17 E2
NORTH DULWICH	LB&SC	40 E4
NORTH ELMHAM	GE	18 E4
North Erewash Jc.	MID.	16 D4
NORTH GREENWICH	Millwall Ex.	40 D3
NORTH GRIMSTON	NE	22 B5
NORTH HAYLING	Hayling	4 E2
NORTH KELSEY	MS&L	22 F3
North Kent East Jc.	SE/L&G	40 D3
North Kent West Jc.	SE	40 D4
NORTH LEITH	NB	30 F2
North London Incline Jc.	MID.	40 B5 (f41)
NORTH LONSDALE CROSSING	FUR.	24 B4
North Mersey (Goods)	L&Y	45 G3
North Pole Jc.	GW/L&NW/WLJt	39 C4
NORTH QUEENSFERRY	NB	30 B3
North Rhondda Col.	SWMin.	43 E2
NORTH RODE JUNCTION	NS	15 B3
NORTH SEATON	NE	27 A5
NORTH SHIELDS	NE	28 B5
NORTH SKELTON	NE	28 E3
North Staffordshire Jc.	L&NW/NS	20 E2
NORTH STOCKTON	NE	28 E5
North Stoke Tunnel	LB&SC	5 F1
NORTH TAWTON	L&SW	2 B5
NORTH THORESBY	GN	22 F2
NORTH WALSALL	MID.	15 F4 (f4)
NORTH WALSHAM	E&M	18 D2
NORTH WALSHAM	GE	18 D2
NORTH WATER BRIDGE	NB	34 C2
NORTH WEALD	GE	11 G3
NORTH WOOLWICH	GE	40 D1
NORTH WOOTTON	H&WN	17 E5
NORTH WYLAM	NE	27 B5
NORTHALLERTON	NE	28 G5
NORTHALLERTON LOW	NE	28 G5
Northallerton Low Jc.	NE	28 G5
NORTHAM	L&SW	4 E4
NORTHAMPTON	MID.	10 B2
NORTHAMPTON BRIDGE STREET	L&NW	10 B2
NORTHAMPTON CASTLE	L&NW	10 B2
Northchurch Tunnel	L&NW	10 E1
NORTHENDEN	CLC	45 A4
NORTHFIELD	MID.	9 A4
NORTHFLEET	SE	5 B5
NORTHORPE	MS&L	22 G4
Northumberland Dock	NE	28 B5 (f8)
NORTHWICH	CLC	45 C5
Northwich (Goods)	CLC	45 C5
NORTHWOOD	MET.	5 A2
NORTON	BIRK. Jt.	45 D4
Norton	L&NW	15 E4
NORTON	L&Y	21 E5
NORTON	NE	28 E4
NORTON BRIDGE	L&NW	15 D3
Norton Bridge (Goods)	NS	15 D3
Norton East & South Jcs.	NE	28 E5
NORTON FITZWARREN	GW	8 F4
NORTON JUNCTION	GW	9 B3
NORTON-IN-HALES	NS	20 F2
NORWICH CITY	E&M	18 F3
NORWICH THORPE	GE	18 F3
NORWICH TROWSE	GE	18 F3
NORWICH VICTORIA	GE	18 F3
Norwood Col.	MID.	41 A3
NORWOOD JUNCTION	LB&SC	40 G4
NOSTELL	WR&GJt	42 C1
Nostell North Jc.	WR&GJt/MS&L	42 C2
Nostell South Jc.	WR&GJt/MS&L	42 C1
NOTGROVE & WESTFIELD	Banbury & Chelt. Dir.	9 D4
NOTTING HILL & LADBROKE GROVE	H&CJt	39 C4 (f27)
NOTTING HILL GATE	MET.	39 C4
NOTTINGHAM	MID.	41 G5
Nottingham (Goods)	MID.	41 G4
NOTTINGHAM LONDON ROAD	N&GR&C	41 G5
NOTTINGHAM RACE COURSE	N&GR&C	41 F5

Station, junction, tunnel, viaduct, etc	Railway	Reference
NOTTON for ROYSTON	MS&L	42 D2
NOVAR	HR	36 C5
NUNBURNHOLME	NE	22 C5
NUNEATON	L&NW	16 F5
NUNEATON	MID.	16 F5
Nuneaton South Leicester Jc.	L&NW/MID.	16 F5
NUNHEAD	LC&D	40 D4
NUNNINGTON	NE	21 A5
NUNTHORPE	NE	28 F4
NURSLING	L&SW	4 D4
NUTFIELD	SE	5 D3
Nuttall Tunnel	L&Y	45 B1
OAKAMOOR	NS	15 C4
OAKENGATES	GW	15 E2
OAKENGATES	L&NW	15 E2
Oakenshaw (Goods)	MID.	42 C2
Oakenshaw Jc.	L&Y	42 C2
Oakenshaw Tunnel	L&Y	42 B4
OAKHAM	MID.	16 E2
OAKINGTON	GE	11 C3
OAKLE STREET	GW	9 E2
Oaklea Jc.	FUR.	24 B5
OAKLEIGH PARK	GN	5 A3
OAKLEY	L&SW	4 B3
OAKLEY	MID.	10 B1
OAKLEY	NB	30 A4
Oakley Jc.	MID.	10 C1
Oakwellgate	NE	28 A1
OAKWORTH	MID.	21 D1
OATLANDS	C&WJn	26 E3
OBAN	C&O	32 F4
OCHILTREE	G&SW	29 F4
OCKER HILL	L&NW	13 B2
OCKLEY	LB&SC	5 D2
OFFORD & BUCKDEN	GN	11 C2
OGBOURNE	M&SWJn.	4 A5
OKEHAMPTON	L&SW	2 B5
OLD COLWYN	L&NW	19 D4
OLD CUMNOCK	G&SW	29 F5
OLD DALBY	MID.	16 D3
OLD FORD	NL	40 B3
Old Ford (Goods)	L&NW	40 C3
OLD HILL	GW	13 C1
OLD KENT ROAD & HATCHAM	LB&SC	40 D4
Old Kent Road Jc.	LB&SC	40 D4
Old Kew Jc.	L&SW/N&SWJn	39 D3
Old Lane Tunnel	H&OJt	42 B5
OLD LEAKE	GN	17 C3
OLD MELDRUM	GNoS	37 E3
OLD NORTH ROAD	L&NW	11 C2
Old Oak Jc.	L&NW/N&SWJn	39 C3
Old Oaks Jc.	MS&L	42 E2
OLD SAGGART ROAD	D&BST	54 C4
OLD TRAFFORD	MSJ&A	45 B3
Old Woods (Goods)	GW	14 A1
OLDBURY	Oldbury	13 B2
OLDBURY & BROMFORD LANE	L&NW	13 B2
Oldbury & Bromford Lane (Goods)	L&NW	13 B2
Oldbury (Goods)	Oldbury	13 B2
OLDCASTLE	GN(I)	57 F4
OLDHAM CENTRAL	L&Y	21 D1
OLDHAM CLEGG STREET	OA&G	21 D1
OLDHAM GLODWICK ROAD	L&NW	21 D1
Oldham Goods	L&NW	21 D1
Oldham Goods	MS&L	21 D1
OLDHAM MUMPS	L&Y	21 D1
OLDHAM WERNETH	L&Y	21 D1
Oldminster Jc.	MID.	9 F2
OLNEY	MID.	10 B2
OLTON	GW	9 A5
OMAGH	GN(I)	60 F4
OMEATH	DN&G	58 C3
OMOA	CAL.	44 A2
Omoa Brick Works	CAL.	44 A2
Omoa Jc.	CAL.	44 A2
ONGAR	GE	11 G4
ONIBURY	S&HJt	14 C1
ONLLWYN	N&B	43 E1
OOLA	W&L	48 B2
ORANMORE	MGW	52 C5
ORDENS	GNoS	37 C2
ORDSALL LANE	L&NW	45 B3 (f24)

Station, junction, tunnel, viaduct, etc	Railway	Reference
Penarth Dock Goods & Harbour	TV	43 B5
Penarth Tidal Harbour	TV	43 B5 (f10)
PENARTH TOWN	TV	43 B5
PENCADER	GW	13 F4
PENCLAWDD	L&NW	7 B3
PENCOED	GW	43 D4
PENDLEBURY	L&Y	45 B2 (f16)
PENDLETON	L&Y	45 B3 (f12)
PENDLETON BROAD STREET	L&Y	45 B3 (f21)
PENDRE	Talyllyn	13 B5
PENGAM	B&M	43 B2
PENGAM	Rhym.	43 B2
PENGE	LB&SC	40 F4
PENGE	LC&D	40 F4
Penge Jc.	LC&D	40 F3
Penge Tunnel	LC&D	40 F4
PENICUIK	NB	30 C2
Penicuik Gas Works	NB	30 C2
PENISTONE	L&Y/MS&L	42 E3
Penistone Viaduct	L&Y	42 E3
PENKRIDGE	L&NW	15 E3
PENMAEN POOL	CAM.	14 A5
Penmaenbach Tunnel	L&NW	19 D3
PENMAENMAWR	L&NW	19 D3
Penmaenrhos Tunnel	L&NW	19 D4
Penmanshiel Summit	NB	31 C2
Penmanshiel Tunnel	NB	31 C2
PENNINGTON	L&NW	45 C3
PENNS	MID.	15 F5
PENNYBURN	L&LS	60 C4
PENPERGWM	GW	43 A1
PENRHIWCEIBER	Aberdare	43 C2
PENRHIWCEIBER	GW	43 C2
PENRHYN	Fest.	19 F2
PENRHYN QUARRIES	Penrhyn	19 D2
PENRHYNDEUDRAETH	CAM.	19 F2
PENRITH	L&NW	27 E1
PENRUDDOCK	CK&P	26 E1
PENRYN	GW	1 F1
PENSFORD	GW	8 D1
PENSHAW	NE	28 C5
PENSHURST	SE	5 D4
PENTEWAN	Pentewan	1 E2
PENTON	NB	26 B1
PENTREBACH	TV	43 C2
Penwithers Jc.	GW	1 E1
Penwortham Jc.	WLancs	24 E3
PENWYLLT	N&B	43 E1
PENYBONT	L&NW	14 D3
PENYFFORDD	WM&CQ	20 E4
Pen-y-Graig	EV	43 D3
PENYGROES	L&NW	19 E1
PENZANCE	GW	1 F4
PEPLOW	GW	15 E2
Perceton Branch	G&SW	29 E3
PERCY MAIN	NE	28 B5
PERRANWELL	GW	1 E1
PERRY BAR	L&NW	13 B3
Perry Bar North Jc.	L&NW	13 B3
PERSHORE	GW	9 C4
Perth (Goods)	NB	33 F5
PERTH GENERAL	CAL.	33 F5
Perth Harbour	CAL.	33 F5
PERTH NORTH (ticket platform)	CAL.	33 E5
PERTH PRINCES STREET	CAL.	33 F5
PERTH SOUTH (ticket platform)	CAL.	33 F5
PETERBOROUGH	GE	17 F2
PETERBOROUGH	GN	17 F2
PETERCHURCH	Golden Valley	14 F1
PETERHEAD	GNoS	37 D5
Peterhead Harbour	GNoS	37 D5
Peter's Marland	Marland Lt.	7 G3
PETERSFIELD	L&SW	4 D2
PETERSTON	GW	43 C4
Peterston East & West Jcs.	GW/BD&R	43 C4
Petterill Jc.	NE/MID.	26 D1
PETTIGO	EB&S	59 F5
PETWORTH	LB&SC	5 E1
PEVENSEY & WESTHAM	LB&SC	5 F5
PEWSEY	GW	4 B5
PHILORTH	GNoS	37 C4
PHILPSTOUN	NB	30 B3
Phoenix Park Tunnel	GS&W	62 C4
PICKERING	NE	22 A5
PICTON	NE	28 F5
PIDDINGTON & HORTON	MID.	10 B2
PIEL	FUR.	24 B5
PIERCEBRIDGE	NE	27 E5
PIERSHILL	NB	30 F1
PILL	GW	8 C2
Pillbank Jc.	GW	43 A3
PILLING	G&KE	24 C3
PILMOOR	NE	21 B4
PILNING	GW	8 C2
Pilsley Col.	MID.	41 D3
Pilton Jcs. East & West	CAL.	30 F3
PIMBO LANE	L&Y	45 D2
PINCHBECK	GN&GEJt.	17 E2
PINCHINGTHORPE	NE	28 E4
PINHOE	L&SW	2 B3
PINMORE	A&W	25 A3
Pinmore Tunnel	A&W	25 A3
PINNER	L&NW	5 A2
PINNER	MET.	39 A1
PINWHERRY	A&W	25 A3
PINXTON	GN	41 E3
PINXTON & SELSTON	MID.	41 E3
PIPE GATE for WOORE	NS	20 F2
Pirbright Jc.	L&SW	5 C1
PITCAPLE	GNoS	37 E3
PITFOUR CURLING PLATFORM	GNoS	37 D4
PITLOCHRY	HR	33 C4
PITMEDDEN	GNoS	37 F4
PITSEA	LT&S	6 A5
PITSFORD & BRAMPTON	L&NW	10 B2
PITTENWEEM	NB	34 G3
PITTINGTON	NE	28 D5
PITTS HILL	NS	15 C3
PLAIDY	GNoS	37 D3
PLAINS	NB	44 A4
Plains Jc.	NB	44 A4
PLAISTOW	LT&S	40 C2
PLAISTOW	SE	40 F2
PLANK LANE for WEST LEIGH	WJn	45 C3
PLAS MARL	GW	43 G2
PLAS POWER	GW	20 E4
PLAS POWER	WM&CQ	20 E4
PLASHETTS	NB	27 A2
PLATT BRIDGE	L&NW	45 D2 (f8)
PLAWSWORTH	NE	27 C5
PLEALEY ROAD	S&WpJt.	14 B1
Plean	CAL.	30 A5
Plean Branch Jc.	CAL.	30 A5
Plean East Pit	CAL.	30 B5
Plean West Pit	CAL.	30 A5
PLEASINGTON	L&Y	24 E2
PLEASLEY	MID.	41 D4
PLECK	L&NW	13 A2
PLESSEY	NE	27 B5
PLODDER LANE	L&NW	45 C2
PLOWDEN	BC	14 C1
PLUCK	Letterkenny	59 C5
PLUCKLEY	SE	6 D4
PLUMBLEY	CLC	45 B5
PLUMPTON	L&NW	27 D1
PLUMPTON	LB&SC	5 F3
Plumpton Jc.	FUR.	24 A4
PLUMSTEAD	SE	40 D1
PLUMTREE & KEYWORTH	MID.	16 D3
PLYMOUTH DOCKS	GW	1 A2
Plymouth Friary (Goods)	L&SW	1 A2
PLYMOUTH MILLBAY	GW	1 A2
Plymouth North Quay	L&SW	1 A2
PLYMOUTH NORTH ROAD (Joint)	GW/L&SW	1 A2
Plymouth North Road Jc.	GW	1 A2
Plymouth West Jc.	GW	1 A2
PLYMPTON	GW	2 D5
Pocket Nook Jc.	L&NW	45 D3
POCKLINGTON	NE	22 C5
POINT PLEASANT	NE	28 B5 (f2)
Point Pleasant Jc.	L&SW	39 E5
Point Quay	Redruth & C'water	1 E1
POLEGATE	LB&SC	5 F5
POLESWORTH	L&NW	16 F5
Polhill Tunnel	SE	5 C4
Pollok Jc.	G&PJt./CoGU	44 F2 (f24)

Station, junction, tunnel, viaduct, etc	Railway	Reference
POLLOKSHAWS	GB&KJt.	44 E3
POLLOKSHIELDS	G&PJt.	44 F1
POLLOKSHIELDS EAST	CD	44 F1
POLMONT	NB	30 B4
Polperro Tunnel	GW	1 E1
POLSHAM	S&D Jt.	8 E2
POLTON	NB	30 C2
POMATHORN	NB	30 C2
POMEROY	GN(I)	60 F2
PONDER'S END	GE	5 A3
Poneil Jc.	CAL.	30 E5
PONFEIGH	CAL.	30 E4
Ponkey Col.	GW	20 F4
PONT LLANIO	M&M	13 E5
PONT MARQUET	Jersey	46 E4
PONT RUG	L&NW	19 D2
Pont Yates	BP&GV	7 A3
PONTAC	JE	46 E2
PONTARDAWE	MID.	43 F2
PONTARDULAIS	GW/L&NW	7 A3
PONTDOLGOCH	CAM.	14 B3
PONTEFRACT	L&Y	42 C1
PONTEFRACT	S&KJt	42 C1
PONTESBURY	S&WpJt.	14 B1
Pontfadog	GVT	20 F5
PONTHIR	GW	43 A3
PONTLOTTYN	Rhym.	43 C2
PONTNEWYDD	GW	43 A3
PONTNEWYNYDD	GW	43 A2
PONTRHYDYFEN	R&SB	43 E3
PONTRHYDYRUN	GW	43 A3
PONTRHYTHALLT	L&NW	19 D2
PONTRILAS	GW	14 G1
PONTSARN for VAYNOR	B&M & L&NW Jt.	43 C1
PONTSTICILL JUNCTION	B&M	43 C1
Pontyberem	BP&GV	7 A3
PONT-Y-PANT	L&NW	19 E3
PONTYPOOL CLARENCE STREET	GW	43 A2
PONTYPOOL CRANE STREET	GW	43 A2
Pontypool North, South, East & Middle Jcs.	GW	43 A2
PONTYPOOL ROAD	GW	43 A2
Pontypool Road (Goods)	GW	43 A2
PONTYPRIDD	TV	43 C3
Pontypridd (Goods)	BD&R	43 C3
PONTYRHYLL	GW	43 D3
POOL	NE	21 C3
POOL QUAY	CAM.	14 A2
POOLE	L&SW	3 F5
Popham Tunnels	L&SW	4 C3
POPLAR	GE	40 D1
Poplar (Cattle)	NL	40 D1
Poplar (Coal)	L&NW	40 D1
POPLAR (EAST INDIA ROAD)	NL	40 D1
Poplar (Goods)	L&NW	40 D1
Poplar Dock (Coal)	NL	40 E1
Poplar Dock (Goods)	GN	40 E1
Poplar Dock (Goods)	GW	40 E1
Poplar Dock (Goods)	L&NW	40 E1
Poplar Dock (Goods)	MID.	40 E1
Poplar High Street Jc.	NL	40 D1
POPPLETON	NE	21 C4
Poppleton Jc.	NE	21 A4
PORCHESTER	L&SW	4 E2
PORT BALLINTRAE	GCP&BV	60 A1 (f10)
PORT CARLISLE	NB	26 C2
Port Carlisle Branch Jc.	CAL.	26 D1
Port Carlisle Jc.	NB	26 D2
PORT CLARENCE	NE	28 E4
PORT DINORWIC	L&NW	19 D2
Port Dinorwic Dock	Padarn	19 D2
Port Dundas (Goods)	CAL.	44 E4
Port Dundas (Goods)	NB	44 E4
PORT EDGAR	NB	30 B3
Port Eglinton Depot	G&SW	44 F1 (f6)
Port Eglinton Jc.	CoGU/G&SW	44 F1 (f1)
Port Elphinstone (Goods)	GNoS	37 F3
PORT ERIN	IoM	23 C1
PORT GLASGOW	CAL.	29 B3
PORT GORDON	GNoS	37 C1
PORT OF MENTEITH	F&CJn	29 A5
PORT PENRHYN	Penrhyn	19 D2
PORT SODERICK	IoM	23 C2
PORT ST. MARY	IoM	23 C1

Station, junction, tunnel, viaduct, etc	Railway	Reference
PORT TALBOT	GW	43 F3
PORT VICTORIA	SE	6 B4
PORTADOWN	GN(I)	58 A4
PORTARLINGTON	GS&W	53 D4
Portarlington Jc.	GS&W	53 D4
PORTBURY	GW	8 C2
Portcreek Jc.	L&SW & LB&SC Jt./LB&SC	4 E2
PORTESHAM	Abbotsbury	3 F2
PORTESSIE	GNoS	37 C1
PORTESSIE	HR	37 C1
PORTH	TV	43 C3
PORTHALL	GN(I)	60 D5
PORTHCAWL	GW	43 E4
Porthcawl Harbour	GW	43 E4
Porthywaen	CAM.	20 G5
PORTISHEAD	GW	8 C2
Portishead Pier	GW	8 C2
PORTKNOCKIE	GNoS	37 C1
PORTLAND	W&PJt.	3 G3
Portland Jc.	GW/W&PJt.	3 G3
PORTLAND ROAD	MET.	39 C5
PORTLETHEN	CAL.	34 A1
PORTMADOC	CAM.	19 F2
PORTMADOC HARBOUR	Fest.	19 F2
Portmadoc Wharf	PC&BT	19 F2
PORTMARNOCK	GN(I)	54 B2
PORTOBELLO	NB	30 G1
Portobello Jc.	GW	39 C1
Portobello Jc.	L&NW	15 E3
PORTON	L&SW	4 C5
PORTPATRICK	P&WJt	25 C1
Portreath (Goods)	GW	1 E5
PORTRUSH	B&NC	60 A1
PORTRUSH	GCP&BV	60 A1 (f6)
Portrush Harbour	B&NC	60 A1
PORTSKEWETT	GW	8 B2
PORTSLADE	LB&SC	5 F3
PORTSMOUTH	L&Y	24 E1
PORTSMOUTH ARMS	L&SW	7 G3
PORTSMOUTH DOCKYARD		
SOUTH RAILWAY JETTY	L&SW & LB&SC Jt.	4 E2
PORTSMOUTH HARBOUR	L&SW & LB&SC Jt.	4 E2
PORTSMOUTH TOWN	L&SW & LB&SC Jt.	4 E2
PORTSOY	GNoS	37 C2
PORTSTEWART STATION	PsT	60 B1 (f1)
PORTSTEWART TOWN	PsT	60 B1 (f5)
POSSILPARK	NB	44 E4
POSTLAND	GN&GEJt.	17 E2
POTTER HANWORTH	GN&GEJt.	17 B1
POTTER HEIGHAM	E&M	18 E2
POTTERHILL	G&SW	44 G3
POTTERS BAR	GN	11 G2
Potters Bar Tunnel	GN	11 G2
POTTO	NE	28 F4
POTTON	L&NW	11 D2
POULTON	L&Y & L&NWJt	24 D4
Pouparts Jc.	LB&SC	39 E3
POWERSTOCK	Bridport	3 F2
POYNTON	L&NW	45 A4
POYNTON	MS&L/NSJt	15 A4
POYNTZPASS	GN(I)	58 B3
Praed Street Jc.	MET.	39 C5
PRAZE	Helston	1 E5
PREES	L&NW	20 F3
PREESGWEENE	GW	20 F4
PRESCOT	L&NW	45 E3
PRESTATYN	L&NW	19 C5
PRESTBURY	L&NW	45 A5
PRESTEIGN	Lm&K	14 D2
PRESTHOPE	Wenlock	15 F1
PRESTON BROOK	L&NW	45 D5
PRESTON FISHERGATE HILL	WLancs	24 E3
Preston Hall Tunnels	LC&D	6 C5
PRESTON Joint	L&Y & L&NWJt	24 E3
PRESTON JUNCTION	L&Y	24 E3
PRESTON PARK	LB&SC	5 F3
PRESTON ROAD	L&Y	45 E3
PRESTONPANS for TRANENT	NB	30 B1
PRESTWICH	L&Y	45 B2
PRESTWICK	G&SW	29 E3
PRIESTFIELD	GW	13 A1
Primrose Hill Tunnel	L&NW	39 B5 (f56)
PRINCE'S END	GW	13 B1

Station, junction, tunnel, viaduct, etc	Railway	Reference
PRINCE'S END	L&NW	13 B2
PRINCES RISBOROUGH	GW	10 F2
PRINCETOWN	Princetown	2 C5
Priory Tunnel	LC&D	6 D2
PRITTLEWELL	GE	6 A4
Proof House Jc.	L&NW/MID.	13 C4
PROSPECT	GS&W	53 B2
PRUDHOE	NE	27 C4
PUDSEY GREENSIDE	GN	42 A4
PUDSEY LOWTOWN	GN	42 A4
PULBOROUGH	LB&SC	5 E1
Pulford (Goods)	GW	20 E4
PULHAM MARKET	GE	12 A3
PULHAM MARY	GE	12 A3
PURFLEET	LT&S	5 B5
PURLEY	LB&SC	5 C3
PURTON	GW	9 F4
PUTNEY	L&SW	39 E4
PUTNEY BRIDGE & FULHAM	MET.-DIS.	39 E4
PUXTON	GW	8 D3
Pwll Col.	BP&GV	7 B3
Pwllcarne Col.	GW	43 D3
PWLLHELI	CAM.	19 F1
PWLL-Y-PANT	Rhym.	43 B3
PYE BRIDGE	MID.	41 E3
PYE HILL	GN	41 E3
Pye Wipe Jc.	GN/GN&GEJt.	16 A1
PYLE	GW	43 E4
PYLLE	S&D Jt.	3 C3
QUAINTON	O&AT	10 E3
QUAINTON ROAD	A&B	10 E3
QUAKERS YARD (HIGH LEVEL)	GW	43 C2
QUAKERS YARD (LOW LEVEL)	TV	43 C2
Quarry Gap Jc.	GN	42 A4
QUARTER ROAD	CAL.	44 B1
QUEENBOROUGH	LC&D	6 B4
QUEENBOROUGH PIER	LC&D	6 B4
QUEEN'S PARK	CD	44 F1
QUEEN'S PARK (WEST KILBURN)	L&NW	39 B5
QUEEN'S ROAD (PECKHAM)	LB&SC	40 D4
QUEEN'S ROAD, BATTERSEA	L&SW	39 E4
QUEENSBURY	GN	42 B5
Queensbury Tunnel	GN	42 B5
QUEENSFERRY	L&NW	20 D4
QUEENSTOWN	GS&W	50 E2
QUEENSTOWN JUNCTION	GS&W	48 E1
QUY	GE	11 C4
RACKS	G&SW	26 B3
RADCLIFFE	L&Y	45 B2
Radcliffe (Goods)	L&Y	45 B2
RADCLIFFE BRIDGE	L&Y	45 B2
RADCLIFFE-ON-TRENT	N&GR&C	16 D3
RADFORD	MID.	41 F4
RADLETT	MID.	11 G1
RADLEY	GW	10 F4
RADNOR PARK	SE	6 D2
RADSTOCK	GW	3 B3
RADSTOCK	S&D Jt.	3 B3
RADWAY GREEN	NS	15 C3
RADYR	TV	43 C4
Raebog	NB	44 A4
RAGLAN	GW	8 A3
RAHENY	GN(I)	62 B1
RAILWAY TERRACE	L&C	1 C4
Rainbow Hill Jc.	GW	9 B3
RAINFORD JUNCTION	L&Y	45 E2
RAINFORD VILLAGE	L&NW	45 E2
RAINHAM	LC&D	6 B5
RAINHAM	LT&S	5 A4
RAINHILL	L&NW	45 E3
RAMAKET	CVT	57 A5
RAMPSIDE	FUR.	24 B5
RAMSBOTTOM	L&Y	45 B1
RAMSEY	MN	23 A3
RAMSEY	Ramsey	11 A2
RAMSEY HIGH STREET	GE	11 B2
RAMSGATE	SE	6 B1
RAMSGATE & ST. LAWRENCE-ON-SEA	LC&D	6 B1
RANDALSTOWN	B&NC	61 E1
Randalstown Viaduct	B&NC	61 E1
Randle Jc.	L&NW	45 E2

Station, junction, tunnel, viaduct, etc	Railway	Reference
RANKINSTON	G&SW	29 F4
RANSKILL	GN	21 G5
RASKELF	NE	21 B4
RATBY	MID.	16 F4
Ratgoed Quarry	Corris	14 A5
RATHDRUM	DW&W	54 F2
Rathdrum No. 1 Tunnel	DW&W	54 F2
RATHDUFF	GS&W	48 F3
RATHEN	GNoS	37 C4
RATHKEALE	R&NJn	48 B5
RATHKENNY	B&NC	61 D2
RATHMORE	GS&W	47 E5
RATHNEW (NEWRATH BRIDGE)	DW&W	54 E2
RATHO	NB	30 B3
RATHO LOW LEVEL	NB	30 B3
RATHVEN	HR	37 C1
RATHVILLY	GS&W	54 F5
Rattery Bank	GW	2 D4
RAUCEBY	GN	17 C1
RAUNDS	KT&H	10 A1
RAVELRIG JUNCTION PLATFORM	CAL.	30 C3
RAVENGLASS	FUR.	26 G3
RAVENGLASS	R&E	26 G3
Ravens Rock Summit	HR	35 D5
RAVENSCOURT PARK	L&SW	39 D4
RAVENSCRAIG	G&WB	29 B3
RAVENSTHORPE	L&Y	42 C4
RAVENSTONEDALE	NE	27 F2
Ravenswood Jc.	NB	31 E1
RAWCLIFFE	L&Y	21 E5
RAWTENSTALL	L&Y	24 E1
RAWYARDS	NB	44 A4
RAYDON	GE	12 D4
RAYLEIGH	GE	6 A5
RAYNE	GE	11 E5
RAYNES PARK	L&SW	39 F4
RAYNHAM PARK	E&M	18 D5
READING	GW	4 A2
READING	SE	4 A2
Reading East, South & West Jcs.	GW	4 A2
REARSBY	MID.	16 E3
Rectory Jc.	N&GR&C/GN	41 F5
RECTORY ROAD	GE	40 B4
Red Hill Jc.	GW/L&NW	9 C1
Red Hills Jc.	CK&P/NE	27 E1
Red Posts Jc.	L&SW/M&SWJn.	4 C4
RED ROCK	LUJt	45 D2
REDBOURN	MID.	11 F1
REDBRIDGE	L&SW	4 E4
REDBROOK	Wye Valley	8 A2
REDCAR	NE	28 E3
Redding (Goods)	NB	30 B4
REDDISH	L&NW	45 A3
REDDISH	S&MJt	45 A3
Reddish Jc.	S&MJt	45 A3
REDDITCH	MID.	9 B4
Redheugh (Goods)	NE	28 A2
REDHILL JUNCTION	SE	5 C3
REDHILLS	GN(I)	57 C3
REDLANE	D&BST	54 D4
REDMILE	GN&L&NWJt	16 D2
REDMIRE	NE	27 G4
REDNAL	GW	20 G4
REDRUTH	GW	1 E5
Redruth	Redruth & C'water	1 E5
Redruth Jc.	GW	1 E5
REEDHAM	GE	18 F2
REEDSMOUTH	NB	27 A3
REEPHAM	GE	18 E4
REEPHAM	MS&L	16 A1
REIGATE TOWN	SE	5 C3
Relly Mill Jc.	NE	27 D5
RENFREW FULBAR STREET	G&SW	44 F4
RENFREW WHARF	G&SW	44 F4
RENTON	NB	29 B3
RESOLVEN	GW	43 E2
RESTON	NB	31 C3
RETFORD	GN	16 A3
Retford (Goods)	GN	16 A3
Retford North & South Jcs.	GN/MS&L	16 A3
Retreat	B&NC	61 C2
RHAYADER	Mid-Wales	14 D4
RHEWL	L&NW	19 E5

Station, junction, tunnel, viaduct, etc	Railway	Reference
RHIWDERIN	B&M	43 A3
Rhondda Branch Jc.	TV	43 C3
Rhos	L&NW	20 F4
RHOSGOCH	L&NW	19 C1
RHOSTRYFAN	NWNG	19 E2
RHUDDLAN	L&NW	19 D5
RHYD-DDU	NWNG	19 E2
RHYDOWEN	W&C	13 F3
RHYDYMWYN	M&DJn.	20 D5
RHYDYRONEN	Talyllyn	13 B5
RHYL	L&NW	19 C5
RHYMNEY	B&M	43 C2
RHYMNEY	Rhym.	43 C1
RHYMNEY BRIDGE	N&RJt.	43 C1
RHYMNEY JUNCTION	GW	43 B3
RIBBLEHEAD	MID.	24 A1
RICCALL	NE	21 D5
RICCARTON	NB	31 G1
RICHHILL	GN(I)	58 A4
RICHMOND	L&SW	39 E3
RICHMOND	NE	27 F5
RICHMOND (NEW)	L&SW	39 E3
Richmond Hill Tunnel	NE	42 A2
RICKMANSWORTH	L&NW	5 A2
RICKMANSWORTH	MET.	5 A2
Riddings Jc.	MID.	41 E3
RIDDINGS JUNCTION	NB	26 B1
RIDGMONT	L&NW	10 C1
RIDING MILL	NE	27 C4
RIGG	G&SW	26 B2
RILLATON BRIDGE	L&C	1 C4
RILLINGTON	NE	22 B5
RIMINGTON	L&Y	24 C1
RINGLEY ROAD	L&Y	45 B2
RINGSTEAD	L&NW	10 A1
RINGWOOD	L&SW	4 E5
RIPLEY	MID.	41 E2
Ripley Spelter Works	MID.	41 E2
RIPLEY VALLEY	NE	21 C3
RIPON	NE	21 B3
RIPPINGALE	GN	17 D1
RIPPLE	MID.	9 C3
RIPPONDEN	L&Y	21 E1
RISCA	GW	43 B3
Risca Jc.	GW	43 B3
Rise Hill Tunnel	MID.	24 A1
RISHTON	L&Y	24 D2
RISHWORTH	L&Y	21 E1
River Dodder Viaduct	DW&W	62 E3
River Shannon Bridge	L&E	48 A3
Riverside Jc.	NE	28 A1
ROADE	L&NW	10 B2
ROADWATER	West Somerset Mineral	8 E5
Roath (Goods)	GW	43 B4
Roath (Goods)	TV	43 B4
Roath Branch Jc.	TV	43 B4
ROBERTSBRIDGE	SE	6 E5
Robertson's Lye	NB	44 A4
Robin Hood Tunnel	L&Y	42 D5
ROBIN HOOD'S BAY	Sc&Wby	28 F1
Robroyston Branch	CAL.	44 D4
Robroyston Branch Jc.	CAL.	44 D4
ROBY	L&NW	45 E4
ROCESTER	NS	15 D5
ROCHDALE	L&Y	45 A1
ROCHESTER & STROOD	LC&D	6 B5
Rochester Bridge Jc.	SE/LC&D	6 B5
ROCHESTOWN	CB&P	48 F2
ROCHFORD	GE	6 A4
Rochsoles	NB	44 B4
ROCK FERRY	BIRK. Jt.	45 F4
ROCKCLIFFE	CAL.	26 C1
ROCKCORRY	GN(I)	57 C5
ROCKINGHAM	L&NW	16 F2
RODWELL	W&PJt.	3 G3
Roe Lane Jc.	WLancs	45 F1
ROGART	HR	36 A5
ROGATE	L&SW	4 D1
Rogerstown Viaduct	GN(I)	54 A2
ROLLESTON JUNCTION	MID.	16 C2
ROMALDKIRK	NE	27 E4
ROMAN BRIDGE	L&NW	19 E3
Rome Street Jc.	M&C/NE	26 D1
ROMFORD for HORNCHURCH, UMPINSTER & CORBET'S TEY	GE	5 A4
ROMILEY	S&MJt.	21 G1
ROMSEY	L&SW	4 D4
ROOKERY	L&NW	45 E3
Rookery Bridge (Goods)	L&NW	20 E2
Rookhope	W&R	27 D3
ROOSE	FUR.	24 B5
ROPLEY	L&SW	4 C2
ROSCOMMON	GN&W	56 G1
ROSCREA	GS&W	53 E1
ROSE GROVE	L&Y	24 D1
ROSE HILL	MS&L/NSJt	21 G1
Rosebush	NP&F	13 F2
Rosehall Pits	NB	44 B3
Rosehill Jc.	C&WJn	26 E3
Rosemill (Goods)	CAL.	34 E5
ROSEMOUNT	CAL.	33 D5
ROSHARRY	CL&RLt	57 E1
ROSHERVILLE	LC&D	5 B5
Roskear	GW	1 E5
ROSLIN	NB	30 C2
ROSS	GW	9 D1
Ross Jc.	CAL.	44 B2
ROSSETT	GW	20 E4
ROSSINGTON	GN	21 F5
Rosslare Pier	W&W	50 D3
ROSSLYN CASTLE	NB	30 C2
ROSSLYNLEE	NB	30 C2
ROSSTEMPLE	GS&W	48 B3
ROSTREVOR	W&RT	58 C3
Rostrevor Quay	W&RT	58 C2
ROTHBURY	NB	31 G4
ROTHERFIELD	LB&SC	5 E5
ROTHERHAM	MID.	42 F1
ROTHERHAM & MASBOROUGH	MS&L	42 F1
ROTHERHITHE	EL	40 D4
Rotherwas Jc.	GW/L&NW	9 C1
ROTHES	GNoS	36 D1
ROTHIE NORMAN	GNoS	37 E3
ROTHIEMAY	GNoS	37 D1
ROTTON PARK ROAD	Harborne	13 C3
ROUDHAM JUNCTION	GE	12 A5
ROUGHAN	CVT	60 G3
ROUND OAK	GW	15 G3
ROWFANT	LB&SC	5 D3
ROWLAND'S CASTLE	L&SW	4 E2
ROWLANDS GILL	NE	27 C5
ROWLEY	NE	27 C4
ROWLEY & BLACKHEATH	GW	13 C2
ROWRAH	WC&EJt	26 E3
ROWSLEY for CHATSWORTH	MID.	41 C1
ROXBURGH	NB	31 E2
Royal Albert Bridge	GW	1 D5
ROYAL ALBERT DOCK CENTRAL	L&IDocks	40 C2
ROYAL ALBERT DOCK CONNAUGHT ROAD	L&IDocks	40 C2
ROYAL ALBERT DOCK GALLIONS	L&IDocks	40 C1
ROYAL ALBERT DOCK MANOR WAY	L&IDocks	40 C1
Royal Border Bridge	NE	31 C3
Royal George Tunnel	L&NW	21 F1
ROYAL OAK	GW	39 C1
ROYDON	GE	11 F3
ROYSTON	R&H	11 D3
ROYSTON & NOTTON	MID.	42 D2
ROYTON	L&Y	45 A2
ROYTON JUNCTION	L&Y	21 F1
RUABON	GW	20 F4
RUAN	WClare	52 F5
RUBERY	Halesowen	9 A4
Ruchill	NB	44 E4
RUDGWICK	LB&SC	5 E2
RUDYARD LAKE	NS	15 B4
RUFFORD	L&Y	45 E1
RUGBY	L&NW	10 A4
RUGELEY	L&NW	15 E4
RUGELEY TOWN	L&NW	15 E4
RUMBLING BRIDGE	NB	30 A4
RUMWORTH & DAUBHILL	L&NW	45 C2 (f11)
Rumworth & Daubhill (Goods)	L&NW	45 C2 (f11)
RUNCORN	L&NW	45 D4
Runcorn Bridge	L&NW	45 D4
Runcorn Dock	L&NW	45 E4
Runcorn Dock Jc.	L&NW	45 D4

Station, junction, tunnel, viaduct, etc	Railway	Reference	Station, junction, tunnel, viaduct, etc	Railway	Reference
SANDGATE	SE	6 D2	SEATON & BEER	L&SW	2 B1
SANDHILLS	L&Y	45 G4	SEATON & UPPINGHAM	L&NW	16 F1
SANDHOLME	HB&WRJn	22 D5	SEATON CAREW	NE	28 E4
SANDILANDS	CAL.	30 E4	SEATON DELAVAL	NE	28 B5
SANDLING JUNCTION	SE	6 D3	SEATON JUNCTION	L&SW	2 B1
Sandling Tunnel	SE	6 D3	Seaton Tunnel	MID.	16 F1
SANDON	NS	15 D4	SEDBERGH	L&NW	27 G2
Sandon Dock (Goods)	MID.	45 G4	SEDGEBROOK	N&GR&C	16 D2
SANDOWN (Joint)	IoW/IoWC	4 F3	SEDGEFIELD	NE	28 E5
SANDPLACE	L&L	1 D4	SEDGEFORD	H&WN	17 D5
SANDSEND	NE	28 F2	Sedgeley Jc.	L&NW	13 B1
SANDSIDE	FUR.	24 A3	SEEDLEY	L&NW	45 B3
SANDWICH	SE	6 C2	SEEND	GW	3 B4
SANDY	GN	11 D2	SEFTON & MAGHULL	CLC	45 F2
SANDY	L&NW	11 D2	SEGHILL	NE	28 B5
SANDYCOVE	D&K	54 C2	SELBY	NE	21 D5
SANDYCROFT	L&NW	20 D4	Selby E. Jc.	NE	21 D5
SANDYMOUNT	D&K	62 D2	SELHAM	LB&SC	5 E1
SANKEY	CLC	45 D4	SELHURST	LB&SC	40 G5
SANKEY BRIDGES	L&NW	45 D4 (f17)	Selhurst Jc.	LB&SC	40 G5
SANQUHAR	G&SW	30 F5	SELKIRK	NB	30 E1
SANTON	IoM	23 C2	SELLAFIELD	FUR.	26 F3
Sapperton Summit	GW	9 F4	SELLING	LC&D	6 C3
Sapperton Tunnel	GW	9 F4	Selling Tunnel	LC&D	6 C3
SARNAU	GW	7 A2	SELLY OAK	MID.	9 A4
SAUCHIE	NB	30 A4	SELSDON ROAD	LB&SC/SE Joint	5 C3
SAUGHTREE	NB	31 G1	SEMLEY	L&SW	3 D4
SAUNDERSFOOT	P&T	7 D3	Serridge Jc.	S&WJt	8 A1
Saundersfoot Pier	Saundersfoot	7 D3	SESSAY	NE	21 B4
SAVERNAKE	GW	4 A5	SETTLE	MID.	24 B1
SAWBRIDGEWORTH	GE	11 F3	Settle Jc.	MID.	24 C1
SAWDON	NE	22 A4	SETTRINGTON	NE	22 B5
SAWLEY	MID.	16 D4	SEVEN SISTERS	GE	40 A4
SAWLEY JUNCTION	MID.	16 D4	SEVEN SISTERS	N&B	43 E1
SAXBY	MID.	16 E2	SEVENOAKS BAT & BALL	LC&D	5 C4
Saxelby Tunnel	MID.	16 E3	SEVENOAKS TUBS HILL	SE	5 C4
SAXHAM & RISBY	GE	11 C5	Sevenoaks Tunnel	SE	5 C4
SAXILBY	GN&GEJt.	16 A1	Severn Bridge	S&WJt	8 A1
SAXMUNDHAM	GE	12 C2	SEVERN BRIDGE for BLAKENEY	S&WJt	8 A1
Saxondale Jc.	N&GR&C/GN&L&NWJt	16 C3	Severn Tunnel	GW	8 C2
SCAFELL	CAM.	14 C3	SEVERN TUNNEL JUNCTION	GW	8 B2
SCALBY	Sc&Wby	28 G1	Severus Jc.	NE	21 A4
SCALFORD	GN&L&NWJt	16 E2	SEXHOW	NE	28 F4
SCARBOROUGH	NE	22 A3	Seymour Jc.	MID.	41 B3
Scarborough (Goods)	NE	22 A4	SHACKERSTONE	A&NJt	16 F5
Scarborough Road Jc.	NE	22 B5	SHADWELL	EL	40 C4
SCARVA	GN(I)	58 A3	SHADWELL	GE	40 C4
SCAWBY & HIBALDSTOW	MS&L	22 F4	Shaftholme Jc.	GN/NE	21 F5
SCHOLES	NE	42 A2	Shakespeare Tunnel	SE	6 D2
Scholes Summit	NE	42 A2	SHALFORD	SE	5 D1
SCHULL	S&SLt	49 G3	Shalford Jc.	L&SW/SE	5 D1
Scole	Scole Tramway	12 B3	SHANKEND	NB	31 F1
SCOPWICK & TIMBERLAND	GN&GEJt.	17 C1	SHANKILL	DW&W	54 C2
SCORRIER GATE	GW	1 E5	SHANKLIN	IoW	4 G3
SCORTON	L&NW	24 C3	Shantonagh Jc.	GN(I)	57 C5
SCORTON	NE	27 F5	SHAP	L&NW	27 F1
SCOTBY	MID.	26 C1	Shap Summit	L&NW	27 F1
SCOTBY	NE	26 C1	SHAPWICK	S&D Jt.	8 E3
SCOTCH DYKE	NB	26 B1	SHARLSTON	L&Y	42 C1
Scotland Street Jc.	CAL./G&SW	44 F2 (f23)	SHARNAL STREET	SE	6 B5
SCOT'S GAP	NB	27 A4	SHARNBROOK	MID.	10 B1
SCOTSCALDER	HR	38 D3	Sharnbrook Summit	MID.	10 B1
SCOTSTOUNHILL	GY&C	44 F4	Sharnbrook Tunnel	MID.	10 B1
SCOTSWOOD	NE	28 A2	SHARPNESS	S&WJt	8 B1
Scotswood Bridge	NE	28 A3	Sharpness Docks	MID.	9 F2
Scout Tunnel	L&NW	21 F1	SHAW	L&Y	21 F1
SCREMERSTON	NE	31 D4	SHAWCLOUGH & HEALEY	L&Y	45 A1
SCROOBY	GN	21 G5	Shawfield Col.	CAL.	30 D5
SCRUTON	NE	28 G5	SHAWFORD	L&SW	4 D3
SCULCOATES	NE	22 A1	SHAWFORTH	L&Y	45 A1
SEA MILLS	BP&P	8 C2	Shawhill Jc.	CAL.	26 B2
Seafield	NB	30 C4	SHEEPBRIDGE	MID.	41 B2
SEAFORD	LB&SC	5 G4	SHEERNESS DOCKYARD	LC&D	6 B4
SEAFORTH	L&Y	45 F3	SHEERNESS-ON-SEA	LC&D	6 B4
SEAHAM	L'derry	28 C5	Sheet Factory Jc.	GE	40 B2
SEAHAM COLLIERY	L'derry	28 C5	Sheet Stores Jc.	MID.	16 D4
SEAHAM HALL	L'derry	28 C5	SHEFFIELD MIDLAND	MID.	41 A2
SEAMER	NE	22 A3	SHEFFIELD PARK	LB&SC	5 E4
Seamer Jc.	NE	22 A4	Sheffield Park (Goods)	MS&L	42 G2
SEAPOINT	D&K	62 E1	Sheffield Pond Street (Goods)	MID.	41 A2
SEASCALE	FUR.	26 F3	Sheffield Tunnel Jc.	MS&L	42 G2
SEATON	C&WJn	26 E3	SHEFFIELD VICTORIA	MS&L	42 G2
SEATON	NE	28 C5	Sheffield Wicker (Goods)	MID.	42 G2

Station, junction, tunnel, viaduct, etc	Railway	Reference	Station, junction, tunnel, viaduct, etc	Railway	Reference
SHEFFORD	MID.	11 D1	SILEBY	MID.	16 E3
SHELFORD	GE	11 D3	SILECROFT	FUR.	24 A5
Shelley Woodhouse Tunnel	L&Y	42 D4	Silkstone	L&Y	42 E3
Shelton	NS	15 C3	SILKSTONE	MS&L	42 E3
Shelwick Jc.	S&HJt/GW	9 C1	Silkstone Jc.	L&Y	42 D2
SHENFIELD & HUTTON JUNCTION	GE	5 A5	SILLOTH	NB	26 C3
SHENSTONE	L&NW	15 F5	SILVER STREET	GE	5 A3
SHENTON	A&NJt	16 F5	SILVERDALE	FUR.	24 B3
SHEPHERDS BUSH	H&CJt	39 D4	SILVERDALE	NS	15 C3
SHEPHERDS BUSH	L&SW	39 D4	Silvermuir Jc. South	CAL.	30 D4
SHEPHERDS WELL	LC&D	6 C2	SILVERTON	GW	2 A3
SHEPLEY	L&Y	42 D4	SILVERTOWN	GE	40 C2
SHEPPERTON	L&SW	5 B2	SIMONSTONE	L&Y	24 D1
SHEPRETH	R&H	11 D3	Simpasture Jc.	NE	27 E5
Shepreth Branch Jc.	GE	11 C3	Sincil Jc.	GN/GN&GEJt.	16 A1
SHEPSHED	CF	16 E4	SINCLAIRTOWN	NB	30 A2
SHEPTON MALLET	GW	3 C3	SINDERBY	NE	21 A3
SHEPTON MALLET CHARLTON ROAD	S&D Jt.	3 C3	SINGLETON	L&Y & L&NWJt	24 D4
SHERBORNE	L&SW	3 D3	SINGLETON	LB&SC	4 E1
SHERBURN	NE	21 D4	SINNINGTON	NE	22 A5
SHERBURN COLLIERY	NE	28 D5	SION MILLS	GN(I)	60 D5
SHERBURN HOUSE	NE	28 D5	SIRHOWY	L&NW	43 B1
SHERRINGHAM	E&M	18 C3	Sirhowy Jc.	GW/L&NW	43 B3
SHERWOOD	Nott. Sub.	41 F5	SITTINGBOURNE	LC&D	6 C4
SHETTLESTON	NB	44 C3	Sittingbourne East Jc.	LC&D	6 C4
SHIDE	IoWC	4 F3	Sittingbourne Middle & West Jcs.	LC&D	6 B4
SHIELDHILL	CAL.	26 A3	SIX MILE BOTTOM	GE	11 C4
SHIELDS	G&SW	44 F1	SIXMILEBRIDGE	L&E	52 G4
Shields Jc.	G&PJt/CAL.	44 F1 (f19)	SIXMILECROSS	GN(I)	60 F3
SHIELDS ROAD	CoGU	44 F1 (f21)	SKARES	G&SW	29 F4
SHIFNAL	GW	15 F2	SKEGNESS	W&F	17 B4
SHILDON	NE	27 E5	SKELMANTHORPE	L&Y	42 D3
SHILLELAGH	DW&W	54 G4	SKELMERSDALE	L&Y	45 E2
SHILLINGSTONE	S&D Jt.	3 E4	Skelton Jc.	CLC	45 B4
SHILTON	L&NW	16 G5	SKEOG	CVT	57 B3
SHINCLIFFE	NE	28 D5	SKERRIES	GN(I)	54 A2
SHINCLIFFE TOWN	NE	28 D5	SKETTY ROAD	Oy.	43 G3 (f7)
SHIPLAKE	GW	10 G2	SKIBBEREEN	IV	49 G4
Shipley	MID.	41 F3	SKIBBEREEN	S&SLt	49 G4
SHIPLEY	MID.	42 A5	SKIPTON	MID.	21 C1
SHIPLEY & WINDHILL	GN	42 A5	Skipton N. Jc.	MID.	21 C1
Shipley & Windhill (Goods)	GN	42 A5	SKIRLAUGH	NE	22 D3
Shipley (Nutbrook Col.)	GN	41 F3	SLAGGYFORD	NE	27 C2
SHIPLEY GATE	MID.	41 F3	SLAITHWAITE	L&NW	42 D5
SHIPSTON-ON-STOUR	GW	9 C5	SLAMANNAN	NB	30 B5
SHIPTON	GW	10 D5	Slamannan Jc.	NB	30 B5
SHIPTON	NE	21 C4	SLATE QUARRIES ROAD	D&BST	54 C4
SHIRDLEY HILL	LS&PJc	45 F1	SLATEFORD	CAL.	30 G3
SHIREBROOK	MID.	41 C4	Slatty Viaduct	GS&W	48 F1
SHIREHAMPTON	BP&P	8 C2	SLEAFORD	GN	17 C1
SHIREOAKS	MS&L	41 A4	Sleaford East Jc.	GN/GN&GEJt.	17 C1
Shireoaks East Jc.	MS&L/MID.	41 B5	Sleaford Jc.	GN	17 C3
Shireoaks South Jc.	MID.	41 B4	Sleaford North & South Jcs.	GN&GEJt.	17 C1
Shireoaks West Jc.	MS&L/MID.	41 A4	SLEDMERE & FIMBER	NE	22 B4
Shirland Col.	MID.	41 D2	SLEIGHTS	NE	28 F2
SHOEBURYNESS	LT&S	6 A4	SLIGO	MGW	56 B3
SHOLING	L&SW	4 E3	Sligo Quay (Goods)	MGW	56 B3
SHOREDITCH	EL	40 C4	SLINFOLD	LB&SC	5 E2
SHOREDITCH	NL	40 C4	Sling	S&WJt	8 A2
SHOREHAM	LB&SC	5 F3	SLINGSBY	NE	21 B5
SHOREHAM	LC&D	5 C4	SLOANE SQUARE	MET.-DIS.	39 D5
SHORNCLIFFE CAMP	SE	6 D2	SLOUGH	GW	5 B1
SHORT HEATH (CLARKS LANE)	MID.	15 F4 (f3)	SMALL HEATH & SPARKBROOK	GW	13 C4
SHORTLANDS	LC&D	40 F2	Smallbrook Jc.	IoW/IoWC	4 F3
SHOTLEY BRIDGE	NE	27 C4	SMALLFORD	GN	11 F2
Shotlock Hill Tunnel	MID.	27 G2	SMARDALE	NE	27 F2
SHOTTLE	MID.	41 F1	SMEAFIELD	NE	31 D4
SHOTTON BRIDGE	NE	28 D5	SMEATON	NB	30 B2
SHOTTS	CAL.	30 C5	SMEETH	SE	6 D3
Shotts No. 1 Col.	NB	30 C5	SMEETH ROAD	GE	17 F4
SHREWSBURY	S&HJt	15 E1	SMETHWICK	L&NW	13 C2
SHREWSBURY TICKET PLATFORM	S&HJt	15 E1	SMETHWICK JUNCTION	GW	13 B2
SHRIVENHAM	GW	9 F5	SMITHBOROUGH	GN(I)	57 B5
Shugborough Tunnel	L&NW	15 E4	Smithfield Goods	GW	40 C5 (f3)
SHUSTOKE	MID.	15 F5	SMITHY BRIDGE	L&Y	21 E1
SIBLE & CASTLE HEDINGHAM	CV&H	11 E5	Snailbeach	Snailbeach Dist.	14 B1
SIBSEY	GN	17 C3	Snailwell Jc.	E&N/GE	11 C4
SIDCUP	SE	40 E1	SNAINTON	NE	22 A4
SIDDICK JUNCTION	L&NW	26 D3	SNAITH	L&Y	21 E5
SIDMOUTH	Sidmouth	2 B2	Snape (Goods)	GE	12 C2
SIDMOUTH JUNCTION	L&SW	2 B2	Snape Jc.	GE	12 C2
SIGGLESTHORNE	NE	22 D3	SNARESBROOK for WANSTEAD	GE	40 A2
Sighthill	NB	44 D4	SNARESTONE	A&NJt	16 E5

Station, junction, tunnel, viaduct, etc	Railway	Reference
SNELLAND	MS&L	17 A1
SNETTISHAM	H&WN	17 D5
Sneyd Park Jc.	BP&P	3 F1
SNODLAND	SE	6 C5
SNOW HILL	LC&D	40 C5
SNOWDON RANGER	NWNG	19 E2
Snydale Jc.	MID.	42 C2
SOHAM	E&N	11 B4
SOHO	GW	13 C3
SOHO	L&NW	13 C2
Soho (Goods)	L&NW	13 C3
Soho Pool Jc.	L&NW	13 B3
Soho Pool Wharf	L&NW	13 B3
SOHO ROAD	L&NW	13 B3
Soho Soap Works Jc.	L&NW	13 C2
SOLE STREET	LC&D	5 B5
SOLIHULL	GW	9 A5
Solway Viaduct	CAL./SJ	26 C2
SOMERFORD	GW	9 G4
Somerhill Tunnel	SE	5 D5
SOMERLEYTON	GE	18 F1
Somers Town (Goods)	MID.	40 C5
SOMERSET ROAD for HARBORNE	MID.	13 D3
SOMERSHAM	GN&GEJt.	11 B3
SOMERTON	GW	10 D4
Soothill Wood Col.	GN	42 B3
SORBIE	P&WJt	25 D4
Sough Tunnel	L&Y	45 B1
SOUTH ACTON	N&SWJn	39 D3
SOUTH BANK	NE	28 E4
SOUTH BERMONDSEY	LB&SC	40 D4
SOUTH BROMLEY	NL	40 C3
SOUTH CANTERBURY	SE	6 C3
SOUTH CARADON	L&C	1 C4
SOUTH CAVE	HB&WRJn	22 D4
South Cobbinshaw Pit	CAL.	30 C4
SOUTH CROYDON	LB&SC	5 C3
SOUTH EALING	MET.-DIS.	39 D2
SOUTH ELMSALL	WR&GJt	42 D1
SOUTH HAYLING	Hayling	4 E2
SOUTH HETTON	NE	28 D5
SOUTH KENSINGTON	MET.	39 D5
SOUTH KENSINGTON	MET.-DIS.	39 D5
SOUTH LEIGH	Witney	10 E5
SOUTH LEITH	NB	30 F1
South Leith (Goods)	NB	30 F1
South Leith Docks	NB	30 F1
SOUTH LYNN	E&M	17 E4
SOUTH MILFORD	NE	21 D4
SOUTH MOLTON	Devon & Somerset	7 F4
SOUTH MOLTON ROAD	L&SW	7 G4
SOUTH QUEENSFERRY	NB	30 B3
SOUTH SHIELDS	NE	28 B5
SOUTH SHIELDS (WESTOE LANE)	SSM&WC	28 B5
SOUTH SHORE	L&Y & L&NWJt	24 D4
SOUTH STOCKTON	NE	28 E4
SOUTH TOTTENHAM & STAMFORD HILL	T&HJn	40 A4
South Tottenham Jc.	T&HJn/GE	40 A4
SOUTH WEST INDIA DOCK	Millwall Ex.	40 D3
SOUTH WILLINGHAM & HAINTON	GN	17 A2
SOUTHALL	GW	39 C1
SOUTHAM ROAD & HARBURY	GW	10 B5
SOUTHAMPTON DOCKS	L&SW	4 E4
SOUTHAMPTON ROYAL PIER	L&SW	4 E4
SOUTHAMPTON WEST END	L&SW	4 E4
Southborough Viaduct	SE	5 D5
SOUTHCOATES	NE	22 A1
Southcote Jc.	GW	4 A2
SOUTHEND-ON-SEA	GE	6 A4
SOUTHEND-ON-SEA	LT&S	6 A4
Southerham Jc.	LB&SC	5 F4
Southfield Jc.	CAL.	30 D5
SOUTHFIELDS	L&SW	39 E4
SOUTHFLEET	LC&D	5 B5
SOUTHILL	MID.	11 D1
SOUTHMINSTER	GE	12 G5
SOUTHPORT ASH STREET	WLancs	45 F1 (f1)
SOUTHPORT CENTRAL	WLancs	45 F1
SOUTHPORT CHAPEL STREET	L&Y	45 F1
SOUTHPORT LORD STREET	CLC	45 F1
SOUTHPORT ST. LUKE'S ROAD	L&Y	45 F1 (f4)
SOUTHREY	GN	17 B1
SOUTHSEA	L&SW & LB&SC Jt.	4 E2

Station, junction, tunnel, viaduct, etc	Railway	Reference
SOUTHWAITE	L&NW	26 D1
SOUTHWATER	LB&SC	5 E2
SOUTHWELL	MID.	16 C3
SOUTHWICK	G&SW	26 C4
SOUTHWICK	LB&SC	5 F3
Southwick (Goods)	NE	28 C5
SOUTHWOLD	Southwold	12 B1
SOWERBY BRIDGE	L&Y	42 C5
SPA	T&F	47 D2
SPA ROAD (BERMONDSEY)	L&G	40 D4
SPALDING	GN	17 E2
Spalding North Jc.	GN/GN&GEJt.	17 E2
Spalding South Jc.	GN/E&M	17 E2
SPAMOUNT	C&VBT	60 E5
SPARKFORD	GW	3 D2
SPEECH HOUSE ROAD	S&WJt	8 A1
Speedwell Siding	GW	8 A1
SPEETON	NE	22 B3
SPEKE	L&NW	45 E4 (f19)
Speke Jc.	L&NW	45 E4
SPELLOW	L&NW	45 F3 (f63)
SPENNITHORNE	NE	21 A2
SPENNYMOOR	NE	27 D5
Spetchley (Goods)	MID.	9 B3
SPETISBURY	S&D Jt.	3 E4
Spiersbridge (Goods)	GB&KJt	44 E2
SPILSBY	S&F	17 B3
Spireslack	CAL.	30 E5
SPITAL	BIRK. Jt.	45 F4
Spitalfields (Coal)	GE	40 C4 (f51)
Spitalfields (Goods)	GE	40 C4 (f49)
Splott Jc.	TV/GW	43 B4
SPOFFORTH	NE	21 C3
SPON LANE	L&NW	13 B2
SPONDON	MID.	41 G2
Spondon Jc.	MID.	41 G2
SPOONER ROW	GE	18 F4
SPRATTON	L&NW	10 A3
SPRING VALE	L&Y	24 E2
Springbank Jcs.	HB&WRJn	22 A2
SPRINGBURN	NB	44 D4 (f7)
SPRINGFIELD	NB	34 F5
Springs Branch Jc.	L&NW	45 D2
SPRINGSIDE	G&SW	29 E3
Springwell Pit	MID.	41 B3
Springwood Jc.	L&Y/L&NW Jt	42 D5
Springwood Tunnel	L&Y/L&NW Jt	42 C5
SPROUSTON	NE	31 E2
Sprouston Jc.	NB/NE	31 E2
Spur Jc.	LC&D/LB&SC	40 F4
STACKSTEADS	L&Y	24 E1
STADDLETHORPE	NE	22 E5
STAFFORD	L&NW	15 E3
STAFFORD COMMON	GN	15 D3
Stafford Jc.	S&WnJt/L&NW	15 E2
STAINCLIFFE & BATLEY CARR	L&NW	42 C3
STAINCROSS	MS&L	42 E2
STAINES	GW	5 B1
STAINES HIGH STREET	L&SW	5 B1
STAINES JUNCTION	L&SW	5 B1
STAINFORTH & HATFIELD	MS&L	21 F5
STAINLAND	L&Y	42 C5
Stainmore Summit	NE	27 F3
STAINTON DALE	Sc&Wby	28 G1
STAIRFOOT for ARDSLEY	MS&L	42 E2
STAITHES	NE	28 E2
STALBRIDGE	S&D Jt.	3 D3
STALEY & MILLBROOK	L&NW	21 F1
STALHAM	E&M	18 D2
STALLINGBOROUGH	MS&L	22 F2
STALYBRIDGE	L&Y	21 A2
STALYBRIDGE Joint	MS&L/L&NW	21 A2
STAMFORD	MID.	16 F1
STAMFORD	S&E	16 F1
STAMFORD BRIDGE	NE	22 C5
STAMFORD HILL	GE	40 A4
Stammerham Jc.	LB&SC	5 E2
STANBRIDGEFORD	L&NW	10 D1
Standedge Tunnel	L&NW	21 F1
STANDISH	L&NW	45 D1
Standish Jc.	GW/MID.	9 E3
Standish Jc.	L&NW	45 D2
STANDON	GE	11 E3

Station, junction, tunnel, viaduct, etc	Railway	Reference	Station, junction, tunnel, viaduct, etc	Railway	Reference
STANDON BRIDGE	L&NW	15 D3	STOKE-ON-TRENT	NS	15 C3
STANFORD-LE-HOPE	LT&S	5 A5	STOKES BAY	L&SW	4 F3
STANHOE	H&WN	18 D5	STOKESLEY	NE	28 F4
STANHOPE	NE	27 D4	Stone Cross Jc.	LB&SC	5 F5
Stanhope Ironworks	NE	27 D4	STONE JUNCTION	NS	15 D3
Stank Mines	FUR.	24 B5	STONEA	GE	11 A3
STANLEY	CAL.	33 E5	Stonebridge Park (Goods)	MID.	39 B3
STANLEY	L&NW	45 F3	STONECLOUGH	L&Y	45 B2
STANLEY	MJt	42 B2	STONEHAVEN	CAL.	34 A1
Stanley Col.	NE	27 D5	STONEHOUSE	CAL.	30 D5
STANNER	K&E	14 E2	STONEHOUSE	GW	9 E3
STANNINGLEY	GN	42 A4	STONEHOUSE	MID.	9 E3
STANSFIELD HALL	L&Y	21 E1	Stonehouse Jc.	CAL.	44 A1
STANSTEAD	GE	11 E4	Stonehouse Pool	L&SW	1 A1
STANTON	GW	9 F5	STONEWALLS	C&VBT	60 E5
STANTON GATE	MID.	41 G3	Stoneywood	CAL.	30 B5
Stanton Tunnel	MID.	16 D3	STONEYWOOD	GNoS	37 F4
STAPLE HILL	MID.	8 C1	Stony Stratford	WSS&D	10 C2
STAPLEFORD & SANDIACRE	MID.	41 G3	Stormstown Jc.	TV	43 C3
STAPLEHURST	SE	6 D5	STOULTON	GW	9 C3
STAPLETON ROAD	GW	3 F1	STOURBRIDGE JUNCTION	GW	9 A3
STARBECK	NE	21 C3	STOURBRIDGE TOWN	GW	15 G3
STARCROSS	GW	2 C3	STOURPORT	GW	9 A3
STAVELEY	L&NW	27 G1	STOW	GE	17 F4
STAVELEY	MID.	41 B3	STOW	NB	30 D1
Staveley & Oakes Co's. Siding	GN	16 D2	STOW BEDON	T&W	18 F5
STAVERTON (DEVON)	BT&SD	2 D4	STOW PARK	GN&GEJt.	16 A2
STAWARD	NE	27 C3	Stowe Hill Tunnel	L&NW	10 B3
STECHFORD	L&NW	15 G5	STOWMARKET	GE	12 C4
STEELE ROAD	NB	27 A1	STOW-ON-THE-WOLD	GW	9 D5
Steelend (Goods)	NB	30 A3	STRABANE	GN(I)	60 D5
STEENS BRIDGE	GW	9 B1	STRAFFAN	GS&W	54 C4
Steeplehouse (Goods)	L&NW	41 E1	STRANGEWAYS & HINDLEY	WJn	45 C2 (f7)
STEETON & SILSDEN	MID.	21 C1	Strangeways & Hindley (Goods)	WJn	45 C2 (f7)
Stenson Jc.	MID.	16 D5	STRANOCUM	Ballycastle	61 B1
STEPNEY	GE	40 C3	STRANORLAR	FV	59 D5
STEPNEY	NE	22 A1	STRANORLAR	WD	59 D5
STEPS ROAD	CAL.	44 C4	STRANRAER	P&WJt	25 C2
STEVENAGE	GN	11 E2	STRANRAER HARBOUR	P&WJt	25 C2
STEVENSTON	G&SW	29 E3	STRATA FLORIDA	M&M	14 D5
STEVENSTON	L&A	29 D3	STRATFORD	GE	40 B3
STEVENTON	GW	10 F4	Stratford Canal Dock	GW	9 B5
STEWARTON	GB&KJt	29 D4	Stratford Central (Goods)	GE	40 B2
Stewarts Lane (Goods)	LC&D	39 F4	STRATFORD LOW LEVEL	GE	40 B3
Stewarts Lane Jc.	LC&D	39 E4	STRATFORD MARKET	GE	40 B2
STEWARTSTOWN	GN(I)	60 F1	Stratford Market (Goods)	GE	40 B2
STEYNING	LB&SC	5 F2	STRATFORD-ON-AVON	E&WJn	9 B5
STILLINGTON	NE	28 E5	STRATFORD-ON-AVON	GW	9 B5
STILLORGAN	DW&W	62 F2	STRATHAVEN	CAL.	29 D5
STIRCHLEY	L&NW	15 F2	Strathaven Jc.	CAL.	44 C2
STIRLING	CAL.	30 A5	STRATHBLANE	BV	29 B5
STIRLING	NB	30 A5	STRATHBUNGO	GB&KJt	44 F1
STIXWOULD	GN	17 B2	STRATHCARRON	HR	35 E2
Stobcross	NB	44 E4	STRATHMIGLO	NB	34 F5
STOBO	CAL.	30 E3	STRATHORD	CAL.	33 E5
STOBS	NB	31 F1	STRATHPEFFER	HR	35 D5
STOCKBRIDGE	L&SW	4 C4	STRATHYRE	C&O	33 F2
STOCKINGFORD	MID.	16 F5	STRATTON	GW	9 F5
Stockingford Col.	MID.	16 F5	STRAVITHIE	NB	34 F3
Stockingford Summit	MID.	16 F5	STRAWBERRY HILL	L&SW	39 F2
Stockingford Tunnel	MID.	16 F5	Strawberry Hill Tunnel	SE	5 D5
STOCKPORT	L&NW	45 A4	Strawfrank Jc.	CAL.	30 D4
Stockport Edgeley (Goods)	L&NW	45 A4	Streamstown Jc.	GS&W/MGW	53 C2
STOCKPORT TIVIOT DALE	CLC	45 A3	STREAMSTOWN JUNCTION	MGW	53 B2
Stockport Wellington Road (Goods)	CLC	45 A4	STREATHAM	LB&SC	40 F5
Stocksbridge Ironworks	Stocksbridge	42 F3	STREATHAM COMMON	LB&SC	40 F5
STOCKSFIELD	NE	27 C4	STREATHAM HILL	LB&SC	40 E5
STOCKSMOOR	L&Y	42 D4	Streatham Jc.	LB&SC/L&SWJt	40 F5
Stockton North (Goods)	NE	28 E4	Streatham North & South Jcs.	LB&SC	40 F5
Stockton South (Goods)	NE	28 E4	Streatham Tunnel	LB&SC	40 F5
Stockwith Siding	GN&GEJt.	22 G5	STREET & RATHOWEN	MGW	57 G3
STOGUMBER	West Somerset	8 F5	STREETLY	MID.	15 F5
STOKE	GE	11 D5	STRENSALL	NE	21 B5
STOKE CANON	GW	2 B3	STRETFORD	MSJ&A	45 B3
STOKE EDITH	GW	9 C2	Stretford Bridge Jc.	S&HJt/BC	14 C1
STOKE FERRY	D&SF	17 F5	STRETFORD BRIDGE JUNCTION	BC	14 C1
STOKE GOLDING	A&NJt	16 F5	STRETHAM	E&Stl	11 B4
STOKE NEWINGTON	GE	40 B4	STRETTON & CLAY MILLS	NS	15 C5
Stoke Summit	GN	16 D1	STRETTON for ASHOVER	MID.	41 D2
Stoke Tunnel	GN	16 D1	Stretton Jc.	NS/L&NW	15 C5
STOKE WORKS	GW	9 B4	STRICHEN	GNoS	37 D4
Stoke Works (Goods)	MID.	9 B4	STRINES	S&MJt	21 G1
Stoke Works Jc.	GW/MID.	9 B4	STROMEFERRY	HR	35 E1

Station, junction, tunnel, viaduct, etc	Railway	Reference
TEMPLEMORE	GS&W	53 G1
TEMPLEOGUE BRIDGE	D&BST	62 E4
TEMPLEOGUE DEPOT	D&BST	62 E4
TEMPLEOGUE MILL	D&BST	62 E5
TEMPLEPATRICK	B&NC	61 E2
TEMPLETON	P&T	7 C3
TEMPSFORD	GN	11 C2
TENBURY	S&HJt	9 A1
TENBY	P&T	7 D3
Tennochside & Bredisholm	CAL.	44 C3
Tennochside Jc.	CAL.	44 C3
TERENURE	D&BST	62 D4
Terminus Jc.	CAL.	44 F1
TERN HILL	GW	15 D2
TERRINGTON	E&M	17 E4
TETBURY	GW	9 F3
Tetbury Road (Goods)	GW	9 F4
TEVERSALL	MID.	41 D3
TEWKESBURY	MID.	9 D3
TEYNHAM	LC&D	6 C4
THACKLEY	GN	42 A4
Thackley Tunnel	MID.	42 A4
THAME	GW	10 E3
THAMES DITTON	L&SW	39 G2
THAMES HAVEN	LT&S	6 A5
Thames Haven Jc.	LT&S	5 B5
Thames Wharf	GE	40 C2 (f 21)
THANKERTON	CAL.	30 E4
THATCHAM	GW	4 A3
THATTO HEATH	L&NW	45 E3
THE COMMON	D&BST	54 C3
THE DYKE	B&D	5 F3
THE LAMB	D&BST	54 C4
THE MONUMENT	MET.-DIS./MET.Jt	40 C4 (f15)
THE MOUND	HR	36 A4
THE OAKS	L&Y	45 B1
THE TEMPLE	MET.-DIS.	40 C5
THEALE	GW	4 A2
THEDDINGWORTH	L&NW	16 G3
THEDDLETHORPE	L&EC	17 A3
THELWALL	L&NW	45 C4
THETFORD	GE	12 B5
THETFORD BRIDGE	GE	12 B5
THEYDON BOIS	GE	11 G3
Thingley Jc.	GW	3 A4
THIRSK	NE	21 A4
Thirsk Town (Goods)	NE	21 A4
THOMASTOWN	W&CI	49 B4
THONGS BRIDGE	L&Y	42 D5
THORINGTON	GE	12 E4
THORNBURY	MID.	8 B1
THORNE	MS&L	21 F5
THORNE	NE	21 E5
THORNE FALCON	GW	8 F4
Thorne Jc.	MS&L	21 F5
THORNER & SCARCROFT	NE	21 D3
THORNEY	E&M	17 F2
THORNEYBURN	NB	27 A2
THORNEYWOOD	Nott. Sub.	41 F5
THORNHILL	G&SW	30 G4
THORNHILL	L&Y	42 C3
THORNIELEE	NB	30 E1
THORNLEY	NE	28 D5
Thornley Col.	NE	28 D5
THORNLIEBANK	CAL.	44 E2
Thornliebank (Goods)	GB&KJt	44 F2
THORNTON	GN	42 A5
THORNTON	MID.	21 C1
THORNTON ABBEY	MS&L	22 E3
THORNTON DALE	NE	22 A5
THORNTON HALL	CAL.	44 E2
THORNTON HEATH	LB&SC	40 G5
THORNTON JUNCTION	NB	30 A2
THORP ARCH (BOSTON SPA)	NE	21 C4
Thorp Gates (Goods)	NE	21 D5
THORPE	GE	12 E3
THORPE	L&NW	10 A1
THORPE	MID.	16 B1
THORPE CULVERT	W&F	17 B4
Thorpe Jc.	GE	18 F3
THORPE THEWLES	NE	28 E5
THORVERTON	GW	2 A3
THRAPSTON	KT&H	10 A1
THRAPSTON	L&NW	10 A1
THREE BRIDGES	LB&SC	5 D3
THREE COCKS JUNCTION	Mid-Wales	14 F2
THREE COUNTIES	GN	11 E2
Three Signal Bridge Jc.	GN/L&Y/L&NW/NE	21 B2
THRELKELD	CK&P	26 E1
THRISLINGTON	NE	28 D5
THROSK	CAL.	30 A5
Throstle Nest Jc.	CLC/MID.	45 B3
THURGARTON	MID.	16 C3
Thurgoland Siding	MS&L	42 E3
Thurgoland Tunnel	MS&L	42 F3
THURLBY	GN	17 E1
THURLES	GS&W	49 A1
Thurles Jc.	GS&W/S(I)	49 A1
THURNBY & SCRAPTOFT	GN	16 F3
THURSFORD	E&M	18 D4
THURSO	HR	38 C3
THURSTASTON	BIRK. Jt.	20 C5
THURSTON	GE	12 C5
Thurstonland Tunnel	L&Y	42 D4
THUXTON	GE	18 F4
Thwaite Flat Jc.	FUR.	24 B5
TIBBERMUIR CROSSING	CAL.	33 E4
TIBSHELF & NEWTON	MID.	41 D3
TICEHURST ROAD	SE	5 E5
Ticknall	MID.	16 E5
TIDAL BASIN	GE	40 C2
TIDDINGTON	GW	10 E3
TIDENHAM	Wye Valley	8 B2
TILBURY	LT&S	5 B5
TILBURY DOCKS	LT&S	5 B5
TILE HILL	L&NW	10 A5
TILEHURST	GW	4 A2
TILLICOULTRY	NB	30 A4
TILLIETUDLEM	CAL.	30 D5
TILLYFOURIE	GNoS	37 F2
TILLYNAUGHT	GNoS	37 C2
TILLYSBURN	B&CD	61 A5
TILTON	GN&L&NWJt	16 F2
TIMPERLEY	MSJ&A	45 B3
TINAHELY	DW&W	54 G3
TINGLEY	GN	42 B3
TINODE POST OFFICE	D&BST	54 C4
TINSLEY	MS&L	42 G2
Tinsley East Jc.	MS&L	42 G1
Tinsley South & West Jcs.	MS&L	42 G2
TINTERN	Wye Valley	8 B2
Tintern Wire Works	Wye Valley	8 B2
TINTWISTLE	Longdendale	21 F1 (f3)
TIPPERARY	W&L	48 B1
TIPTON	GW	13 B1
TIPTON	L&NW	13 B1
Tipton Basin	GW	13 B1
TIPTON ST. JOHN'S	Sidmouth	2 B2
TIR PHIL & NEW TREDEGAR	Rhym.	43 B2
TIRYDAIL	GW	43 G1
TISBURY	L&SW	3 D4
TITLEY	Lm&K	14 E1
TIVERTON	GW	2 A3
TIVERTON JUNCTION	GW	2 A2
TIVETSHALL	GE	12 A3
TIVOLI	GS&W	48 F2
TOCHIENEAL	GNoS	37 C1
TODMORDEN	L&Y	21 E1
TOKENBURY CORNER	L&C	1 C4
Tolcarn Jc.	Cornwall Minerals	1 D1
TOLLER	Bridport	3 F2
TOLLERTON	NE	21 B4
TOMKIN ROAD	CL&RLt	57 C3
TONDU	GW	43 D4
TONGE	MID.	16 D4
TONGHAM	L&SW	4 B1
Tonteg Jc.	BD&R	43 C3
Tonyrefail	EV	43 D3
TOOME BRIDGE	B&NC	61 E1
TOOTING JUNCTION	LB&SC/L&SWJt	39 F5
TOPCLIFFE	NE	21 A4
TOPSHAM	L&SW	2 B3
Topsham Harbour	L&SW	2 B3
TORKSEY	MS&L	16 A2
TORPANTAU	B&M	43 C1
Torpantau Tunnel	B&M	43 C1

Station, junction, tunnel, viaduct, etc	Railway	Reference
TORPHINS	GNoS	37 G2
TORQUAY	GW	2 D3
TORRANCE	NB	44 D5
TORRE	GW	2 D3
TORRINGTON	L&SW	7 G3
TORVER	FUR.	26 G2
TOTNES	GW	2 D4
Totnes Quay	BT&SD	2 D4
Toton Sidings	MID.	41 G3
TOTTENHAM HALE	GE	40 A4
Tottenham North & West Jcs.	T&HJn/GE	40 A4
Tottenham South Jc.	GE	40 A4
TOTTERIDGE & WHETSTONE	GN	5 A3
TOTTINGTON	L&Y	45 B1
TOTTON for ELING	L&SW	4 E4
Touch Jcs.	NB	30 A3
TOVIL	SE	6 C5
TOW LAW	NE	27 D5
TOWCESTER	N&BJn.	10 C3
TOWER BRIDGE	C&MLt	48 G3
TOWER HILL	L&SW	1 B5
Towiemore (Goods)	GNoS	37 D1
TOWN GREEN & AUGHTON	L&Y	45 F2
TOWNELEY	L&Y	24 D1
TOWYN	CAM.	13 B5
Towyn Wharf	Talyllyn	13 B5
TRABBOCH	G&SW	29 F4
TRALEE	GS&W	47 D3
TRALEE	L&K	47 D3
Tralee Jc.	GS&W	47 F4
TRAM INN	GW	14 F1
TRAMORE	W&T	49 E5
Tranent	NB	30 B1
TRAWSCOED	M&M	13 D5
TRAWSFYNYDD	B&F	19 F3
Treamble	Cornwall Minerals	1 D1
TREBORTH	L&NW	19 D2
TREDEGAR	L&NW	43 B1
TREDEGAR JUNCTION	GW	43 B3
TREDEGAR JUNCTION	L&NW	43 B3
TREETON	MID.	42 G1
Trefeglwys	Van	14 C4
TREFEINON	Mid-Wales	14 F3
Treferig Railway Jc.	TV	43 C3
TREFNANT	L&NW	19 D5
TREFOREST	TV	43 C3
TREGARON	M&M	14 D5
TREGARTH	L&NW	19 D2
TREHARRIS	GW	43 C2
TREHERBERT	TV	43 D2
Tremadoc	GJ&P	19 F2
TRENCH CROSSING	L&NW	15 E2
TRENHOLME BAR	NE	28 F5
TRENT	MID.	16 D4
Trent Jc.	MID.	16 D4
Trent Valley Jc.	L&NW	15 E3
TRENTHAM	NS	15 C3
TREORKY	TV	43 D2
Tresavean	GW	1 E5
Treverrin Tunnel	GW	1 D3
TREVIL	L&NW	43 B1
TREVOR	VoL	20 F5
TREW & MOY	GN(I)	60 G1
TRIANGLE	L&Y	21 E1
TRILLICK	GN(I)	60 G5
TRIM	MGW	54 A5
TRIMDON	NE	28 D5
Trimsaran (Goods)	BP&GV	7 A3
TRING for WENDOVER	L&NW	10 E1
Tring Summit	L&NW	10 E1
TRINITY & NEWHAVEN	NB	30 F2
TROEDYRHIEW GARTH	GW	43 E3
TROEDYRHIW	TV	43 C2
TROON	G&SW	29 E3
Troon Harbour	K&T	29 E3
TROOPER'S LANE	B&NC	61 E3
TROUTBECK	CK&P	26 E1
TROWBRIDGE	GW	3 B4
TROWELL	MID.	41 F3
Trowse Upper Jc.	GE	18 F3
TRURO	GW	1 E1
TRURO TICKET PLATFORM	GW	1 E1
TRUSHAM	GW	2 C3

Station, junction, tunnel, viaduct, etc	Railway	Reference
TRYFAN JUNCTION	NWNG	19 E2
TUAM	A&T	52 A4
Tuam Jc.	MGW/A&T	52 A4
TUBBER	A&EJn	52 E4
TUE BROOK	L&NW	45 F3
Tuffley Jc.	GW/MID.	9 E3
Tufts Jcs N. & S.	S&WJt	8 A1
TULLAMORE	GS&W	53 C3
TULLIBARDINE	CAL.	33 F4
TULLOW	GS&W	54 G5
TULLYMURRY	B&CD	58 B1
TULLYVAR	CVT	60 G3
TULSE HILL	LB&SC	40 E5
Tumble	L&MM	7 A3
TUNBRIDGE JUNCTION	SE	5 D5
TUNBRIDGE WELLS	LB&SC	5 D5
TUNBRIDGE WELLS	SE	5 D5
Tunnel Jc.	GW/MID.	9 B3
Tunnel Jc.	L&SW	4 C5
TUNSTALL	NS	15 C3
TURNHAM GREEN	L&SW	39 D3 (f24)
TURRIFF	GNoS	37 D3
TURTON	L&Y	45 B1
TURVEY	MID.	10 B1
TUTBURY	NS	15 D5
TUXFORD	GN	16 B2
TWEEDMOUTH	NE	31 C3
TWENTY	E&M	17 E2
TWERTON	GW	3 A3
Twerton Tunnel	GW	3 A3
TWICKENHAM	L&SW	39 E2
TWIZELL	NE	31 D3
TWYFORD	GW	4 A1
TWYWELL	KT&H	10 A1
TY CROES	L&NW	19 D1
Tycoch Jc.	GV/BP&GV	7 A2
TYDD	E&M	17 E3
TYDU	GW	43 A3
TYLDESLEY	L&NW	45 C2
Tyler Hill Tunnel	SE	6 C3
TYLOR'S TOWN	TV	43 D2
TYLWCH	Mid-Wales	14 C4
TYNAN	CVT	58 A5
TYNAN & CALEDON	GN(I)	58 A5
TYNDRUM	C&O	32 E1
Tyndrum Summit	C&O	32 E1
TYNE DOCK	NE	28 B5
Tyne Dock	NE	28 B5 (f9)
TYNEHEAD	NB	30 C1
TYNEMOUTH	NE	28 B5
TYNEWYDD OGMORE VALE	GW	43 D3
TYTHERINGTON	MID.	8 B1
TYWITH	GW	43 E3
UCKFIELD	LB&SC	5 E4
UDDINGSTON	CAL.	44 C3
UDDINGSTON	NB	44 C3
Uddingston Jc.	CAL.	44 C3
UDDINGSTON WEST	NB	44 C3
UDNY	GNoS	37 E4
UFFCULME	GW	2 A2
UFFINGTON	GW	10 F5
UFFINGTON & BARNACK	MID.	17 F1
UFFORD BRIDGE SIDING	S&E	17 F1
ULCEBY	MS&L	22 E3
ULLESKELF	NE	21 D4
ULLESTHORPE for LUTTERWORTH	MID.	16 G4
ULLOCK	WC&EJt	26 E3
Ullock Jc.	WC&EJt	26 E3
Ulster Jc.	GN(I)	61 B4
ULVERSTON	FUR.	24 B4
Ulverston (Goods)	FUR.	24 A4
UMBERLEIGH	L&SW	7 F3
UNION MILLS	IoM	23 B2
UNSTON	MID.	41 B2
UP EXE & SILVERTON	GW	2 A3
UPHALL	E&B	30 C3
Uphill Jc.	GW	8 D3
UPMINSTER	LT&S	5 A5
Upper Abbey Mills Jc.	LT&S	40 C3 (f48)
UPPER BANK	MID.	43 G3
UPPER BATLEY	GN	42 B3
UPPER BROUGHTON	MID.	16 D3

Station, junction, tunnel, viaduct, etc	Railway	Reference	Station, junction, tunnel, viaduct, etc	Railway	Reference
WATERFORD	W&L	49 D5	WEST AUCKLAND	NE	27 E5
WATERFORD	WD&L	49 D4	WEST BAY	Bridport	3 F1
WATERFORD THE MANOR	W&T	49 D5	West Benhar Col.	CAL.	30 C4
Waterhall Jc.	TV	43 B4	WEST BRIGHTON	LB&SC	5 F3
WATERHOUSES	NE	27 D5	WEST BROMPTON	MET.-DIS.	39 D5
WATERINGBURY	SE	6 C5	WEST BROMPTON	WLEJt	39 D5
WATERLOO	L&SW	40 D5	WEST BROMWICH	GW	13 B2
WATERLOO	L&Y	45 F3	WEST CALDER	CAL.	30 C4
WATERLOO JUNCTION	SE	40 D5	West Creech	Furzebrook	3 G4
WATERSIDE	G&SW	29 F4	WEST CROSS	Oy.	43 G3
Waterside Jc.	NB	44 C5	WEST CROYDON	LB&SC	40 G5
Watford Crossing Jc.	Rhym.	43 B3	WEST DERBY	CLC	45 F3
WATFORD HIGH STREET	L&NW	11 G1	WEST DRAYTON	GW	5 B2
WATFORD JUNCTION	L&NW	11 G1	WEST END for KILBURN & HAMPSTEAD	MID.	39 B5
Watford Tunnel (Herts)	L&NW	11 G1	WEST END LANE	L&NW	39 B5 (f26)
Watford Tunnel (Northants)	L&NW	10 A3	WEST FERRY	D&AJt	34 E1
WATH	MS&L	42 E1	WEST GREEN	GE	40 A4
WATH & BOLTON	MID.	42 E1	WEST GRINSTEAD	LB&SC	5 E2
Wath Road Jc.	MID./S&KJt	42 F1	WEST HALLAM	GN	41 F3
WATLINGTON	GW	10 F3	WEST HAMPSTEAD	MET.	39 B5 (f55)
WATNALL	MID.	41 F4	WEST HARTLEPOOL	NE	28 D4
Watnall Col.	MID.	41 F4	WEST HOATHLY	LB&SC	5 E3
Watnall Sidings	GN	41 F4	West Holmes Jc.	GN/GN&GEJt.	16 A1
WATTEN	HR	38 D2	West India (Coal)	MID.	40 C3
WATTON	T&W	18 F5	WEST INDIA DOCKS	GE	40 C3
WAVERTON	L&NW	20 E3	WEST JESMOND	NE	28 A1
WAVERTREE	L&NW	45 F4	WEST KENSINGTON	MET.-DIS.	39 D4
Wavertree (Goods)	CLC	45 F4 (f59)	West Kensington Goods	MID.	39 D4
WEAR VALLEY JUNCTION	NE	27 E5	WEST KILBRIDE	G&SW	29 D2
Wearmouth Dock	NE	28 C5	WEST KIRBY	BIRK. Jt.	20 C5
Weasal Hall Tunnel	L&Y	21 E1	WEST KIRBY	SH&D	20 C5
WEASTE	L&NW	45 B3	WEST LEIGH	L&NW	45 C3
Weaver Jc.	L&NW	45 D5	West London Extension Jc.	WLJt/WLEJt	39 D4 (f22)
WEAVERTHORPE	NE	22 A4	West London Jc.	GW	39 C4
Weddington Jc.	A&NJt	16 F5	West London Jc.	L&NW	39 C4
WEDNESBURY	GW	13 A2	WEST MILL	GE	11 E3
WEDNESBURY	L&NW	13 A2	WEST MOORS	L&SW	3 E5
Wednesbury Goods Branch Jc.	GW	13 A2	WEST NORWOOD	LB&SC	40 F5
WEDNESFIELD	MID.	15 E3	West Norwood Jc.	LB&SC	40 F5
WEEDON	L&NW	10 B3	WEST PENNARD	S&D Jt.	8 E2
WEELEY	GE	12 E3	West Pit	Middleton	42 B3
WEETON	NE	21 C3	West Riding Jc.	MID./WR&GJt	42 C2
Weir Bridge	SL&NC	57 B2	West Road Jc.	MGW/GS&W	62 C3
WELBURY	NE	28 F5	West Rosedale (Goods)	NE	28 G3
WELDON & CORBY	MID.	16 G1	WEST ROUNTON GATES	NE	28 F5
WELFORD & KILWORTH	L&NW	16 G3	WEST RUNTON	E&M	18 C3
WELFORD ROAD	MID.	16 F3	WEST ST. LEONARDS	SE	6 F5
Welham Jc.	L&NW/GN&L&NWJt	16 G2	West Stanley (Goods)	NE	27 C5
Welland Viaduct	MID.	16 F1	West Street Jc.	LC&D/MET.	40 C5 (f2)
WELLFIELD	NE	28 D5	WEST TIMPERLEY	CLC	45 B4
Wellhouse Tunnel	L&Y	42 E3	WEST VALE	L&Y	42 C5
WELLINGBOROUGH	L&NW	10 B2	WEST WEMYSS	NB	30 A2
WELLINGBOROUGH	MID.	10 A2	WEST WICKHAM	SE	40 G3
WELLINGTON	GW	8 G4	WEST WORTHING	LB&SC	5 F2
WELLINGTON	S&WnJt	15 E2	WEST WYCOMBE	GW	10 F2
WELLINGTON COLLEGE	SE	4 B1	West Wylam Jc.	NE	27 B4
WELLOW	S&D Jt.	3 B3	WESTBOURNE PARK	GW	39 C1
WELLS	GE	18 C5	WESTBOURNE PARK	H&CJt	39 C1
WELLS	GW	8 E2	WESTBROOK	Golden Valley	14 F2
Wells Harbour	GE	18 C5	WESTBURY	GW	3 B4
WELLS PRIORY ROAD	S&D Jt.	8 E2	WESTBURY	S&WpJt.	14 A1
Wells Tunnel	SE	5 D5	WESTCOMBE PARK	SE	40 D2
WELNETHAM	GE	12 C5	WESTCOTT	O&AT	10 E3
WELSH HARP	MID.	39 A4	WESTCRAIGS	NB	30 C4
WELSHAMPTON	CAM.	20 F4	WESTENHANGER	SE	6 D3
WELSHPOOL	CAM.	14 B2	Wester Pits	NB	30 B4
WELTON	GW	3 B3	WESTERFIELD	GE	12 D3
WELTON for GUILSBOROUGH	L&NW	10 A3	WESTERHAM	SE	5 C4
WELWYN	GN	11 F2	Westerleigh Jc.	MID.	8 C1
Welwyn North & South Tunnels	GN	11 F2	WESTFIELD	NB	30 B4
Welwyn Viaduct	GN	11 F2	Westfield Oil Works	NB	30 A2
WEM	L&NW	20 G3	WESTGATE-ON-SEA	LC&D	6 B2
WEMYSS BAY	G&WB	29 C2	WESTHOUGHTON	L&Y	45 C2
WEMYSS CASTLE	NB	30 A2	WESTHOUSES & BLACKWELL	MID.	41 D3
WENDLING	GE	18 E5	WESTMINSTER BRIDGE	MET.-DIS.	40 D5
Wenford Bridge	L&SW	1 C3	WESTMOOR	MID.	14 E1
WENHASTON	Southwold	12 B2	WESTON	E&M	17 E2
WENNINGTON	MID.	24 B2	WESTON	MID.	3 A3
WENSLEY	NE	27 G4	WESTON & INGESTRE	NS	15 D4
Wensum Jc.	GE	18 F3	WESTON-ON-TRENT	MID.	16 D5
Wenvoe Tunnel	BD&R	43 C4	WESTON-SUPER-MARE	GW	8 D3
Wern (Goods)	CAM.	19 F2	WESTPORT	GN&W	55 F4
Werrington Jc.	GN	17 F2	Westport Quay	GN&W	55 F3

Station, junction, tunnel, viaduct, etc	Railway	Reference
WESTPORT QUAY	GN&W	55 F4
WESTWOOD	MS&L	42 F2
WETHERAL	NE	27 C1
WETHERBY	NE	21 C4
Wetmoor Jc.	MID.	15 C5
WETWANG	NE	22 C4
WEXFORD	DW&W	50 C3
WEYBRIDGE	L&SW	5 C2
WEYHILL	M&SWJn.	4 B4
WEYMOUTH QUAY	GW	3 G3
WEYMOUTH TOWN	GW	3 G3
WHALEY BRIDGE	L&NW	15 A4
WHALLEY	L&Y	24 D2
WHAPLODE	E&M	17 E3
WHARRAM	NE	22 B5
WHATSTANDWELL BRIDGE	MID.	41 E2
WHAUPHILL	P&WJt	25 C4
WHEATHAMPSTEAD	GN	11 F2
WHEATLEY	GW	10 E3
Whelley (Goods)	L&NW	45 D2
Whelley Jc.	L&NW	45 D2
WHERWELL	L&SW	4 C4
WHIFFLET	NB	44 B4
WHIFFLET (HIGH LEVEL)	CAL.	44 B3
WHIFFLET (LOW LEVEL)	CAL.	44 B3
WHIMPLE	L&SW	2 B2
WHIPPINGHAM	IoWC	4 F3
Whiskerhill Jc.	MS&L	16 A3
WHISSENDINE late WYMONDHAM	MID.	16 E2
WHITACRE JUNCTION	MID.	15 F5
WHITBURN	NB	30 C4
WHITBURN COLLIERY	SSM&WC	28 C5
WHITBY TOWN	NE	28 F2
WHITBY WEST CLIFF	NE	28 F2
WHITCHURCH	DN&S	4 B3
WHITCHURCH	L&SW	4 B3
WHITCHURCH (SALOP)	L&NW	20 F3
WHITE BEAR	LUJt	45 D1
WHITE HART LANE	GE	5 A3
WHITE NOTLEY	GE	11 F5
WHITEABBEY	B&NC	61 F3
Whiteball Tunnel & Summit	GW	8 G5
WHITECHAPEL	EL	40 C4
WHITECHAPEL (MILE END)	MET.-DIS.	40 C4
WHITECROFT	S&WJt	8 A1
WHITEDALE	NE	22 D3
WHITEFIELD	L&Y	45 B2
Whitegate (Goods)	CLC	20 D2
WHITEHAVEN BRANSTY	L&NW/FUR.	26 E4
WHITEHAVEN CORKICKLE	FUR.	26 E4
Whitehaven Preston Street (Goods)	FUR.	26 E4
WHITEHEAD	C&L	61 E4
Whitehead Tunnel	C&L	61 E4
WHITEHOUSE	B&NC	61 A4
WHITEHOUSE	GNoS	37 F2
Whitehouse Jc.	L&Y	24 E3
Whiteinch	Whiteinch	44 F4
Whitemoor (Goods)	GE	17 F3
WHITERIGG	NB	44 A4
WHITEROCKS	GCP&BV	60 A1 (f8)
Whitestripe Col.	NB	30 C5
WHITHORN	P&WJt	25 D4
WHITLAND	GW	7 A1
WHITLEY	NE	28 B5
WHITLEY BRIDGE	L&Y	21 E5
WHITLINGHAM	GE	18 F3
WHITMORE	L&NW	15 C3
WHITNEY-ON-THE-WYE	MID.	14 E2
WHITRIGG	SJ	26 C2
Whitrope Summit	NB	31 G1
Whitrope Tunnel	NB	31 G1
WHITSTABLE	SE	6 B3
WHITSTABLE-ON-SEA	LC&D	6 B3
WHITTINGHAM	NE	31 F4
WHITTINGHAM	Whit.	24 D3
WHITTINGTON	CAM.	20 F4
WHITTINGTON	GW	20 G4
WHITTINGTON	MID.	41 B2
WHITTLESEA	GE	11 A2
WHITTLESFORD	GE	11 D3
Whitton Jc.	L&SW	39 E1
WHITWELL	MID.	41 B4
WHITWELL & REEPHAM	E&M	18 E4
WHITWICK	CF	16 E4
Whitwood Jc.	NE	42 B1
WHITWORTH	L&Y	45 A1
Wichnor (Goods)	MID.	15 E5
Wichnor Jc.	MID./L&NW	15 E5
WICK	HR	38 D2
WICKENBY	MS&L	17 A1
WICKFORD JUNCTION	GE	6 A5
WICKHAM	GE	12 F5
WICKHAM MARKET	GE	12 C2
WICKLOW	DW&W	54 E2
Wicklow Jc.	DW&W	54 E2
WICKLOW MURROUGH	DW&W	54 E2
WICKWAR	MID.	9 F2
Wickwar Tunnel	MID.	9 F2
WIDDRINGTON	NE	27 A5
WIDFORD	GE	11 F3
WIDMERPOOL	MID.	16 D3
WIDNES	L&NW	45 D4
Widnes (Goods)	MID. & MS&LJt	45 D4
WIDNES CENTRAL	MID. & MS&LJt	45 D4
Widnes Dock	L&NW	45 D4
Widnes Jc.	CLC/MID. & MS&LJt	45 D4
Widnes West Bank Dock	MID./MS&L	45 E4
WIGAN	L&NW	45 D2 (f22)
WIGAN	L&Y	45 D2 (f18)
Wigan (Goods)	L&NW	45 D2
WIGAN DARLINGTON STREET	WJn	45 D2 (f9)
WIGSTON	MID.	16 F3
Wigston Central & South Jcs.	MID.	16 F3
WIGSTON GLEN PARVA	L&NW	16 F4
Wigston North Jc.	MID./L&NW	16 F3
WIGSTON SOUTH	MID.	16 F3
WIGTON	M&C	26 C2
WIGTOWN	P&WJt	25 C4
WILBURTON	E&Stl	11 B3
WILKINSTOWN	MGW	58 F5
WILLASTON	L&NW	20 E2
WILLBROOK	WClare	51 E5
WILLENHALL	L&NW	15 F4 (f6)
WILLENHALL MARKET PLACE	MID.	15 F4 (f2)
WILLERBY & KIRK ELLA	HB&WRJn	22 D4
Willersley Tunnel	MID.	41 D1
WILLESDEN GREEN	MET.	39 B4
WILLESDEN JUNCTION	L&NW	39 C4
WILLINGDON	LB&SC	5 F5
Willingdon Jc.	LB&SC	5 F5
WILLINGTON	NE	27 D5
WILLINGTON for REPTON	MID.	16 D5
Willington Jc.	MID./NS	16 D5
WILLINGTON QUAY	NE	28 B5 (f1)
WILLITON	West Somerset	8 E5
WILLOUGHBY	GN	17 B4
Willow Walk (Goods)	LB&SC	40 D4
WILMCOTE	GW	9 B5
WILMINGTON	NE	22 A1
WILMSLOW	L&NW	45 A5
WILNECOTE & FAZELEY	MID.	15 F5
WILPSHIRE	L&Y	24 D2
Wilpshire Tunnel	L&Y	24 D2
WILSDEN	GN	42 A5
WILSONTOWN	CAL.	30 C4
Wilsontown N. Jc.	CAL.	30 C4
Wilsontown S. Jc.	CAL.	30 C4
Wilsontown W. Jc.	CAL.	30 C4
WILSTROP SIDING	NE	21 C4
WILTON	GW	3 C5
WILTON	L&SW	3 C5
WILTON	NE	22 A4
Wimberry	S&WJt	8 A2
WIMBLEDON & MERTON	L&SW/LB&SC	39 F4
WIMBLEDON PARK	L&SW	39 E4
WIMBLINGTON	GN&GEJt.	11 A3
WIMBORNE	L&SW	3 E5
WINCANTON	S&D Jt.	3 D3
WINCHBURGH	NB	30 B3
WINCHELSEA	SE	6 E4
WINCHESTER	L&SW	4 D3
Winchester (Goods)	DN&S	4 D3
WINCHESTER CHEESEHILL	DN&S	4 D3
Winchester Jc.	L&SW	4 C3
WINCHFIELD	L&SW	4 B1
WINCHMORE HILL	GN	5 A3

Station, junction, tunnel, viaduct, etc	Railway	Reference
WINCOBANK	MID.	42 G2
WIND MILL HILL	NE	31 D4
WINDER	WC&EJt	26 E3
WINDERMERE	L&NW	26 G1
WINDERMERE LAKE SIDE	FUR.	24 A4
Windmill Bridge Jc.	LB&SC	40 G4
WINDMILL END	GW	13 C1
Windmill Road Jc.	DN&G/GN(I)	58 D3
WINDSOR	GW	5 B1
WINDSOR	L&SW	5 B1
Windsor Street Wharf	L&NW	13 B4
WINESTEAD	NE	22 E2
Wing Tunnel	MID.	16 F2
WINGATE	NE	28 D5
WINGFIELD	MID.	41 E2
Wingfield Tunnel	MID.	41 E2
WINMARLEIGH	G&KE	24 C3
Winning Col.	NE	28 A5
Winnington & Anderton (Goods)	CLC	45 C5
WINSCOMBE	GW	8 D3
WINSFORD	L&NW	20 D2
Winsford & Over	CLC	20 D2
Winsford Jc.	L&NW	20 D2
WINSLOW	L&NW	10 D2
WINSLOW ROAD	A&B	10 D3
WINSON GREEN	L&NW	13 C3
Winsor Hill Tunnel	S&D Jt.	3 C3
WINSTON	NE	27 E5
Winterbutlee Tunnel	L&Y	21 E1
Winterset Jc.	MS&L	42 C2
WINTON	NB	30 B1
Winwick Jc.	L&NW	45 D3
WIRKSWORTH	MID.	41 E1
WISBECH	E&M	17 F3
WISBECH	GE	17 F3
Wisbech Harbour	E&M	17 F3
Wisbech Harbour	GE	17 F4
WISBECH ST. MARY	E&M	17 F3
WISHAW CENTRAL	CAL.	44 A2
WISHAW SOUTH	CAL.	44 A2
WISHFORD	GW	3 C5
WITHAM	GE	12 F5
WITHAM	GW	3 C3
WITHCALL	GN	17 A2
WITHERNSEA	NE	22 E2
WITHINGTON	GW	9 C1
WITHINGTON & ALBERT PARK	MID.	45 A3
WITHNELL	LUJt	24 E2
WITHYHAM	LB&SC	5 D4
Withymoor Basin	GW	13 C1
WITLEY & CHIDDINGFOLD	L&SW	5 D1
WITNEY	Witney	10 E5
Witney Jc.	GW/Witney	10 E4
WITTON	L&NW	13 B4
WITTON GILBERT	NE	27 D5
WITTON-LE-WEAR	NE	27 E5
WIVELISCOMBE	Devon & Somerset	8 F5
WIXFORD	MID.	9 B4
WOBURN SANDS	L&NW	10 C1
WOKING JUNCTION	L&SW	5 C1
WOKINGHAM	SE	4 A1
WOLFERTON	H&WN	17 D5
Wolfhall Jc.	GW	4 B5
WOLSINGHAM	NE	27 D4
Wolvercot Jc.	GW	10 E4
Wolverhampton (Goods)	MID.	15 E3
WOLVERHAMPTON HIGH LEVEL	L&NW	15 E3
WOLVERHAMPTON LOW LEVEL	GW	15 E3
Wolverhampton Victoria Basin	GW	15 E3
Wolverhampton Walsall Street (Goods)	GW	15 E3
WOLVERTON	L&NW	10 C2
Wolverton Viaduct	L&NW	10 C2
Wombridge (Goods)	L&NW	15 E2
WOMBWELL	MS&L	42 E1
WOMERSLEY	L&Y	21 E4
WOOBURN GREEN	GW	10 F2
WOOD GREEN (ALEXANDRA PARK)	GN	40 A5
WOOD GREEN (OLD BESCOT)	L&NW	13 A2
WOOD SIDING	O&AT	10 E3
WOOD STREET, WALTHAMSTOW	GE	40 A3
WOODBOROUGH	GW	3 B5
WOODBRIDGE	GE	12 D3
WOODBURN	NB	27 A3
Woodburn Jc.	MS&L	42 G2
WOODBURY ROAD	L&SW	2 B3
WOODCHESTER	MID.	9 F3
WOODENBRIDGE & SHILLELAGH JUNCTION	DW&W	54 F2
Woodend Col.	NB	30 C4
WOODEND for CLEATOR & BIGRIGG	WC&EJt	26 F3
WOODEND for HUCKNALL HUWTHWAITE	MID.	41 D3
WOODFORD	GE	5 A4
WOODHALL SPA	H'castle	17 B2
WOODHAM FERRIS	GE	11 G5
WOODHAY	DN&S	4 A3
WOODHEAD	MS&L	42 F5
WOODHEAD DAM	Longdendale	21 F1 (f1)
Woodhead Tunnel	MS&L	42 E5
Woodhead Tunnel Summit	MS&L	42 E4
WOODHOUSE	MS&L	41 A3
WOODHOUSE MILL	MID.	41 A3
WOODLAND	FUR.	24 A4
WOODLANDS	S&SLt	49 G3
WOODLAWN	MGW	52 B3
WOODLESFORD	MID.	42 B2
WOODLEY	S&MJt	21 G1
Woodley Jc.	NB	44 C5
Woodmuir Col.	CAL.	30 C4
WOODSIDE	CAL.	33 E5
WOODSIDE	GNoS	37 F4
WOODSIDE	SE	40 G4
Woodside (Goods)	L&NW	45 E4
Woodside Jc.	SE/LB&SC&SE Joint	40 G4
WOODSIDE PARK	GN	5 A3
WOODSTOCK ROAD	GW	10 E4
WOODVILLE	MID.	16 E5
WOODVILLE & AINSDALE	CLC	45 F1
WOOFFERTON	S&HJt	9 A1
WOOKEY	GW	8 E2
WOOL	L&SW	3 F4
WOOLASTON	GW	8 B1
WOOLER	NE	31 E3
Wooley Col.	NE	27 D5
WOOLFOLD	L&Y	45 B1
Woolley Tunnel	L&Y	42 D3
Woolsthorpe	GN	16 D2
WOOLSTON	L&SW	4 E4
WOOLWICH ARSENAL	SE	40 D1
WOOLWICH DOCKYARD	SE	40 D2
WOOPERTON	NE	31 E4
WOOTTON	IoWC	4 F3
WOOTTON BASSETT	GW	9 G4
WORCESTER FOREGATE STREET	GW	9 B3
WORCESTER PARK	L&SW	39 G4
WORCESTER SHRUB HILL	GW/MID.	9 B3
Worcester Wharf	GW	9 B3
Worgret Jc.	L&SW	3 F4
WORKINGTON	L&NW	26 E3
WORKINGTON BRIDGE	L&NW	26 E3
WORKINGTON CENTRAL	C&WJn	26 E3
Workington Lonsdale Dock	C&WJn	26 E3
WORKSOP	MS&L	41 B5
WORLE	GW	8 D3
Worle Jc.	GW	8 D3
WORLESTON	L&NW	20 E2
WORMALD GREEN	NE	21 B3
WORMIT	Newport	34 F2
Wormit (Goods)	NB	34 F2
WORMWOOD SCRUBS	WLJt	39 C4
WORPLESDON	L&SW	5 C1
Worsborough (Goods)	MS&L	42 E2
Worship Street (Goods)	L&NW	40 C4 (f4)
WORSLEY	L&NW	45 B3
Worsley Jc.	L&NW	45 B2
WORSTEAD	GE	18 E2
Worth Valley Bch. Jc.	MID.	21 D1
WORTHING	LB&SC	5 F2
WORTHINGTON	MID.	16 E5
Worting Jc.	L&SW	4 B3
WORTLEY	MS&L	42 F3
WORTLEY & FARNLEY	L&NW	21 C1
Wortley Jc.	MID./NE	21 B2
Wortley S. Jc.	GN	21 C2
Wortley W. Jc.	GN	21 C1
WOTTON	O&AT	10 E3
WRABNESS	GE	12 E3

Station, junction, tunnel, viaduct, etc	Railway	Reference	Station, junction, tunnel, viaduct, etc	Railway	Reference
WRAFTON	L&SW	7 F3	YARMOUTH BEACH	E&M	18 F1
WRAGBY	GN	17 A1	Yarmouth Fishmarket	GE	18 F1
Wrangaton Summit	GW	2 D4	YARMOUTH SOUTH TOWN	GE	18 F1
Wrawby Jc.	MS&L	22 F3	Yarmouth South Town (Goods)	GE	18 F1
WRAYSBURY	L&SW	5 B1	YARMOUTH VAUXHALL	GE	18 F1
WREA GREEN	L&Y & L&NWJt	24 D4	YARNTON	GW	10 E4
WREAY	L&NW	26 C1	Yarwell Jc.	L&NW	11 A1
WRENBURY	L&NW	20 E3	YATE	MID.	8 C1
Wrenthorpe North Jc.	GN	42 C2	YATTON	GW	8 D3
Wrenthorpe South Jc.	GN/WR&GJt	42 C2	YAXHAM	GE	18 E4
WRESSLE	NE	21 D5	Yaxley (Goods)	GN	11 A2
WRETHAM	T&W	18 G5	YEATHOUSE	WC&EJt	26 E3
WREXHAM	GW	20 E4	YELDHAM	CV&H	11 D5
WREXHAM CENTRAL	WM&CQ	20 E4	YELVERTOFT & STANFORD PARK	L&NW	10 A3
WREXHAM EXCHANGE	WM&CQ	20 E4	YELVERTON	GW	2 D5
WRIGHT GREEN	WC&EJt	26 E3	YEOFORD JUNCTION	L&SW	2 B4
WROTHAM & BOROUGH GREEN	LC&D	5 C5	YEOVIL JUNCTION	L&SW	3 E2
WROXALL	IoW	4 G3	YEOVIL PEN MILL	GW	3 D2
WROXHAM	GE	18 E2	YEOVIL TOWN Joint	GW/L&SW	3 D2
WRYDE	E&M	17 F3	YETMINSTER	GW	3 E2
Wycombe Jc.	GN/MID.	16 D2	YNISCEDWYN	N&B	43 E1
WYE	SE	6 D3	Yniscedwyn Col.	MID.	43 F1
Wye Valley Jc.	GW/Wye Valley	8 B2	YNISHIR	TV	43 D3
WYKE	L&Y	42 B5	Ynisygeinon Jc.	MID./N&B	43 F2
Wyke Tunnel	L&Y	42 B5	YNYS	L&NW	19 F1
WYKEHAM	NE	22 A4	YNYSDDU	L&NW	43 B3
WYLAM	NE	27 B5	YNYS-LAS	CAM.	13 B5
WYLDE GREEN	L&NW	15 F5	YOCKLETON	S&WpJt.	14 A1
WYLYE	GW	3 C5	YOKER	GY&C	44 F4
WYMONDHAM	GE	18 F4	YORK	NE	21 A4
WYNYARD	NE	28 E5	York Goods	NE	21 A4
WYRE DOCK	L&Y & L&NWJt	24 C4	York North Jc.	NE	21 A4
Wyre Dock (Goods)	L&Y	24 C4	YORKHILL	NB	44 E4 (f15)
Wyre Dock Jc.	L&Y & L&NWJt/L&Y	24 C4	YORTON	L&NW	15 E1
WYRE FOREST	GW	9 A2	YOUGHAL	GS&W	49 G1
WYRLEY & CHURCH BRIDGE	L&NW	15 E4	YSTALYFERA	MID.	43 F1
WYVENHOE	GE	12 E4	YSTRAD	Rhym.	43 B3
			YSTRAD	TV	43 D2
YALDING	SE	5 C5	YSTRADOWEN	TV	43 D4
YARM	NE	28 F5			
YARMOUTH	FY&N	4 F4	Zig-zag Lines Jc.	TBJt.	43 C2